Coincidence
+
Synchronicity
=
'Guidance'

A personal journey

by

Linda Watson

Copyright © 2017 Linda Watson

ISBN: 978-0-244-30085-2

All rights reserved, including the right to reproduce this book, or portions thereof in any form. No part of this text may be reproduced, transmitted, downloaded, decompiled, reverse engineered, or stored, in any form or introduced into any information storage and retrieval system, in any form or by any means, whether electronic or mechanical without the express written permission of the author.

ACKNOWLEDGEMENTS

First and foremost I would like to thank my Higher Self, Guides and Inspirers in Spirit for turning my life into a magical roller-coaster ride that so far has been wild beyond my imagining.

Thanks to all the wonderful people mentioned by name or pseudonym in the forthcoming pages whether they are still living in 'The 3rd Dimension' or are now residing 'beyond the veil' because without my interaction with them too I would have no story to tell.

Thanks also to my life long friend Christine McGeehan for helping with the 'loose' editing of this book, her humour and encouragement along the way has been invaluable.

Also many thanks must go to my patient and talented friend, Bruno Cavellec for all his technical help, I would have been lost without him.

I would also like to acknowledge Andrew Mayovskyy for the beautiful cover photograph that I feel symbolizes our pathway in life guiding us 'Home' into the light of our true essence.

And finally many thanks to another dear friend, Rosie Allison, who kindly donated the photograph on the back cover.

To Barbara

with Best wishes.

Linda

I lovingly dedicate this book to my father

Frederick Albert Fletcher

FOREWORD

I am honoured and excited to write this foreword for Linda's second helping of her extraordinary spiritual adventures. You have ahead of you a truly inspiring and oftentimes thrilling read.

I met Linda in person in 2004 at The Inner Light Spiritual Library in Andreas, the inspiration and setting up of which you will read about here in these magical pages. Already having read her first book, My Journey to the 4th Dimension…and beyond, I was enthralled by her wondrous stories and further enchanted by her delightful presence. Since then I have come to trust the flutter of *knowing* from my own spiritual exploration.

One of the many things that Linda generates with her written and spoken words alike is a pure joy in the mysterious experiences of her life which, over many years of search and refinement she has learned to take seriously, and thank goodness she does! The underlying message here is one of encouragement, and by sharing her stories Linda invites us to witness the magic evident in our own lives. She shows how we too can acknowledge and therefore allow for the positive influence of Spirit into our every day existence.

Linda's experiences have played an important role for me and I am so grateful to now call her a dear friend. I never feel anything less than uplifted and inspired when I have the good fortune to be in her warm and bubbly presence.

I know you too will feel the tingle of recognition and amazement as I did when reading the incredible accounts of her spiritual adventures. And, despite her humility and protestations, I for one cannot wait for Volume III.

With Love, Light and the deepest respect I know you will be as thrilled as I am with Linda's latest book. Enjoy!

Christine Collister-Miller

I was delighted when Linda asked me to contribute to the foreword of her book as I have known her all my life. I have many happy memories of our shared, and to me idyllic childhood, when times were much simpler than today, a time when childhood was just that…childhood, with all the simple pleasures that came with it.

Linda always had an interest in 'other worldly' topics even in her youth, but as she grew older and shared her adult experiences with me they 'blew my mind', sending shivers up and down my spine, never failing to amaze me.

I know throughout the past 30 years or so she has inspired and given comfort to countless people she has met on her spiritual journey and has captivated audiences with her stories—as I'm sure you will be captivated too when you read this book. Enjoy the journey!   *Christine McGeehan*

I was thrilled to be invited to write a few words for Linda's book, which I have to say I found utterly amazing. It is a real joy to read, full of inspirational adventures prompted by her guidance from Spirit.

For me to have been a part in her experiences in a small but wonderful way has been fantastic as you will read. And I hope that like me, once you pick this book up and start reading you will find it very hard to put down until you've finished it. Thank you for sharing your life and your love Linda.   *Maggie Collister*

I have been a close observer of Linda's life since our first meeting more than twenty-five years ago. Her 'journey' has both fascinated and entranced me on many occasions and I always love to hear about her latest adventures.

Linda is not only very human with all the trials and tribulations it brings, but also compassionate and warm hearted, filled with humour and love. To me she is an 'Earth Angel' emanating Love, Light and Joy wherever she goes!   *Margaret Wilson*

INTRODUCTION

I would like to begin the introduction for this book by informing you what it is *not,* before I explain to you what it *is*. Firstly, this book is *not* about religion, organised or otherwise, and even though I may use the word 'God' in places it is just a term I am happy using to refer to a Higher Power. Nor is it a training manual on 'how to meditate' or 'how to live a spiritual life' and it most definitely is *not* a literary work of art as you will see as you read through the coming pages.

This book is just a simply written account of the process of becoming aware of my 'Higher Self' or my 'Spiritual Self' if you prefer. I will refer to this 'being' throughout the book as 'HS' or 'spirit'. It is that essential part of us that is pure spirit which is forever constant and loving, operating from a higher vibration than our physical selves while all the while interacting with and through us.

Within these pages you will read about many extraordinary sequences of events that have awakened me spiritually and over the years the beauty and magic of these experiences have instilled in me a faith to love and trust in a 'Higher Power' guiding me ... as it guides us all through this life.

For many years I have visualised my life as a three dimensional map or game board. At the top of the map, the entrance point, my birth, is marked by the letter 'A' and my exit point or physical death, is marked at the bottom of the map by the letter 'Z'. Between these two points I imagine a jungle dotted with small red flags, all of which pinpoint the places I need to visit on my journey through this life as Linda.

My own personal experience has taught me that no matter what choices we make or what deviations we take along the way to those little red flags, we will, without doubt, be guided to meet all the people we need to meet and visit all the places that we require to visit on our journey through this life. This I believe is to work through whatever life challenges *we* ourselves have chosen to experience ...

choices we made long before we arrived here on Planet Earth. Sometimes the choices I've made have led me into the dark interior of life's jungle and I've felt lost, alone and very vulnerable. In effect, failing to notice the nearest red flag, when miraculously, as if guided by the invisible hand of some Higher Power I find my way and 'know' that all will be well.

Life here on the earth plane is very much a place of personal growth on every level of our being. A place of learning and understanding the lessons *we* have chosen. If we don't learn the lesson the first time around you can guarantee a similar situation will be presented to you and you will be required to re-sit the exam. In fact I've found life to be very much like school, but unfortunately without the holidays!

Once acknowledged, your HS gifts into your life a wonderful kind of magic that brings back a childlike sense of wonder and you will start to perceive your life and the events that arise for you in a very different way. This is the moment when you begin to *follow* and learn to **trust** in the guidance you are receiving, even if you are unsure of where your belief is taking you. You may find it will lead you into many potential adventures and also into what might appear to be misadventures! Just know that everything experienced in this life, good and bad, is designed especially for *you* ... to help you grow on a spiritual level.

Many years ago when I consciously set out upon this journey little did I realise that life would be a series of 'Aha' moments helping me to understand who I truly am. Over time and experience I have come to know that ***all*** our challenges and life experiences are about 'waking up' to **remember** that we are all just a small drop of the mighty ocean that is the 'Universal Consciousness of Spirit'.

Guidance may come in many different ways and is dependent on the individual and their degree of awareness. For instance you may feel compelled to pick up a book, and opening it at random read something you needed to know, or sing a song that is meaningful to you only to hear the same tune being played moments later when you switch on the radio. Even a 'chance' meeting with someone you have just been thinking about may be meaningful. The key to this guidance is to hone your awareness and your intuition and be open to the messages and nudges you receive from Spirit. If these occurrences ever happen for you stop for a moment and appreciate the experience as it may *not* be as you think, 'just coincidence'.

I'm sure a lot of you who choose to read this book will be able to relate my journey to your own personal experiences of working with your HS/Spirit. And for those of you who are just awakening, you may find after reading this book that you too no longer believe in coincidence, but choose instead to accept and *trust* in the guidance that comes through your own open loving hearts.

And just a final word to all those potential readers who are wondering how a book such as this has come into their life. Remember there is no such thing as 'coincidence' because this book has found its way into your hands for a reason. Maybe now, this very moment, is the perfect time for *you* to awaken. So, before you read any further I would ask that you suspend your judgement, just imagine putting it into a little sealed box at the back of your mind, choosing instead to open your heart and feel the love and truth with which this book has been written. Thank you.

Linda Watson   March 2017

Footnote: Throughout this book you will find a number of poems which were channeled through me over a period of days during August 2004. Never having written poetry before I was amazed when each one was complete in the space of a few minutes so I choose to believe they were 'heaven sent'.

'The Creator' has a dream,

And the dream comes true,

Each time one of us awakens!

Volume I

My Journey to 'The 4th Dimension'

… And beyond

CHAPTER 1

ARRIVAL

'Let's start at the very beginning it's a very good place to start'
The words from that famous Mary Poppins song are drifting into my mind as I begin to write, so maybe that is the best place to start my story... at the very beginning.

"Hang on Joan, the taxi is on its way," my father called breathlessly as he stepped through the front door. For the second time that evening he had pedalled up the hill from the village phone box on his bicycle, but unfortunately for him, Mum was less than impressed.

"That's what you said an hour ago Fred, if that taxi doesn't arrive soon this child will be born here, so you'd better prepare yourself".

My mother would recall that my father looked horrified at the prospect and attempted to cajole her by assuring her everything would be alright and asking her to hold on. Quite a difficult request when you're about to give birth!

Having gone into labour earlier that evening with her second child, me, she was not unduly panicked until the contractions became a lot closer together and there was still no sign of the taxi.

Our family home was in the small village of Andreas situated on the northern plain of the Isle of Man. For anyone who has not heard of the Isle of Man it is a small island in the middle of the Irish Sea, like a stepping stone between England and Ireland. Back then in 1954, there were only two taxi cabs in Ramsey, our nearest town, and after summoning one it was a further twenty five mile journey to the only maternity home in Douglas, the Island's capital.

A further twenty minutes elapsed after the above exchange before the taxi finally arrived and in Mum's words Dad was sweating profusely at the thought of what he might have to do.

"About bloody time too" Dad yelled at the taxi driver on his arrival, "How the hell has it taken you so long to get here? Don't you know my wife's about to have a baby?"

"Very sorry sir, had a bit of business on the way," the taxi driver replied, tapping the side of his nose conspiratorially and smelling suspiciously of extra strong mints to disguise the smell of alcohol. As you can imagine, this was long before drink driving laws and breathalysers.

"Are you fit to drive?" Dad questioned him angrily.

"Oh yes, I'm fine, thank you sir."

"Come on then, let's get my wife to hospital before she gives birth to our baby right here."

Dad bundled Mum into the back seat of the taxi and jumped in beside her, leaving Nana to look after my sister who was then two years old. They raced into Ramsey at top speed before starting their ascent over the infamous mountain road that led to Douglas. This road is part of the Tourist Trophy Course known to motorcycle and TT fans all over the world.

It was a beautiful July night down on the northern plain, but as they wound their way speedily up the mountain they ran into fog … **thick fog**! Mum would recall that she spent the entire journey with her eyes tight shut praying that they made it to the hospital safely.

The taxi driver did not ease his pace, his foot pressed to the floor on the throttle as they hurtled over the mountain through the impenetrable gloom of the fog. With every minute that passed the air in the taxi became more fetid with the smell of alcohol, the driver not daring to take his hands of the steering wheel to reach for another mint.

With each passing minute Mum's contractions were getting closer and closer together, but thankfully as 4 o'clock chimed they screeched to a halt outside the main entrance of the Jane Crookall Maternity Hospital in Douglas. The matron was waiting in the doorway with a midwife in attendance, and Mum would recall that she could still hear the matron's shrill voice ringing in her ears, "My God, this woman's about to give birth, get her into the delivery room at once."

I'm sure my father and the taxi driver must have wiped the sweat from their brows thinking, 'That was a close shave'. Only five minutes later the matron appeared in the doorway of the waiting room and announced to Dad that his wife had given birth to a bouncing baby girl, tipping the scales at just less than 8lbs.

Mum's prayers had been answered and fate had decreed that her baby arrived safely against all odds. The soul to be known as Linda Jean Fletcher, born at 4.05 a.m. on the seventh day, of the seventh month 1954 had made her entrance into the world. It seems I couldn't wait to get here and I feel as if I have been racing through life at break neck speed ever since.

The above was my mother's account of how I entered the Earth plane in this lifetime, but this life was going to be different from other lives I may have lived because this time I'd come to awaken spiritually, and what an exciting journey it would turn out to be.

The Gift of Life

The gift of life is precious, a spark of Love Divine,
It dwells down deep within the heart, yours as well as mine.
The gift of life is precious because its school you see,
A time for learning lessons, for you and just as much for me,
The gift of life is precious, not a moment must we waste,
But sometimes things get in the way in our eternal haste.
Some lessons we find easy and others extremely hard,
When tragedy befalls us we feel our lives are scarred,
We want to turn the clock back or run away and hide,
But we know that's not the answer, so we stand firm and face the coming tide.
Emotions, they may threaten to overwhelm us, I can tell you this is true,
"What have I done to deserve this? What is it I must do?"
These lessons are the hardest and take all our strength to bear,
This is the time to look inside and feel the 'Love' that's there.
This Love is our connection to the source of All-That-Is,
That wondrous spark of Love Divine, of God's eternal bliss,
Understand we're not alone and never so have been,
Help is always there to call on, even though 'It' remains unseen.
And when at last our lessons are done and school is out once more,
It's time to make the journey 'Home' and we'll pass through the 'Exit' door.
On the other side will be souls we have met along the way,
They'll gather round to greet us and cheer us on that day.
That's when we get the 'Bigger Picture' of our passage through this life,
The happiness and sadness the trouble and the strife,
The lessons we have faced and learned to help our soul to grow,
Won't it be amazing, how much more we'll know,
The gift of life is precious, a spark of Love Divine
It dwells down deep within the heart, yours as well as mine,
The gift of life is precious, it's funny, but it's true,
A life well lived is wonderful, for me, and just as much for you.

Chapter 2

DEPARTURES

In the early 1960's post war Britain was still littered with active air force bases, one of which was located at Jurby where my father worked, three miles away from our home in Andreas.

My father was tall and slim with wavy brown hair and sparkling blue eyes, sporting a thin moustache, which I am led to believe was very fashionable in the fifties and early sixties. During my fanciful teenage years I would often gaze dreamily at old photographs of Dad and compare him to Errol Flynn, thinking that he too could have been a film star with his handsome good looks.

Dad would cycle the three miles to the air force base at Jurby and back every day and appeared extremely fit until he developed a hacking cough which continued to plague him through the day and kept us all awake night after night. After a number of weeks with no respite, and no sleep, Mum decided enough was enough and sent him off to see our family doctor. After a referral and many tests his condition deteriorated so rapidly that he was admitted to the local cottage hospital in Ramsey.

A kindly neighbour who just happened to own a car, quite a luxury in those days, would drive Mum, and on occasion me and my sister to the hospital for visiting time. Unfortunately in those far off days children were not allowed on the hospital wards, so we could not even visit Dad for a hug. Only for the compassion of that very kindly neighbour, who would take it in turns to lift us up onto his shoulders so that we could wave to Dad through the high windows of the ward we would never have seen him again. The last and most enduring memory that I have treasured all my life is the image of my father sitting in a bed beneath the window waving and blowing kisses to us.

We were to discover that Dad was suffering from an acute

condition of the heart which unfortunately robbed him of his life and he passed away at the very premature age of thirty-nine.

So deep was Mum's grief after my father's passing she was utterly inconsolable and so consumed with her own pain and despair that she shut everything out, including her children. In her fragile state of mind she was unable to give us the solace we craved, she couldn't see that we were hurting too. I didn't understand it then how could I? I was only a child. It was not until I married and had two children of my own that I tried to put myself in my mother's position and I have to say I can't even begin to imagine what she must have gone through or how hard life must have been for her.

We were told that Dad had gone 'to be with Jesus', but for some reason I felt he was still with me and derived some comfort from believing that he was still alive somewhere around me even though he remained invisible.

After this traumatic episode my sister and I naturally turned to our grandparents who lived just a few doors away on the same housing estate. We loved them both very much and of course they were now more important to us than ever.

My grandfather was quite a character, round of face with a ruddy complexion and the most beautiful, kind, twinkling blue eyes. He always wore blue dungarees with his shirt sleeves rolled up to the elbows, looking every inch a typical Manx labourer of the 50's and early 60's. Having worked most of his life on local farms his latter years were spent on the high roads cutting the hedges and keeping the ditches clear. Hard work had been his watchword and he had been no stranger to it throughout his life as his weathered appearance and huge rugged hands bore testimony to. Like my father he was also very popular and well liked among his workmates and the village community and if anyone needed a haircut or their boots cobbled Tom Cannell would be their first port-of-call.

We loved to spend time with our grandparents and we always knew we could find Grandad at home on Saturday mornings. Most Saturdays as soon as we'd finished our breakfast we would run excitedly across the estate to their front door and knock as loud as we could on the little door knocker. Nana would open the door and step back as we raced past her into the kitchen where Grandad, more often than not, would be found sitting in an armchair by the range. We would throw ourselves at his knee both trying to climb on board at the same time, which was no mean feat as he had quite a paunch. Laughing he would say, "C'mon now girls, there's plenty of room for both of you" as he hauled us both up onto his lap. Then he would wrap his huge protective arms around us in a bear hug and say lovingly, "There now, what did I tell you? Room enough for both my best girls".

However, just after my eighth birthday our lovely grandfather collapsed having suffered a massive stroke and the last few miserable weeks of his life were spent bedridden in the front parlour. It was heartbreaking to see our once strong and indestructible grandfather reduced to a crumpled paralysed shell. Nevertheless we still loved him and would climb onto the big double bed in the parlour to tell him our stories and confide in him just the way we had always done, even though he was unable to cuddle and tease us any more.

On the 6th of August 1962 my grandfather passed away, and by way of explanation we were informed by the adults in the family that Grandad had gone to join Dad, 'to be with Jesus'.

The night before his funeral we were led crying into Nana's front parlour to say our final 'goodbyes' to our beloved Grandad. The coffin was resting on a trestle in the middle of the room and in childlike innocence I vividly remember peering over the edge to take one last look at my grandfather. Instantly recoiling at the sight that greeted me and thinking that whoever 'it' was laying there it was only my grandfather by virtue of the fact that it looked like him. The life-force and personality were now missing from his body, but I remember being overwhelmed with the same feelings as when my father had passed away just eighteen months previously, somehow I just 'knew' that my lovely Grandad still existed ... somewhere.

When I look back on these two events I see they were the trigger for my spiritual awakening and soon my 'HS' albeit unconsciously at first, would start to nudge me in the right direction.

CHAPTER 3

THE OUIJA BOARD

As I grew older my mind seemed to be very open on the subject of anything paranormal and my friends would often seek me out to tell them stories, usually ghost stories. But, that was only the tip of the iceberg because inside my head the question about life after death, and what, if anything, was on the 'other side' dominated my thoughts.

Finding the answer to this question and others in a similar vein had become not only a quest, but almost an obsession. All these 'weird' thoughts were spinning around inside my head and I'm sure if I'd spoken of them to my mother and grandmother they would have thought I was completely mad and suffering from some psychotic illness.

If school had offered lessons on the paranormal I'm sure I would have been an A* student, but unfortunately I was bored and totally unimpressed and as I entered my teens I looked upon it more and more as a social occasion where I met and had fun with my friends. Needless to say the teachers had conflicting ideas to mine about how I should spend my time whilst I was within their domain, but as a result I left school the day I was fifteen without sitting any formal exams and lacking any qualifications. This was a decision I might add that I did regret later in life, but as the saying goes, 'Life is for the learning' and I have to say like all of us the learning really starts when you leave school.

In the summer of 1969 I left school and was fortunate enough to secure employment as an apprentice hairdresser, something I thought I would enjoy, but how wrong I was! I hated every minute of it and after a six week trial the owner and I decided this was not my vocation and we should go our separate ways. As I couldn't expect my mother to keep me I had to find a new job as quickly as possible and fortunately a vacancy for an assistant in a local newsagent was advertised at just the right moment.

The newsagents shop was in an old building on the main shopping street in Ramsey which housed the printing press and reporters' offices for our local newspaper 'The Courier'. My Uncle Walter had been a linotype operator in the printing works before emigrating to New Zealand and I remembered he'd once told me a story about there being a ghost in the linotype room above the printing press. The ghost was supposedly one of the old linotype operators who had been witnessed on many occasions bending over his linotype machine and going about his business, just as if he were still alive. Of course, to me, with my unusual interests, that would be an added bonus in acquiring the position and to my delight I did in fact secure the job. Being a people person I actually found I enjoyed the shop work and immediately became friends with Eileen, the girl who already worked there.

In no time at all Eileen and I got into the habit of having our lunch together upstairs in the boss's office whilst watching the world go by in the street below. On a rainy lunchtime a few weeks into my new job I was enjoying lunch with Eileen when my eyes were attracted to the unfamiliar word 'Ouija' printed on a box wedged between files on a high shelf. This was a word that I'd never seen or heard of before and I was surprised to find myself attracted to it like iron filings to a magnet. Approaching the manager after lunch I just had to ask, "What is Ouija?" Frowning at me as he peered over the top of his half moon spectacles, he asked why I needed to know. Not being a very good liar I replied honestly and admitted to seeing the Ouija box in his office. Enlightening me to the fact that it was a Victorian parlour game whereby you could receive messages from the dead, but also with the information that all boards had been withdrawn from sale and that was why the last one in stock was now on the shelf in his office.

Increasingly interested I couldn't stop myself from asking why we were no longer allowed to sell the boards and to my surprise discovered that a youth, not much older or smarter than myself had become so obsessed with the information he received from the Ouija that it was blamed for his subsequent suicide.

The boss, shaking his finger in my direction, left me reeling in the certain knowledge that there were things I knew nothing about that should be left well alone. But, instead of being frightened I was spellbound deciding then and there I just had to try it for myself and I'm afraid the stern advice I'd been given had no effect on my fifteen year old enthusiasm.

Thankfully, the boss went out for his lunch most days otherwise Eileen and I would not have dared to even contemplate what we planned to do in *his* office. The very next day we ate our lunch in double quick time before removing the Ouija board from its resting place on the high shelf. My heart was beating like a drum with anticipation and also with the fear that our manager might come back early and catch us doing something he'd advised against.

Following the instructions we laid the contents of the Ouija box on the desk. The board contained all the letters of the alphabet printed in a semi-circle with the words 'Yes' and 'No' printed beneath. A strange teardrop shaped pointer on wheels, described as a planchette had to be placed in the centre of the board and each player had to rest a finger lightly upon it before asking the question, 'Is there anybody there?'

Not really expecting anything to happen I advised Eileen that it all looked simple enough and as all thoughts of the trouble we may get into had dissolved from my mind I was ready to start the game. After all we were only playing... weren't we?

Eileen and I sat opposite one another our fingers resting lightly on the planchette as requested. Then, in the spookiest voice I could conjure up I asked if there was anybody there. We were amazed when after only a few moments the planchette very slowly started to move, and creeping across the board came to rest on the word 'Yes'. Laughing nervously I accused Eileen of pushing the pointer because I knew I hadn't, but one glance at my friend's face told me she was not guilty of my accusation as the look on her face was one of sheer fright.

The planchette now picking up speed started to whizz from one letter to another, spelling out a name ... a name that neither of us knew. All too soon lunchtime was over and packing the board away we carefully replaced it in its original position then made our way back downstairs before being caught by the boss. Throughout the afternoon my thoughts kept straying to the amazing experience we'd had at lunchtime and wondering who the owner of the name we'd been given could be.

Calling in on my great Aunt Mary after work that evening I asked her quite innocently, or as innocently as I could, if she knew anyone by the enigmatic name the Ouija had supplied us with. I was excited beyond belief when she admitted to knowing the name and even more amazed when she informed me that he'd been a linotype operator where I now worked. A very religious lady, she would not have approved of the method I'd used to procure the name of someone who had presumably 'passed on' and I have to say I felt very guilty about lying to her when I told her I'd overheard someone mention his name at work.

Leaving Aunt Mary deliberating on our strange conversation I ran for my bus home, cold shivers running up and down my spine because the stories my uncle had told me about the ghost were true, and I now had proof. Throwing myself onto the departing bus I was overcome with excitement, my mind racing and my only thought was to try and contact Dad as my next step. The poor obsessed boy who had allegedly sacrificed his life to the Ouija was totally forgotten as all I could think about were my own selfish reasons for using it.

On arriving home I immediately set about making my own Ouija board by printing the letters of the alphabet on squares of cardboard and replacing the planchette with an upturned wine glass. Delighted with my homemade Ouija board I then invited those friends who loved my ghost stories to join me in my search for the unexplained. My friends and I played with the Ouija on a regular basis over the next few months, totally and utterly obsessed with the information we would receive. That was until the day it all came to a terrifying end when the information we received told me I was going to die in the most horrific way and the wine glass flew off the table and smashed into a thousand pieces on the floor. The experience frightened us all so much we vowed never to play with it again.

When I look back to that time in my life I find it hard to believe how irresponsible and naïve I was and the sad thing was Dad never did contact me through the Ouija.

CHAPTER 4

THE REVOLVING DOOR

After the frightening experience with the dreaded Ouija board I thought it was about time I conformed and became an ordinary teenager, so I put aside the weird thoughts that had filled my mind for so long and immersed myself in teenage pursuits. Meeting the drummer from the group at the local Saturday night dance we dated for a number of years before marrying in August 1975, and in all that time the thoughts that had haunted me as a child about life-after-death, and where my Dad and Grandad now resided were completely pushed to the back of my mind.

Two years later, in April 1977, I received the sad news that my beloved Nana had passed away which left me totally bereft. I don't think I have ever felt so sad because other than Mum she had been the most important person in my life. I'd always turned to Nana for comfort and advice and now she wasn't there any more. What was I going to do without her? At the time to even contemplate that question was impossible for me.

Depressed for weeks after her passing I just couldn't seem to lift myself out of the dark pit of despair I'd fallen into. Even though I believed my grandmother now resided in the afterlife I missed her in the 'here and now' and had to go through that awful grieving process. My dreams would often feature her and I would wake with tears in my eyes conscious that I'd only just kissed her soft, pink cheeks goodbye, even the perfume of the Ponds face powder she always wore in life lingered into wakefulness.

Three months after her passing I was pulled out of my misery when I found out I was pregnant and my focus was finally taken from my loss as I dealt with this new discovery. There is an old saying, 'As one soul leaves the Earth, another will step in to take its place' very much like a revolving door, and at that time in my life I felt sure that this was true. Nana had left, but a new soul was about to enter.

Julie was born in March the following year and it was a particularly traumatic birth that took me a long time to recover from, but I am now aware that my grandmothers passing and the difficult delivery of my new daughter were both triggers from my 'HS' which was seeking attention once more.

Having relinquished my curiosity when I abandoned the Ouija board I now found new questions floating into my consciousness. Who am I? Where did I come from? Where will I return to? What is the meaning and purpose of life? What am I here to do?

I couldn't tell Dickie because I didn't think he would have understood my thought processes as we had never discussed the subject before. In fact there was no one in my circle of friends at that time I could approach on the subject. It was obviously destined to be a lone quest, but I was happy with that scenario because even though I am quite gregarious I also like my own company.

Often I would find myself skulking about in a local second-hand book shop and when no one was looking I would dive into a small room at the rear of the store. This dusty little room contained all the literature deemed to be radical in the 1970's, but for me it was bliss to secrete myself, unnoticed, for as long as possible while I thumbed through the collection of old books on offer. Always fascinated in anything paranormal or other worldly I would immerse myself in all the available literature on life-after-death, mediumship, spirituality, metaphysics and other related topics... even UFO's.

Back in the 1970's these subjects were not as openly discussed or accepted as they are nowadays and this was the only place I knew of that I could 'feed my habit' like a craving drug addict. Choosing my books carefully, paying only a few pence for them as they were very old, and guiltily hiding them when I got home and only taking them out of their hiding place when I was alone, like some kind of closet spiritualist!

Over time I have come to understand that this was not an obsession, but part of my awakening. Like a thirst I could not quench or a love I could not understand fully until I had dissolved myself into it ... Like a cube of sugar melting into a hot cup of tea, immersing and dissolving myself completely.

Again it is only looking back on my life that I have come to understand the information I sought then was all part of my spiritual path and the questions I asked then are slowly being answered through my life experiences.

Two years later I gave birth to my second daughter, Christine. On her arrival I felt my family was complete and that I would soon be able to continue with my spiritual exploration. However, Christine had other ideas, as she was never very fond of sleeping, day or night, and unintentionally put my spiritual adventure on hold for a few more years. Remaining at home, a full-time mum until both Julie and Christine were at school, by which time I was more than ready to return to work and join the human race again.

Before the children were born I'd worked for some years as an assistant in a local pharmacy and had enjoyed the work there and got on well with the other members of staff, in fact over the years they had become like an extended family. Now that I felt it was time for me to return to work I approached my old boss to see if he could offer me something part-time that would fit in with the girls' school timetable. Unfortunately, he had nothing to offer me in the pharmacy at that time, but I'm happy to say there was a vacancy in their sister shop, a cut-price cosmetics outlet, housed on the ground floor of an old Victorian building just across the street from the pharmacy.

On my first morning the manageress sent me upstairs to the stockroom armed with a list of items that I was to retrieve and bring down to fill the shelves in the shop. Minutes later as I searched the upstairs room for the items on my list the temperature seemed to drop a few degrees, the hairs stood up on the back of my neck and I was overwhelmed with the sensation that I was not alone. It felt as though someone was watching me, which was quite un-nerving, but I told myself that it was *only* my imagination and shrugging my shoulders carried on about my work.

The funny thing was that every time I had cause to enter the stockroom from that day on I had the same feeling and it would be accompanied with an image in my minds eye of an old man wearing a cloth cap and tweed jacket. He always seemed to be standing on the small landing at the top of the stairs, just watching me go about my business, no doubt wondering who the strange young woman was in *his* home. And on evenings when I was left to cash-up I would often hear footsteps walking across the floor above me in the stockroom and knowing I was in the building on my own I came to believe the essence of the old man must still be residing in the space that he had occupied in his physical lifetime.

At the time I experienced the above events I chose to ignore them because it had been some years since I had thought about such things. In effect I had turned my back on my spiritual searching, allowing life and all its tedium to get in the way, as we all do from time to time.

However, my life was about to change as I gently and almost unwittingly pushed the door open between me and my 'HS' and the Spirit world.

My Soul's Journey

I set out on a journey, to where? I didn't know,
I only knew it was my soul telling me to go.
I happened on a landscape, grey and alien to me,
Nothing looked familiar, not land or sky or sea.
The place I'd left was not like this, of that I felt quite sure,
My only recollection was to continue and endure,

*

I travelled many lifetimes over dale and moor and bog
Shrouded as I went in a thick and gloomy fog,
My heart was heavy laden as I plodded through the gloom,
My thoughts were deep and dark with prophecies of doom
Where is this place? Where can I be? Where is the 'Light' I know?
As I asked these questions a light began to glow,

*

My heart it leapt and missed a beat as the little light grew stronger,
The light then spoke in lilting voice, "You need stay here no longer"
"But who are you?" I asked, and "Where did you come from?"
"I am your friend and guide dear child, until it's time for Home."
"Is it time to return now?" I begged the light to tell,
"No, not yet my darling child, but I promise all is well."

*

At once I looked around me on a new and beautiful land,
The sun was shining brightly and someone held my hand,
I turned to see an angel of radiant, shimmering 'Light',
And I knew in that very instant, I'd lived through my darkest night.
Smiling peacefully and so serene, exuding blissful Love,
These words they seemed to sing to me, as if coming from above.

*

"The mission you have chosen is just about to start,
So listen to the guidance of your open loving heart."
From that very moment my life was born anew,
I listened to my guidance and knew just what I had to do.
Love is the key to All-That-Is, the message I must share,
Love is the key to every ill and all of mans' despair.

*

I've met with souls along my path and spoke to them of Love,
Some accepted it with grace and some were left unmoved.
Love and Light have led me on and I have followed in true faith,
All I have ever wanted was to Love and in this Light to bathe.
My mission is not yet over, I have many more to tell,
But my angel is beside me and I *know* that all is well.

*

CHAPTER 5

THE OPEN DOOR

In the summer of 1989 I shared my beliefs with a friend who was a nurse at the local cottage hospital. Amazingly it came as no surprise to her and I discovered that we were both singing from a similar hymn sheet. Not long afterwards that same friend told me she had spotted a flyer advertising meditation classes pinned on the notice-board at the hospital. Although I didn't realize it then this truly was to be the 'conscious' beginning of my spiritual journey.

Congregated in the small designated room at the local hospital with half a dozen other like minded people, that first evening of meditation class I didn't quite know what to expect, but Lena, the lady who was taking the class was really friendly. In fact the moment we met I felt an instant rapport, like I'd known her all my life.

Lena began with an explanation of the concept of meditation before leading us into a beautiful visualization which I still remember to this day ... I loved it. Afterwards she invited us all, one by one, to share what we had witnessed or experienced in our meditation. Excited beyond belief I waited for my turn to speak, eager to share with everyone what I'd witnessed. Finally, my turn arrived, and I exuberantly shared with everyone the beautiful vision I'd seen in my meditation, but commented on the fact that I was a little disappointed to find myself alone.

"My dear," Lena said, looking directly *into* me, "you have not been on your own all evening, you've been accompanied by an elderly lady ever since you arrived."

The group sat in stunned silence as Lena proceeded to describe in detail the lady she could 'see'. Listening intently I could feel the emotion building inside me to an almost overwhelming level which threatened to spill out of my tear ducts at any moment. Without any doubt, Lena was describing, and in perfect detail, Nana who had passed away twelve years previously.

After the class Lena took me to one side and explained she was a medium, like I hadn't already guessed! Whispering, so as not to be overheard by the others she offered to meet with me privately, explaining that she felt my grandmother had much more she wanted to tell me. Feeling very excited at the prospect of hearing from Nana again I arranged to meet Lena at her home for a 'one to one' the following week.

That evening after the meditation class was over I felt as if I'd discovered something special, something I'd been searching for all my life and I knew that I wanted to repeat the experience. For the first time in my life I'd met people who thought like me and who seemed to understand the 'seeker' in me as I understood it in them.

The following week I found myself walking up Lena's drive wondering what on earth to expect. Was she going to appear in full gypsy dress complete with crystal ball and chanting 'Cross my palm with silver'? Or would I find myself sitting in a darkened room partaking in a full-blown séance? Was there any chance she could conjure up all my ancestors known and unknown and parade them like specters appearing out of the darkness? My stomach was in knots as I approached the door, but I had no need to fear as Lena answered the door with a smile and welcomed me in like an old friend.

Settling ourselves in the lounge, where nothing at all seemed out of the ordinary, we chatted easily with one another for a few minutes as Lena gave me time to relax into her company. 'Out of the blue' Lena suddenly announced that my grandmother was with us and informed me that Nana was standing directly behind me. My initial response was to turn my head in the hopes of seeing my beloved grandmother, but of course I couldn't see her and without any warning the sitting had assuredly commenced.

Nana, the same as she had been in her physical life, did indeed have a lot to say that day. Through Lena, as medium, she gave me proof on countless occasions, that it could be none other than her in Lena's sitting room on that auspicious afternoon. Towards the end of the sitting Lena went very quiet and she began looking *into* me, her eyes glazing just like she had at the meditation class and enquiring if there were any questions I would like to ask, informing me that the moment was appropriate.

Without hesitation I asked, "Is my Dad here?" But I could read the pity in her eyes before she answered. Obviously she knew how much this question meant to me and I got the distinct impression that she had been in this position with many of her clients' on previous occasions. Parting her lips to speak I was already aware that her answer was not going to be what I wanted to hear. With a great deal of honesty she admitted that my Dad was not with us at that particular moment, but I was amazed to be told that his brother was and his name was either Tim or Tom. As Lena continued I was to learn that he had passed over when only very young, under tragic circumstances, emphasizing that this brother had been the only blond child in their family and stressing that this information was of real significance. She also wanted me to know that he was very excited about getting through to me because he had agreed to help as a guide on my journey and was adamant that now he'd made contact he would find a way of proving his existence.

Puzzled by the information I'd just been given, because I'd only ever been aware of four other siblings in Dad's family and none of them had been called Tim or Tom, but I thanked Lena all the same for making my first ever sitting with a medium such a wonderful experience. Lena hugged me as we reached the door and became very insistent that I make some enquiries about the formerly unknown brother, stressing once again the importance of his existence.

As my mother was the only person I could ask I sought confirmation the very next day just as Lena had requested. Never backward at coming forward I posed the question as we drove into town and on reflection asking such a question whilst my mother was driving was probably never a good idea. Narrowly avoiding a collision with the hedge and a meeting with *all* our deceased relatives the elusive Tim or Tom included, my mother came to an abrupt halt. Looking decidedly pale she asked who I'd been talking too and informed me that apart from herself and my father's immediate family no one knew about 'Tom'.

Conveniently dodging the question about my source of

information I excitedly bombarded Mum with questions about Tom and was surprised to learn that he had indeed been the only blond haired child in the family and had sadly died in infancy. She even knew the circumstances of his demise and told me that whilst suffering from some childhood ailment the boy had collapsed against the cast iron bed frame and fractured his skull. The poor little soul had only been three years old and had never regained consciousness after the accident. All of this had been relayed to my mother, second hand, by Dad, as it had happened some years before he was even born.

Lena had been absolutely correct in everything she had told me. The story of Tom was true in every sense and without doubt, he had, and still did exist. In only one week I had joined a meditation class and been kick started on my renewed journey in search of understanding and enlightenment. And my first visit to a medium had given me wonderful evidence of survival in a dimension I could only yet guess at.

Little was I to know that I had just stepped on board a roller coaster ride that had not been fitted with brakes!

CHAPTER 6

'RAGAMUFFIN'

It was now 1989 and Julie and Christine were 11 and 9 respectively and both with very different outlooks and temperaments, but one thing they did have in common was their love of animals. During their primary years we had inherited a cat called Charlie along with the acquisition of various rabbits, gerbils and goldfish. These vied for attention with cat-molested wild birds, hedgehogs and even a half-dead butterfly that Christine had found on her way home from school. Desperate to keep it as a pet, she begged me to nurse it back to health, however, along with the majority of wild birds the unfortunate creature eventually succumbed to natural causes.

Having a very sensitive nature Christine was distraught each time there was a death, whereas Julie on the other hand, the more philosophical of the two, was much more matter of fact about such things. As far as Christine was concerned every death required a decent burial, each with its own cross made out of an iced lollie stick to mark the final resting place and over time the garden became littered with a myriad of wooden memory sticks. Both girls were only too happy to feed and play with their pets, but they were never around when hutches needed mucking out or the goldfish tank required cleaning and fresh water. Over the years I had gotten used to the fact that once the novelty had worn off it was me that was left to do the dirty jobs.

Having run the gamut of the above they turned their attention to acquiring something a little larger and more playful and the 'puppy' word now entered their vocabulary being bandied about on a daily basis. Never having owned a dog I was reluctant to take on the long term responsibility or give in to their persistent badgering. After some months of pestering I'd got my stock answer of '*No*' down to a fine art when for some unexplained reason I started to warm to the idea of bringing a puppy into the family. Looking back I'm not sure if it was some form of Chinese torture I'd been subjected too, like water dripping on a stone the girls had worn me down, but I decided I would go ahead and get their puppy.

Once I'd agreed to their request there was the question of what kind of dog we would look for. The girls wanted a puppy that would grow into a big dog, but I put my foot down and told them it would be a small breed of dog which would fit easily into the family and our small bungalow. Thankfully, they agreed to my stipulations because to them a puppy was a puppy, now they knew Mum had given in and that they had won.

By 'chance' a couple of weeks later I heard about someone who bred Yorkshire terriers locally and thinking a little Yorkie might be the ideal size for us and our small home I rang to make enquiries and was informed by the lady breeder that there was a new litter to choose from.

The night before we were due to see the pups I had the most vivid dream where I found myself sitting in front of a roaring fire with Nana. Comfortable in her company and her home as we had been in life, we were talking and laughing having a lovely conversation and I felt as though we had never been apart. During the dream she pointed to the hearthrug where to my surprise a little puppy was curled up fast asleep. The same colour as its background the pup was so well camouflaged I hadn't noticed it resting on the black and tan rag rug that I remembered so well from my childhood. Not taking my eyes of the pup I heard my grandmother say, "Linda, I am sending you this puppy, she is a very special gift and is meant for you, her name is Rags. Look after her well."

On waking I recalled the lovely dream of Nana which had left me feeling all warm inside. That warmth remained with me throughout the day and I thought to myself many times that it had been a long, long time since I'd had such a vivid dream about Nana and it had left me as excited as the girls to see the puppies.

Later that day we found the breeder's home with ease following the directions she'd given us, and as we were expected the owner was waiting to welcome us in. To our delight, just inside the porch door, was a dog bed filled with little squirming black puppies no bigger than my hand. We were pleased to find that we had first choice of the new litter of eight puppies, but they all looked exactly the same so how on earth could we choose?

Leaving the girls with the puppies I was invited into the sitting room for a cup of tea and to my surprise, curled up on the hearthrug, was the puppy from my dream the previous night! Pricking up her ears as I entered the room she lifted her sleepy head and looked in my direction wagging her little docked tail as she ambled over to me with a look of instant recognition in her eyes. The look on her face melted my heart and picking her up I sat her on my lap where she immediately curled up and went back to sleep. The owner smiled at the sleeping puppy as she entered the room with our tea, "I see you've found a friend," she remarked.

Secretly hoping the answer would be 'no' I asked if she was keeping the little puppy to breed from. You can't imagine the joy I felt when I discovered that the pup had been the 'runt' from the previous litter and had only been kept reluctantly. Not able to imagine why such a sweet little thing had not been homed, I knew I could not go home without her and found myself asking the incredulous woman if she would be prepared to sell her to me. The breeder not sure why I would possibly want a runt in preference to a puppy from a new litter didn't quibble and happily agreed.

Delighted with Nana's choice, although they weren't aware of it, the girls were only too happy to take Rags home with us. As for myself, I believe Rags knew I was the person she was meant to be with from the very first moment her knowing little eyes saw me and because of my dream I could not have left her behind.

Very soon it became obvious that Rags was very much 'my' dog as the girls' interest quickly waned, which I knew it would, so of course, the dog walking was left to me, not that I minded, I loved it!

Never having owned a dog before I couldn't quite believe how quickly this little creature had cast such a loving spell over my heart. Rags or Ragamuffin as we registered her on her pedigree certificate was indeed destined to become a very special part of my life just as Nana had predicted.

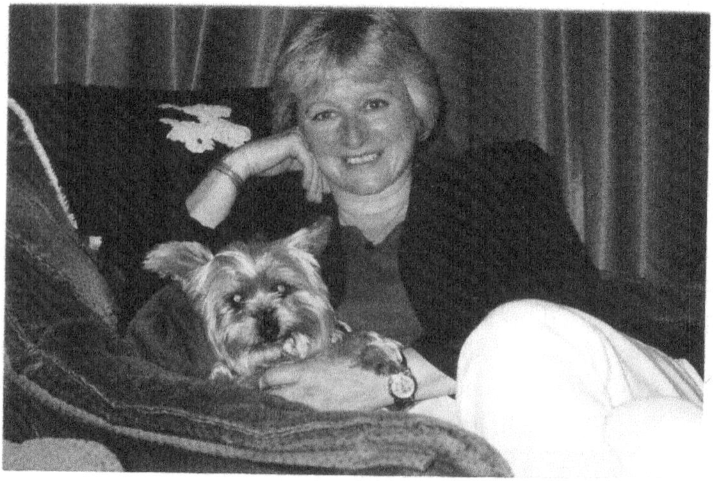

CHAPTER 7

THE CRYSTAL MAZE

On a beautiful sunny Sunday afternoon shortly after Rags joined the family we took a drive out to the old airport base at Jurby accompanied by Mum and Julie, with Rags riding shotgun on the parcel shelf, a habit she had adopted from her very first journey in the car.

The old nissan huts that had once been home to the Royal Air Force were now a collection of shops selling second-hand furniture, bric-a-brac and books. Wandering in and out of the various huts we came upon a store which was magically named Merlin's Cave and peeping through the door its appearance was more like that of Aladdin's Cave with its vast array of merchandise and items of interest on display.

Feeling as though the shop was beckoning me in for a closer look we entered, although I had my work cut out as Rags, even on her lead, was anxious to chew anything within easy reach. Not wanting to upset the shop owner, who was keeping a beady eye on me and my wayward puppy, I eventually picked Rags up tucking her under my arm.

Julie, who in the company of my mother had followed me into the shop called me over to where her attention was focused on a selection of small wicker baskets, each one full to the brim with brightly coloured polished stones. Never having come across anything similar I was surprised to find myself telling Julie that they were crystals and semi-precious stones used for healing purposes and suggesting she should close her eyes for a few moments before choosing a stone. Knowing, but without knowing how I knew, Julie was surprised to be told by me, with 'authority', that the crystal she would choose had actually chosen her. We each chose a different stone in the way I had suggested and making our purchases we left a much relieved shop owner who I'm sure was glad to see me exit with Rags.

Leaving the house for my meditation class a few days later a thought popped into my mind to take my stone with me to hold whilst I meditated and following my internal prompt I slipped the little stone into my pocket. A little while later as I entered the meeting room I could hardly believe my eyes as every surface was covered with crystals and tumble stones in many different colours, shapes and sizes.

Lena, without informing the class, had invited her friend who was a crystal healer to take the meditation that evening and she had brought with her the beautiful collection of crystals on display. On the main table there were chunks of natural quartz, rose quartz and amethyst displayed around a huge dish filled with highly polished tumble stones, just like the ones we'd seen in Merlin's Cave.

We were all invited by the crystal healer to choose a crystal from the table and instructed to hold it while we meditated. At this point I put my hand in my pocket and pulled out my shiny new stone, showing it to Lena and her friend and telling them the story of how I had come to find it. Smiling knowingly at one another, but saying nothing to me I was requested to choose another stone so that I could hold one in each hand during the meditation. Without hesitation I closed my eyes for a few moments and when I opened them the only precious stone obvious to me in the bowl was a beautiful piece of purple amethyst. Feeling very pleased with my choice I plucked it from the bowl and sat down to ready myself for the meditation.

It was a lovely meditation and I remember what a strange sensation it was to feel the flow of energy moving from one crystal to the other through my body. After the meditation I returned the amethyst to the bowl when another stone 'winked' at me. It was very small with the appearance of solid mercury and I felt completely overwhelmed with the urge to pick it up. Lena was able to tell me it was called Hematite and bestowed her strange knowing look on me as she placed it in my palm. Smiling, she closed my fingers over the small piece of hematite and said, "I am giving you this stone with much love as they will mean a great deal to you in the future."

Whilst driving home that evening I found myself pondering on the coincidence that had introduced me to crystal healing only days after finding the crystals in Merlin's Cave. Now in possession of two healing stones with no real understanding of their abilities and Lena's enigmatic message floating around my head I was questioning what it all meant.

The next day was Wednesday which I really looked forward to as I worked with my friend Betty and not having seen her since the previous week I had lots to tell her about my experiences with the crystals.

Betty was already taking her coat off as I entered the staff room and looking up she said, "Oh, Linda, before I forget, I've got something for you, it's in my bag." Pulling a small parcel wrapped in white tissue paper from the depths of her enormous handbag she handed it to me. Opening the package I could scarcely believe what I was seeing as lying resplendent on the white tissue paper was a piece of amethyst almost identical in size, colour and shape to the piece I had chosen the night before at meditation class.

Overwhelmed at another unexplained coincidence I asked where it had come from and why she was giving it to me. To my absolute amazement I learnt Betty had brought the stone back from Africa some years previously and had come across it the day before whilst cleaning out some drawers. Without hesitation or embarrassment on her part she told me the moment she had picked it up a little voice inside her head had told her to give it to Linda.

Staring wordlessly at the piece of amethyst lying in my palm I listened to Betty explaining that 'the voice' had been so insistent that she had to wrap it up and put it in her handbag straight away lest she forget. Looking up from the crystal Betty suddenly enquired if I was feeling alright as my face had completely drained of colour. Struggling with the fact I now had three stones and none of these occurrences could be deemed coincidence I retold my story of the last few days to my amazed friend who was as excited and puzzled as I was.

On Friday of that same week I was checking stock when I heard the shop door open and a cheery voice call out, "I'm glad your here today Linda I've got something for you." Turning around I discovered it was Vera, my colleague Liz's mum, and she was offering me something wrapped in white tissue paper.

"It's only a little gift," said Vera, smiling disarmingly, unable to disguise her excitement and waited for me to take the little parcel. Eventually thrusting it into my hand she persuaded me that she genuinely wanted me to accept it. Somewhat surprised at the gesture because it was not my birthday or any other significant occasion that I could think of and couldn't imagine why Vera would want to give me a gift.

Carefully, I un-wrapped the tissue paper to reveal something that made my heart miss a beat because it was the most beautiful crystal pendant I'd ever seen. Fondling the pendant lovingly in my hand I told Vera how much I appreciated her gift and I could see how delighted she was by my obvious enthusiasm. Questioning Vera as to why she had given me the pendant I was excited to discover that she had bought it at a charity event some years before, but had never felt comfortable wearing it herself, and that it had lain undisturbed in her jewelry box until the day before when she had come across it and had been overwhelmed with the desire to give it to *me!*

Arriving home after visiting his mother that Sunday afternoon Dickie placed a carrier bag full of glossy women's magazines on the coffee table. My mother-in-law, not wanting to throw them out had passed them on for me to read. Never having really been interested in these types of magazines I wouldn't have bought them for myself, but pulling one out of the pile and opening it at random was amazed to discover it was an interview with a *crystal healer*! Reading through the page I was even more amazed when I read the very words I myself had spoken in Merlin's Cave the previous Sunday on how to choose a crystal!

There could be no denying I was being fed little pieces of a jigsaw puzzle, some of which seemed to fit together, but what was it all trying to tell me? And when would the missing pieces appear?

CHAPTER 8

THE DEVIL'S CLAW

After a week of strange events you would think I was prepared for the unexpected, but not so. Early in the week a man unknown to me entered the shop and asked my colleague Liz if we stocked Devil's Claw tablets. Liz looked over at me pulling one of her funny faces saying, "This sounds like something you'd know about Linda." Shaking my head I had to admit I'd never heard of Devil's Claw before and pointed the stranger in the direction of the health food shop with a feeling he would find what he was looking for there.

A couple of days later a friend called into the shop for a chat and as she was leaving handed me a book that she'd bought especially for me in the local charity shop. Taking the small volume from my friend's outstretched hand I could feel my hands begin to shake and my knees buckle as I read the title, 'All about The Devil's Claw'! As the unfamiliar name rang a familiar bell in my consciousness I asked her why she had bought me this particular book only to discover that having run her fingers along the bookshelf she had thought of me when reaching this volume and just knew she couldn't leave the shop without it.

Placing the thin volume in my handbag I shook my head in disbelief and made a mental note to read it during my lunch break. I was amazed to learn the Devil's Claw is a prickly plant that only grows in the Kalahari Desert and the pulped root, when ingested, can help relieve the symptoms of psoriatic arthritis. This was incredible information to me as I had been struggling with the curse of psoriasis and joint pain since I was sixteen and at that precise time I was in the middle of a flare-up.

My joints were aching and the skin, especially on my face, was a mess with patches of angry red and disfiguring psoriasis. Believe me my body did not feel or look good and I was willing to try anything. Luckily the one and only health food shop in town did stock Devil's Claw tablets and I bought some absolutely certain in the knowledge I had been given this information to help me. While I was there I described the man who had visited the shop asking for Devil's Claw a couple of days earlier, but the girl who owned the shop shook her head and told me she had never seen anyone fitting that description and that I was the only person to have bought Devil's Claw that week!

A few days later whilst walking Rags along the disused railway line near my home I noticed a plant growing wild on the hedge with a beautiful blue star shaped flower. It was a plant I had never spotted before, but for some reason I was fascinated with it and made a mental note to find out its name.

Later that week the girls' school was holding a Victorian exhibition and as a mum I was dragged along to give my support. In the corner of the assembly hall where the exhibition was taking place there was an arrangement of plants which was meant to be a replica of a Victorian herb garden. There were lots of potted herbs with little name stickers in each one and there right in the middle of the display was the beautiful blue star shaped flower I'd seen on the railway lines earlier that week. Knowing I just had to see what it was called, and to my daughters' obvious dismay and cries of protest I climbed over the little rope barrier and waded into the sea of plants triumphantly plucking the label from the pot only to discover its name was 'Borage'.

Standing knee deep in what was once a pristine display and ignoring the embarrassment of my children I stared at the word 'Borage' as tingles ran up and down my spine, accompanied with a sure knowing that there must be a reason why I felt so attracted to this plant. By the time I had disentangled myself from the perimeter rope my girls were beating a hasty retreat out of the assembly hall thoroughly ashamed of their mother for having shown them up.

As I have already mentioned my psoriasis was very active at the time, red and scaly and not a pretty sight. On the advice of my doctor I could use only un-perfumed cream on my face, the effects of which lasted only minutes before my nose was bright red and shining like a beacon. Believe me it was so bad I was seriously considering changing my name to Rudolph!

Making my way to the health food shop, yet again, hoping against hope that I would find some natural cure that would help my condition. Smiling at the girl behind the counter I pointed to my face asking her if she could suggest anything other than a bag to put over my head. Despite the distress the psoriasis caused me I always tried to keep a sense of humour even when things were bleak. Passing me a small brown jar of cream from the box she was unpacking she said, "Try this, it's new in today, but you must read the leaflet before applying it for the first time."

Needless to say I bought it willing to try anything that might help. That evening after cleansing my face I read the leaflet before applying the cream and imagine my amazement when I discovered that the main ingredient of the cream was 'Borage', purported in the leaflet to be 'the skins natural healer.'

Within a few days of taking the Devil's Claw and applying the Borage cream both my arthritis and psoriasis were unbelievably well under control. By now I was beginning to think that the meditation classes must have something to do with the things that were happening to me. These coincidences, as I chose to call them then had never taken place before in my life, or if they had I'd been totally unaware.

YOGA, MEDITATION and 'ALL THAT JAZZ'

Feeling slightly under the weather and out of sorts one day,
I called in on my doctor to see what he would say,
After taking temperature and pulse and looking in both eyes,
Peering over his spectacles, he said, "My dear, this comes as no surprise.
My diagnosis is very clear this is a 'bout of stress."
I had to look on the bright side, at least he hadn't asked me to undress!
With a few well chosen words, he scribbled on a docket,
Smiled as he held it out to me and I shoved it in my pocket,
Pills I thought, and rolled my eyes, I hated taking pills,
There must be another way to cure me of my ills.
Yoga, that would help to become more relaxed and calm,
To sit cross-legged for hours would be a beneficial balm.
I bought a book on Yoga and studied every page,
Took up the 'Lotus' position, and sat there like a sage,
After only five minutes both feet were completely numb,
And that is not to mention a word about my bum!
It took another half an hour to undo my tormented frame,
I was totally tied up in knots, and thought,
"I'll not try that again."
Still searching for a remedy to cure this general malaise,
Once more I visited the bookshop, this time in a desperate daze.
There were books on many subjects all claiming to de-stress,
Some of them were most bizarre I really must confess.
Anything from hanging upside down resembling a bat,
To being wrapped in seaweed and stewing in a vat!
No, these were not the answers of that I felt quite sure,
If I had to go to those lengths I'd never find a cure.
Indian Head Massage I was told was gentle and not taxing,
I thought that I would give it a go and 'yes' it was ever so relaxing,
I was a little disappointed though when the therapist came in,
I was expecting an Indian chief, but what I got was a guy named Glynn!

Next I tried Pilates and was given a rubber band,
I had to put it round my feet and hold it tightly in my hands,
We then progressed to lying prostrate upon the floor,
But, Oh dear me, I lost my grip and the band flew out the door!
Following my wayward band I exited the room,
I never did return, I thought my efforts doomed.
So much for Pilates, Yoga and Indian Head massage,
For all the success I'd had I might well have taken up equine dressage,
I thought I'd give it one more go, this time meditation,
I bought a tape and took it home, a beautiful visualization,
It took me on a journey far away from every day,
Through leafy lanes and meadows and fields of yellow hay,
This was much more like it, I felt calm and so serene,
Hooray! I've found the answer, now I was super keen.
Meditation is the remedy, for me it works a treat,
It wasn't long before I was dancing down the street.
This journey may have taken a few twists and turns along the way
But all is well, that ends well, is all that I can say.

CHAPTER 9

THE OLIVE BRANCH

Things seemed to be happening on an almost daily basis, one so called 'coincidence' after another and it gave me such a buzz. Even minor things like thinking of someone I'd not seen in a while only to meet them in the street a few minutes later or turning on the radio to find I was already singing the song that was being played, but on other occasions they would be momentous events like the next story.

During the summer of 1990 my Uncle Walter arrived home on holiday from New Zealand to stay with his sister, my mother Joan. Some years earlier he'd fallen out with their brother who is also resident on the Island and try as we might to reconcile them both Walter was very much against the idea.
   Some days after Walter had arrived on the island I received a very strange phone call from my other uncle apologizing for missing Joan and Walter's visit. It seemed he had found their note on arriving home with my aunt and requesting that they call again before they left for their holidays that weekend. Happy to think Walter had had a change of heart I relayed the message to Mum who gaped at me in surprise and informed me that she hadn't been able to get Walter anywhere near their brother's farm.
   A week or so later Walter called at my home to see if I would spend the afternoon with him and leafing through a copy of the local paper spotted an advert for a new sheltered housing development in Ramsey. Asking if we could perhaps go and take a look that afternoon, remarking on the fact that if it was nice he wanted to take video footage back to New Zealand to show my aunt in the hopes she would be enticed to come back 'home' to retire.
   Minutes later, after parking the car at the new development we followed the signs to the show house when simultaneously we

became aware of a large lady with her hair in curlers watching us from her kitchen window. Beckoning us by waving she called from her back door that she thought the show house was closed, but telling us she would be happy for us view her own recently completed house. Thanking her, we told her we would come back if there was no one in the site office. Retracing our steps a few minutes later after finding the show house closed we were once again assailed by the large lady in rollers who would not take 'no' for an answer and ushered us into her home.

Apologizing for the accumulation of dust everywhere due to their absence from home for a few days she offered to show us upstairs first. Walter enquired if she had been on holiday, whereupon she was happy to tell us that she and her husband had been 'farm sitting' for some friends. Winking at me, Walter asked if their friends name happened to be Cannell. Almost losing her grip on the banister, which would have been a disaster for those of us following her up the stairs, the poor woman asked how he could possibly know that. Smiling back at her Walter shrugged his shoulders and told her it had been a wild guess! Although I felt his comment had come as much of a surprise to him as it had to me, and gathering his thoughts quickly explained he was the brother of their friends.

Squealing with delight the woman shouted down the stairs to her husband, telling him to phone my aunt and uncle from the farm immediately. Walter gave me a horrified look as this was the last thing he wanted, but there was nothing we could do to halt events. Making our way downstairs behind a very excited large lady, curlers bouncing with every step she took, we entered the living room to find an elderly gentleman with the phone in his outstretched hand. Grabbing the phone our excitable hostess held it out to my mortified uncle. Walter took the phone and we all looked on in agonized silence as a frosty exchange ensued between the brothers, obvious to all parties by now that things were not as they should be.

After the phone was placed back on the receiver Walter explained the situation and apologized for their embarrassment and thanking them for their hospitality politely enquired their names. You can imagine our surprise when they introduced themselves as **Joan** and **Walter**. Suddenly we began to make all the connections and finding out that they had indeed visited my aunt and uncle on the farm a couple of weeks previously and had left a note, the mystery was finally solved.

When you take into consideration the huge odds of the above sequence of events the outcome can only be described as truly miraculous.

To my delight my uncles' did indeed make up, after all life is too short to hold grudges ... wouldn't you agree?

CHAPTER 10

GERALDINE

One evening after our meditation class Lena announced that she was in the process of organising a weekend dedicated to all aspects of spirituality and metaphysics, adding that we were all welcome to attend. My name was first on the list, as it had to be admitted she would have had trouble keeping me away.

Lena had invited two of her friends from the mainland to teach and about a month later fifty or so spiritually-minded people from all over the island met to take part in what turned out to be a wonderful spiritual weekend. It was absolutely fascinating and I met a lot of new people who, like me, were all awake or awakening spiritually.

One woman in particular, a lovely serene lady, probably about twenty years older than myself seemed to gravitate towards me, introducing herself as Mary. We just 'clicked' and spent the rest of the weekend sitting together in the auditorium and sharing lunch and tea breaks discussing excitedly what we had been learning. The weekend flew by and I for one did not want it to end as prior to this workshop much of what I knew had been self taught or inherently 'known', but now the gaps in my knowledge were being filled and my thirst for more information was even greater.

Hugging Mary as we parted I thanked her for her friendship over the past couple of days and her eyes twinkled in response as she assured me we would be meeting again very soon. Asking her how she could be so sure I was puzzled to hear her say it was already 'in our destiny'.

Only a few weeks after this event I was distressed to learn that Lena was moving to the other end of the island and unfortunately the meditation classes would cease. Devastated, I wondered what I was going to do without the support of the group, but had to come to terms that things change in the blink of an eye and accepting the situation realised this was all part of my spiritual journey too.

During the summer of 1993, an advert in the local paper leapt off the page at me as it was offering spiritual healing at an address in Douglas, something I'd never ever seen advertised before. Desperately wanting to find out more as this I felt was an important 'first' for the Island, but somehow not able to pluck up the courage to go on my own.

By 'chance' shortly after reading the advertisement I met an old friend who suffered from Multiple Sclerosis and was only able to walk with the aid of two sticks. He asked if I could think of anything that might help and the advert for spiritual healing popped straight into my mind, so I discussed with him the possibility of trying it. Although he was a little reluctant at first he eventually agreed to let me take him the following week.

Arriving shortly after the hall opened I helped my friend through the door, only to be greeted by a familiar face. It was Mary, the lady I'd met at Lena's workshop. Surprised to meet Mary again in these surroundings she held her arms out wide and hugged me giving me that same twinkly eyed look I remembered. I had not known she was a healer, in fact her first name was the only thing I knew about her. She, on the other hand, explained that she had realized I was a healer from the moment we'd met at Lena's spiritual weekend and that it would only be a matter of time before my 'guides' would draw me in the same direction as herself. I must confess at this point in my life I didn't agree with her and definitely did not see myself in the role of a healer.

Mary led my friend off to a quiet corner to administer healing while I found myself somewhere to sit that looked out on to a tranquil garden at the rear of the premises. Sitting quite happily entranced with the antics of a family of blue-tits I suddenly realised someone was speaking to me. Turning around I found a very charismatic looking lady in her 50's was introducing herself as Geraldine and asking me if I would like some healing. Politely declining, telling her I was only there as moral support for a friend and nodded in the direction of Mary and her charge. Geraldine was nothing, if not persistent or should I say persuasive as she seemed to think I would really benefit from a healing session, so, eventually I agreed, mainly out of curiosity.

Having never actually received healing before this was another wonderful new experience for me and was glad I'd let Geraldine talk me into it. When the healing session was over she came to sit by me and very soon we were deep in conversation and I found myself telling her about all the strange 'coincidences' that were happening to me. Adding that I knew something special was happening in my life, but I was not sure what *'it'* was, or where *'it'* was leading me.

Feeling supremely peaceful and calm, cocooned in the tranquil atmosphere of the place I felt confident that I could ask any questions that came into my mind and requested of Geraldine if she could shed some light on the things I'd told her about. She confirmed that something special was indeed happening, but her advice was to take things one day at a time and the things I needed to know would all be revealed when 'the time was right'.

Feeling a little bit let down by Geraldine's non-specific answer, I was about to take the conversation further when I spotted Mary and my friend approaching and immediately decided against it. Thanking Mary as she led another client away for healing she winked and smiled sweetly in my direction. Little did I know it then, but I was never to see Mary again as shortly after this meeting I discovered she had passed on. Yet for some reason I didn't feel sad as I had a feeling deep inside that I already knew her very well, even though our acquaintance in this earthly plane had been destined to be brief.

Only a week or so after meeting Geraldine at the healing centre she walked into the chemist shop where I worked. Noticing her as soon as she entered, I knew at that point she had not seen me. Smiling when she recognized me behind the counter, we spent a few minutes chatting as she informed me she was a qualified aromatherapist and reflexologist and ran her business from her home which was only a few hundred yards away.

Geraldine enquired if I was interested in complementary therapies and was delighted when I shared with her that I had just enrolled on a home study course in anatomy and physiology as a forerunner to learning reflexology myself. She laughed at what she deemed to be another coincidence, but before leaving the shop she suggested we make a date to meet at her home where she would give me a free reflexology treatment and any help and advice I needed with my forthcoming anatomy and physiology course.

By now I really thought I must have a guardian angel working for me behind the scenes. It all seemed too good to be true, as I was just about to embark on an Open University course, the prospect of which absolutely terrified me because I hadn't studied since leaving school at fifteen. Having already received the first batch of notes and questions I thought I'd accidently been enrolled on the wrong course, as to my mind they had to be the notes for a trainee brain surgeon! And then seemingly by chance, the very person who could help me had just popped up in my life, as if by magic.

Calling at Geraldine's home as scheduled she gave me a lovely relaxing reflexology treatment. During the session we talked about various aspects of complementary therapies, and by the end of the evening she'd encouraged me to enrol on a First Aid course to run alongside my anatomy and physiology studies. I was becoming a glutton for punishment as that would mean even more study on my agenda.

The First Aid courses were held in Douglas through the Red Cross and consisted of one training night a week for twelve weeks and it appeared Geraldine and I were in luck as a new course was due to start in two weeks time and interestingly there were only two places left. The week before the course started Mum and I were going on holiday to Cornwall, so the dates fitted in perfectly. How strange that everything appeared to slot into place without any problem ... as easy as a child's jigsaw.

Mum and I had a lovely week in Cornwall and as it was a coach trip we got to see all the sights and the beautiful countryside. On our last full day the excursion was to Truro which turned out to be a beautiful sunny day just as it had been all week. We were dropped off at a coach park and told to be back in three hours time which would give us enough time to visit the cathedral and tour the shops. Finding our way to the cathedral was easy because it was so big you couldn't miss it. We wandered around inside soaking up the atmosphere before taking some photographs on the steps outside then headed to the shops. The hours slipped by very quickly and before long Mum remarked it was time to find our way back to the coach park. But which way was it? Direction has never been my strong point; in fact if you were to blindfold me and spin me round three times in my own garden it is highly unlikely I would be able to find the way out! Sadly, this appears to be an inherited trait as Mum is no better than I am.

Making our way up a couple of back streets we both thought we were heading in the general direction of the coach park, but were far from sure when I recognized a middle aged woman pushing a pram who was accompanied by a young man. They walked past us with no recognition on their part and as they passed I commented to Mum that I thought I knew the woman and was sure she worked at the Cottage Hospital in Ramsey. Mum commented that it couldn't possibly be anyone I knew and thought the woman was probably just a look-a-like or doppelganger. Not convinced with her explanation I felt certain that I'd been meant to notice the woman, but with little time to deliberate on the subject we continued up that street and thankfully found the coach park and our coach, with the engine running.

The following Monday night Geraldine and I attended our first lecture at the Red Cross Centre. What a shock I got when I entered the lecture room as there were only fifteen people enrolled on the course and one of those just happened to be the very woman I thought I'd seen in Truro the week before!

After the class I tapped her lightly on the shoulder and asked the surprised lady if she had enjoyed herself in Truro the previous week. Spinning around with a startled look on her face she immediately wanted to know how I, a stranger, was aware of her comings and goings. Reassuring her that I was not a private detective and only holidaying with my mother in the same locale as herself she visibly relaxed and explained her visit to Truro was to spend time with her new grandchild. Thanking her and apologising for startling her I was relieved when she laughed and said she just found the whole episode quite bizarre.

Perhaps a year or so prior to this I would have thought it bizarre too, but not now, as I was beginning to see these 'coincidences' all had meaning. The sequence of events that had just taken place involved two strangers who both lived in close proximity on an island with a population of some 80,000 inhabitants. That our paths should cross on more than one occasion when both of us were out of our normal environment cannot be considered as anything as mundane as coincidence! I was learning that these events were predestined to happen, remember the little red flags in the jungle ... to be in the right place at the right time. In effect I feel we had kept our appointment in this life, although at least one of us was not aware of this fact and even I still remained puzzled by the mysteries I was encountering. Life was certainly becoming a real adventure or perhaps it always had been only now I was noticing it more.

CHAPTER 11

THE ROLLER COASTER PICKS UP SPEED

During the summer of 1994 I received my quarterly copy of Kindred Spirit, a magazine to which I had subscribed for some time. Flipping through the pages I searched for the article which grabbed my attention the most and coming across a photograph of a man I felt strangely drawn to I settled down to read the accompanying article. The interviewee was James Redfield, a very charismatic looking man with a beautiful aura about him and he'd written a book called 'The Celestine Prophecy.'

A new age novel, his interest was centered on people who were experiencing meaningful coincidences or synchronicities and were convinced they were being guided from one experience to another. Although the article said the storyline of the book was fiction, James pointed out that the essence of his writing was fact and although it wasn't common knowledge, these 'coincidences' were now happening to a large number of people around the world.

Knowing I had to get my hands on a copy of this book because I felt it would somehow shed light on what was taking place in my own life I began a search of all the book shops I could find. To my dismay I drew a blank at every book-seller as no one had even heard of The Celestine Prophecy, let alone had a copy.

One Saturday towards the end of November, Dickie and I set out with a long list of items to begin our Christmas shopping. The said list ended with a visit to our local bookshop to buy a book that Julie had requested. I love book shops and could spend hours in them, but unfortunately my dear husband does not. Entering the shop I remember thinking what a perfect opportunity I had to search some more for my elusive book. Searching the shelves thoroughly in all the sections where I thought I might find a copy of 'The Celestine Prophecy' sadly I remained empty handed.

Never patient under such circumstances an irritable Dickie asked me to find the book we had come to buy so we could finally go home. Explaining that I was looking for a particular book I'd been searching for all year had little effect and I could tell by the expression on his face he'd had enough of Christmas shopping!

Resignedly, I made my way to the fiction section as Julie had requested a book by Terry Pratchett. Terry, being a prolific writer had a whole shelf devoted to his books alone, some of which were spine out and some were face on. Running my finger along the shelf I quickly located the book Julie had requested and lifting it down was amazed to find a copy of 'The Celestine Prophecy' directly behind it.

Jumping up and down on the spot with excitement I exclaimed to my astonished and extremely embarrassed husband that I'd found the book I'd been searching for with a passion for months. Looking less than impressed Dickie gave me a withering look as I'm sure he considered me completely mad.

Clutching both books and feeling very pleased with myself I made my way to the counter to pay. The assistant frowned and asked me if I had dropped the re-order slip from my copy of 'The Celestine Prophecy' as there was not one to found within its pages. Retracing my steps I searched the floor, but could find nothing. On my return to the counter, a very puzzled assistant having checked the stock on her computer, told me there was no record of the book or it ever having been ordered! Obviously completely flummoxed by the whole episode and after telling her I'd been searching for it for months, I'm happy to say, she did let me buy it.

Despite its apparent non existence in the records at the book store the copy I was now proud owner of gave every appearance of being brand new. At this point on my spiritual journey it would have been impossible for me to explain how the book had materialized right behind the very book I had gone into the shop to buy! To me, it seemed as though an invisible hand had placed it there knowing that I would be the one to find it.

Not pondering on the circumstances of my ownership I can only say that The Celestine Prophecy changed my view of what was happening to me and I know it has been a catalyst for countless thousands of other spiritual seekers. Needless to say I read the book in less than 24 hours and have read and re-read it on numerous occasions since also having lent it to countless others whom I have come across in the course of my journey, who were, like me, experiencing similar coincidences.

After reading The Celestine Prophecy I learnt that through my positivity and connection with nature I had raised my energies to a higher vibration whereby the synchronicities I was experiencing were being magnetized towards me propelling me along my path of destiny.

In effect I had waved the green flag for *'Go'...* now without any doubt I became aware that my 'HS' was not only going to accompany me, but was actively pushing me along my path.

CHAPTER 12

'ILLUMINATION'

The very next week another crazy, wonderful thing happened. As I have already mentioned it was coming up to Christmas and I was struggling to find a gift that would please my 'down to earth' husband. Leafing through a friend's home shopping catalogue for ideas I came upon clock radios, one of which caught my eye. Not only was it a radio alarm clock it could also be used as a bedside light and seeing the proverbial 'light' at the end of my shopping tunnel I considered this a useful and practical present for the no-nonsense man in my life.

As a result of my mother's perpetual insistence that I should only buy electrical equipment from a local supplier who could be relied upon to repair faults should they arise, it has left me with an aversion to shopping for electrical items via catalogue. So, with Mum's advice in mind I set off in search of the clock radio with the light. I visited practically every electrical outlet on the island, describing the item I was searching for and the brand name. On plenty of occasions I was offered alternatives, but I had a real 'bee in my bonnet' and for me it had to be the one I'd seen in my friend's catalogue.

As with my search for the book I drew a blank everywhere I went and had almost given up hope of ever finding it when I found myself walking through the door of a dusty little electrical repair shop. Practically every surface in the small shop was filled with televisions and radios with their innards hanging out and numerous other unidentifiable items of electrical equipment lay about in the course of repair. Wondering what had brought me on such a fool's errand into this shop with only a handful of new products I had almost convinced myself that I was not going to find my husband's elusive gift. Undaunted, I walked over to the counter and described to the owner what I was looking for and was unsurprised when shaking his head he apologized and told me he couldn't help. Thinking my intuition had failed me I turned to leave when he produced a thick catalogue of electrical products and dropped it on the counter with a loud thud. Tapping the large tome he said, "If you can find it in here I will try and get it from my supplier, but don't hold your breath."

Flipping through the pages of clock-radios there were dozens of little photographs advertising different makes and designs when to my absolute delight I eventually found the one I'd been searching for and pointing to it excitedly I asked if he could order it for me as soon as possible. I think he felt sorry for me more than anything, but he did promise he would try and obtain the item, stressing that he hoped I'd not be too disappointed if he couldn't get one. It was at this point he explained the catalogue was two years out of date!

Feeling I had little other hope of tracking one down I asked the nice man to try and obtain the clock, telling him I would call again in a week's time. Leaving the store with a warm feeling towards the eccentric owner because at least he had tried to help me, which was more than the bigger stores had done.

Later that day Christine had just arrived home from school when the phone rang and running to answer it, expecting it to be one of her friends, was disappointed to find a male voice requesting the presence of her mother. Coming through to answer her call I was surprised to find myself speaking to the nice man from the electrical shop, although my heart sank when I heard his voice as I expected him to tell me he could not get my clock radio. Imagine my surprise when he told me he was in possession of the radio I'd ordered earlier that day! Thanking him for such quick and efficient service the poor man began to stutter and there was every chance that any further conversation with him was going to be rather garbled. Calming him down I managed to ascertain that a delivery van had rolled up at his store shortly after I'd left and delivered a parcel that just happened to contain my clock radio, which at that point he hadn't even tried to order.

The poor man was completely bemused as the parcel contained no delivery note or invoice of any description. Informing me that he had no clue as to how this had happened I didn't have the heart to tell him these experiences had become everyday occurrences for me, but

I did assure him that I would call in a week's time and collect the clock by which time he may have received an invoice.

Entering the shop the following week I was not surprised to find the nice man disemboweling a radio at the counter. Having spotted me as I walked in he reached under the counter and lifted out a brown box which he placed proudly in the only clear space left in sight and proceeded to open it. To my delight, he produced the exact clock radio I'd been searching for. Magic!

The poor man was still in a dilemma as to its arrival advising me that his suppliers knew nothing about it and were unable to supply him with a price, so he had therefore decided that the fairest thing would be to charge me the price in the two year old catalogue where we had originally found the clock. Paying the man I thanked him very much for his help, although I knew I was leaving him in a rather perplexed state. To this day I never went back to see if he received an invoice, but a little voice in my head tells me that he did not.

For some unexplained reason my wish had been granted yet again and I knew that I must keep following my 'nudges' and allow myself to be guided.

CHAPTER 13

HELLO AGAIN .... TO ANOTHER PART OF ME!

In the late summer of 1994 Mum asked me to accompany her on a visit to an old friend who lived in Fleetwood. The elderly lady in question was very ill and Mum really wanted to see her one last time before she passed on.

Realising that we would only be a few miles from my father's family I reminded her that we hadn't seen any of them since I was 8 years old and expressed the desire to look them up, without any real understanding of why I should want to see them again.

As I mentioned earlier Dad had passed on when I was only six years old, but I could still remember his sisters and their families staying with us when I was a child. After Dad's death we seemed to lose contact with his remaining siblings and his assorted nieces and nephews, I suppose because their brother was no longer there the pull to come the Island was not as strong. However, Dad had been particularly close to his sister, my Aunt Ursula, and Mum had made the effort to keep in touch with her over the intervening years, usually at Christmas, but even that slight contact had petered out a number of years before. Nervously ringing the only number Mum had for my aunt, which she suspected may no longer be valid was relieved when Ursula answered the phone. Absolutely delighted that her sister-in-law had eventually reconnected Ursula immediately invited us to stay with them before we travelled on to Fleetwood.

Arriving at my aunt's home the following week we were given a wonderful welcome by her and my Uncle Joe and remembering their home from childhood visits more than 30 years before the feeling of déjà vu was intense. Later that afternoon Dad's older sister, Gertrude called by and joined in the reminiscing and the room quickly filled with laughter as they all seemed to have a lot of memories to share.

It wasn't long before we were joined by two younger women who were introduced as Elaine, my cousin, who I barely recognised and Karen the wife Elaine's brother, Greg. For some unexplained reason I was disappointed Greg was not with them because I really wanted to meet him again. The last time I'd seen him he was 3 years old and I was sure he would be as unrecognisable to me as Elaine had been. Having only called in to invite me on their evening out, the girls soon left with the promise they would keep me out of the way while the oldies recalled happier times in peace.

Returning a couple of hours later to pick me up I was disappointed once again to find Greg was not with them and was beginning to think he didn't want to meet me. Assuring me that was not the case they dragged me off to the nearest pub where they expected him to join us as soon as he could get away from work.

Their local pub was huge by Isle of Man standards, very busy and noisy, but we managed to find a table and sitting down with our drinks started to chat and get better acquainted. In no time at all we were getting along really well and at ease in each other's company. Suddenly I was overcome by a very strange sensation as everyone around me appeared to become immobile and the noise ebbed away to silence. I stopped talking mid-sentence and found myself turning in slow motion to look towards the door as a young man entered. Not able to take my eyes of him he walked past our table on his way to the bar without any acknowledgment. To me he seemed to be the only person in the pub who was moving, but as he reached the bar the strange sensation passed and the pub burst back into life again and the sound of everyone chatting and laughing was almost overwhelming as if the volume had been turned up.

Turning my attention back to my companions I was surprised to see a look of concern on their faces and couldn't understand why as in unison, they asked if I was feeling alright. Dismissing their worries I was more interested in finding out if the young man at the bar was Greg. Looking at one another and laughing they admitted it was a 'set up' that had been arranged by the three of them to see if I could pick Greg out in the crowd.

Calling him over the girls had no need to introduce us and I stood up leaning forward to kiss Greg in what turned out to be more of an embrace because I felt as if I didn't want to let him go! After he'd sat down the two of us just talked and talked and talked. Karen and Elaine must have wondered what was going on as we behaved as if we were the only two people at the table and remained wrapped up in our conversation for the rest of the evening.

Meeting Greg that evening felt like meeting another part of me, a part that had been absent for a long, long time and the realisation dawned on me that this almost total stranger meant something much more to me than *just* a long lost cousin. At the end of an evening full of fun and laughter we arranged to visit their local club the following night and take the oldies with us for a full family reunion and on returning to my aunt's home she was thrilled to find us all getting along so well, especially myself and Greg.

The following evening every five minutes or so one of the older generation commented on how alike Greg and I were and also how much we resembled my Dad, minus the moustache in my case. Feeling very pleased with myself for encouraging Mum to look the family up and give us all a chance to get reacquainted I went to bed that night full of excitement knowing that this was another part of my amazing journey through life.

Uncle Joe had offered to drive us to the train station for the next leg of journey to Fleetwood and we were just about to leave when Greg arrived unexpectedly and said he would like accompany us. A short while later we were standing on the platform saying our 'goodbyes' when Greg threw his arm around me and hugged me close making me promise it wouldn't be another 30 years before we met again. Without any hesitation on my part I invited both him and Karen to come and stay with me on the Island any time they wished.

Boarding the train I found myself waving madly at someone I **knew** I would see again....very soon and completely intrigued by the depth of feeling I had for this man and also the fondness I had for his wife Karen, who in many ways reminded me....of me!

Mum and I stayed in Fleetwood for a couple of days, long enough for her to see her friend before catching the return ferry from the Pier Head in Liverpool. Standing up on deck I watched the receding

Liverpool skyline as the ferry sailed down the Mersey, a lovely warm feeling of belonging welled up inside of me and thoughts of the family I had just been re-united with after some 30 years filled my mind. Especially my thoughts of Greg, as I already knew there was some other connection between us and I was confident that given time all would be revealed.

The wind picked up as we sailed out into open water away from the land and it soon became to cold for me to stay outside, so retreating below decks I went in search of Mum and the seat she was reserving for me. Stopping off at the 'ladies' to comb my tangled hair I looked in the mirror and gasped in horror when I discovered my right eye was totally covered in blood. What a fright I looked! This was the first time my eye had bled and it was to be some years before I found out why this happened, but from that day forward it bled every month during the week of my 'monthly'. It was to become quite a talking point with the girls from the pharmacy and they used to tease me about it every month, and it became affectionately known as 'my womb with a view'.

A couple of months after this trip I received a call from Greg asking if he and Karen could come and stay for a few days and telling him I would be delighted to see them both again we arranged for them to visit the following week. Feeling a little concerned as to how Dickie and the girls, who had never met Greg and Karen, would react to their visit and I couldn't help but wonder how we would all get on. But, I had no need to worry as they blended into the family straight away and they both loved the Island so much I knew after that first visit they would keep coming back.

The following summer we arrived home from our holiday in Spain to be met with the news that Aunt Ursula had passed away and although feeling sad I also felt happy that we'd made the effort to reconnect the year before. It had obviously been the right thing to do and once again I had that strange feeling of pieces being placed in a puzzle.

Inviting Greg and Karen to come and stay for a few days after my aunt's funeral I quickly became aware of how close he had been to his mother and I knew he was grieving badly. Hardly through the door on the day of their arrival, Greg announced he had something for me and opening his suitcase produced a large envelope that had been laid flat beneath his clothes, a huge smile lighting up his face as he handed it to me. Peering inside the envelope I was delighted to discover a beautiful black and white portrait photo of Dad in his Air Force uniform which was in pristine condition, although it must have been almost 60 years old.

Explaining how he had come by the photo Greg told me he had been given the un-envious task of sorting through his mother's personal belongings and had found this photograph hidden in a box in her wardrobe. As I mentioned earlier Dad and Ursula had been extremely close so it did not seem strange for her to have kept this memento of him, but Greg had yet another surprise for me and produced a small cream-coloured envelope edged in black which had the appearance of being very old. Taking the envelope from Greg and opening it very carefully I pulled out a small card and gasped in utter shock and disbelief as I read the following:-

In Loving Memory of Thomas,
Beloved son of William and Gertrude Fletcher,
Died February 5th 1913 aged 3 years.

Held between my shaking fingers was undeniable proof of the existence of 'Little Tom', my father's brother, the little soul that Lena had told me about in my sitting. Eventually, Greg spoke telling me he believed his mother had placed both items together knowing that he would be the one to find them and give them to me.

This was becoming quite a story and as promised, 'Little Tom', with Greg's help, had confirmed his identity. The strong and magical feeling of some wonderful energetic connection between us all was overpowering and intoxicating.

Weeks later while I was visiting Greg in St. Helens we enjoyed lunch at a local eatery during which we decided to spend the afternoon at the St. Helen's annual show. Stepping out into the warm sunshine Greg suggested we take a short cut to the park and a little way down the road steered me through the gates of an old churchyard. We meandered down the pathway between the graves reading the odd inscription here and there and soon found we were walking through the oldest part of the churchyard which was very overgrown and unkempt.

The memorials in this part of the churchyard dated back 150 years or more and were very weather worn with some broken in half and others leaning like the tower of Pisa. As if by magic we suddenly found ourselves staring in quiet disbelief at an ancient headstone. The headstone we were both silently reading bore very familiar names to us as it was the grave of my father's maternal grandparents and etched beneath their names read the following:-

Thomas Fletcher grandson of the above, died aged three years, 5th February 1913.

My body was tingling from head to foot as it appeared 'Little Tom', not content with the evidence already supplied had now led us to *his* very grave in a sea of thousands, in a churchyard I had never entered before in my life!

Standing in silence for a few moments I thanked 'Little Tom' for making himself known to me in such a special way, understanding now what an important part he was playing in my destiny. Instigating all of the events since my reading with Lena, I was sure in the knowledge that he had guided me to Greg and although I was still unaware of the outcome of this journey I knew in my heart of hearts that the puzzle was not yet complete.

Linda (left) with Greg and Karen on our first meeting

CHAPTER 14

WHEN THE STUDENT IS 'READY' THE TEACHER WILL APPEAR

One morning during the early spring of 1996 I was in the local supermarket and bumped into Geraldine whom I'd not encountered for a couple of years. Geraldine was very pleased at our 'accidental' meeting telling me she was going to call me when she got home. Proceeding to tell me she was organising a workshop on behalf of The National Federation of Spiritual Healers as an introduction for probationary healers and that I was the first person she had thought to invite.

Feeling very reticent at first she encouraged me by saying Spirit had been working through me long enough for me to realise that this would be my inevitable 'next step'. Not convinced because I certainly didn't see myself as a healer in any way, but felt that I couldn't say no to her request as Geraldine had been such a help to me in the past. Delighted with my acceptance she strode off telling me she'd be in touch as soon as she had more details.

Ringing me a few days later to confirm the dates and the venue I was delighted to discover the event would be held at the home of Joy, a local complementary therapist whom I already knew well and considered a good friend.

On the day of the workshop I arrived early with a friend and after depositing our contributions for the bring-and-share lunch in the kitchen I took up position at the front door to watch for anyone who might be having difficulty in finding the house. Within minutes a smiling Geraldine pulled up outside accompanied by two men who were strangers to me. Introducing them as John and Michael it became apparent that they were the lecturers from the UK who would be facilitating the workshop.

John, the younger of the two looked at me with smiling eyes and said, 'Hello'. Immediately overwhelmed with a very strange feeling of déjà vu I found myself transfixed and struck dumb, unable to move or speak. John must have thought I was very odd because I just stared at him for what seemed like ages before mumbling a feeble 'Hello' in return, eventually managing to drag my gaze away from his as they entered the house.

A little while later whilst assisting my friend in the kitchen with the preparations for lunch I asked if she had met the lecturers and wasn't a bit surprised when she told me she'd had the strangest sensation when she'd met John, commenting on the fact that she felt she already knew him. We were as perplexed as one another wondering where we could have met this man before.

John was the first lecturer to speak that morning and standing up he introduced himself and told us that this was his very first visit to the Isle of Man. Shooting a sideways glance at my friend I'm sure she was wondering the same as me, 'Where could we have met this enigmatic man before?'

I puzzled over this question all morning and I can tell you my curiosity was well and truly piqued. A little while later my friend and I made our way into the lounge with our lunch when we met John stepping into the hallway. Smiling at us both with a serene, knowing smile I asked him if we'd met before and was amazed to be told that he **had** met us **both** before. John then explained to us that we had worked together before and had 'agreed' to reconnect in another life and this workshop provided the opportunity for us to meet and work together again! This comment made a tingle run up and down my spine which I was to learn as I moved further along my spiritual path that it represents a confirmation from your H/S or spirit when 'Truth' is spoken.

As the first day of the workshop came to a close Geraldine announced that John and Michael were available for healing sessions should anyone wish to partake and as I was experiencing a medical problem which had troubled me for some time I thought some healing might help so remained seated. Inviting me into the therapy room a little while later John never asked me any questions about my problem and without touching me scanned my body with his hands. What followed was incredible. It was as if my medical record and life history had been placed in front of him and without any input from me he was able to tell me the times in my life when certain experiences had scarred me physically, mentally and emotionally! A strange sensation began to stir deep inside of me as he spoke and suddenly an incredible surge of emotion overwhelmed me as I relived those painful events and released them in a torrent of tears.

Thanking John after the session I told him I felt more than a little foolish for breaking down, but had to admit I felt so much better as if some heavy weight had been lifted from my shoulders. Smiling, he told me I'd just let go of something I'd been carrying for many lifetimes and for me to move forward on my spiritual path it had been necessary for me to release it.

Although not aware of it at the time I had just met someone very special on my spiritual journey, someone who from that day on would keep entering my life at intervals to help me in every area of my growth. Over a period of time John became not only my teacher, but also my friend, exerting a positive influence on my spiritual, mental, emotional and physical well being.

The workshop continued and we all successfully completed Stage 1 of the NFSH training with arrangements made to follow it with Stage 2 in July a few months later. Five of us on the training course had gravitated to one another and decided to form a meditation and healing group which would meet once a week for that purpose.

July and the second workshop soon arrived and I was really looking forward to meeting John again, as we all were, because the five girls in our group all felt this strange affinity with him. Unfortunately, John could not make it on that occasion and another lecturer was sent in his place, we were disappointed, but the weekend went well and we all received our certificates.

Ringing a few weeks later Geraldine told me that John would be coming to the Island for a few days and asked if any of us would like to meet him again. The group including myself all said we would love to see him again and so it was arranged that we would meet him one evening during his visit.

When we met with John again we told him we had formed a group for the express purposes of meditation and healing. Delighted with this news he informed us he would be visiting the Island every few months to work with some large 'Earth Keeper' crystals that were situated nearby. Offering to meet with our group each time he was on the island to see how we were getting along, John true to his word did exactly that.

By the summer of 1997 John had become a good friend to us all and he kindly invited the whole group to visit him and his wife Lynn in Wales. Fortunately one of the meditation group members made all the arrangements and as she didn't mind driving in the UK booked her car on the ferry. Unfortunately, one of the girls couldn't make it so there was only going to be four of us. Like giddy schoolgirls on our first trip away from home with not a care in the world we set off in gorgeous weather arriving at John and Lynn's home later in the day without too many wrong turns on the way.

At that time they lived in a remote converted cottage high in the hills up above Denbigh in North Wales. John and Lynn made us very welcome in fact they were the perfect hosts and took us out and about and showed us the sights of North Wales. One day we took a trip to Llanberis and set out to climb Mount Snowdon and two of the girls actually made it to the top, but as for the rest of us we got as far as the lower slopes and decided that was far enough and settled for the view there instead. We also visited Caernarfon Castle and Betws-y-Coed, which was beautiful and so picturesque, especially Swallow Falls which were absolutely breathtaking and exhilarating.

It was supremely quiet, calm and tranquil where John and Lynn lived, the sort of place you could retreat from the world and never miss the hustle and bustle. Each evening I would creep outside and stand alone to watch the sun set over the beautiful green Welsh hills and gaze in awe as the huge red ball of fire slid slowly second by second out of sight turning the sky many different shades of red and gold. Just to be there drinking in that view was food enough for my soul.

The ritual after sunset had us meeting in the lounge for either meditation or discussions on spiritually-related topics. We learned a lot about spirituality and how the Universe works on that holiday and those few days gave me a much deeper understanding of what was happening in my life. Even though some of what we discussed went completely over my head at the time I was beginning to see the world through very different eyes.

Footnote: The day I arrived home from Wales the cupboards were bare so I made my way to the supermarket to re-stock. Arriving home laden with supplies one of which happened to be a box of tea-bags and on opening the box discovered a free coaster, the picture on it was none other than that of Mount Snowden the very place I had just visited for the first time in my life only days before.

I laughed to myself and looked heavenward as I took this to be a sign from my helpers in Spirit that I had indeed been in the right place, at the right time, with the right people.

CHAPTER 15

THE STORY OF THE STONES

During the spring of 1995, the year before I met John, I found myself drawn to a particular little road just a few miles from home. It meanders through softly undulating countryside for about a mile before it joins the main road again at a lovely un-spoilt village on the northern plain. Thankfully this area has remained almost untouched throughout the building boom of recent years as it is designated farmland.

Drawn to this little road, as I thought, because it was nice and quiet and safe for Rags to walk off the lead and sniff to her heart's content. From the very first time we walked along that road I knew she loved it as much as I did. I loved it so much in fact that it became an absolute obsession and every time I had an hour to spare that is where I *had* to go.

Walking along that stretch of road I would be filled with the most incredible feelings of love, peace, joy and belonging and would experience the sensation of being ten feet tall, expanding into all I could see and hear. It truly was the most magnificent feeling, my heart felt so full like it could burst with joy as I became part of the landscape, melding into the animals, the sky, the trees and every blade of grass.

The seasons ran into one another as summer and autumn had come and gone whilst Rags and I continued to enjoy our country walks along our favourite little road. Taking our usual route the week before Christmas 1995 a friend passed us in her car waving and smiling as she went by. A few days later, on Christmas Eve, I met the same friend in Ramsey when she stopped to ask who I'd been walking with on the day she'd seen me in the country. Looking at her blankly I told her I'd been alone with Rags and staring back at me as if I was mad or purposely lying, she then proceeded to describe in detail a person she'd seen with me. Apparently this mystery person was wearing a long flowing tunic-style suit and had shoulder-length silver blonde hair, although she had been unable to make up her mind if it had been male or female. Despite my protestations to the contrary she was certain of what she'd seen. Totally mystified, because I knew I'd been on my own I had no explanation to offer my friend, so we parted company none the wiser.

The following week Julie and I decided to walk Rags, I think more to get out of the house and blow the cobwebs off after the festivities of Christmas. Calling to pick up Mum we then drove to my favourite stretch of road for our walk. A couple of hundred yards down the road Julie produced her camera and had us pose in the gateway of a nearby field. It was a cold, grey afternoon with what is known here on the Isle of Man as a 'lazy wind' because it doesn't stop to go round you, it goes straight through you! It was biting cold and not the sort of day to stand posing for photographs, but we did as we were asked and Julie snapped the shutter a few times before we objected to the freezing conditions and insisted on moving in the hopes we'd warm up.

A couple of weeks later Julie gave me the film to be developed telling me she needed them for Friday as they were part of her college project. Picking the processed film up a few days later I gave them to Julie without looking at them. Excitedly opening the packet Julie checked the photographs she needed for her project, and thankfully they'd all turned out, as had the last few on the film, which were of her friends and classmates at college. However, the snaps we'd taken on our walk at Christmas had an odd light in the shape of a diamond on each one and these photographs were in the middle of the reel and were the only ones affected. Taking them back to the photography shop I asked the technician if he could give me any idea as to what the marks were, but he was as mystified as the rest of us and could offer no explanation at all.

Taking them out to view again, I realized the gateway we'd been standing in was exactly the spot on the road where my friend had seen the mystery person with me. I was now beginning to think that these happenings were connected, but what was it all about?

Some time after the episode with the photographs I started to have a recurring dream or rather a nightmare, it was the same dream that had haunted me as a child and now some 40 years later it had returned for no apparent reason:

I would be alone on my friend's farm, in reality I'd played there often as a child. The dream always began with me standing at the farmhouse door before getting the most incredible urge to run as if something monstrous was chasing me. I would always run along the same path, leaving the farmhouse behind, heading through the orchard then across a small bridge over a stream. Once over the stream I would run into a circle of grassland surrounded by trees. The trees were old and gnarled with what I imagined were grotesque faces and I always felt threatened by them before finding myself rooted to the spot with fear on a small grassy hillock in the centre. The unimaginable horror that had been chasing me was about to catch up when I would wake bathed in sweat and very, very frightened. The horror never revealed itself and the dream had only altered in the respect that I was now an adult and not a child.

A few weeks after the nightmare recommenced I was at the meditation group when one of the girls told us a story about a man she had nursed until his passing, some years before. Telling us he had rambled on many times about a stone that was supposedly buried on his land and his family had experienced extreme bad luck over the years and had blamed this on the supposedly 'cursed stone'. I was amazed to discover the land she was talking about was none other than the land I was dreaming about!

The dreams continued through the following week until the group met again when I was surprised to find one of the other girls had something to add to the story. Recounting the previous week's tale to her husband he had enlightened her to a tale of his grandfather's. It seems when he was a young boy his grandfather had told him about a stone supposedly buried on **his** land and this stone was a third of a very much larger stone that had been broken into three and buried in three different locations in the north of the island hundreds of years before. He had been able to name the three locations of the stones, two of which were familiar to me, but I hadn't a clue as to the whereabouts of the third.

The following week one of the girls from the meditation group was going away to spend a few days in Wales with John and Lynn and I was hoping she would return with some meditation tapes for the group. Having written a list of titles I had seen in a magazine, I then forgot to give it to her and had to ring her at John's home.

Dialing the number it rang only twice before Lynn answered and I was just about to explain my reason for calling when Lynn cut in to tell me Jo had recounted the tale of the three stones. Lynn is a medium and having meditated on the subject she had received insight from her guide with a message for *me*!

The conversation that followed was incredulous as Lynn informed me that I'd promised, on a spiritual level, to carry out what was needed to be done with the energy of these stones. Two of these places I had to visit physically, but the third, the one I had been dreaming about, I had to visit in meditation. She went on to explain that this was the reason I had been haunted by this dream as a child, because it was part of the work I'd promised to do before I came on this journey to Earth. Now that the dream had returned it was telling me the time had come to carry out what I subconsciously knew I'd promised to do.

When Lynn had finished speaking I tried to protest, telling her I didn't know what she was talking about and that I certainly didn't know what I had to do, quite apart from the fact that I didn't know where one of these locations was to be found. Assuring me any information needed would be given to me and I would most definitely know what to do when the time came, Lynn said goodbye and put the phone down! Staring at the receiver in my hand I sat for a while trying to remember why I'd rung in the first place, the tapes were completely forgotten, all I could hear were her words ringing in my head, "This is something you promised to do".

That night I tossed and turned finding it difficult to sleep, but by morning I had put Lynn's message to the back of my mind thinking it all a bit far-fetched. Anyway there were other things to think about as Dickie and I were going to an anniversary party that evening and by all accounts it was going to be a big affair with a live band and over a hundred guests, so I told myself I didn't have time to dwell on what Lynn had said the night before and got on with my day.

We were a bit late arriving at the function that night and there was only one table left with any vacant seats so we joined a couple already seated and a few minutes later another middle-aged couple sat down beside us. Falling into easy conversation with the man we had the most unusual chat given the surroundings we were in as he told me about a house he and his wife had lived in some years earlier. Without any encouragement from me and without any prior knowledge of my interests he told me of their experiences with poltergeist activity and paranormal phenomena of all kinds.

When he had finished recounting his tale he then turned his attention to the rest of the table telling us all a story about a motorcycle accident he'd been involved in some thirty years before and to my utter disbelief his accident had occurred at the location of the third buried stone! Finishing his story the man remarked that the location of the accident was no longer known by the name he had used before informing us of the modern day name for the place. Amazingly within twenty-four hours of speaking to Lynn I had met someone who had furnished me the final piece of information required for fulfilling the 'task' spirit had set me.

The very next day I bought a map of the island and to my amazement when I looked up the three place names, I discovered that two of them were on the stretch of road I'd been drawn to the year before and where the mystery person had appeared to my friend and where the unusual photographs had been taken. Both places were marked by a tumulus sign (burial mound) and the third, the place of my nightmares was also marked as a burial mound. All of the above had taken over a year to come to fruition and it was now pre-Christmas 1996.

On my Christmas night out with work colleagues one of the girls remarked that a man across the room was staring at us and asked if I knew him. Looking across the room I discovered it was the gentleman I'd met and enjoyed the metaphysical conversation with at the anniversary party. Making eye contact with him he beckoned me over telling me he'd been trying to attract my attention for some time as he just wanted to thank me for listening to his stories the week before. He then admitted he'd never told another living soul about the things he'd quite willingly discussed with me the previous week.

Smiling in response I had to enquire why he'd felt it necessary to tell me and was amazed to learn he'd been drawn to me by a bright light he'd seen hovering above my head accompanied with an overwhelming sensation that I was the right person to tell.

Feeling I needed more information I asked him why he had recounted his tale of the motorcycle accident and pulling a face and shrugging his shoulders he admitted that he had no idea as hadn't thought about it for years, the memory had just popped into his head and he felt it necessary to share his experience. (This is another example of 'Spirit' guiding an unwitting participant to help in their work.)

Thanking him, I was able to tell him that he'd helped me with something important, although I did not enlighten him as to what. Even though this man was unconsciously working with 'Spirit' I think it would have been too difficult for me to explain. Now I had a little bit more to go on, but I still didn't know what was required of me and the dream/nightmare kept on replaying every night.

A few days later whilst vacuuming the lounge carpet, I suddenly 'found' myself in the place of my nightmare standing on the little grassy hillock surrounded by those grotesquely gnarled trees. Pouring down from the sky was a beautiful ray of pink light and I could actually feel this light coursing its way through my body and out through the soles of my feet. The ground soaked up the 'light' like a sponge soaking up water turning the grass around me pink as it seeped and spread in every direction. It was a wonderful feeling and I found myself suspended in time completely unaware of how long I remained in that place before finding my awareness back in the lounge and wondering what had just taken place.

The following night was our final meditation meeting before Christmas so we decided to call John and wish him and Lynn a happy holiday. We took turns to speak to him, me being the last in line, and after wishing him a happy Christmas I took the opportunity to recount the events of the last couple of weeks, finishing with what had taken place the day before.

A resounding *'Congratulations'* came down the line from John and on enquiring what I'd done to deserve his praise he told me I had just released my first earthbound spirit! Speechless for a moment, before garbling that I didn't know what I'd done only to be told that I had channelled 'Spiritual Love' into an area of negative energy and released an earthbound soul.

John then informed me that my constant walks around the little loop road had delivered the same result as the distant meditation/vision the day before. Thanking him, I put down the phone and the words of John Lennon's immortal song rang in my ears, *'ALL YOU NEED IS LOVE'*.

However, this story was not quite over and meeting a friend for coffee the next day we exchanged Christmas gifts. My gift from her was what appeared to be a book cunningly disguised as a Christmas present and deciding not to keep them until Christmas Day we opened our gifts over coffee. Un-wrapping my present eagerly to find that it was indeed a book by a local author and opening it at random can you imagine my surprise as the first words I read were,

'The Stones' are happy and *I AM* happy. Thank You'

Staring in disbelief, the feelings I had inside of me at that moment were overwhelming. I felt as if the soul who'd been released was speaking directly to me through the words it chose to show me in that book and I felt humbled and very, very blessed.

From that day to this the nightmares that had dogged me in my childhood and again in the past few weeks disappeared and have never returned. Apparently, my job was done.

Footnote: I have not named the places in this story because when I first wrote this chapter I included all the place names and for some unexplained reason the whole story was deleted on completion. Taking this as a sign from Spirit that I should not divulge the whereabouts of these sacred places you will find that I have continued that theme throughout this book.

The above photographs travelled to Japan with my friend Eva to be shown to a Japanese priest whose particular field of interest is spiritual phenomena captured on film. He has a huge collection taken by time lapse cameras during services in temples throughout Japan. It is his considered opinion that my photographs are definitely evidence of Spirit caught on film and that the diamond shape is one of the rarest and most significant examples, being reminiscent of a spinning 'Merkebah' field or energetic Lightbody.

Guided through this incredible adventure by the mystery being my friend witnessed accompanying me in 1995 I'm sure Spirit were also responsible for the light above my head that summoned the one man capable of providing me with the information I required to carry out my 'mission'.

CHAPTER 16

PUBLIC SPEAKING

The years were passing so quickly I could hardly believe it, time seemed to have speeded up somehow and my girls were all but grown. Having survived their teenage years I felt was nothing short of a miracle, as any mother of two teenage girls reading this will appreciate.

By the winter of 1996 Julie was 18 and had left college to work in an office and spreading her wings she'd flown the nest and was now living independently in her own flat. I say independently, apart from the odd sack of laundry that appeared as if by magic hoping to be washed and the occasional plea for a sub to keep her going until pay day, she was effectively off my hands.

Christine was now in her first term at college and apparently enjoying it and getting on well with her tutor Ms.Roney. Never having been inside the Isle of Man College until the day I had to pick her up for a dental appointment I was glad she'd given me directions on how to find her classroom. Reluctant to disturb the class, I knocked quietly and waited for someone to answer and after a couple of minutes a booming voice from inside the room called out 'Enter'. Ms. Roney I presumed.

All eyes appeared to be on me as I entered the room and Ms Roney looked me up and down in such a strange fashion making the comment that I looked 'quite normal'. The look on my face must have given me away and laughing the tutor told me not to take her remarks personally. I then discovered that Ms Roney, by way of getting to know her students had set an essay on their home and family life at the beginning of term. Christine, unbeknown to me, had left no details of her mother's strange interests and unusual coincidences out of her lengthy discourse. Obviously my rather mundane appearance didn't have quite the flamboyance she was expecting for the person Christine had described in her essay.

Warming to the woman immediately I was pleased when she asked me to call her Jacqui and rather taken aback when she informed me the class had all been looking forward to meeting me! Feeling myself blushing I was even more surprised when she asked if I had time to tell the class about one of my experiences. Apologising, I reminded her I'd only come to collect Christine for an appointment and we had to leave immediately, but thanked her for her interest before making a quick getaway.

The following week Christine arrived home from college telling me Jacqui wanted to know if I would give a talk to the class the following week, after their exams. Christine's insistence that I comply surprised me as I thought she would have been very embarrassed at the mere suggestion of her mother talking to her classmates. Promising I'd give her my answer in the morning I talked to my invisible helpers before going to sleep that night asking them to give me a sign or a feeling that what I'd been asked to do would be appropriate. The next morning I awoke feeling totally positive that this would indeed be the right thing to do and informed Christine of my decision.

On her arrival home from college that evening Christine told me I would be expected on Friday afternoon straight after lunch. By the time Friday arrived I was really nervous and wondered why I'd agreed to the invitation as I'd never spoken in public before. But, having promised Christine I knew there was no way I was going to let her or myself down. With that thought in my head I set off for another 'date with destiny' aware that my life was subtly changing because I was beginning to look at life differently, accepting the things that were happening to me with a deep knowing that these circumstances were being placed on my path for a reason.

Arriving at college around lunchtime I was pleased to find Christine waiting for me and followed her into the canteen to meet her classmates. After lunch we made our way upstairs to Christine's classroom, my heart beating like a drum with miscellaneous thoughts of what could go wrong racing around my mind. My head buzzed with the notions that I would be booed out of the classroom or that I would freeze with nothing to say as I hadn't made any notes to support my talk. Finally to save my sanity I just told my brain to shut up and get on with it.

Thankfully the class were very enthusiastic and interested in what I had to say and the afternoon was a great success with more questions than I had time to answer. In what seemed like only minutes the home bell rang, two and a half hours after I'd started to talk! Even then the students were reluctant to let me go and a number of them stayed behind to talk, commenting on how much they had enjoyed it. I too had enjoyed every minute and loved the fact that the students were anxious for more knowledge and I felt extremely honoured when Jacqui told me the entire class had been free to go home at lunchtime when their exams had finished, but had all chosen to stay.

Some weeks later Christine arrived home with a surprise invitation for *me* to attend the end-of-year party at Jacqui's home. The day of the class party was a beautiful summer's day and Jacqui was able to hold it in her garden where I was surprised to find that I was the only mum present. As the afternoon progressed I discovered that my invitation was special, as I was presented with a beautiful bouquet of flowers as a 'thank you' from the whole class.

My first attempt at public speaking had evidently been a success, but as I was to find out this was just dipping my toe in the water as Spirit had yet more up their sleeve for me.

CHAPTER 17

WHAT'S IN A NUMBER?

Part of my spiritual awakening involved a growing awareness of numbers and as I progressed on my journey the significance and meaning each number holds and how it affects you became more and more important. This is the story of how it all began and how I fell in love with numbers.

I remember having a conversation with Dickie quite a few years ago now about the number 22 and how strange it was the amount of times it showed up in our lives. Reeling off the occasions where 22 cropped up he was surprised when I was able to tell him that not only did we live at number 22, but so did my mother and his sister. Our daughter Christine and my nephew both had birthdays on the 22nd, not to mention that our car registration added up to 22, and so did his work vehicle.

Once we'd had the above conversation it was like a green flag had been dropped at the start of a race and every invoice, bill, receipt, raffle and lottery ticket that came my way was numbered 22 or added up to 22. It was as if the number 22 had to be continually brought to my attention at every conceivable opportunity.

Shortly after this discovery we happened to be looking for another car and my heart was set on an ice blue Honda Civic hatchback. Scouring every second-hand car dealership on the Island we unfortunately drew a blank everywhere as there was nothing in our price range to be found. Unhappily I resigned myself to the fact I would have to settle for something else and putting it to the back of my mind I set off to stay with friends on the mainland.

Greeting me with a kiss and an enigmatic smile on my return the following week Dickie asked if I'd like to go for a test drive in a Honda Civic. Knowing there to be nothing in our price range on the Island I queried how he was going to manage that. Quickly enlightened to a conversation Dickie had with our neighbour about the car we were looking for only to discover his employer who lived not more than five miles away was selling his car privately and it just happened to be an ice blue Honda Civic!

What a lovely surprise I got when I returned home the next day to find the car we had searched all over the island for and in the colour I desired sitting on our drive. It was love at first sight, and the owner was asking exactly the amount we had to spend on our new car, but not only that, we were absolutely amazed to notice the registration number was 796 which of course adds up to 22! For me that was the icing on the cake as my wish had been granted and the number 22 had turned up trumps yet again.

Not long after we received my dream car someone gave an old car to Dickie which he decided to keep in his works garage to restore. The day he brought it home for the first time I couldn't believe my eyes as the registration number added up to 22. At this point I thought I would run my own survey to see how many cars had registration numbers that added up to 22 and for weeks after when I was out driving I would automatically add up the numbers of the car travelling in front of me, and I have to say very few added up to a total of 22.

By now I was obsessed with numbers and found I was adding up sequences of numbers wherever I went. My old math's teacher would have been very impressed if he'd known what an interest I was taking because I'd never shown any aptitude for mathematics whilst at school!

The 22 obsession continued unabated for quite some time until it became 11:11 when every time I looked at a clock or timer it would be showing 11.11 which of course adds up to 22. Glancing randomly at the time display in my car or video it would more often than not be 11.11 or 22.22 and on the occasions I checked the mileage in the car it would often be 11 or 22.

By now, I'm quite aware you probably think I'm barking mad and I thought I was too, until quite by 'chance', someone gave me a book about different types of divinatory methods and the answer to my dilemma was found within its pages, a whole chapter on numerology the science of numbers.

I was amazed to learn that our whole life, personality, character, health, career etc. can be divined by numbers that correspond with the letters in our name. I was even more excited when I discovered that 11 and 22 are Master numbers in numerology as they have a special significance and are extremely high spiritual numbers. From that moment on I was hooked on Numerology and after reading that book it all began to make sense why the numbers 11 and 22 were cropping up in my life as spiritual portents guiding me, but this was only the beginning as I was to discover even more about numbers as my journey progressed.

The next story is about allowing myself to be guided by Spirit using numbers. This experience happened not long after I'd read the book and had developed a little more understanding about what was happening.

Healing with Numbers

One beautiful sunny morning I was taking Rags to the local vet who lives in the countryside just a couple of miles from town. Turning in to the parking area I had a very clear vision of walking up my friend's drive. As I hadn't previously been thinking about her and had not seen her for some time I found it a little strange as to why she should pop into my thoughts at that moment. Shrugging the thought off I entered the waiting room which was packed with a dozen different kinds of dogs, some cowering and trembling at the thought of what they may have to endure when they got through the dreaded doors into the surgery, others barking their protest, plus various cats in cages meowing and hissing. Much to Rags relief, and deciding I didn't want to spend this beautiful morning in such noisy surroundings I picked her up and tucking her under my arm we made our way back to the car.

Turning into my drive a few minutes later once again I got the strong impression of walking up to my friend's house. Unlocking the door and stepping inside I was overwhelmed with a desire to check if there had been any calls in the twenty minutes I'd been out. Unbelievably the very friend I'd been thinking about had called during the short time I'd been away from home. Immediately I rang her back and was disappointed to be greeted by the answering machine, so leaving a short message I carried on with my jobs around the house.

Later on that morning I found myself standing in the hallway staring at the telephone, rooted to the spot, my eyes focused on the time display, completely hypnotized by the time flashing 11:11! Without knowing why I suddenly became aware that my friend needed my help and decided to visit her after lunch. Once the decision to visit her had been made I found myself released from my previous hypnotic state and returned to my work.

After lunch I set off to visit my friend, requesting the company of my invisible helpers to accompany me, because I was certain that my friend needed help of some kind. Arriving at her home minutes later I parked the car on the road and walked up the drive fulfilling my premonition from earlier that day.

Answering the door Rachel beckoned me in although she was already in conversation with someone. The situation that unfolded was quite funny as Rachel's other guest took one look at me as I entered and beat a hasty retreat, disappearing through the door in double quick time almost as if some invisible person had grabbed them by the scruff of the neck and unceremoniously ushered them out!

As soon as we were alone Rachel dissolved into tears and blurted out her problem and all I had to do was sit and listen whilst my friends in Spirit did the rest. This was a lovely healing and one I would not have had the privilege to witness if I had not been aware of 11.11 and how that usually signifies 'Spirit' are at work.

CHAPTER 18

'THE HEALING RUNES'

In the summer of 1997 I accompanied my mum-in-law, Beryl, to Blackpool. Having not been on holiday for a number of years since losing her husband, Blackpool was the obvious choice as it had been their favourite holiday destination.

The weather the week we visited Blackpool was glorious and hotter than on the continent. We did all the usual touristy things in the daytime, visiting the pleasure beach and laughing at the youngsters hurtling around the various rides screaming and shouting as they went. We ate candyfloss and fish and chips and we even spent an afternoon being entertained by the dancers in the tower ballroom. Our original plan was to go to the top of the tower, but Beryl chickened out using the excuse that the queue was too long, however, she couldn't pull the wool over my eyes, I'd already guessed she was scared of heights and teased her about it for the rest of the day.

We spent our evenings in the hotel where the entertainment was excellent and during the week we took a trip to the Freeport at Fleetwood on the tram. Deciding to return by bus we managed to catch the wrong one and spent a couple of hours travelling around the countryside before finally being dropped off back on the seafront in Blackpool weary and exhausted. Of course there was plenty of retail therapy to be had in such a resort and we spent almost every afternoon walking up and down the main shopping street. By the end of the week I think we must have been in almost every shop at least three times and I felt as if I knew the street like the back of my hand.

On the day we were due to come home Beryl declined to join me for one last wander down the street saying she was worn out and it would take her weeks to recover from all the walking and shopping. Leaving Beryl to enjoy her morning coffee, promising I would be back in a couple of hours, I headed off for my last sojourn to the shops. During the week on one of our many shopping expeditions I had spotted a big bookshop that I wanted to browse in, but had resisted the temptation as I felt the time should be devoted to Beryl. Now free to go wherever I pleased the book tokens I'd been given a few weeks previously for my birthday were burning a hole in my handbag. The book shop was enormous, spread over two floors it contained books on every conceivable topic and I knew I'd find something that would interest me.

On entering the shop I immediately started to look for the metaphysical book section and after twenty minutes or so had almost given up hope of finding one when I was approached by a member of staff, my furtive behaviour having marked me out as a potential shop-lifter I think! However, the girl was very pleasant and helpful directing me up the stairs and to the very far end of the upper floor overlooking the street.

Oh joy! There were so many metaphysical books to choose from I didn't know where to begin. Closing my eyes and asking to be led to the book I most needed I stretched out my hand and plucked a book from the shelf. Opening my eyes in expectation I read the title and was puzzled to find I'd chosen 'Zen and the art of Motorcycling'. After reading the flyleaf I decided that it wasn't the book for me and wondered why Spirit had directed me to choose it. Placing it back on the shelf my hand strayed across a dozen books or so and came to rest on a volume with the title 'Out of the Blue', a book about a fresh approach to synchronistic sequences, which of course was right up my street!

Clutching my chosen book I strode over to the counter where two overworked staff were very busy serving a long queue of people. Taking my place and waiting patiently in line I was a little annoyed when a very irate lady pushed to the front of the queue asking if someone could help her. Looking up wearily one of the harassed counter assistants told her she would have to wait her turn like everyone else. Huffing and puffing she took her place behind me and began to moan about the length of time she'd wandered about the store looking for a particular book her friend had requested as a birthday present.

Not really wanting to get involved with the angry woman I none the less found myself asking her the title of the book she was looking for. Imagine my surprise when she told me it was none other than Zen and the art of Motorcycling! Leaving the queue I asked her to follow me and led her over to the bookshelf I had been looking at moments earlier and retrieving the said copy handed it over to the disbelieving woman. The irate lady immediately deflated and smiled sweetly in my direction with a bemused and puzzled look on her face, no doubt wondering how I knew where to find it.

Walking out of the book shop I glanced at my watch only to discover that I'd been in there for an hour and a half, although it had only felt like minutes. Making my way back up the street in the direction of the hotel my intention was to visit a small shop where I'd bought a set of runes a couple of days earlier with the intention of purchasing a second set thinking they would make a nice gift for my friend.

The day Beryl and I had first entered the little shop we had been drawn in thinking we might bag a bargain as it had the appearance of being a souvenir shop that was closing down. In the centre of the shop was a table piled high with dozens of what appeared to be books, but on closer inspection turned out to gift sets of Runes. Never having come across Runes before I had no real idea of what to do with them, but at only £4.99 a set which was accompanied by a book of interpretations and a small velvet bag to keep them in they seemed a bargain and I was immediately compelled to buy some. Beryl had laughed when I bought them saying, 'You and all your weird stuff Linda I don't know what you will be up to next'.

Having examined my purchase later that day and discovered them to be a tool for divining your path to healing I thought they were so good that my friend would appreciate a set. Now on my way back to the hotel I felt I could afford to take five minutes to revisit the little shop, but imagine my surprise when I discovered the shop had disappeared. Knowing exactly where it **should** have been on the street I was amazed to find it had not closed down, but had quite simply **vanished** into thin air!

CHAPTER 19

THE DREAM

Returning to work after our week in Blackpool I felt more unsettled than ever in my job at the pharmacy, where I had resumed work some years previously when a position had become available, but I knew something was missing from my life although I could not put my finger on it. I still belonged to the meditation group with the girls and we met regularly each week to carry out our spiritual work, but there was something more I felt I should be doing and kept questioning myself as to what it was. Every week in meditation and each night before sleep I asked Spirit what I needed to be doing and requested to be guided in the right direction.

    The word *communication* was all I received from my meditations and over time it repeated itself like a mantra, until one morning I awoke with an internal voice repeating a sentence over and over again in my head saying, *'This is the day you will change your life'*.

    Accompanying this repetitive mantra was a very clear memory of the dream I'd had the night before. In my dream I owned a shop. I could see the shop clearly and knew exactly where it was to be, even how it was to be arranged and what it would sell. It was a spiritual shop. The dream showed me an old winged chair sitting in the corner, without a doubt it was the one my mother had owned for at least 35 years, but in the dream it was draped in a beautiful throw. Along the back wall there was a small library of spiritual books with beautiful calming music playing in the background. The shop was full of natural crystals, candles, flower remedies and incense and hanging from the ceiling were Native American Indian Mandalas, dream-catchers, coloured chakra scarves and beautiful ornamental crystals. The air hung heavy with the scents of essential oils and the place was alive with an 'energy' all of its own.

    In the dream I had become aware that someone was standing

next to me, it was my friend and colleague Betty, who had passed away the year before. Pointing to the small counter she attracted my attention to my set of healing runes and encouraged me to take on the challenge of the dream shop as it was time for people to hear the stories I had told her about my spiritual awakening. She continued by telling me that 'The Runes' and the chair were the most important items in the shop as their purpose was for healing. Betty then sat down in the healing chair her legs crossed in an easy fashion and her fingers entwined loosely resting on her lap. Looking up she smiled at me serenely and told me she knew I would be successful and that this was my 'next step'.

I was unable to mention the dream to Dickie, but none the less I knew it had been very special and I found myself in a state of high excitement and anticipation.

That night was our meditation evening and I shared the dream with the girls as we gathered together in the kitchen over a cup of tea. Telling them this dream had been so real I felt it was already manifest and I had every intention of living it. Encouraged by the fact they all thought it was a really good idea the conversation then turned to what I would call the enterprise. "The 4th Dimension, Body, Mind and Spirit Shop" I declared, as the name just popped into my head, even though I was not all together sure at that point in my understanding what the 4th Dimension entailed, but I knew without doubt that it was the right name for this brave new venture.

CHAPTER 20

FOLLOWING THE DREAM

The next morning I went to work as usual, but feeling so different, like a new me. Walking into the pharmacy I smiled at my boss and Barbara, my friend and colleague, who glancing sideways at me made the statement that something about me had changed. Anxious to maintain an aura of secrecy I told her I had no idea what she meant, even though I knew exactly what I was going to do that day I wasn't ready to let the 'cat out of the bag' just yet.

My anticipation seemed to make the morning drag and when coffee break finally arrived I asked Barbara to cover the shop for a few minutes whilst I went on a message. Making my escape she remarked on my furtive behaviour saying, "I know you're up to something Linda."

Looking over my shoulder as I made my exit I couldn't resist making her even more suspicious by replying, "I'm off to change my life, that's all."

And that is exactly what I did. Running down the street I dashed into the estate agents and blurted out, "I've come to find out about one of the empty shops in the mall."

The estate agent informed me that they had just been notified by the owners that the empty units were to be offered at an initial rent of £10 per week for the first 6 months, in an attempt to attract new business. Trotting happily back to work with the details of the shop I'd seen in my dream stowed safely in my pocket I knew I was going to follow that dream. The question of how I was going to fund this venture or where I would find the stock I required were mere practicalities in my highly charged state, but I was sure that if Spirit wanted me to do this 'they' would help. This venture would be a 'leap of faith' for me, a leap into the unknown, but what an exciting faith to be leaping towards!

By lunchtime I thought I'd better tell Dickie and dropping the subject of my dream into the conversation told him it was my wish to follow it and open a shop in the mall. I'd had reservations about telling Dickie the nature of the business as he does not always go along with my mode of thinking, especially about spiritual matters. However, by now I had no choice but to tell him that I intended it to be a spiritual shop and the only drawback I could see was my lack of funds to finance the venture. Looking up from his lunch I expected him to tell me what a stupid idea it was, but what he actually said took my breath away. Without hesitation he offered me the thousand pounds he'd saved for our annual holiday telling me if that was really what I wanted to do it was mine. Dumbstruck, I realized that there was indeed a much greater force than I could imagine working in my favour.

The 'magic' continued as the very next day Dickie and I went to lease the shop I had seen in my dream and once that was taken care of we visited the bank to open a business account. The bank manager asked what sort of venture it was going to be, and when I told him he laughed, calling me a 'space cadet', but I didn't take offence as I'd known him for years.

Having rung John and Lynn the night before to tell them my plans, John was delighted and offered to pick me up at Liverpool airport to take me to a few suppliers he knew where I could purchase some of the stock I needed. Only three days had passed since I'd had the dream and my life was changing by the minute, so rapid was the speed at which Spirit seemed to be pushing me.

On Friday of that week I thought I had better hand in my notice and come clean with my workmates about my plans. Making my announcement at coffee break I was happy to find the girls I worked with were as excited as I was and Barbara hugged me and whispered in my ear that she had known there was something going on with me as I'd looked so different ... 'so alive'.

The reaction I got from my boss though was less than enthusiastic as he thought I was making the biggest mistake of my life ... and told me so. Undaunted, I carried on with my plans, as in truth, I could not have done otherwise, I was so inspired I found couldn't stop, not even if I'd wanted to.

Calling to see my friend who was working her shift at a local charity shop I took her to a quiet corner and gave her my news and she was as excited as I was and we ended up laughing, hugging and jumping up and down together in the corner. Another lady who was working there came over to see what all the excitement was about and introduced herself as Rosemary and she, on hearing my plans, ended up hugging me as well, telling me it was just the sort of shop the town needed.

Although I'd never met this woman before I was to find out she too was very much awake and aware of her spirituality and offered to donate a number of metaphysical books for my second-hand library. Turning to my friend I enquired if they had any small wicker baskets, having just priced them in the high street I was beginning to understand my limited funds were not going to stretch very far. Laughing, she escorted me to the back of the shop and showed me a pile of wicker baskets that were just the right size and were only 10p each. Counting the baskets we found 22, and I knew for definite then that this was not coincidence, but *guidance*.

There were still lots of things I wanted for the shop, but I had no idea where to purchase them so I turned to the advertisements in my back copies of Kindred Spirit magazine for help where my eyes were immediately drawn to a small advert offering music tapes for sale. Having already found my music supplier I had no idea what attracted me, but I felt I had to ring the number. A very nice man answered the phone only to tell me that he did not supply wholesale, which was just as well because I didn't need anything! Chattering on, as I usually do, I found myself telling him I was planning to open a spiritual shop, but was having difficulty finding a supplier who could supply me with the merchandise I required? Guess what? He did, and proceeded to give me the name, address and telephone number of a company in Dorset.

Contacting the suppliers the very next day I received their catalogue in super quick time and duly put in an order for the remainder of the items I wanted. My thousand pounds now spent I had to hope custom would be brisk when I opened the shop. The company in Dorset became my sole suppliers of everything spiritual and it appeared everything I wanted just seemed to be falling into my lap. It was hard to believe it had only been two weeks since my fateful dream and because I'd chosen to follow it the whole enterprise seemed effortless.

The following week would be my last at the pharmacy and the week after that I would be working in my own shop! It seemed incredible, too good to be true and I had to keep pinching myself to make sure I wasn't dreaming, but I still had a few practicalities to see to. As I couldn't afford to advertise in the paper a friend had offered to run off some flyers for me and I was also telling as many people as possible hoping they would pass the information on to other interested parties, but I was always careful not to mention my shop to any customers during working hours at the pharmacy, it just didn't seem the right thing to do.

About ten days before I was due to open I found myself breaking my rule when a lady came into the pharmacy looking for aromatherapy oil. Apologizing for not stocking it I ventured to tell her about my own shop which was due to open soon and that I would be selling essential oils and hoped she would come along and see me. Another woman who was waiting for a prescription stepped forward and apologized for eavesdropping, expressing an interest in where the shop would be, and requested any flyers I might have. Offering her the half dozen I had in my bag I was surprised when she said, "Oh, I was hoping for about a hundred or so!" Recovering my composure I enquired why she wanted a hundred flyers and learnt she was organizing a complementary therapies evening at the Isle of Man College that weekend. Assuring me that the people coming to the event were bound to be interested in my shop and that she would hand out the flyers personally.

My final days at the pharmacy flew by and before I knew it the time for me to leave had arrived. For me this was a happy, yet sad occasion, leaving a company and colleagues which had spanned almost 27 years.

During a lull in the afternoon the girls I had worked with for many years presented me with a large square box. Laughing, I questioned its contents and asked if perhaps this could be my very own 'ball of golden light'. The girls gasped in collective disbelief as I lifted the lid and there nestled on a bed of tissue paper was a large golden globe! Mesmerized, my colleagues wanted to know how I'd known what the box contained before I'd even got the wrapping paper off, but I'm afraid I couldn't tell them because the words had just been dropped into my mind.

Resembling a large Christmas tree decoration I knew the beautiful golden ball was known as a 'Witch's Ball' and the purpose was to deter negative energy by being hung at the entrance to your home. Thanking the girls for their thoughtfulness I told them the ball would be hung in pride of place in the doorway of my new shop, deciding there and then that this globe would be my trade-mark. Picking the ball out of the box, sadly, I noticed it was damaged which disappointed the girls, but I reassured them that I still loved the gift and would exchange it for one identical as soon as I could. The only problem was when I went to exchange it the shop had no golden balls left and I was offered the only remaining globe they had in stock which was electric blue. It was absolutely stunning and inexplicably felt so right when I held it that I couldn't leave the shop without it.

This was to become the trademark for The 4th Dimension a blue ball of healing light welcoming **all** spiritual seekers.

CHAPTER 21

THE 4ᵀᴴ DIMENSION ......MANIFEST

After leaving the pharmacy I only had a week to get the shop ready for opening. Picking up the keys from the estate agents I almost ran to the shopping mall where my new enterprise was to be found in the exact location I had seen in my dream. The shop was very small, about the size of a single bedroom with windows onto the mall all along one side. Letting myself in it felt so strange to be standing in what was from that moment my shop. Lucky for me the unit contained a counter, shelves and cupboards, which meant no further outlay was necessary, only a quick wash down was required. When I'd finished cleaning I stood for some time and surveyed the empty shop wondering how I was going to suspend the lovely window crystals and dream catchers I'd purchased to show them off to their best effect.

That afternoon, walking along the banks of the Sulby River with Rags, I spotted some men lopping branches off nearby trees and discarding them on the riverbank. A picture flashed through my mind, I could see branches suspended from the ceiling in the shop and my beautiful window crystals, dream catchers and coloured chakra scarves draped and decoratively woven through them. Ah! Divine Inspiration! Approaching one of the men I asked if he would mind if I took some of the branches, happily he agreed, expressing that it would be less for him to clear up. Returning later with the car I bundled as many branches into the boot as I could before setting off for home like a small mobile forest.

All the cleaning necessary was now complete and it was time to decorate the shop with the branches and display the stock. When I was satisfied that I'd achieved a natural woodland effect I displayed the crystals, scarves and Indian items just as I had seen them in my minds eye while walking by the river the day before. Displaying the rest of the stock on the shelves and titivating until I was satisfied with the overall effect I finally took time to stand back and admire my handiwork. It was just as well the shop was on the small side because the meagre amount of stock I had didn't go very far and after spreading everything out as much as possible I filled in the remaining gaps with fossilized stones collected from the beach.

To one side of the door, behind the counter, was a small window where I placed a little display in memory of my dear friend Betty who after all had played a significant role in this venture or should I say adventure? I'd filled a small, open treasure chest with a selection of crystals and tumble stones and placed on top a beautiful paua-shell bracelet that Betty had given me and finished off by suspending my blue healing ball, my trademark, directly above. Now the shop was ready for opening, it looked lovely and was literally my dream come true. When I looked at the display of tumble stones in their little wicker baskets I thought of Lena and the prediction she'd made all those years ago as she'd given me the piece of Hematite and thought, it may have taken a few years, but her words had finally come true.

Arriving early Dickie and I laid out glasses of complementary juice and I took a final glance around the shop before opening the door to my new life at the stroke of 10 o'clock. 'The 4th Dimension, Body, Mind and Spirit Shop' opened its doors to the public for the first time on Saturday the 4th day of the 4th month 1998, which although I hadn't planned it felt like a very auspicious numerological date.

To my amazement there was already a queue outside, mainly friends and relatives who had come along to wish me well. Many brought cards wishing me success, some even brought flowers that quickly filled the available spaces and I was completely overwhelmed by the love, support and good wishes I received throughout the day.

Within minutes of opening the door a woman almost fell into the shop and looking slightly puzzled she glanced at her worried partner before saying, "It felt as though someone just pushed me through the door." Catching her breath she looked up and around the shop before exclaiming, "This is lovely just my kind of shop. How long have you been here?"

Glancing at my watch I replied, "Oh, about 20 minutes."

Laughing, she said "No, I mean how long have you been in business."

I glanced at my watch again, "about 20 minutes and 40 seconds, you see I've just opened the doors for the first time this morning. This is my first day in business."

Introducing herself as Jan and her partner as Peter she informed me they were from Port St Mary, adding that they hadn't visited Ramsey in over two years. By now I was beginning to understand how Spirit worked and wasn't the least bit surprised to find she had been 'compelled' to visit Ramsey that day and had only walked twenty-five yards from their car before literally being pushed through my door.

Pleased to find Jan was on the same wavelength as me and even more delighted to discover that she was a medium, we hit it off straightaway. In the future she would visit the shop regularly to administer healing and give messages of comfort to my customers and I believe it was no accident that Jan found herself in my shop that first day. We often laughed about it and came to the conclusion that Spirit had a 'hand' in our meeting if not the middle of her shoulder blades as she was pushed through the door!

That first day 5 o'clock came far too quickly as it had been a wonderful and extremely busy day and there was no question in my mind that I had done the right thing by following my dream.

The next week would be my first full week and I was not sure what to expect, but if Saturday was anything to go by it would be all right. How wrong can you be? Opening the shop on Monday morning and standing behind the counter I was suddenly beset by total and utter panic. Questioning my motives and what I thought I was doing, giving up a steady job in the pharmacy, I was kidding myself if I thought this was going to work. These and many other negative thoughts buzzed around my head and I felt as if I'd come back into my body after being absent for some weeks. It was as if the person who had been making all the arrangements and coming up with all the good ideas had decided to leave me.

Oh my God! What was I going to do now?

Trying not to let the outside world see the fear that was welling up inside of me I busied myself dusting and reading and drinking cup after cup of coffee. Outside in the mall passers-by would stop and stare in the window cracking what they thought were funny jokes, "Body, Mind and Spirit shop? Excuse me love, where do you keep the bodies? I could do with new one!" and other such comments in a similar vein.

Sitting there listening to the jibes I tried desperately not to take them on board, but something my old boss had said to me was repeating over and over in my head, "There's nothing more depressing than sitting in a shop with no customers." That was a vote of no confidence I could have well done without because now his words were replaying over and over in my head. But all these negative thoughts would change very soon with the advent of what happened next.....

CHAPTER 22

THE 4TH DIMENSION ..... NO ORDINARY SHOP

Eleanor's story

Even though I was concerned about how many customers I didn't have I felt an excitement that I just couldn't explain because I *knew* deep inside I had embarked upon the adventure of my life.

 The following week remained quiet, dusting the shop for the third time that day and on to my fourth cup of coffee. I found myself quietly willing someone to come into the shop, if only for a chat. No sooner had the thought entered my head when a frail old lady opened the door, she was a stranger to me, but I welcomed her in and asked if I could help. She was very direct and told me she hadn't come in to buy anything although she did have a story to tell, and she knew that *I* was the person she needed to share it with!

 Inviting her to sit down I settled into my chair and prepared to listen to her story. After all what else did I have to do? She proceeded to tell me about a near-death experience she had undergone some years before. It was a beautiful story and when she had finished she looked at me and said, "I know I don't have much longer here on Earth as my body is old and weak, but I have no fear of death because I have seen the place I am going to, and let me tell you dear it is a place of great beauty with so much Love and Light that I will welcome death with open arms when it arrives."

 Introducing herself as Eleanor she accepted my invitation to stay for a cup of tea and whilst chatting over our cuppa she told me about her life and how she had worked at Jurby airport during the 1950s.

Pricking up my ears at the mention of Jurby I couldn't help but ask if she'd known a man called Fred Fletcher. Eleanor's eyes misted and tears welled up threatening to spill over as she replied rather dreamily, "Oh yes, I knew Fred he was the loveliest man I have ever met. What made you mention him? He's been dead for years"

Smiling encouragingly I told her that I was his daughter, whereupon Eleanor, unable to control the emotion she was feeling stood up and threw her arms around me in the tightest of hugs. Returning the hug from this woman I had only just met, I felt a strong sense of sadness within her. When we released our hold on one another, her eyes still glistening with tears she told me she'd had an overwhelming desire to come into my shop that morning and couldn't believe it had led her to Fred's daughter. Like me she found the whole episode intriguing and rather wonderful.

A rather misty eyed Eleanor began to recall times long ago when she had worked with my father and I got the distinct impression from the way she was talking that she'd had a real crush on him. Those far off days at the air base seemed to have been the highlight of her life as the remainder had been occupied with looking after her brother and infirm parents. She told me she'd never married and I felt quite sad for her as she'd put her own happiness on hold and lived her whole life for everyone else. However, she gave no evidence of regret and told me she had enjoyed her life.

Leaving the shop that morning she told me she would call in the following week as she had something to show me, expressing again how glad she was to have found me. Having no idea as to what she wanted to show me I had no alternative, but to wait patiently for her next visit when hopefully all would be revealed.

Calling to see Mum that weekend I told her about Eleanor's visit and whilst chatting it occurred to me how nice it would be to have some photos of Dad to show Eleanor when she called again. Persuading Mum to get out the old albums we sorted through the family pictures until I came across some old black and white prints taken whilst Dad was working at Jurby. One of the photographs had been taken at a function in the Officers' Mess where Dad was waiting on tables. Looking very smart in his white waiter's jacket and black Dickie-bow I couldn't help thinking how handsome he'd been with his little Errol Flynn moustache. Mum then unearthed another photograph of a group of waiters lined up behind a banquet table, in the centre of this line-up was a young woman smiling and posing for the camera. Placing the snaps in an envelope I put them in my handbag making a promise to Mum that I would look after them and return them the following weekend after I'd shown them to Eleanor.

True to her word Eleanor returned to see me the following week and hardly through the door when she produced a large hard backed book from her handbag. Passing it to me I noticed the book was called "The Truth in the Light" by a Dr Peter Fenwick and his wife Elizabeth. It was an in depth study into near-death experiences which included many personal experiences from members of the public. A book mark had been placed between the pages and with Eleanor's prompting I turned to that page only to find it catalogued the story about Eleanor's own near-death experience. She told me after having answered an advert in the newspaper requesting stories from people who'd had near-death experiences she had been invited to take part in the investigation and had penned her story which was accepted by Dr. Fenwick and printed in this very book. I could see how thrilled she was to have people believe her story and that it had been worthy of being included in such an important investigation.

Settling Eleanor into the 'healing chair' I pulled the photographs from my handbag with a flourish saying, "Now I have something to show you, Eleanor." Tears welled up in her eyes as she gazed at the pictures of Dad looking so young and vibrant, and leafing through the collection, she eventually found the group photograph and squealing with delight pointed at the line up and exclaimed, "That's me in the middle."

Staring incredulously at the grainy black and white image I really had to study the photograph, but could see that it was indeed a young and attractive Eleanor, not the stooped and bent old lady that sat before me. Tears of joy streamed down her wrinkled cheeks as she told me how happy she felt seeing the photographs' and admitted that her time working at Jurby with my father had been the happiest days of her life. It was obvious that Eleanor was going to be a regular visitor to the shop and I resolved to have the old photographs copied so she could look at them whenever she wished.

Just prior to meeting Eleanor I'd been talking business with a young man when he shared with me that he was terminally ill and had asked me did I believe in life-after-death. My heart went out to him and I spoke at length on my beliefs, which seemed to comfort him, but it was obvious to me that he was searching for an answer before his final day arrived.

A few days after Eleanor's second visit I received a letter from the unknown young man. He had contacted me because he thought I would be interested in a doctor who was coming to the Island to lecture on the subject of life-after-death saying that his studies could prove to science that there actually was life after physical death. The letter went on to say that the lecture was to be held at The Manx Museum the following week and this doctor had written a book about his investigations, his name was Dr Peter Fenwick, and the book was called 'The Truth in the Light'

Was this a coincidence? I think not. Reading the contents of the letter again I knew exactly why I had been given this information and immediately booked two seats at the lecture, telling Eleanor to be ready at 7pm the following Friday night. Questioning me on where we would be going I told her it was a secret, but she would need to bring her copy of 'The Truth in the Light.'

I had also mentioned the talk to Harold, Betty's husband, who had taken to calling at the shop most days for a cup of coffee and a chat. He had been so lonely since Betty's passing and on hearing about the lecture was anxious to attend, kindly offering to drive us all to Douglas.

Picking up an excited Eleanor, she told us it was a rarity for her to go out at night and was really looking forward to it even though she didn't have a clue where she was going! Arriving at the museum with just enough time to take our seats before the start of the lecture, poor Eleanor was still at loss to know the purpose of the evening. The lights dimmed and a young man walked up to the podium on stage and I recognized him instantly as the young man who had sent me the letter. Introducing himself to the assembly I learnt that it was he who had organized the evening and invited Dr. Fenwick to the Island on the strength of a conversation he'd had with a lady he knew to be in the audience! Finishing his introductory speech he then welcomed Dr. Fenwick onto the stage. Eleanor gasped in surprise, smiling at me through her tears she reached for my hand, squeezing my fingers tightly and mouthed a silent 'Thank You'. Fascinated by the topic the three of us sat opened mouthed and listened to the lecture after which the doctor invited anyone who wished to buy his book or speak to him to come forward.

Nudging Eleanor I told her the moment had arrived and now was her chance to introduce herself and get her book signed. Joining the queue of people waiting to speak to the doctor she kept glancing over her shoulder at Harold and me, her excitement quite evident. Finally, reaching the front of the queue Eleanor engaged the doctor in animated conversation for some time before handing her book over for signing. Moments later she made her way back to us beaming from ear to ear holding the book aloft in triumph. I can tell you, there was a lump in my throat the size of a golf ball just to see the look of happiness on that old lady's face.

Offering me the book as she sat down she told me she wanted me to have it. Protesting, I declined, saying that now that her book was signed by the author she must keep it herself. However, Eleanor insisted, telling me she'd just enjoyed one of the most magnificent evenings of her life and as she wasn't planning on being around for too much longer she couldn't think of anyone she would rather leave the book to than Fred Fletcher's daughter! Thanking her I felt the golf ball in my throat grow to twice the size and kissed her on the cheek promising I would keep her book and treasure it always, which I have.

Eight weeks later Eleanor passed on peacefully in her sleep and the young man who'd organised the talk has since passed on too. "God bless you both and thank you for the parts you played on my journey and also for giving me the opportunity to play my part in yours.

CHAPTER 23

'TIEME RANIPIRI'

As the weeks drifted by I became accustomed to my new role as the proprietor of The 4th Dimension. At this stage I did not think it very likely I would be there any longer than my initial six month lease as business remained very slow, but on the plus side I'd met lots of new and interesting people and I was thoroughly enjoying myself which made it all worthwhile. It was a real joy to be there as so many wonderful things seemed to happen on an almost daily basis.

For example I'd become very friendly with Rosemary the lady I'd originally met in the charity shop. She had been very kind to me, bringing in a vast amount of metaphysical books for my second-hand book section and I know without her contribution the shop would have appeared much emptier than it already was!

Rosemary and her husband lived in a cottage a few miles out of town and had invited me to call and see them if I was ever passing. I remember vividly the first time I called at their home when Rosemary had showed me into the lounge where Les was watching sport on the television, before disappearing into the kitchen to make tea. Not wanting to disturb Les, who was obviously engrossed in a snooker match, I let my eyes wander around the room. Instantly drawn to a picture frame that contained a poem, hanging on the opposite wall which I read it from where I was sitting. Not knowingly having drawn Les's attention to my interest I spent the rest of the afternoon wondering how I could ask these people I hardly knew if they would let me have a copy of the poem as it had touched me so deeply.

The following week Rosemary and Les called at the shop and approaching the counter with a huge grin on his face Les produced a paper bag from his inside jacket pocket. Handing it over, he excitedly told me to open the package and sliding a small picture frame out of the bag I squealed with delight as I turned it over and found it to be a copy of the poem Tieme Ranapiri. Les obviously hadn't been as engrossed in the snooker as much as I'd thought and I accused him of reading my mind, an accusation he readily admitted to.

Reading through 'Tieme Ranapiri' once again after Rosemary and Les had left the shop I placed it under the counter and considered getting some copies made because I was sure a lot of people would be interested and love it as much as I did.

Minutes later a friend came in and placed a couple of books on the counter for my second-hand library and by way of conversation I shared with them the lovely gift I'd just been given and produced the framed poem. I was more than a little taken aback when my friend began to smile and I told her in no uncertain terms it was not meant to be funny. "I'm not smiling at the poem, I'm smiling at this," she replied, picking up one of the books she'd just brought in and there printed on the inside cover was the poem Tieme Ranipiri!

The next day was quiet yet again so closing the shop for a while mid-morning I went to the copy shop to have some prints made of Tieme Ranapiri. On my return I could see a woman trying the shop door and anxious not to lose a prospective customer I broke into a trot through the mall. Arriving breathlessly at the shop door just as she was about to turn away I apologised for being closed. Asking if I could help, she told me she had been admiring some beautifully worded cards on display in the window and wondered if I had any more inside. It seems she was looking for a particular poem she wanted to send to a friend who was terminally ill. Yet again I found myself apologising telling her all my stock was on display.

However, as she turned to leave the shop a voice inside my head was shouting, 'What about Tieme Ranapiri?' and calling her back I produced a copy of the poem from the sheaf I'd just had printed. Reading silently for a few moments before looking up at me in disbelief, she told me that it was the very poem she had been searching for! I cannot tell you how pleased I was to be able to help her, nor can I tell you how many copies of this poem I have given away since that day or the countless times it has provided comfort for those in need.

My Law.....Tieme Ranipiri

The sun may be clouded, yet ever the sun,
Will sweep on its course till the 'Cycle' is run,
And when into chaos the system is hurled
Again shall the Builder reshape a New World?
Your path may be clouded, uncertain your goal,
Move on, for your orbit is fixed to your soul.
And though it may lead into darkness of night
The torch of 'The Builder' shall give it new light.
You were. You will be! Know this while you are;
Your spirit has travelled both long and afar.
It came from the Source, to the Source it returns…
The Spark which was lighted eternally burns.
It slept in a jewel. It leapt in a wave.
It roamed in the forest. It rose from the grave.
It took on strange garbs for long eons of years
And now in the soul of your self it appears.
From body to body your spirit speeds on
It seeks a new form when the old one has gone
And the form that it finds is the fabric you wrought
On the loom of the Mind from the fibre of Thought,
As dew is drawn upwards, in rain to descend
Your thoughts drift away and in Destiny blend.
You cannot escape them, for petty or great,
Or evil or noble, they fashion your Fate.
Somewhere on some planet, sometime and somehow
Your life will reflect your thoughts of your Now.
My Law is unerring, no blood can atone …
The structure you built you will live in … alone!
From cycle to cycle, through time and through space
Your lives with your longings will ever keep pace
And all that you ask for, and all you desire,
Must come at your bidding, as flame out of fire,
Once 'list to that Voice and all tumult is done,
Your life is the Life of the Infinite One.
In the hurrying race you are conscious of pause

With love for the purpose, and love for the Cause.
You are your own Devil; you are your own God
You fashioned the paths your footsteps have trod.
And no one can save you from Error or Sin
Until you have harked to the Spirit within.

CHAPTER 24

ENTER EVA.... AND A QUICK COURSE IN FENG SHUI!

About four months into my lease I was becoming really worried about the finances of the shop and wondered if I would be able to survive for more than the initial six months. The company who owned the mall wanted to know if I would be renewing my lease by the time I had been in business for 5 months. Having benefitted from a reduced rent and a short six month lease I had to take into consideration that the lease would be for much longer and there would be a significant hike in the rent if I was to renew.

Although wonderful things were happening and I didn't want to let the business go I was letting the financial worries crowd in on me. The question was: Would I be able to pay the full rent and did I want to commit for a further three years? I was concerned that if I extended the lease there may come an occasion when I would not be able to meet the rent and not only would I go out of business, but would be sued for the outstanding amount. Talk about being in mental chaos I felt as if I were going crazy and all because I'd followed my dream, a dream I might add that I loved and had made manifest, but the turmoil inside my brain made this all feel so unfair.

As if in answer to my thought processes and 'out of the blue' a medium, who was a total stranger to me came into the shop and gave me the message, "Don't worry about the finances of the shop, I had followed my guidance and all would be well." By now I was used to such occurrences and I listened, but did not heed the message I had been given! Instead I thought that the messenger had the easy job as she wasn't in my position, so I paid little heed. A few days later a second stranger came in and gave me exactly the same message, then a third and a fourth, before I finally stopped and listened to what my

HS had to say. To my detriment this has not been the only lesson in trust that I have ignored until it was staring me in the face, by which time I had a mental picture of my guides wiping the sweat from their brows and shaking their heads in despair.

The week I received the above messages was the first time I met Eva when she breezed into the shop one day and stood with her back to the counter browsing through the second-hand books. The first thing I noticed about her were her clothes and shoes as she was wearing an oversized colourful mohair cardigan with black leggings and the most beautiful pair of gold slipper type shoes and completing the ensemble dangling from her ears were the biggest pair of chunky gold ear-rings I'd ever seen. Immediately I fell in love with her shoes and felt they would be a good starting point to strike up a conversation, because for some reason I felt I had to talk to this flamboyant woman.

Opening the conversation with, "What a beautiful pair of shoes" we had a short discussion about her shoes and where to purchase them before she shared with me she'd been itching to get into my shop for some time, but was currently nursing her elderly mother, which took up most of her day. Chatting for some time she told me she thought the shop was lovely and gradually we became acquainted and discovered more about one another. Asking about her accent she informed me that she was of Swedish parentage although she had spent the early part of her life in Japan where her father had been employed during the final years of World War II. She told me that Japan had been reluctantly left behind when she'd married in the 1960's and had lived in various countries until she settled on the Isle of Man during the 1980s.

I soon found myself telling Eva that business was very slow and if it didn't pick up in the next few weeks I wouldn't be able to continue any longer than my initial six month lease. With a wave of her hand she informed me she was a Feng Shui consultant and told me not to worry about my business. Not knowing what a Feng Shui consultant was and looking expectantly to her for an explanation, I told her I had no idea what she was talking about, expressing that it was all 'Double Dutch' to me. Smiling, she explained it was the ancient Chinese art of placement and offered to show me how it would work to attract more customers into the shop. Asking if I had a small mirror, I produced one I kept under the counter and handed it to her, whereupon she immediately stuck it on the wall behind the till! Although I couldn't see how this could possibly make any difference I decided to humour her and thanked her for the tip.

This was to be the beginning of a very special and spiritual friendship as Eva is larger than life and twice as colourful with a heart as big as a house and a laugh that's bigger, even bigger than her ear-rings! I can honestly say a room is never empty when Eva is in it.

To this day I'm not sure if it was Eva's Feng Shui mirror, the messages from Spirit, or a combination of both, but the shop took off from that moment and I never looked back. However, there were a lot more surprises in store for me and they would be 'winging' there way towards me very soon.

CHAPTER 25

A DREAM FROM THE ANGELS

After meeting Eva and receiving the messages from Spirit I allowed myself to relax, and the more I relaxed the better the business became as spiritually minded people from all over the Island were finding the shop and obviously telling one another as more people made their way in my direction.

Just as I had begun to breathe more easily and put my financial worries on the back burner I began to have a dream. Every night I would have the same dream, a dream about the shop, the only difference being it was not the shop I was in, but another one. The dream shop was 50 yards away from my own, outside the mall bordering the car park. It was a corner shop with lots of windows and the beautiful window crystals were displayed on branches and the whole shop was alight with rainbows as they caught the sunlight.

In my waking hours I would relive this dream and thought how lovely it would be in that particular shop as it was out in the sunshine rather than being tucked away in the gloom of the mall. I had long since become accustomed to leaving the mall at close of business with my eyes smarting as I came out into the daylight, like a mole emerging from its tunnel!

The dream had been replaying nightly for almost two weeks when I received a letter from the owners of the mall asking me for a decision on whether I was going to renew my lease and wanting to know by the end of the following week. The lease they wanted me to sign was for three years which I have to say struck fear in my heart. The business was just getting on its feet and the future still seemed so uncertain to me and whether I liked it or not this was crunch time and I had to make a decision.

To complicate things further I'd heard a rumour that the shop I'd been dreaming about was closing down so I decided to make tentative enquiries at the leasing agents. Confirming the shop would be closing in two weeks time I found myself asking for details of the lease and after furnishing me all the relevant information I went home rather puzzled as to why I'd asked for them. Reading through everything I discovered my 'dream shop' was almost twice the size of the one I was already in, so of course it would be twice the rent.

Wondering what on earth I was doing, having followed one dream I now found myself chasing another and spent many hours making one financial calculation after another, but was still no nearer to making a decision. My head spinning I decided to leave my worries at home and take Rags out for a walk in the country. It was a beautiful afternoon and driving into the countryside I parked the car on a favoured little road where Rags and I often walked. Rags usually shot out of the car as soon as I opened the door, eager for a walk, but on this occasion she remained sitting on the parcel shelf head cocked on one side staring at me as if to say, "I'm not coming Mum, you can go and walk on your own today." No matter how I enticed her she would not budge so finally I gave up and got back into the car.

Sitting for a while to appreciate the beautiful Manx countryside that I love so much, taking in the softly rolling hills, the lush green fields where the sheep and cattle grazed contentedly, the seagulls flying overhead calling to one another against a beautiful canopy of clear blue sky and warm sunshine, I breathed deeply, giving thanks and sighed to myself, 'What a perfect day'

Suddenly I was jolted out of my reverie by the rogue thought of the shop and despite having come out to get away from my worries I found them breaking through my consciousness. Sending up a plea to my HS I asked for help with my decision, explaining I personally didn't have a clue what to do for the best and prayed that my HS would send me a sign that I could understand.

Turning the key in the ignition we set off once more, but I had barely driven a mile when Rags set up a commotion demanding to be let out. Just having turned off the main road I was now driving along a country lane resembling a narrow ribbon with nowhere to park! Abandoning the car as close to the hedge as possible I opened the door and Rags shot out, like a bullet from a gun, hurtling off down a farm track. Immediately I gave chase whilst cursing under my breath about what I would do to her when I caught her. This behaviour was very out of character as she ran wildly up the road like something possessed when suddenly Rags stopped abruptly about thirty yards ahead of me.

Slowing to catch my breath I was grateful she had decided to wait for me although I was still intent on giving her a good scolding. Walking towards her something lying in the road caught my eye as it glinted in the sunlight. Rags had stopped right beside the shining object and appeared to be staring down at it. Reaching her I discovered it was a piece of Manx quartz crystal shaped like a pyramid and lying next to it was a small, pure white feather. According to a book I'd only just read a white feather always denotes a sign from an angel! Thanking the angels at the top of my voice as my request of only a few minutes previously had surely been answered. What better sign could I have wished for?

My anger at Rags disappeared completely as I knew she had been used to help me reach the sign and without a doubt she is much more adept at communicating with Spirit than I am. Racing back to the car with Rags now chasing me, I drove straight into town, running into the leasing agents and rather breathlessly telling them that I would be taking the lease on the shop unit I had enquired about. Not another thought of how I was going to pay for it entered my mind I just knew I had to do it.

The very next day I rang the gentleman in charge of the mall, enquiring if it would be possible to have the shop unit on the car park instead of re-leasing the unit I already occupied. Thankfully I received the answer I hoped for and was told they would draw up the lease immediately. Finding the courage from somewhere, I took the opportunity to request a one year, rather than a three year lease, and although I was told it was against company policy, could hardly believe my ears when he agreed.

The following day David, the local Tarot reader called by the shop, I'd only met him once before, a couple of months previously, and was surprised to find he'd come in especially to give me a 'message'. Telling me 'the move would go well' I initially pretended not to know what he was referring to as at this time Dickie was the only person I'd told. In his broad Irish accent David continued by saying he was aware that Spirit had been encouraging me for weeks to move to another shop because that was where they wanted me to be!

Flabbergasted, this was the confirmation I needed, so I went ahead with my plans, much against the advice of friends and well-wishers who all thought I was mad to move to the new venue. They came up with many reasons why I should not move to the new location, some even resorting to pleading that I'd be making a big mistake as it was out of the main walkway. I'm glad to say I didn't take on board any of the negative comments, being happy with the decision I'd made with the help of 'the angels' and knowing deep inside that this was the move I had to make.

CHAPTER 26

GOODBYE AND THANK YOU

As soon as I'd made the decision to move I could sense a subtle change in the atmosphere of the shop, it was still beautiful and calming although to me it felt very different, but thankfully I seemed to be the only one to feel the energetic shift.

Jon, the son of my friend, was opening up spiritually and had become a regular visitor to the shop calling in most days for a chat. Dear Jon, he proved to be an invaluable friend, because without him coming into my life at that moment in time I don't know how I would have managed. Turning to him in panic on the day I received the keys I remember asking what I was possibly going to display my stock on as there were no shelves and counters and I couldn't afford to buy any. Without hesitation Jon came up with the solution as his best mate was just having a new kitchen fitted and Jon persuaded him to let us have the old units to fit out my new shop.

Working like a Trojan every night for the next two weeks he successfully turned a few old kitchen units into my beautiful new shop and it did look beautiful by the time he was finished. We painted the work surfaces gold and the counter deep blue with stencilled silver stars, draping the cupboard fronts with cream voile decorated in golden cherubs and finally suspending branches above the windows to display the window crystals.

My last day in the little shop soon arrived and as I unlocked the shop that morning I was acutely aware that the atmosphere in the shop was now vastly changed. Everything was still in place and ready for the days trading, but as I stood in the middle of the shop I was filled with a strange desolate feeling of emptiness, almost desertion, as a mixture of emotions swept over me. Did I really want to say goodbye to my little shop? What lay ahead? And was I really ready for what the future might hold?

Putting aside these questions as the first customers of the day arrived and I settled in to what proved to be a very busy day as lots of friends stopped by to wish me well, although many still expressed their doubts as to whether a move was the right thing for me to do. To everyone who voiced a worry I gave the same reply, "I am just following my guidance."

As the day wore on I could feel the energy draining from the shop more and more and felt as if it was deserting me. It was quite a depressing feeling I can tell you. By 5 o'clock the mall had gone completely quiet and I dropped the catch on the door for the last time as Dickie arrived to help me move the stock the 50 yards up the mall to where the new shop was located. Billy and Pearl friends of mine had come to wish me well as I closed and decided to stay and help us move. Dickie and Billy armed themselves with shopping trolleys from nearby Safeway while Pearl and I filled them with stock before the lads wheeled them the short journey up the mall to their new home.

When we had finished I thanked Pearl and Billy for their help and they left me standing on my own in the empty little shop near to tears, but instead of crying I gave thanks for the time I'd spent there and for all the wonderful memories I was taking with me. Stepping outside I turned the key in the lock for what would be the last time before making my way up the mall to the new shop.

A few moments later I entered my new premises piled high with stock which looked like a huge jumble sale and I almost wept, but that was not the reason I felt like crying. It was not from sadness, but from joy, as the feeling in the shop was one of tremendous and overwhelming *'LOVE'* that wrapped itself around me like a warm and welcoming blanket. In that instant the 'light bulb' came on in my brain and understanding flowed through me as I realized the energy that had imbued my little shop had transferred itself and was waiting for me to take up residence in these new premises! In that moment I knew everything was going to be all right I had come home, and yes, I was more than ready to face whatever the future had in store for me.

CHAPTER 27

THE 4TH DIMENSION # II .... PASTURES NEW

The weekend I moved premises was a really busy one as you might imagine and spent mainly at my new shop sorting out all of the stock and finding new homes for everything. Unfortunately Dickie had to sacrifice his weekend to help me as I had to be open as usual the following Monday morning because now I could definitely not afford to be closed. Despite the effort involved the weekend flew by and it didn't seem like hard work at all, in fact, for me at least, it was a labour of love, and the satisfaction I received from seeing the finished result was well worth the effort.

The shop had windows on three sides which made you feel as if you were in a goldfish bowl. Inside the door on the left was a small counter where I displayed my Native American Indian section, next to that at the back of the shop was an elevated bay shaped display window facing directly into the cafeteria next door. Coming out of the bay window we had positioned a bookshelf in the corner to be stocked with my second-hand books, next to the bookshelf and directly behind the small counter was a sliding door that led into what had once been a very small changing-room, beyond that was a small back room cum kitchen, compact and bijou are the words that spring to mind where thousands of cups of tea and coffee would be made over the coming years.

Placing my wing chair/ healing chair in the corner at the back of the shop between the Native American section and bookshelf thinking to myself it would be a comfortable place to sit and read when the shop was quiet, which as it turned out was almost never! Having hung a large mirror opposite the door Eva was incensed when she saw it, immediately telling me it was extremely bad Feng

Shui, but as it felt right to me we agreed to disagree and the mirror stayed put despite her protestations! I'd placed a small cherub water fountain in the window and much to my relief Eva informed me that this was very good Feng Shui, or if you like just good luck on my part. My final job was to hang my large blue Witches' Ball in the window on the right-hand side of the door, my trademark.

With the stock laid out and decoration complete I took a few moments to look around, finding I was well satisfied with the result and was instantly rewarded by a shaft of sunlight beaming through the windows. The sunlight caught the dangling crystals and the whole place lit up with dozens of beautiful rainbows just like in my dream. Once again I felt I was experiencing confirmation from Spirit that I was doing the right thing and I was on the right path.

I could hardly wait for the next day when I would open the doors to the world and let seekers in to what I felt was going to be a very special place. Lacking the funds to advertise I'd pinned a notice on the old shop door to let my existing customers know where to find me, and thankfully, find me they did, as the new premises turned out to be the perfect venue for a spiritual meeting place.

The business really took off after the move as people started to arrive from all over the Island and much to my delight I was to find what a wonderful thing word of mouth is as I believe it is the best form of advertising in the world, and certainly the least expensive. My little shop soon made a name for itself throughout the spiritual community on the island and it never ceased to amaze me the wonderful healings and all manner of magnificent things that took place there, some of which I will recount in further chapters.

I was in 'Seventh Heaven' this was definitely not work or at least not work as I had ever known it, because managing the 4th Dimension was a sheer joy.

CHAPTER 28

GOING PUBLIC

More and more people were finding the shop and spreading the word amongst other like-minded souls and although it hadn't been my original intention, my little shop was becoming a meeting place of kindred spirits and the energy in the place was wonderful. Knowing the plan spirit had intended for me was coming to fruition I also knew they hadn't finished with me yet and there would be many more surprises to come.

In an effort to retain some semblance of being a caring housewife I only opened the shop four days a week remaining closed on Monday and Wednesday.

One Wednesday morning whilst busy doing the housework I answered the phone to find it was the organiser of a forthcoming psychic and healing evening, which was to be held at one of the largest hotels on the island. She was calling to invite *me* to take part! She wanted me to give a demonstration of clairvoyance, no less! Almost laughing down the phone on hearing her request I told her that I definitely was ***not*** a clairvoyant and wanted to know who had told her I was. Careful not to let the informer's name slip she insisted that she'd been told that I was clairvoyant and it was obvious to me at that point I was not going to get rid of her that easily. When it became evident I had no intention of displaying my non-existent mediumistic talents she wanted to know what else I could do and telling her I ran a spiritual shop I found myself explaining the details of my dream and how the shop had come into being. The more I told her the more excited she became insisting that I come and talk about my spiritual journey and finally promising her I'd think about it I eventually managed to get her off the phone.

When Dickie came home for lunch that day I told him about the phone call and was a little hurt when laughing at the possibility he questioned whether I was actually considering doing it. Telling him I intended to send it up to Spirit and see how I felt in the morning, but I had already made my mind up that if it felt right, Spirit would expect me to comply. My poor husband shrugged his shoulders and rolled his eyes heavenward, it was patently obvious he thought I was absolutely mad. He is a very quiet, reserved man and does not enjoy being in the spotlight, so the scenario of his wife talking about her weird exploits in front of a large audience would be one of his worst nightmares.

The next day I awoke with a very positive feeling that I should take part and the same emotions were flowing through me as when I'd been asked to speak for Christine's class. The organizer of the event was pleased when I rang and told her I would take part telling me she would send a programme of events for the evening in due course.

The very next day the programme arrived in the post and to my horror I was billed on the front page as a Psychic Artist!!! Staring at the programme in utter disbelief as there was no way I had given the woman any indication of my abilities in this direction, I couldn't draw a straight line let alone someone's deceased Aunt Fanny!

Without further ado I got straight on the phone to the organiser and told her she had made a terrible mistake and that I was definitely not a psychic artist and she would have to change the programme or people would be misled. In a breezy sing-song voice she informed me that as all the programmes had been sent out there was nothing she could do! I was in a mental quandary thinking Dickie had been right all along in telling me not to do it. However, something inside of me was calm and reassuring telling me that everything would be all right and that on the night I would just apologise for the mistake in the programme before I began my talk.

The day before the event Dickie asked if I had written my speech and was surprised when I told him I hadn't which I realise must have sounded very egotistical or just plain stupid. Somehow I didn't feel the need to write down what I was going to talk about, I liked to think I could trust my memory and also my connection with Spirit. My husband was absolutely astounded, telling me I must be mad if I was planning on giving a speech without any notes. So, in an effort to relieve his worries I told him I'd probably jot down a few headers as a prompt, although this was more for his benefit than my own as I knew he would be mortified if I stood up and made a fool of myself. Within a few minutes I'd made all the notes I felt necessary and triumphantly told him I'd finished. Looking at me in utter disbelief he shook his head from side to side probably thinking he'd had his say and now he had to leave me to my fate.

Feeling I needed a little moral support I'd invited Eva and Rosemary to accompany me and they were really looking forward to an evening full of clairvoyants, Tarot readers, healers and complementary therapies. Arriving in good time we were directed to a large conference room where row upon row of seating was laid out. They must have been expecting about eighty people by the number of chairs and I realized in that moment that this was going to be a whole lot different than speaking to a class full of students. Seemingly unfazed, I busily set out a display of crystals on a table at the side of the room whilst being utterly amazed at how calm I felt.

All the speakers had been given a timetable to tell them when they were due on and in what order. Perusing the list I noticed I was the third speaker of the evening with a 10-minute slot to fill. Anxious not to miss anything my friends had found us seats near the front by the platform and glancing behind me as the first speaker took the podium I was astonished to find that most of the seats were now taken.

The first speaker began very nervously and was obviously quite relieved when her time was up and almost ran of the stage. The second speaker droned on a bit and lost the attention of the audience as a lot of people wandered into the adjoining rooms where other therapies and demonstrations were taking place. Looking behind me again I saw a lot of empty seats and thought to myself, "Phew, that's good, not so many people, it's my turn next."

As my name was being announced I sent up a silent prayer to my HS asking for assistance then made my way to the platform. Taking up position at the podium behind the microphone, armed with my few scribbled notes, I began to talk and was very aware my voice was wavering with nerves for the first few sentences, but once I got into my stride it just flowed. During the talk people started to drift through from the other rooms, more and more people filed in until the seats were all full again. Continuing to talk, (well I've been told on many occasions once I start it's difficult to stop me!) the room was soon full to capacity with people even standing along the back wall who couldn't get a seat and throughout my speech I was constantly being made aware of certain people in the audience that my words were touching on a deep level.

Eventually my ten minutes were up and the lady organiser attracted my attention by waving to me from the side of the stage. Thanking the assembled audience for their patience and bidding everyone goodnight I made my way off the platform to rapturous applause! I was overwhelmed. Taking up position next to my crystal display I was busy for the rest of the evening with numerous people wanting to share their own experiences. It was just magic!

On the way home I remarked to Rosemary and Eva that my stint on stage was the quickest ten minutes of my entire life and they both laughed, saying as one, "That wasn't ten minutes, you were on stage for almost three-quarters of an hour!"

I could hardly believe it, but one thing I do know, I could not have done it without the help of my HS/Spirit as they orchestrated the whole thing, of that I'm sure.

Over the course of the next few weeks the shop became busier than ever, thanks to word of mouth, which of course is the best advertising in the world. This was my first real experience of being in the public eye, but Spirit was going to make sure it was not going to be my last as later that summer the local press contacted me asking for an interview.

Asking the reporter what had I done to warrant an interview, he commented that he had been told many stories about this unique shop called 'The 4th Dimension' and its owner and was intrigued and wanted the opportunity to see it for himself and write an article, reminding me that all advertising is good and this would be *free.*

Agreeing to the interview we made arrangements to meet at the shop the following Wednesday which just happened to be my birthday. An interview with the local press on my birthday what a unique birthday present I thought with a laugh.

Arriving at the shop a few minutes early the following

Wednesday I didn't switch the lights on so as not to attract attention, but people still looked through the windows and tried the door during the interview. Even with no lights on the shop seemed to emanate a 'Light' and 'Life' of its own.

The journalist was very polite and asked me lots of questions; "How did you come to start a shop like this? What do you hope to achieve? What is it all about?" How long do you expect to be here? And many, many more questions in a similar vein.

Furiously scribbling my replies in his notebook I could see he was having difficulty with some of the things I was telling him. When the interview was over he thanked me saying it had been an interesting and informative meeting and although he had acted graciously throughout I could see he had been struggling with some of the philosophy I had expounded. Promising he would send a draft copy for my perusal before it went to press he then inveigled me into having a photograph taken sitting in the 'healing chair', telling me that an interview without a picture to relate to would be of little use.

The following week the draft copy arrived accompanied by a note from the nice journalist to say that if I didn't agree with anything he had written to change it into my own words. Reading through the draft I found, to my horror that he continually referred to me as a spiritualist instead of someone who was in touch with and exploring their spirituality, which are in fact, two very different things. Making my corrections with a red pen I changed a lot of what he'd written into my own words and when I was satisfied I sent it back to him apologising for all the changes I'd made. Bless that journalist because he printed it exactly as I had worded it, a full page spread of free advertising which did wonders for the shop as more and more people now knew where to find it and what it was about.

Once again I believe this event was orchestrated by Spirit and I was learning to understand the prompting of my Soul or whatever you choose to call this Higher Power that was helping me with the practical things in life by orchestrating these situations for my benefit.

CHAPTER 29

GERONIMO! ..... INDIANS AND ANGELS

I'm aware that the title of this chapter might mislead you into thinking you had picked up a book on cowboys and Indians by mistake, but I assure you that is not the case. Not long after moving in to my new premises I purchased a very large Native American Indian shield to display in the window. It was a beautiful shield depicting the head and shoulders of the Red Indian, Geronimo. The perimeter of the shield was bound in suede with a multitude of beautiful pure white curled feathers hanging from strips of suede around the lower edge making it a spectacular window display and was also one of the most expensive items for sale in the shop.

Just prior to buying the shield I had acquired a new customer called Colin. When I first met him I thought he was a rather gruff and aggressive character, but as I got to know him better I realised this was just his protective persona as the real Colin was quite a softie underneath. Over the next couple of years I grew very fond of him, but during the early days of our relationship he knew just how to wind me up with his abrupt manner. On his first visit to the shop he told me how delighted he was to find a shop that stocked Native American Indian merchandise, but wasn't remotely interested in any of the other 'weird stuff'.

When I enquired as to how long he had been interested in the subject of Native Americans he told me he'd suffered a heart attack some years earlier when his heart had actually stopped beating for a few minutes. In his own words he described himself as being as 'dead as a Dodo', but on recovery, for some unexplained reason he'd found himself drawn to all things related to Native Americans.

Trying to explain his sudden obsession I implied that it may have been his Spirit Guide who had drawn close to him at a time of great trauma and was trying to attract his attention. Colin, not being particularly spiritually minded pooh-poohed this idea telling me he'd never heard such a load of rubbish in his life.

After our initial conversation Colin would call in most days for a chat and to see if I had anything new, but to be honest I think the energy of the shop was casting its spell over him. From the first time he set eyes on the Indian shield he wanted it, but had remarked that it was too expensive for him to buy. Each time he came into the shop he would remark on how magnificent it was and tell me that he knew exactly where he would hang it in his home. Unfortunately, I couldn't afford to sell it at the price he was prepared to pay so it remained hanging in the window.

The shield had been on display for some weeks when Colin called in on his usual visit and remarked that I still hadn't sold his favourite item. Feeling a bit jaded at the thought of going another conversation on the subject of reducing the price I had to agree there didn't seem to be many interested parties out there. Colin then drew my attention to a feather missing from the very end of one of the suede strips which gave it a distinctly lop-sided appearance and laughing, told me that I would have no choice other than to reduce the price. Still reluctant to reduce the price to what Colin was prepared to pay I told him I'd search the shop for the missing feather and if I couldn't find it I would rethink the price.

After Colin had left the shop I turned the place upside down looking for the missing feather, but couldn't find it anywhere. Puzzling over it's disappearance I wondered where I could get a feather the appropriate size, colour and shape to replace it. Almost resigning myself to letting it go to Colin at a ridiculously low price I decided to ask Spirit for help, so standing alone in the shop I voiced my concerns to Spirit telling them I couldn't afford to reduce the shield and could they please help.

Opening the shop the next day I noticed a book called, 'Working with Guides and Angels' had fallen off the bookcase and picking it up placed it back on the shelf without a second thought. I was more distracted dreading the thought of Colin coming in and my having to sell the shield for much less than it was worth, but lucky for me

Colin never showed up. The following day when I entered the shop I was surprised to find the same book lying on the floor again, only this time a little further from the bookshelf. Considering it a little strange I returned it to the bookshelf only to find it on the floor every day for the rest of the week! Each day the book managed to be further and further away from the bookshelf, but the book on the floor was only one of the unusual events of this particular week as Colin, normally a daily visitor, was conspicuous by his absence all week.

On Saturday morning I awoke to the sound of a howling gale as a storm had blown up during the night and our poor little house was being buffeted with each huge gust. Reluctantly prising myself out of bed I walked into the lounge and paused to open the curtains in the bay window. As the curtains parted I caught my first glimpse of the wind swept garden and couldn't believe my eyes, because clinging on to a bush right outside the window was a pure white feather and it appeared to be waving to me, inviting me to come outside and collect it. Squealing with delight I rushed into the garden wearing only my dressing gown and slippers, struggling as the wind wrapped my dressing gown tightly round my legs. Plucking the feather from the top of the bush I came charging back into the house, feather clasped tightly between my fingers. Dickie, looking heavenward as I was blown back through the door shook his head, but didn't say a word as the look on his face said it all, 'My wife is mad, totally mad'.

All I could think about was the feather in my hand and attracting my husband's attention to my find, I shouted, "Look it's my feather". Rolling his eyes he agreed that it was indeed a feather and questioned me as to why it was so special. Telling him I'd asked Spirit for this particular feather a few days earlier I had to clarify my explanation by recounting the story of the shield. Happy that I was happy Dickie continued with his breakfast giving the impression that understanding my motives for doing anything any more were totally beyond him.

Popping the feather into the safety of an envelope I set off to work early with the intention of sewing it on to the shield before opening time. Arriving at the shop I wasn't a bit surprised to find my 'mobile' copy of 'Working with Guides and Angels' lying on the floor, this time directly under the shield ... at least six feet away from the bookshelf!

No longer in any doubt that my guide and Guardian Angels were working in my best interests I could only class what had happened as a miracle and sending up a silent prayer I stood in the shop and said, "Thank you" to the Angels.

The shield was obviously never meant for Colin and was eventually purchased by someone else, although he never bore a grudge and remained a very good customer over the next three years until he passed on.

The day after his passing I was driving into town when I became acutely aware of Colin's presence in the car beside me and I could hear him 'telling' me that I'd been right about his spirit guide and he'd come back especially to tell me that his Indian Chief had been waiting for him when he passed over. This gave me a lovely warm feeling inside and I was very happy for Colin because he had made his final transition *with* the help of his Indian Guide.

CHAPTER 30

MY ANSWERED PRAYER

Now that I was in larger premises I obviously needed more stock including gift items that were conventional as well as spiritual, but I had no existing knowledge of where to find suitable merchandise. Living on a small island where there were no wholesalers supplying the sort of stock I required, sourcing produce for the shop was a bit of a headache. So once again I found myself standing in the middle of the shop sending up a plea to Spirit for help and as an afterthought, I added, "If I had the bare faced cheek I would ask the owner of my favourite gift shop 'Faeries' where they get their stock, but I don't have the cheek so that's out of the question, *please help*."

Letting the above thought go just as the door flung open, and Shelagh, one of my regular customers entered the shop. Shelagh was an elderly and very eccentric lady, almost blind and with a very blunt way of expressing herself, but to my mind an extremely lovable character all the same. Dear Shelagh she believed in calling a spade 'a bloody spade' and she was never backward in coming forward when expressing her opinion on *anything* and practically every sentence she uttered was usually peppered with expletives. That day Shelagh was accompanied as she usually was by her friend Madge who very kindly brought her into town each week to do some shopping. Madge was a beautiful lady with a very patient and serene nature and believe me she needed all those virtues and more to cope with Shelagh.

After making her grand entrance, Shelagh stood stock still and very quiet, which was most unlike her, head cocked to one side as if listening to something. Telling whoever happened to be listening that she could hear the sound of running water and saying, 'Where the hell is that coming from?" The ever patient Madge led her over to the small cherub fountain I'd just switched on and Shelagh bent down for a closer look. Poor Shelagh her nose was almost in the fountain before she could see anything and turning to her friend she expressed her delight at what she imagined as much as saw. Continuing in the usual Shelagh vein she turned to me and said, "I'd like one of those, but without the bloody cherubs on it. Can't you get me one that's bloody ugly, the uglier the better?"

Laughing at a typical Shelagh statement I told her if she really wanted one, I'd try and get her one with gargoyles instead of cherubs, but I had to warn her the one I had in mind was pretty grotesque. Anxious for her to view it in the catalogue before I ordered it, she told me if it was ugly I should just order the 'bloody thing' and let Madge know when it arrived so she could collect it. Madge, smiling at her eccentric friend managed a silent 'thank you' to me behind Shelagh's back as they left the shop.

Madge came to collect the ugly fountain the following week and I was so glad she did because I was sure I would never be able to sell it to anyone else. Even Madge was a little taken aback when she saw it, but laughing said it was typical Shelagh and was sure she'd love it. Madge had come into town without Shelagh on this occasion as she wanted to pay for the monstrosity and give it to her as a gift. Questioning if it was Shelagh's birthday I was to learn that Madge was terminally ill and wanted to give Shelagh the hideous water feature as a memento before she passed over. The pair of them had been good friends for so many years Madge knew instinctively that Shelagh would get immense pleasure from the reactions of visitors to the grotesque gift, such was her sense of humour.

Studying Madge while she spoke to me I couldn't get over how beautiful this elderly, terminally ill woman appeared, her eyes glowing, and her demeanour calm, serene and radiant, she was someone who had definitely come to terms with her imminent demise.

The very next day, another of Shelagh's friends appeared in the shop clutching the water pump from the gargoyle fountain and telling me in no uncertain terms that it was faulty. It seems he had arrived at Shelagh's the night before just as she'd turned on the fountain and to the accompaniment of a great spluttering sound followed rapidly by spurting water. Trying not to laugh he informed me they'd had to switch it off very quickly before the whole of the front room was soaked. Knowing Shelagh's use of expressive language I could imagine the scene from the previous evening. Promising to get Shelagh a replacement as soon as I could and asking for her address before he left telling him that I would deliver the new pump myself.

On Wednesday of that same week I awoke with the most incredible urge to visit Shelagh. As it was my day off there was nothing really stopping me apart from the fact the new pump for her fountain had not yet arrived. After lunch, undeterred, having fought the desire to visit Shelagh all morning, I donned my coat and boots and got myself ready to take Rags for a walk and soon found myself driving in the direction of her home, but not really knowing why, I only knew that somewhere inside of me was a sense of purpose.

Following the instructions her friend had given me I soon arrived at the end of a dirt track road and taking one look at the unmade lane full of deep ruts and muddy puddles knew there was no way I was driving any further. I'd only been through the car wash the day before so I parked at the top of the lane as tight in to the hedge as I could so as not cause an obstruction. Rags and I set off down the muddy track slipping and sloshing for what seemed like an eternity. Rags being a small Yorkshire terrier and very close to the ground was soon covered in mud as some of the puddles were so deep she practically had to doggy paddle through them.

We were well down the lane when a huge smart car with an English registration plate appeared around the corner, heading straight towards us. The car was as wide as the lane and the only course of action I could take was to pick Rags up and climb onto the hedge. The car passed, the driver smiled and mouthed a 'thank you' while Rags and I descended back down onto the boggy track, unfortunately both a little the worse for wear as my coat was now covered in muddy paw marks. Now looking as though I had been sleeping rough for weeks I sent a silent prayer into the ether that I would not meet anyone other than Shelagh on reaching the cottage.

Proceeding on around the bend we were confronted by a huge bog, the muddy track skirting around the edge of it and on the far side was a small Manx cottage, presumably Shelagh's home. Suddenly, I experienced a strange feeling of déjà vu as I recognized this place from a dream I'd had some ten years earlier. Gazing at the scene I relived my dream in which I'd been searching for someone and the cottage in front of me was the place I had found them. This place was identical in every detail to the memory of my dream and I questioned how that could be as I had never been to this place before in my life and it was far too remote a place to stumble on, surely I would have remembered visiting it before?

Rags barked urgently, jerking me out of my reverie and looked up at me knowingly, as if to say, "C'mon, let's get going and find the person we're looking for."

Edging our way gingerly around the bog slipping and sliding on the muddy track I wondered how on earth Shelagh survived in these conditions all the way out here, on her own, with her sight almost gone. Escaping the bog and walking on firmer ground Rags spied an assortment of hens and ducks pecking about in the yard and took great pleasure in dispersing them with a display of frenzied barking. Clucking and quacking they disappeared over the hedge into the adjoining fields and onto the bog in a flurry of feathers.

Taking a deep breath I knocked on the cottage door and waited nervously for Shelagh to answer, still not knowing why I was there, and wondering what she might think about my unannounced arrival. Moments later the door opened and peering intently through me with her almost blind eyes, Shelagh barked, "Who is it now?" in her usual gruff manner. Answering somewhat timidly I told her it was Linda from the crystal shop and having no other excuse for being there explained I'd come to tell her I'd ordered a new pump for her fountain. Feeling more than a little foolish that I didn't actually have the pump to give her I stood on the step waiting for whatever she was likely to say next. Completely unfazed by my unwarranted arrival Shelagh invited me in saying, "Come in Linda, today must be my day for visitors as I've just had an old friend call."

Leading me into a small lounge where a very smartly dressed lady was sitting I felt myself being given the 'once over' by the stranger who must have thought Shelagh had let a mud covered tramp into her home, although I felt this lady was far too polite to comment on the fact.

Introducing her friend as Doreen, Shelagh continued by telling me they had taught together at the same school on the mainland some thirty years previously and now only saw one another very infrequently when Doreen came to the Island on business. Shelagh felt that the two of us might have a lot in common as she explained Doreen also owned a shop on the Island, and leaving us to get acquainted shuffled off to make some tea.

Feeling very self conscious about my muddy appearance I tried to make conversation with this elegant stranger whom I couldn't imagine would possibly have anything in common with myself. Smiling politely Doreen asked how long I'd been in business and I found myself telling her my short and exciting journey into commerce had only been about eight months and that I'd recently moved into bigger premises and was still in the process of building up the stock and gaining recognition.

Doreen then asked me what type of shop I ran and I explained to her that it was a spiritual shop and how it had come into being. Listening very intently she didn't pass any comment until I'd finished speaking, but her next question almost blew my mind. Without any prompting she enquired if I was having difficulty finding the right suppliers for the stock I wanted to keep and I admitted that was my biggest problem to date. Almost fainting at her reply when she told me she might be able to help as she was the owner of 'Faeries' at St Johns! I couldn't help wondering, what were the odds of our meeting without Divine Intervention? I would hazard a guess at zero.

Invited to join Shelagh and Doreen for tea and cake, but excusing myself shortly afterward I left them to catch up. Once outside the cottage the excitement having built inside me to an explosive level I punched my arm into the air in victory and shouted "Thank you" into the ethers for having guided me to this place. Much to the disapproval of the hens and ducks who once again scattered in all directions clucking and quacking, only this time I was to blame and not Rags.

The next day a man came into the shop with an armful of trade catalogues and recognizing him instantly as the man who had passed me the day before in Shelagh's muddy lane, he was obviously Doreen's husband. Apologizing profusely for making me stand in the hedge he introduced himself and placed the catalogues on the counter saying, "These are for you from Doreen with her love." Forgiving him for making me climb the hedge was easy. How could I be cross? It so obviously was all meant to happen.

CHAPTER 31

40 YEARS ON

Eva's mum passed away only a few months after we first met and from that day on Eva became a regular visitor to the shop calling in for a chat most days, her visits became longer and longer until she was almost a permanent fixture! She was a great help to me, and my customers got used to accepting her advice on Feng Shui, whether requested or not. And when I became unwell, necessitating a month off work, Eva took over the day-to-day running of the business and if it had not been for her there would have been no business to go back to, so I have a lot to thank her for.

One day I asked Eva how she had come to settle on the Isle of Man, after all it is a long way from Japan. I was surprised to find it was because of someone she'd met whilst living in Karachi (Pakistan) in 1965. Telling me she had become good friends with a lady named Sheila who was originally from the Isle of Man, and who used to talk about the Island all the time. Years later after Eva divorced and left Pakistan she and her mother decided to visit the island and both of them fell in love with the place choosing to settle here. Asking what happened to Sheila and if she was still in Pakistan I discovered that she and her husband now ran a quail farm just outside Manchester and that Eva was still in regular contact with her old Manx friend.

Not long after this conversation Eva and I decided to go to the mainland for a couple of days on a buying trip and to visit some new suppliers in the Manchester area. Eva offered to drive which was wonderful as I did not relish the prospect, so we decided that she would drive and I would navigate. On the first night of our trip we checked into a motel just off the M62 outside Manchester and Eva remarked on the fact that her friend Sheila lived only a few miles away and it was a pity we wouldn't have time to call in. Sadly we were on a very tight schedule as once our business in Manchester was finished we had to drive to Yorkshire to meet with another supplier then get back in time for the return ferry to the Island.

Despite our frantic agenda we had a very successful trip and I know we both enjoyed every minute. Unfortunately, the crossing back to the Island was extremely rough. Thankfully, we'd booked a cabin, because poor Eva suffered from the most horrendous seasickness while we were tossed for four hours across the Irish Sea. I'm sure the journey must have seemed endless for her and I did feel sorry for her because she was booked to travel by ferry to the mainland the following week to visit her daughters in Oxford. If I'd been Eva I would have had to cancel the forthcoming trip as the thought of going on a ferry only a week after being so seasick would have finished me off completely, but Eva is made of sterner stuff than me because one week later she was on the high seas yet again.

The morning after she left I answered the phone to a bright and breezy Eva telling me she was fine and the crossing had been without mishap before asking me a strange question …What was my maiden name? Wondering what on earth she could possible want my maiden name for I argued the toss for a moment or two, but as she persisted I eventually told her it was Fletcher. I could hear her relay this information before coming back on the line to tell me she had someone who wanted to speak to me. My head whirled as I tried to bring to mind possible people Eva could be with who knew me, because I didn't know anyone who lived in Oxford, which is where I thought she was.

A voice came down the line, "Hello Linda, it's been a long time since we spoke. Do you know who this is?" Telling the unknown caller they had the advantage over me the voice asked me to cast my mind back forty years. *Forty years!* I would have been five and I had to admit to not having a clue who I was talking to. Laughing, the mysterious voice decided to give me a prompt and told me to think of my primary school. Light was dawning and into my mind came the vision of my very first teacher at Andreas School.

"Is that Miss. Kneen?" I asked.

"The very same," came the reply.

Absolutely stunned, I couldn't begin to understand how Eva was with my very first teacher, someone I'd not seen in 40 years. Stammering in disbelief at speaking to Miss Kneen after so many years I just had to ask her what she was doing with Eva. Much raucous laughter came from the other end of the line as she told me that she was Eva's old friend Shelia from Pakistan. Eva had called in on her way to Oxford and during conversation she had recalled her recent exploits with me on the mainland. Sheila, reminding Eva that she had started her teaching career on the Island in Andreas encouraged her to ring up and ask my maiden name to see if I could have been a pupil of hers. And of course I was.

We had quite a chat and when I put the receiver down I just sat and stared at it incredulously. My life never seemed dull these days Spirit were making sure of that and I was finding that there was magic in every day if you looked, and sometimes even if you didn't! The last person in the world I thought I would be talking to that day was my teacher from 40 years ago, but that was not quite the end of the story.

On Eva's return she rang to let me know she was home and asked if I would come to her apartment, telling me quite enigmatically, "I have something for you."

Arriving at her home, Eva answered the door in bare feet bedecked in a beautiful, brightly coloured Japanese kimono belted around her waist with a huge sash and wearing her trademark very large shiny gold earrings. Eva's apartment was full of unusual things collected from her extensive travels, oriental antiques, Japanese silk wall hangings, crystals in all shapes and sizes too numerous to mention, and a myriad of other interesting items, I loved it!

Hugging me warmly she led me through into the lounge where without further ado she presented me with a gift from Sheila, a beautiful hand embroidered, pure wool, pashmina all the way from Pakistan, accompanied by a white sealed envelope bearing my name. Eva told me that Sheila had been amazed at the coincidence of us all knowing one another and wanted me to have something to remember her by.

Touched by the gift I could feel a lump rising in my throat as I carefully slit open the envelope and pulled out a card. Withdrawing the card a photograph fell onto the floor and retrieving it I discovered it was actually a photograph of me and my classmates in our first year at Andreas School. It had been taken when I was only five years old and I couldn't believe that Sheila had kept it all these years. Turning my attention to the contents of the card it read as follow;

Hello Linda,

Is this not the most amazing coincidence, the two oldies having the common acquaintance of the young one! You will notice how I place Eva in the oldies category! It was wonderful to speak to you after all these years and learn that you are so busy enjoying your new venture, and also to hear news of your family. I remember you and your parents very well from my 2 year sojourn in Andreas. It is unusual because one does not remember the mass of people, just the few. Please remember me to your Mum and sister with all good wishes. As you know, we are very close to the M62 so do please call to see me, there is always a bed available if you need one. I thought you would like this photograph. I have kept an album with a picture of each class I have ever taught over the years. I recognise the children, but the names escape me. By the way my nails are pink now! It really has been lovely to find you.

Love Sheila.

Miss Kneen remembered our family because of the tragic circumstances of losing Dad while we were in her charge which was something we had spoken about during our telephone conversation. The lump in my throat felt like a golf ball because this was just the best experience ever. I had loved Miss Kneen, she had been very caring to me and my sister during a very traumatic period of our lives and I could still remember her kindness even after so many years. The last remark about her nails was something I had mentioned on the phone as the abiding memory I have of Miss Kneen circa 1960 was of a huge beehive hairdo backcombed to within an inch of its life and the longest manicured nails I'd ever seen, which were always immaculately painted in bright red nail varnish.

Thanking Eva for being the messenger we talked about the meaning of such a big coincidence and both felt it was Spirit letting me know that if ever I needed to go to Manchester again I would have welcome accommodation with Sheila instead of staying at a B&B. There is just a little bit more to this story. I had my class photograph copied and wrote the names of all my classmates on the back sending it back to Sheila with a thank you for the lovely gift. A few days later I came home to find a postcard lying on the doormat addressed to me and it read:

Dear Linda,

Lovely to have all the children's names, senility departed when I read them and was able to attach names to faces. I received a beautiful book from Eva today the title of which is, "Spirit of Man" with wonderful pictures of the magical Isle of Man, I still think of it as home even after all these years.

Much love to you and hope to see you soon.

Sheila.

It wasn't so much the content of what Sheila had written, although I feel there was a clue in the title of the book Eva had sent her. The surprise for me came when I turned the postcard over because the picture on the front was a copy of an old painting of Clifford's Tower in York. Now you are probably wondering what that could possibly have to do with anything, but the strange thing is that I have travelled very, very little in England, but the one place I have been and I have a photograph of me there to prove it is the top of Clifford's Tower in York.

My old school photograph from Sheila (Linda 2nd right front row)

134

CHAPTER 32

FROM CYPRUS WITH LOVE

As I mentioned earlier I always wore my 'Friendly Crystal' the pendant Vera had given me right back at the beginning of my awakening and was often asked the significance of my wearing it. It was a difficult question to answer as I didn't really know, only that I felt comfortable wearing it and by now it had got to the stage where I didn't feel dressed without it.

One morning shortly after moving into the new shop I picked up my pendant and slipped it over my head giving myself a cursory glance before leaving the house, but something was wrong. For some reason I was compelled to take it off and replace it with a necklace I'd been given for my 40th birthday, a very pretty necklace with a faceted crystal sphere set into a golden eagle's claw, suspended on a gold chain.

Before lunch a middle aged couple came into the shop and smiled at me, before proceeding to look around. Nothing unusual about that I can almost hear you say, until they reached the counter with their purchases. The lady spoke first and commented on what a lovely little shop I had and how she felt the atmosphere was very spiritual, warm and welcoming. Thanking her in my normal way as I was becoming used to comments like these and I found it very rewarding that other people felt the same as I did about The 4th Dimension.

As I packaged their purchases I felt the woman staring at me and before excusing herself asked if she could have a closer look at my necklace. Leaning over the counter I was surprised to be pulled forward as she gently took hold of the sphere and turned around to attract the attention of her husband. Looking at one another knowingly they said no more on the subject other than to remark what a pretty necklace it was. The woman then informed me that she and her husband were originally from the Isle of Man although they now lived in Cyprus and only managed to get home for a visit every couple of years. After further conversation I was to learn that they were both Reiki Masters and ran a practice from their home in Cyprus.

Compelled to ask this woman if she knew who her guide was which surprised her somewhat as a regular client had asked her the very same question the previous week before she'd left for the Island. Telling me that she sometimes got a name in her head while giving Reiki treatments and although it was not a name she was familiar with she assumed that it might be the name of her guide. Feeling as if I had to give this woman confirmation I told her if she was repeatedly being given a name the chances were it was her guide, who would no doubt take further steps to make 'themselves' known to her.

Now engrossed in our conversation she continued by telling me of a strange occurrence that had taken place the night before they left Cyprus. She and her husband had gone for a meal to their favourite restaurant and chose to sit outside as it was a beautiful evening. During the course of their meal a Cypriot woman sitting a few tables away seemed to be trying to attract her attention finally approaching their table and telling her that she had the most beautiful visible aura and that her guide was around her. She also told her that they would be visiting another island where her guide would lead her to someone who would produce the answers to her questions.

When she had finished her tale she asked me if I didn't think the whole affair was very enigmatic. Well used to such goings on by now I agreed, telling her this was the way spirit worked, advising her to stay open and expectant for more guidance to come in. As they left the shop she asked did I know where she could buy a copy of The Psychic News as the Cypriot medium had told her to obtain a copy while she was on the Island. Amazingly, I was able to help her having been given a copy by a friend only the day before, and apologizing as I handed it to her because it was three months out of date. Thanking me the pair set off for lunch promising me faithfully that they would return the magazine directly they'd finished eating.

Thirty minutes later they burst through the door the woman excitedly waving the copy of the Psychic News in the air and shouting, "I've found him, I've found him." Explaining to me the name she had kept receiving during healing sessions was 'Barbanell' and as it was such an unusual name she'd thought she was imagining it. Waving the paper in front of me she drew my attention to the back page where in large bold print was a notice acknowledging the editor in Spirit who was **Maurice Barbanell**.

Telling her how pleased I was in playing a small part in the confirmation of her guide's name she interrupted, "Yes, but that's not all," and retrieving a small diary from her handbag she showed me some notes she'd scribbled down after her meeting with the Cypriot medium. Opening the paper once more she turned to a particular article that mirrored exactly what the medium had told her she would find. Her questions had been answered just as predicted, in an out of date magazine. Truly amazing!

Still unaware of their names and total strangers to me she asked me if I hadn't wondered a little at her interest in my necklace, before telling me she'd had a dream the night before where she had been talking to someone with a necklace just like mine! Recalling the dream vividly on waking she'd shared it with her husband, happily admitting that she felt her 'guide' had led her straight to me, just as the medium had predicted.

At last it all made perfect sense to me as I explained that I'd had to change my pendant before leaving home that morning, but not knowing why. Hugging me like a long lost friend, the woman, who was still a stranger to me, concluded the conversation by saying, "I'm so happy I found your shop today."

Telling her as seekers on a similar path, neither of us actually had any choice in the matter as Spirit wouldn't have let her miss the shop ... or me. Wishing them well for a safe journey home I stood alone in the shop and laughed out loud as I sent a great big 'Thank You' to my HS. How perfect everything was, just perfect!

CHAPTER 33

SHONA'S ARRIVAL and HAROLD'S RE-AWAKENING

A few months after opening the shop Harold remarked upon how he would love to be part of a meditation group because since losing Betty his interest in the spiritual side of life had blossomed and he was 'opening up' and wanted to learn more. Often I would find this to be the case when speaking to people who had lost someone close or had experienced a close shave with death themselves.

Harold, I was to learn had taken part in séances with his mother and father when he was a young man as this was a popular pastime in the days before television. It seemed the young Harold would go into trance very easily and take on the image of deceased persons (transfiguration) and not remember anything about it afterwards.

Unfortunately, when he was enlisted in the army these events were very definitely left behind and Harold told me sadly that he was much too busy learning how to kill people and survive himself. Being such a gentle man the army must have been a nightmare for him and the spiritual side of his life had been effectively put on hold. By the time he was back on 'civvy street' those long gone days of séances in the parlour with his parents were well and truly buried. By then he had met and married Betty and was busy providing for his family as a technical engineer working in many far-flung places around the world.

Now that Betty was no longer here and the children grown up he had a lot of time on his hands. Having been introduced to the local Spiritualist Church by his son's friend he had visited many times since Betty's passing and had derived great comfort from it. I'd accompanied him on a few occasions when Anita, one of Harold's favourite mediums was visiting from the mainland. Anita was good, very good indeed and I'd remarked to Harold after one such visit how much I would love a sitting with her, but it was nigh on impossible as she was usually fully booked on every trip. However, Harold, being the angel that he is managed to arrange a sitting for each of us on her next visit which was three months away. Now I'm not normally in the habit of consulting mediums, but this was a very strong urge within me and I knew it was Anita I needed to see.

In the meantime, my friend Carol and I met once a week at Harold's home to meditate. Harold loved to play host and looked forward to these evenings spending the whole day cleaning and polishing in preparation for our arrival. There was always a welcoming fire in the lounge ready for us to retire to after our meditation and the elegantly decorated dining room where we meditated always had candles and incense lit in preparation for our spiritual work.

However, it soon became clear to Carol and I that it was going to be more than just meditation as Harold would go into trance almost as soon as he closed his eyes. The crunch came one night when we were about to begin our meditation when Harold suggested we all hold hands to see if we could experience the same thing. Totally naïve and not knowing we shouldn't touch anyone who is in trance, we each took one of Harold's hands and moved silently into meditation.

Within minutes Harold was in trance, shaking and jerking violently and breathing in a very erratic fashion. Carol and I opened our eyes as there was no way we could meditate, but Harold on the other hand seemed totally oblivious to it all. The jerking got worse and worse and we feared he may have a seizure as he is no spring chicken, so we just stared at each other in the candle light, not daring to speak lest we make matters worse.

What happened next was unbelievable, as a breeze seemed to spring up from nowhere and whistled around the room blowing out the candles, leaving us in complete darkness, whilst from the corner of the room we could hear the sound of running water! Carol and I were absolutely petrified as we hadn't a clue as to what was likely to happen next. This extreme paranormal activity felt quite scary and was completely out of our league as neither of us knew how to handle the situation. Just then Harold came out of trance, back from who knew where? In unison we asked Harold if he was alright and were rewarded with the most beautific smile we'd ever seen. Harold was quite unaware of what had just taken place telling us he was absolutely fine having just been with Archangel Michael and asking if *we* had seen him!

In Harold's opinion the experience had been wonderful and he'd had the time of his life while Carol and I were nervous wrecks. He was absolutely amazed when we told him what had taken place because he had been totally oblivious to it all being so wrapped up in the dimension he was exploring. At this point I felt completely out of my depth as it was obvious something was happening to Harold that required expert help and I was no expert.

Wondering what to do next I immediately thought of Lena as being the most likely person to have the experience necessary to help Harold. Not having been in contact with her for a long time I rang and explained the situation, breathing a sigh of relief when she told me that she knew the very person who could help. Very kindly Lena arranged for the three of us to visit her home the following week to meet her American friend Shona who was a medium and teacher of metaphysics, the only metaphysical teacher on the Island. After our initial meeting with Shona she agreed to hold metaphysical development classes at Harold's home once a week on the understanding that we find three more people to join the group. This was an easy task because we knew exactly who to ask, almost like it had been pre-ordained.

After making the arrangements for our development class Shona shared with us that she was due to move house within the next few weeks and that she would be moving to the north of the Island, remarking on how convenient that would be for all the group members as we all lived within easy reach of one another in the north.

Discovering she was about to move to a renovated Manx cottage a couple of miles out of Ramsey I asked it's location and was surprised to find it was a property I knew that had been on the market some years earlier.

*When it was originally advertised the picture in the paper was of a neglected little Manx cottage, but with such charm and character I had immediately been drawn to it. Not being able to place it's location I had eventually consulted the estate agents and discovered it was situated at the end of a private unmade lane, half a mile off the main road. The estate agents had informed me that the old lady who'd lived there for many years had passed on and they'd been requested to sell the property, which was in a very bad state of repair.

It seemed the old lady had been something of an eccentric, not mixing with anyone, but caring more for wild birds and animals and growing strange herbs. I felt strongly this lady had been an herbalist/healer although the estate agent had merely described her as 'a bit of a recluse'. Intrigued, once I knew for sure that there was no one living there I knew I had to go and see the cottage to try and understand the strange fascination it held for me. Making my way directly to the cottage after leaving the estate agents I had followed the instructions I'd been given and found myself bumping and jolting over the pot-holes on a winding unmade road that wound deeper and deeper into the softly undulating green Bride hills. At one stage the road and I use that term loosely, was almost perpendicular with the car slipping and sliding as the loose gravel and shale spat up from the back wheels as they tried to make purchase on the uneven ground. Just as I thought I was about to roll back down the hill the car made a leap forward as the wheels gripped a section of solid ground and rounding a corner there on my left was the cottage tucked away under the hill with only the sheep and cows in the surrounding fields as company.

Getting out of the car I had looked around me sensing the sheep in the field opposite halt their grazing for a moment as they looked up to see who the stranger was. Half a dozen young rabbits scampered over the field and into the hedge their white bob-tails bouncing as they went. The feeling of deep peace engulfed me, this I knew was a special place, I could feel it, but I still couldn't explain why I had been compelled to come.

The poor little cottage was very dilapidated, just like the estate agent had told me. Thinking to myself if only I had the money I would buy it there and then because it felt magical and I completely understood how the old lady had become a recluse because I knew if I'd ever had the good fortune to live there I probably wouldn't have wanted to leave it either.

Visiting the cottage many more times while it was up for sale I found it to be a magical, peaceful place, where time seemed to stand still. It made me feel as if I was the only person left on Earth and I loved it, but once it was sold I felt I could no longer visit. *

Now years later I could not believe that my new spiritual teacher had bought the little cottage I had been so attracted to. Although I was a little disappointed when Shona told me it was no longer the quaint Manx cottage I remembered and that over the intervening years it had been extensively renovated and extended by the couple she was buying it from. Feeling quite saddened by this information I asked what had attracted her to such a place and I could have worded her reply myself as she told me she loved the feelings of 'deep peace and timelessness' that it emanated.

Happy that Shona was obviously experiencing the same feelings as I had myself with regard to the cottage I instinctively knew that we hadn't met by chance and the events detailed above were just confirmation of the way forward for me and my friends.

CHAPTER 34

THE POSITIVE NEGATIVES

During the spring of 1999 I met Tom Sawyer and his wife Brenda which led me to another interesting phase in my life. One Saturday morning an elderly couple came into the shop, the gentleman making a beeline for the table with the natural crystals, exclaiming to his wife that he never thought he'd come across a shop like this on the Isle of Man. Benignly smiling her agreement his wife proceeded to browse whilst he made a full perusal of the crystal table before asking if I had any magnetite, telling me he needed a nice large chunk for an experiment he was conducting. Not having been asked for magnetite before I had to apologize for not having any and offered to order some. Unfortunately, I discovered he and his wife were only on the Island for a few more days and would probably have left by the time it arrived.

Introducing himself as Tom Sawyer and his wife as Brenda he told me it had been rather a long shot as he'd been looking for a piece for ages and had been unable to find it anywhere. It transpired they were on holiday from Devon and had made two bus journeys that day to get to Ramsey from their hotel in Port Erin. On hearing this I invited them to stay for a cup of tea as they were not young and the journey they had just undertaken was quite a tedious one.

Returning with the tea I found Tom had ensconced himself in the 'Healing Chair' and was extolling the comfort of it to his wife, whilst she had perched herself on my high stool behind the counter. Making conversation whilst they drunk their tea Tom asked how a shop such as this had come into being and for the hundredth time since going into business I explained the details.

Fascinated by my story he proceeded to tell me that he and Brenda were both healers and that Brenda was also a medium, travelling around the south of England to various churches and meeting halls where Brenda would take the platform and give demonstrations of clairvoyance. Needless to say I found them to be a really interesting couple and was glad I had taken the time to get better acquainted. Quite sometime later they left to start their long bus journey back to Port Erin and thanking me for the tea and my company off they went, as I thought never to be seen again.

The following Tuesday as I rounded the corner of the car park I found Tom and Brenda waiting at the shop door. Telling them how surprised I was to see them again so soon I was to learn they'd made the journey from Port Erin the previous day only to find the shop closed. I was amazed when Tom told me they had made the journey especially to see me again and I felt rather guilty that the shop had not been open.

Tom, being the talkative one, continued by telling me that he'd been unable to get me out of his mind since our first meeting and having meditated on the subject had felt compelled to come back and ask me to take part in an experiment he was conducting, hence his urgency in seeking me out before they went home.

Intrigued, to say the least, I didn't at this point know what the experiment was about, but I felt I would be unable to refuse after all they had made two extremely tiring bus journeys on my behalf and used up the last two days of their holiday trying to locate me.

Resigning myself to the part I felt I had to play I asked Tom what the experiment entailed and learnt that his research hoped to scientifically prove beyond a shadow of a doubt, that there is such a thing as life-after-death and that we could interact with spirit. On hearing this I was bewildered to know how I could possibly help him with this task, but he was ready with the information I sought. Telling me all I had to do was hold a specially sealed unexposed Polaroid negative whilst meditating, having asked Spirit beforehand to prove their existence by leaving their mark on the negative. Any colours and shapes imprinted on the negatives once exposed after meditation were deemed to be the evidence of Spirit and looked upon as a positive result.

In my usual fashion, putting myself down at every turn, instead of having faith in myself and my connection with Spirit, I immediately dismissed the possibility of being able to help Tom. Giving myself a smack on the wrists I reminded myself how human we all become when arriving in the 3rd dimension and how much we inadvertently limit our potential to achieve the impossible.

However, Tom's dealings with Spirit had been for much longer than my own and he wasn't about to give up that easily, so after giving myself a further talking to I agreed to help him. Beaming from ear to ear, Tom thanked me for agreeing and told me he'd send me the film equipment with details of what to do as soon as he got home.

Waving them goodbye I could tell from his demeanour that my agreeing to take part in his experiment meant a lot to him and true to his word, only a matter of days later, I received a letter from Tom with the sealed negative enclosed, explaining exactly what I was to do and to send it straight back to him in the self-addressed envelope.

*At this juncture I will include a quote from Tom: **'To get anything at all on a negative which has not been in a camera or exposed to light or any external material interference can be construed as a miracle.'***

As I've already mentioned I'm a 'Doubting Thomas' by nature and I thought that this would be a total waste of my time and Tom's, but I'd promised to take part so I had no other option than to do it. That night I sat quietly in my bedroom and meditated whilst holding the negative after which I slipped it into the envelope provided and posted it back to Tom.

Within a couple of days Tom was on the phone to tell me the negative was completely blank and how disappointed he was as he'd felt so sure there would be a good result from me. Confident that this was only a minor blip he told me he'd carried this experiment out with some of the top mediums in the British Isles and sometimes they had drawn a blank too. I have a feeling he was trying to make me feel better by telling me that before pleading with me to give it one more go. Finally agreeing I received another sealed negative a few days later, but this time I had the distinct impression I was to carry out this experiment in the shop.

Later that evening, once it was dark, and the mall was quiet I crept into the shop and sat down on the 'Healing Chair' the only light being the twinkle of the window crystals reflecting the light from the street lamps outside. Feeling completely at peace and surrounded with *'LOVE'* I opened myself up to meditate. After sitting quietly in meditation for about twenty minutes I slipped the sealed negative back into the envelope popping it into my handbag to post and thanking Spirit for being present, before quietly letting myself out, locking the door behind me. On the way home I posted the envelope in the nearest letterbox with a deep *knowing* that this negative would be different to the first.

A few days later the phone rang and it was a very excited Tom on the line informing me of the brilliant result my meditation had achieved, telling me that he'd known all along that I could do this. After chatting for some time about my result and his work he promised to send a photocopy for me to keep, but not before dropping his next bombshell which would involve taking the experiment a step further. Asking if he could send me another negative to meditate with, but this time he would be providing me with two negatives as he wished to demonstrate a connection in Spirit between myself and Rags. Somewhat buoyed by my apparent success, but a little dubious at the prospect of getting Rags to meditate I agreed.

On the day the negatives arrived I pondered for some time as to how I was going to accomplish this new task, but it all came to me quite easily. Whilst putting Rags to bed I explained to her Higher Self that we would be working together that evening, before slipping her sealed negative under the blanket in her bed. Clasping my own negative I began my meditation with the intention of our Higher Selves communicating in Spirit and guess what? Both negatives produced a positive result, which pleased Tom no end and set him off on even greater experimentation.

For the third part of his experiment he wanted me to visit a past life in my meditation and I was to ask for confirmation on the negative. Once again I found myself sitting in the darkened shop and asking the new question. (I will speak of this meditation in chapter 37).

Within a couple of days of this meditation Tom was on the phone again to say he'd received another wonderful result, he was over the moon with the information on the negatives and could scarcely believe his good luck in finding The 4th Dimension and presumably, me. Our conversation then turned to my development group with Shona and without hesitation Tom begged that we all to take part collectively. I'm happy to report that not only were we all willing and able, we all provided him with more superb results making him a 'very happy bunny' indeed.

Believe me I was truly overjoyed at my cooperation with Spirit on the above occasions and so were the rest of the group, but I couldn't finish this chapter without a little footnote.

Footnote: A couple of weeks after we had concluded the experiments for Tom the Daily Mail ran a serialisation of a ground breaking new book, *'The Scole Experiment'* which had just been released. It was about the findings of a group of people who met regularly to carry out investigations into paranormal phenomena.

It was absolutely fascinating, but even more so when I came across a paragraph that mentioned a certain Tom Sawyer who was invited to join the group as part of their investigative team. As I read I thought surely this couldn't be the same Tom Sawyer that I knew because if it was he'd never mentioned being a part of any such big experiment in all the phone conversations we'd had. My curiosity having being aroused I had to call Tom and find out if he was the Tom Sawyer mentioned in the book. Tom's reply to my question was simply, *"Yes, I am."*

We had a long conversation about the findings of the 'Scole' group and I couldn't believe my luck that I was hearing it first-hand from someone who'd actually taken part in it all. That he, Tom Sawyer investigative reporter for such an important book had actually walked into my shop months earlier and that I had also had the privilege of taking part in one of his experiments. Just at that moment a well known quote from an old film played through my mind: "Of all the bars, in all the world, you had to walk into mine." Laughing to myself I thought for at least the hundredth time how wonderful and perfect life had become since I had been blessed with being caretaker of The 4th Dimension, because that is the way I thought of the place, I may have brought it into being, but it belonged to everyone and I was *only* the caretaker.

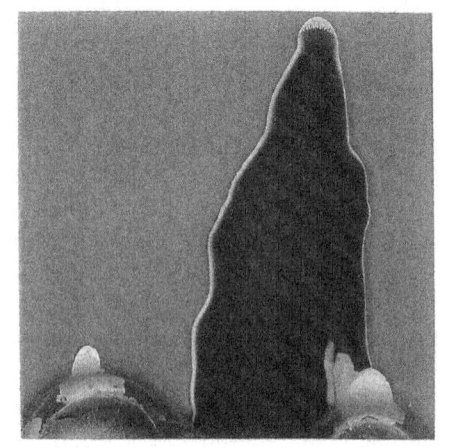

LINDA   14.3.2000

166
RAMSEY I.O.M.   OD4M

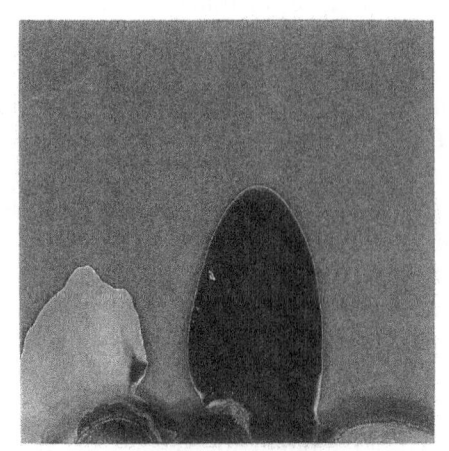

DOG (Linda's)   14.3.2000

167
RAMSEY I.O.M.   OD4M

CHAPTER 35

'HELLO DAD'

Our development group with Shona was in full swing and we were all enjoying the classes very much, especially Harold. He thrived in this environment and looked forward to the classes even more than the rest of us as it was his opportunity to play host, and what a wonderful host he was. We were all learning so much not only about Spirit, but also about ourselves and just how much we were developing would be proven to me by a wonderful experience between myself and Harold.

One morning Eva and I were in the shop when Harold called in for his daily cuppa and leaning against the long counter opposite the door we all chatted easily for a few minutes before Harold suddenly clutched his chest and gave a groan crying out, "Oh, I've got a terrible pain in my chest."

Poor Harold had gone a funny shade of grey, yet for some reason I didn't feel alarmed as I thought he might have someone in Spirit with him. Ushering him to the healing chair he sat down heavily saying, "I can't explain it, but I feel this pain doesn't belong to me."

After a few moments with little change in Harold's demeanour I had the overwhelming feeling that he was trying to channel someone who had passed over with a heart problem, believing Harold was quite correct in assuming the pain wasn't his. Closing his eyes Harold tried to glean some more information before glancing over at Eva and saying, "I think it's your father, he is saying it's Dad."

Eva grew very excited, but unfortunately for her it was short lived as Harold began to describe in detail the man who was with him ... tall and handsome with dark brown wavy hair, a slim moustache and dressed in a white waiters' jacket sporting a black Dickie bow tie.

Standing stock still staring at Harold, not daring to believe what I desperately wanted to believe, the whole place seemed to be holding its breath, even Eva, whom I'd almost forgotten was there.

As far as I was concerned Harold and I were the only actors in this scene. By now Harold was in full trance, completely unaware of his surroundings. Standing up and in a semi-dreamlike state walked the few steps to where I stood. His eyes fixed on me, but I was aware Harold was seeing nothing, the look was not his. Wrapping his arms around me the essence now controlling Harold whispered in my ear, "I'm sorry I never got to say goodbye, but don't ever forget, I Love You."

Standing like a statue, icy cold, not able to move I was having difficulty in believing what had just taken place, while Harold in the meantime had staggered backwards flopping down onto the chair and was beginning to come round. Eva, for once was speechless and as for me I was totally speechless, and believe me that is quite something! When I had recovered sufficiently enough to speak I thanked Harold for bringing my Dad through in such a wonderful and unexpected way, his face lighting up as I spoke, I could see he was very pleased with himself, but he was even more pleased for me. Ever the 'Doubting Thomas' (damn it) I still needed some kind of confirmation, even though I knew in my own mind it had been my lovely Dad that Harold had brought through.

That weekend I sorted out some old black and white snaps of me as a child, sliding a print of Dad, whom Harold had never seen, between the other photographs and placed them carefully in my handbag. The photographs of my father were taken whilst he worked at Jurby and showed him amongst a group of colleagues dressed the way Harold had described.

The following week Harold came in for his usual chat and during our conversation I pulled the envelope from my bag saying, "Oh by the way Harold, I almost forgot, I found these snaps of myself at the weekend and I thought I'd bring them in to show you."

Handing over the pile of photo's I watched as he started to leaf through them and listened to him chuckling to himself at the sight of me as a child in the 1950s, especially one picture where I wore a huge bow in my hair that was almost as big as my head! Coming across the photograph with Dad in the group his face lit up and pointing at Dad said, "Oh my God, this is who was with me in the shop last week, this is your Dad Linda, its your Dad, I just know it's him."

Sure enough Harold had picked out my father from the collection of similarly dressed colleagues. In that moment a wonderful feeling of warmth and love crept over me and I knew I was acknowledging Dad's energy.

"Yes Harold, that's my Dad, you have just confirmed to me that it really was him that was with us last week. Thank you so much for bringing him through to me after all these years. You can never know how much this means to me."

Wrapping my arms around Harold we hugged and held each other close in the love we shared for one another and our connection in Spirit.

The following week Harold and I were looking forward to our long-awaited sitting with Anita the medium. We set off for Douglas on the day of our appointment with high hopes and in great anticipation of what Anita would have to tell us. Harold especially was very excited hoping Betty would come through with a message for him. Although he felt her presence on a daily basis, he, like me, wanted confirmation of the fact. And as for me, well, what more could I expect now that Dad had already made a connection with me just the week before?

Arriving at the Spiritualist Church where Anita took her sittings we waited patiently in the hallway with a few others. Being called in one at a time it felt rather like waiting to see the headmistress at school for some unknown wrongdoing. When it came to my turn I sat down opposite Anita and we chatted for a few minutes until I felt myself relaxing and almost immediately Anita's voice and demeanour changed as her guides took over and the sitting commenced.

Announcing that two gentlemen had joined her, both of whom had passed over many Earth years ago, she proceeded to give me a wonderful description of both Dad and his father, my paternal grandfather, just as I remembered them. Anita continued, "The taller man is extremely handsome and is telling me he is your father."

I nodded in agreement with her finding, but what she said next nearly blew my socks off.

"He is telling me he never got the chance to say goodbye and tell you that he loved you before he passed away, but recently he has managed to do just that through one of your friends, but he says you are the biggest Doubting Thomas he has ever come across."

Bowing my head and cringing at this statement I knew exactly what Dad was telling me, by not accepting facts the first time round and having to question and have things proven to me time and again, even going so far as to test Harold with those old photographs. Feeling slightly guilty after this admonishment from Dad and for deceiving Harold in such a way, even though he came through with flying colours, it was just the need of confirmation on my part and I knew Harold would understand that.

Personally I don't see anything wrong in questioning guidance, because in my experience if it truly is genuine guidance, a confirmation will be given in some way when asked for.

"But, for all of that." Anita continued, "Your father is very proud of what you are doing and he is telling me there is much more in store for you and to go forward with an open heart as he will be guiding you every step of the way."

There was much more to this sitting, but this was the most important part. My lovely Dad was with me and has been with me always, this I now knew beyond a shadow of a doubt....

CHAPTER 36

GREAT AUNT MAY

Late one Sunday evening during the spring of 2000 Dickie and I retired to bed for what I thought would be a peaceful night's sleep as we were both tired after what had been a busy weekend. Dickie was sound asleep in minutes and snoring, much to my annoyance, whereas I on the other hand seemed to come wide awake as soon as I'd gotten into bed and switched off the light.

Closing my eyes I thought I'd will myself to sleep, so I lay there in the darkness waiting to 'drop off', but after ten minutes or so I was still annoyingly wide awake. Opening my eyes I was shocked to discover an elderly woman sitting at the bottom of the bed! I could see her as plain as day, dressed in twinset and pearls, she appeared solid and physical, but with a kind of luminescence about her. Staring intently at me with an expression on her face like she was trying to impart information of some sort, but there was something else about her that captured my attention because she looked vaguely familiar. Thinking lack of sleep was playing havoc with my imagination I closed my eyes tight shut before opening them again with the expectation of her disappearance, but she was still there, she was definitely *not* a figment of my imagination. Then I made a big mistake, in my excitement I shook Dickie saying, "Wake up there's a woman sitting on the bed," to which she disappeared into thin air.

For the hundredth time in recent years my poor husband must have thought I'd lost the plot.

"What are you on about now," he said sleepily. Telling me I was imagining things and complaining I'd woken him from a deep sleep to stare into thin air he turned over and was asleep and snoring again in seconds.

Knowing what I'd seen I lay awake for some time afterwards kicking myself for having frightened her off and wondering who she was and why had she looked so familiar, and what had she been trying to tell me, but finally the questions melted away as I drifted off to sleep.

Approaching the shop the following Tuesday morning I could see a woman standing by the door obviously waiting for me to open and recognised her instantly as Janice, a medium I'd met at some of the spiritual events I'd attended.

"I'm glad your open today" Janice remarked, "I've come all the way from Douglas this morning as my guide was very insistent that there was a specific crystal in your window that I have to get for someone."

Entering the shop Janice made a bee-line for the main window obviously knowing exactly which crystal she had come for and plucked it from the display. Making her way back to the counter I was quite taken aback when she told me there was an elderly lady standing by me. Asking her to describe the lady I was pleased, if not a little surprised, to receive a description in great detail of the lady who had been sitting on my bed the night before! Anxious to know who this visitor from Spirit was I took the opportunity to ask Janice if she could tell me any more about this woman and what she wanted.

"I feel she is on your mother's side of the family, not your grandmother, but maybe her sister. She is telling me she left the Island 'under a cloud' some years ago and the reason she has come to you is that now you are 'open' she wants to ask you as part of her family for forgiveness."

Informing Janice about what had taken place the night before I thanked her finding it all very intriguing. Before Janice left the shop she remarked on the fact this was the first time she had been to Ramsey in years, telling me she had wanted to visit my shop for some time, but it was always closed on her days off. It just so happened that her days had been changed that week just prior to receiving the insistent message from her guide to come that very morning!

After Janice left the shop the name 'May' dropped into my mind. Knowing that it couldn't possibly be my mystery woman's name as I knew Nana had two sisters, but neither of them had been called May, and both had passed away when they were young, before I could even remember them. Once again there was only one person to ask … Mum. Fortunately, the following day she visited me at the shop and I asked her did Nana have any other sisters apart from the two I knew about.

"Yes" she replied. "She had another sister called May who left the Island 'under a cloud' when she was only young."

Mum had used the same expression, 'under a cloud', that Janice had used when telling me about May. Mum then proceeded to tell me the story about May.

It seems May had fallen in love and had become pregnant to a man from the north-east of England whom she'd met whilst he was working on the Island. Her parents didn't approve and forbade her to marry him, but May had gone against their wishes and had eloped to England with the man she loved. The family had received a letter from May some time later informing them of the birth of her son and asking for forgiveness, but her parents, my great-grandparents, had refused to have anything more to do with her and effectively made her an outcast. Her name was never mentioned again within the family and she never returned to the Island.

Mum finished her story by saying all this had taken place when she herself had been only eight years old, which would have been by my calculations about 1936. No wonder I'd never heard of poor May.

Standing quietly in the shop after Mum had left I spoke out loud telling May she was forgiven and asked her to please move on in peace. The words had barely left my lips when what felt like a breeze brushed past my cheek and with the most delicate of kisses May was gone!

On Saturday morning of that same week a family member came into the shop with a large brown envelope asking if I would pass it on to Mum, telling me it was a copy of my grandfather's family tree. I knew he had been working on this project for months and he was hoping Mum could help with a couple of missing pieces.

Giving me permission to look through if I wished I slid out a large pile of foolscap sheets from the envelope and spread them onto the counter. Flicking through the sheets of paper I came across a page with Nana's maiden name where she had married my grandfather. I felt in that moment that May had brought Nana's name to my attention because it was Nana that she had reminded me of when I'd seen her sitting on my bed.

This to me was just final proof of her existence as it had been her maiden name also and wanted me to know that she was Nana's sister and part of the family no matter what had gone before. She had already proven herself to me and I had forgiven her on behalf of our family which was the outcome she'd desired and I took this to be her way of saying, 'Thank You.'

Footnote

Whilst I was preparing this book for publication my Mum sadly passed away and sorting through her personal belongings I came across a very old black and white photograph. You can imagine my surprise when I discovered it was of great Aunt May and her husband on their wedding day, after being banished from the Island.

May obviously sent it to my grandmother (her sister) back in the 1930's as it was amongst old photographs that had originally belonged to Nana. What a treasure and another wonderful confirmation for me!

CHAPTER 37

PAST LIVES - PRESENT PROBLEMS

This chapter is a collection of past lives that have been made known to me during my period of awakening. Each life that I've uncovered helped me understand the things that were happening in the present day and where they had come from originally. I believe these experiences were given to me by Spirit so that I could see their origin and release any negative effects on me, thereby enabling my progress in this life. This was to be very much an illuminating and healing process and not without its share of pain on every level of my being. I will sub-title each life separately as they took place over a number of years.

MARY
I had been interested in the subject of reincarnation for many, many years and had read a few books on the topic, finding it a fascinating and far reaching subject. To acknowledge that we have lived many times throughout history in many parts of the world, as both men and women was something I was greatly intrigued by.

For some years I'd felt I would like to be regressed to see what would surface under hypnosis, surely I would then know whether it was me making up a story or a genuine memory of a passed life that my current consciousness had no knowledge of. The chances of fulfilling this wish were slim in the 70's and 80's because as far as I was aware there was no one on the Island who undertook this kind of therapy and if there was they were certainly not advertising the fact.

During the wonderful spiritual weekend Lena organised I finally got my first opportunity to be regressed when the lecturer announced he was going to take us all through a mass regression. The entire audience had the opportunity to take part and those that did not want to were told they could wait in another room until we were finished, but no one left, so I have to assume that everyone was as fascinated by this subject as me.

Before commencing the regression the shutters in the auditorium were closed and the main overhead lights switched off, the only light was from a small lamp placed on a table in the centre of the stage that issued a dim orange glow. Collectively we were guided into a relaxed state after which the lecturer asked us to imagine we were standing at the top of a flight of steps. With no hesitation at all I found myself conjuring up the vision of the stairs, old stone steps covered in moss and lichen. In the distance I could hear the facilitator asking us to proceed very slowly down the steps allowing our consciousness to expand into our surroundings. With every step I took I could feel a sense of panic rising up inside of me, my heart was pounding so loudly I thought everyone around me in the auditorium must be able to hear it, but I kept my eyes closed and carried on with the visualisation. The voice, now very far away, was telling us we had reached the bottom of the steps and asked us to notice what we were wearing. What kind of shoes and clothes were we wearing? How did we feel and were we alone?

By now I was totally immersed in the visualization and was somewhere and sometime a long, long way from the auditorium. Looking down at myself I was horrified to see that I was wearing a very shabby, dirty dress covered by an equally grubby pinafore, the shoes on my feet were two sizes too big and appeared to be of broken down black leather with cock eyed buckles. Clearly I was very poor and I felt the time frame was maybe somewhere in the 1500s, history never having been my strong point.

The name Mary dropped into my consciousness completely out of the blue and I felt the place I had found myself in was Leeds. Why? I had no idea. Just then the feeling of fear overtook me again as I quickly dragged my attention away from the state of my dress and started to run down what appeared to be a narrow cobbled street with bow-fronted shops on either side. My fear almost reaching fever pitch I felt as though my heart was about to burst as I knew my life was at stake and that I was being chased, but by whom and for what reason? Those were questions I had no answers for. Thank God, just as I felt all would soon be lost and my pursuers, whoever they were, would catch me, I heard a familiar voice telling me I was once again at the bottom of the flight of steps and it was now time to come back. With each step I took back up the staircase my heart slowed down and the feeling of fear subsided, and by the time I'd reached the top step I felt back to normal again.

"Phew! That was quite an experience." I thought, as I opened my eyes to the comforting orange glow of the auditorium. The emotions and the level of fear I'd felt had seemed very real to me, yet the entire time I'd been living through my experience as Mary I'd been aware, on another level, of sitting amongst the other people in the auditorium. My first ever regression had been the very strange sensation of being two people in the same body or should I say in the same mind, but both with different thought patterns and living hundreds of years apart!

A few days after this experience I put my faithful, infuriating old 'Doubting Thomas' head on and told myself I'd not witnessed a past life at all and convinced myself it had been a figment of my imagination, and the name Mary had come to me because I'd been sitting next to someone who'd shared that name.

Putting the whole emotionally charged episode behind me, not understanding that I'd just been given the opportunity of releasing an old fear, which in the future I'm sorry to say, would come back to haunt me! And come back to haunt me it did, long after I'd all but forgotten about the experience in the auditorium.

During the spring of 1997 having suffered for a number of weeks not being able to move my head without considerable pain the doctor diagnosed the problem as arthritis of the cervical spine. Almost having given up hope of ever being free of the terrible pain in my neck I received an unexpected phone call from John asking if he could come and stay that weekend.

Telling him there was no problem with his impromptu visit and that I'd be more than happy to pick him up from the airport. But, I was more than a little amazed when he went on to tell me he was aware of the current problem with my neck and the terrible pain I was experiencing. Gasping at the incredulity of what he had just said I asked him how he knew and was rewarded by being told I'd visited him in meditation the previous evening and asked for his help! Admitting that I hadn't been aware of my actions the previous evening John laughingly told me that another level of my being had come to him in meditation.

John continued by telling me he had followed up my 'request' by taking his meditation into the 'Hall of Records' where he was given access to my 'Akashic File' (a record of all the lives I've lived) and he now needed to make me aware of something he had discovered. John was insistent that it could not be discussed over the phone and that I would have to wait until we met in person, hence the reason for his impromptu visit. Intrigued to say the least, I couldn't imagine what he could possibly want to tell me, or why he could not discuss it over the phone.

Friday dawned bright and clear only by now the pain in my neck was so bad I was almost at screaming point, but I had promised to meet John at the airport and that was exactly what I was going to do 'come hell or high water'. However, my journey to the airport was not that simple as I encountered one obstacle after another, traffic lights on red, the road being dug up with heavy construction vehicles travelling very slowly, and to top it off I even encountered a herd of sheep!

My humour was not at its best at the outset of my journey and after so many hold ups I was less than a 'happy bunny' by the time I reached the airport only to find John already waiting for me. It had taken him less time to fly from Liverpool to the Island than it had taken me to drive from Ramsey to the airport!

We chatted amiably all the way home, neither of us touching on the subject he had mentioned over the phone, but knowing when the time was right all would be revealed. However, I didn't have too long to wait because as soon as we arrived home John followed me into the kitchen while I filled the kettle to make tea.

"This can't wait any longer Linda I need to tell you what I discovered from your Akashic Record."

Turning to look at him, or as much as I could turn my head, I agreed, and told him I was ready to hear whatever he had to say.

Although the information John gave me came as a bit of a surprise when I discovered I'd been hung in a previous life. This was not something I expected to hear whilst putting the kettle on for tea!

As John spoke I experienced the strangest sensation as my neck, beyond my control, was pulled painfully to one side while inside my head I heard a huge crack, just as I imagine it would if you were being hung and your neck had broken. Into my mind came the vision I'd had all those years ago at the mass regression where I was Mary, running down those dirty streets being hunted like a criminal, quite rightly in fear for her life. In that moment I knew John was telling me the truth and I was recognizing it.

Getting over the shock I had to ask if he knew what I had done to warrant being hung. Replying, he asked me to take myself back 500 years and remember what they did to people with my beliefs in those times. Instantly a light bulb had been switched on inside my head and I was able to see what John, in his diplomatic way, was trying to tell me, that I'd been hung as a witch! Although he preferred to use the term healer and described the actions of my less enlightened contemporaries in those historic times as barbaric.

For the remainder of that day I felt really unwell, nauseous and in pain, but the following day I bounced out of bed feeling absolutely wonderful, totally and utterly different from the days and weeks before. There was a lightness of being about me just as if I was floating on air and realization soon dawned on me as to why I felt so good. I was no longer in pain! Knowing John would have the answer to my current elated state of well-being, because I knew he'd been observing my energy field intently, I asked how this unexpected and much improved state had come about.

"You brought into this life a cellular memory of being hung in your life as Mary and the pain in your neck was letting you know it was now time to address this problem and release it from your memory banks. The only way you could do this was to realize where it had come from originally and understand that it no longer serves you. It was time to let it go."

Pulling a face at my invisible Doubting Thomas who unfortunately is so much a part of me, I said, "I was right after all, Mary was real and now I know her secret I can let her rest in peace."

JANE

This life was shown to me during the time when I was a part of the meditation group with the girls I had met at the National Federation of Spiritual Healers (NFSH). At one of our meetings someone had brought a meditation tape which we had followed for that evening's work, on the reverse side of which was a visualization to regress you into a past life. Of course I was anxious to try it, but unfortunately the others were not that interested so they made their way to the kitchen and the kettle instead!

Telling them I would join them when I'd listened to the regression side of the tape I pressed the play button and began my journey through time. Listening intently to the voice guiding me I was soon feeling very far away, distant and dreamy as if hypnotized. The only sound in my consciousness was that of the voice telling me to imagine I was drifting far out in the universe way above the Earth. Instantly into my minds eye I could see the Earth as a blue and green globe spinning through space far below. The voice then instructed me to feel myself coming back down to Earth, landing gently, to find myself in new and different surroundings.

Immediately I was aware of standing on a bridge, looking down into the water, totally captivated by my reflection because the face that stared back at me was that of a young woman with a mane of golden blond hair and to my amazement I was sylph-like, unfortunately not the figure I brought with me on this occasion! Wearing a button through powder blue tea-dress, my legs were bare and on my tiny size 3 feet I wore brown pig skin high-heeled shoes with a matching brown felt hat, complete with a little veil. All very 1940s I thought as I lifted my head to take in my surroundings where my eyes were met with a familiar, yet very unfamiliar skyline with large buildings. This vision was accompanied by the name Jane along with the place name of Boston.

Jane/me looked down into the water again and I was utterly overwhelmed with sadness and despair knowing with alarming certainty that I was about to take my life! As this knowledge dawned on me the voice cut in again, "You now find yourself standing at a door."

As if by magic I found myself standing in front of an old fashioned arched door made from heavy wooden panels and set into a high stone wall, the type of door you would find in a Victorian walled orchard. Reaching out my hand to touch the twisted wrought iron handle I was surprised that I could actually feel it in my grasp, the experience was so real. My other hand gently pushed against the door and I noticed it was the hand of a young woman with the most beautifully manicured nails painted in bright red varnish and wearing a very large ornate amber ring. It was not the sort of jewellery I myself would wear, but it made a lasting imprint on my memory.

Pushing the door open I found myself in a beautiful countryside of rolling green hills and fields of corn. This was a place of extraordinary 'Light' that seemed to emanate from everything around me, even though there didn't appear to be a sun. Was this heaven?

I then became aware of a figure walking across the field towards me. The mystery person was wearing a cream coloured robe and as they came closer I felt a surge of recognition in my energy field. I could see/feel the person was smiling, apparently happy to see me. It was the most wonderful feeling in the world because I knew then that this was to be a reunion.

Recognizing him as a young man whom I'd had a deep relationship with in my teens I wondered what he was doing here in my regression. But, before my question could be answered the voice on the recording broke into my consciousness telling me it was now time to come back.

A few days after this regression I happened to be on an errand to the other end of town and crossing the street I was drawn to look in the window of a jeweller's shop. This was very unlike me as I have no real interest in jewellery, but peering through the window my eyes immediately homed in on a certain object. There in the middle of a display of second-hand jewellery was an unusual amber ring, identical to the one I'd seen on my own finger in my regression! In that instant I made a mental note that I'd not looked in that particular shop window for at least a year, maybe even more.

However, that was not the only surprise I was to receive that week as a few days later browsing through a copy of the 'Daily Mail' I was amazed to see an article about Boston accompanied by an old black and white photograph. Unbelievably, the skyline on the photograph was the same as the one I had seen in my regression and in the foreground was the very bridge I had been standing on!

This again I felt was confirmation from my Higher Self/Spirit to let me know I had indeed been Jane in a previous existence, but what I didn't understand and what was perplexing me was why I had taken my life?

JANE - Part II

As I mentioned earlier I took part in some Polaroid experiments with a gentleman named Tom Sawyer and one of the positive results I will recount below as it ties everything together.

Sitting quietly in the darkness of the closed shop ready to meditate, holding the sealed Polaroid film between my hands just as I had on previous occasions the only difference being on this occasion the question posed by Tom was for me to be shown a happy past life memory and impregnate some aspect of it onto the sealed Polaroid negative.

Almost immediately I found myself on a 'sidewalk' where I took a minute to take in the surroundings and it soon became obvious that I was somewhere in America and instantly the word Boston came to mind. Within seconds I was gliding down a flight of steps that took me into some sort of club below street level where I found myself hovering at ceiling height in my energy body.

Looking down on the scene below inside the nightclub there were booths around a small dance floor where groups and couples sat talking and laughing, while others were enjoying themselves gliding around the small dance floor to the sound of a live 40's Glen Miller-type band.

My focus was then drawn to one of the booths where a couple were sitting laughing and joking, obviously very much in love. The woman was a very pretty slim blonde lady and the man, dressed in a US Air Force uniform, had broad shoulders and dark wavy hair with a ruggedly handsome face. Floating down from the ceiling, apparently invisible, I 'merged' energetically with the beautiful woman I'd been observing. My heart began to pound as soon as I entered her body as I realised it was Jane from my regression a few years earlier. As soon as I entered her body I instantly 'knew' that we had only recently been married and this was our last night together before my husband was drafted to England. Not only was I privy to this information, but also to the facts of how the two regressions were joined together.

'Jack' had gone off to war and I'd been left in Boston only to receive a letter sometime later telling me he had been shot down, presumed dead. Life to me was not worth living without him and I had decided to take my own life, thinking we would be reunited in death, but Jack was not dead, and returned home to America only to discover I had committed suicide. This information had left him a broken man who in turn took his own life.

Footnote: I hope the footnote to this story will be as interesting to you dear reader as it is to me.

1. In this life I've always had a deep fear of drowning, it being the theme of a recurring nightmare that haunted me when I was a child.

2. In this life I've always had a fixation with the 1940s. When I was in my teens in the 60s and everyone was going mad about the Beatles and the Rolling Stones by contrast I would be playing Glen Miller which my friends found quite hilarious.

3. In this life I dislike flashy jewellery and very rarely wear nail polish and the one colour I cannot bear to see on myself is bright red!

4. I have always had a strange fascination with the roar of the old WWII planes at air shows because it would make my stomach turn over and reduce me to tears, a happy, yet sad emotion that I always found quite disturbing until I uncovered this particular life. Now it all makes so much sense.

5. As for the man Jack, his identity is that of the young man in my first regression as Jane where we were reunited in the rolling countryside of the afterlife. We both must have realized our mistake

at taking our lives at such an early age in our 1940s existence because we were both back on Earth living new lives by the early 1950s. Throughout the years of my spiritual journeying I have come to understand that we never lose anyone we love and I look forward to our reunion in the afterlife when all will be known and understood.

THE EYES TRULY ARE THE WINDOW OF THE SOUL

This particular story is quite fragmented so I will do my best to make it easily understandable.

Shortly after opening the 4th Dimension I met an Irish lady named Gillian who loved the shop from the first moment she found it and we just clicked becoming friends immediately. She told me she had only recently qualified as a hypnotherapist which of course I found very interesting. Gillian also has the most beautiful, soft lilting Irish accent I've ever heard, which I thought would be perfect as a hypnotherapist. Obviously I must have appeared very enthusiastic because she invited me to come to her home the following week for an introductory session. As you can imagine I did not need to be asked twice.

Arriving at Gillian's home the next week as arranged she showed me through into a comfortable lounge and after explaining the procedure to me she then invited me to close my eyes in preparation for my journey.

Gillian's soft and lilting voice invited me to find myself in a favourite place of my choice and in my mind I was immediately there on a stretch of beach that I loved. Through Gillian's prompting I invited my spirit guide to accompany me on the journey and soon I found myself enclosed in a large shimmering bubble that traversed the Earth until it came to rest.

Finding myself at the edge of a clearing in a wood I was guided to step out of the bubble into the landscape. Immediately I could see what appeared to be a small woodcutter's cottage in the clearing and I knew instantly that was where I had to go. At this point 'information' was coming to me about the location which felt like it was either Austria or Germany, maybe sometime in the Middle Ages.

Walking towards the open cottage door I could feel a deep emotion rising up inside of me, uncertain at this stage as to what it was. Standing on the threshold, peering into the gloom of the humble one-roomed cottage, the vision made freeze and sent shudders of emotion rippling through my whole body. So moved by the sight in front of me I broke down into floods of tears rendering me speechless. I was looking at a young woman dressed in the garb of a poor peasant, wearing a rough bonnet on her head with long blond hair tumbling from beneath it. She was bending over a handmade, roughly hewn crib, where a baby of about three months of age lay, but to my horror I could see the baby was dead and already turning blue. The young mother was distraught and believe me at that precise moment, so was I.

Gillian's soothing voice cut in, "You are completely safe. You are only an observer." At this juncture Gillian didn't know what I was 'seeing' because the emotions I was going through couldn't and wouldn't allow me to speak! Once more I heard her soft lilting voice cut through my vision. "Detach yourself from the emotion you are feeling because it is now time to come back."

But, before I came back something caught my eye in the gloomy interior of the cottage. It was a man. A tall very roughly dressed young man with a head full of dark unruly hair with a huge beard. He was standing in the corner of the room of this humble dwelling sobbing quietly, his shoulders heaving under the strain of his emotion.

Once again I heard Gillian repeat herself, telling me it was time to come back. This time I obeyed and when I'd recovered enough and could finally speak I shared the vision I'd had, commenting on the fact that I could shed no light as to why I should have been taken back to that particular life, or that vision.

That weekend Dickie and I had been invited to my aunts 60th birthday which was to be an open day at her and my uncle's farm. Family and friends from all over the Island had been invited to call throughout the day to celebrate her birthday. It had been some years since I had last visited their home and I was to discover that they had made a great many changes since my last visit.

Arriving mid-afternoon there were already a lot of guests milling about taking in the afternoon sunshine and strolling around the beautiful gardens. The place was a joy to behold, my aunt being an inveterate gardener and lover of DIY. Dickie and I were wandering around the gardens enjoying ourselves meeting family and friends when my cousin came over saying, "C'mon Lin, you must come and look at the cottage aunt has restored."

Leading me down the yard at the back of the farmhouse to what appeared to be a small cottage. My cousin explained that aunt had restored what had originally been an outbuilding into a replica of a humble Manx cottage.

"You must see inside Lin, it's fantastic it's all laid out just as if someone is actually living there."

By now my cousin and I were standing in the open doorway of the cottage peering into the gloom of the interior when a vague feeling of déjà-vu swept over me as we stepped into the main room of the small dwelling. Although a little gloomy inside the only light coming through a very small window, it felt cosy and inviting with a peat fire smouldering in the range. A homemade rag rug lay on the compacted earthenware floor with a rocking chair placed in front of the fire and a varied collection of jars and jugs of bottled produce lined up on a shelf erected on the far wall. Sweet smelling herbs and lavender hung to dry above the range accompanied with many other items of antiquity too numerous to mention, altogether giving the distinct feeling of having stepped back in time.

Turning away from the range towards the back of the cottage I noticed a curtain screening off what must be the sleeping area and pulling it to one side to have a closer look I almost fainted at the sight before me. In the small bedroom area was an old bed with a lumpy horsehair mattress covered in a patchwork quilt, but on the floor next to the bed was a roughly-hewn hand-made crib identical to the one I had seen in my regression earlier that week with Gillian. Not only that, there was a baby lying in the crib, and yes, I know it was only a doll, but at first sight it looked just like the dead baby, even being the same size of the child I'd witnessed in my regression!

Once more I could feel the emotion welling up inside of me and thought I was going to break down as my whole body was tingling from head to toe and I knew then I'd not been brought here without reason.

AN EYE FOR AN EYE

Remember me telling you, what seems like ages ago, about my 'bleeding eye', and no, I'm not swearing!

Having been reunited with my cousin Greg after 30 years and within hours of our parting my right eye became bloodshot and continued to bleed once a month every month for the next few years. It became affectionately known among my good friends and work mates as my 'menstrual eye' or my 'womb with a view'. I'd already been diagnosed with endometriosis and was to learn that this debilitating complaint wasn't restricted to the womb and could, and in my case, did affect other organs in the body, hence the name for my bloodied eye.

For one week every month I looked like something from a cheap horror movie which was making my life a misery. Desperately, I struggled to find a solution to my problem when the unthinkable and improbable happened. As I was hanging out some washing the spring broke in one of my plastic pegs and flew back hitting me in my already bloodied eye! In extreme pain I rushed to the optician, who, after a complete examination told me I'd scratched the surface of my eye, which would take a week or so to heal.

A week went by and then another, but still the pain in my eye remained acute. Feeling this couldn't possibly be right I made my way back to the optician who gave my eye another thorough examination, explaining to me that everything appeared to be back to normal and couldn't come up with any explanation for my discomfort.

Another couple of weeks passed and the pain eased during the day, but at four o'clock every morning I was awoken with the most terrible stabbing pain in my eye and would roll around the bed in sheer agony until it eventually subsided.

Dickie was very concerned and begged me to see the doctor. After examining my eye the doctor came up with the same conclusion as the optician, "Absolutely normal, I can't see anything amiss." Consultation over I went home distraught, the doctor must have thought I was neurotic and making it up, but this pain was real, very real indeed. The pain continued day after day and week after week and I was woken every morning at 4am to roll around the bed in the most excruciating and exquisite agony I have ever known in my life.

Over the months I'd begun to think about the problem I'd experienced with my neck a few years earlier and wondered if this was something similar, maybe I'd brought this pain from a past life injury. Considering that the doctor and optician hadn't been able to find a problem I was now so desperate that I felt any theory was worth exploring. Deciding to call a good friend, whom I will refer to as J.W, a gifted complementary therapist and hypnotherapist I poured out the entire story to him and made arrangements to meet for a hypnotherapy session to see if together we could shed any light on the 'sorry' subject of me!

Arriving at his therapy rooms the following evening J.W invited me to sit in a huge wing chair and make myself comfortable. After outlining the procedure, which by now I was very familiar with, we began the session as he took me through the basic relaxation procedure before moving me deeper into trance.

Once at the required level he asked me to recall a memory from my 30s, then my 20s, and finally my teens. I couldn't quite believe the ease with which I could remember such far distant events, but his next question shocked me to the core as it was one I didn't expect. J.W asked me to go even further back to explore the interlude before I was born into my current life! Before asking, where I found myself? Who was with me? And what was happening?

Without hesitation I heard myself telling him I was in a place of 'light' and was with my parents in the process of agreeing to come into their lives as their daughter. My father was informing me that he would return to Spirit early in my life, although he would be my guide throughout this incarnation as I was agreeing to come into this life to work for Spirit! I can remember being very surprised by my answers as I'd never consciously thought of *life before birth!*

Continuing doggedly J.W asked me to go back and visit the life where my eye problem originated and almost instantly I found myself in the middle of a battlefield. The trench I was standing in was knee deep in mud and although it was very dark the first glimmer of daylight was appearing on the horizon. Feeling very cold and very frightened I knew without doubt that I was a young man during the First World War.

J.W's voice broke into my consciousness enquiring where I found myself and I had no hesitation in my response, but stopped mid-sentence as I became aware of a whistle being blown inside my head, closely followed by the barking command of a voice yelling, "Over the top lads"

My fear knew no bounds as in my vision I scrambled out of the muddy trench along with dozens of other young men. Aware that my brother was standing next to me, we ran across the battlefield, shoulder to shoulder to meet our destiny. Out of the gloom and noise I spotted a young man looking equally as frightened as me, he was the enemy, bayonet at the ready, and heading straight for my brother. My last thought was, "Oh My God, I can't let him die, I love him too much," and stepping out in front of my brother I took the full force of the bayonet through my eye and into my brain, dying instantly.

The session had come to its natural ending and I discovered as I came round that my sweater was wet through because I'd been crying so much. Throughout this whole experience I was completely aware of my surroundings in the present day, but also acutely aware that the visions/thoughts were from somewhere else in my being. The emotions attached to these visions were very real which I believe sets them apart from mere make-believe.

On this occasion my 'Doubting Thomas' didn't get a chance to make me believe it was just a figment of my imagination because the very next day it was proven to me that the life I had recalled the day before was in fact true:

The shop was unusually quiet when the atmosphere suddenly became very still and I was compelled to sit down in the 'Healing Chair', something I rarely if ever got the chance to do. Obeying the guidance I was receiving I sat down heavily in the comfortable chair where I remained for a few minutes in a semi-meditative state. Opening my eyes I turned to look at the shelf of second-hand books and one little book in particular seemed to be calling out to me, one I may add that I had never read. Reaching out I lifted it off the shelf and started to read as the aura of calm and stillness still permeated the shop. The book detailed the life of a medium and how she'd first started to work for Spirit and before meeting her guide for the first time she'd experienced excruciating pain in her right eye! Trying unsuccessfully to attract her attention by other means her guide manifested the problems with her eye and in due course she realized what was happening and eventually allowed her guide to speak through her. This is the information she received and I quote from the book;

"I was in the holocaust of the First World War where men, God bless them, died like flies, and I never forget even now. At 4 o'clock one morning we had the order to go 'over the top' and I was in charge of some fine chaps and I knew in that moment many of them wouldn't return. It was too audacious a thing for them to do. I remember being terrified and within the first two minutes I was mortally wounded with a bayonet through my right eye."

I finished reading the paragraph then closed the book with a sigh, sending up a silent 'Thank You' to Spirit for giving me the confirmation I needed.

But, this was not to be the end of the saga with my eye, there was still more to come. Yes, I had uncovered another life that was causing problems in this one, but the pain in my eye did not disappear overnight although I would like to report that it did. It did subside somewhat after uncovering my life in World War 1, but it didn't completely disappear and the bleeding still continued on a monthly basis. There was obviously more clearing to be done as I knew I had not uncovered all the pieces yet and this particular jigsaw was still incomplete.

THE FINAL PIECE

Quite sometime after I'd had the above regression my eye started to bleed on a more permanent basis, in fact it was bleeding for almost three weeks every month! It was hideous, and I knew it was telling me to look deeper within myself and address the situation.

At the time I was sitting in the development class with Shona and after discussing my problem with her she agreed that there was still something that hadn't come to light. Deciding that we should do some energy work I made arrangements to call at her home, 'The Magic Cottage' a few days later.

Arriving at Shona's home as arranged I was a little nervous, but I also felt more than ready for whatever lay ahead because I knew the time was right for something to be revealed. Leading me upstairs to her workroom which I was delighted to discover was a beautiful country-cottage bedroom, complete with stripped pine bedroom furniture which complemented the old world charm of the cottage. The bed was draped in a cream linen throw and covered with dozens of plump hand-embroidered cushions. It looked so inviting I couldn't wait to try it out and see if it was as comfortable as it looked.

Shona invited me to relax on the bed and close my eyes in preparation for the journey ahead. Almost as soon as I lay down I became aware of a strange sensation within me as something appeared to be stirring deep inside my being and I knew without doubt that this was going to be a journey of discovery and enlightenment. Just listening to Shona's voice, which I was well used to by now, and knowing she was an expert at this kind of work made me feel completely relaxed and at ease.

Guiding me into a meditative state she invited me to look within and see if I could see anything attached to my chakras. Immediately finding my awareness inside my body I answered her question by telling her I could see a nasty, bloody looking cord and it appeared to be attached to the sacral and the heart chakra. She responded by asking me to follow the sacral cord first to see where it took me. I remember trying to focus on the horrible bloodied cord only to discover it was inextricably linked with the lesion from my heart. Following the slimy, bloody cords that were intimately bound together, a vision began to unfold before me and I found myself walking towards the open door of a woodcutter's cottage! Sudden realization dawned on me that this was the place I had visited in the regression I had experienced with Gillian which was quite some time before.

Relaying this information to Shona the vision remained clear and focussed within my inner sight the entire time. Confident in Shona's abilities, although full of fear and trepidation, I stepped inside the gloomy cottage when she asked me to. My emotions were coming to the boil and I could feel the blood rushing through my body and the sound of my heart pounding in my ears. What was I going to witness this time?

Shona's soothing voice broke into my consciousness reminding me that I was an impartial witness to what I was about to see and that I would always be in control of my emotions. Her words made all the difference as I could feel my emotions subside and with a clear head I allowed the vision to materialize.

Now inside the humble cottage my vision became clearer and I looked on in disappointment at the little tableau which was no different to the first time I'd seen it. The woman was still bent over the crib, distraught at the sight of her dead baby, while her husband remained in the corner of the room sobbing.

Sharing the unsettling scene with Shona I was advised to remain objective and look closely at each person in turn in the hopes that I would recognize someone from my current life. Remaining with the vision I focused on the woman first mentally asking her to lift her head so that I could see her face. Very calmly as if my request had dried her tears the woman obeyed and lifted her tear stained face to look at me. Gasping in disbelief the face that looked up at me was not mine, but the eyes were, and I knew in that instant that she was me!

Shona, realizing that I was being absorbed by the moment prompted me to move on. I moved across the room towards the man, his huge shoulders hunched and shuddering as he sobbed. Once again I mentally asked that he turn around and look at me and in what seemed like slow-motion the young man obeyed my request. Had I not already been physically lying down I think I'd have keeled over because the person who stared back at me was none other than my very own father! Although unlike him in stature and looks I was certain it was him, the recognition was instant and overwhelming. Smiling at me, his tears gone, and apparently knowing exactly why I was there, he nodded in the direction of the crib indicating that I should go and look at the baby.

Moving slowly and deliberately towards the crib I could feel my heart expand as if it was about to burst with love. Gazing down at the lifeless little form my heart felt heavy, but so full of love for the little soul because it was my baby, and I knew in that instant who it was. It was Greg, my cousin Greg! At last the little tableau had revealed its secret and I knew beyond doubt that I'd been given the answer to the question that had haunted me for so long. Now I knew who Greg had been to me and why I'd always felt that he was a part of me, because in that life my father had obviously been my husband and Greg my son.

Shona explained that I'd brought into my present life the memory on a cellular level of having lost Greg (heart chakra—Love) in infancy. Somewhere in my consciousness I'd blamed myself for his death and had willingly taken on endometriosis which affected my reproductive system (sacral chakra) and crying tears of blood at the loss of my child. Our reunion in this life had been the trigger that had set everything in motion, and that was why my eye began to bleed from the moment Greg and I were reunited.

With the help of 'Little Tom' and my HS who had guided me to Greg I'd been given the opportunity to understand and release the debilitating affects of the life I had just uncovered on the life I am now living.

Now I know beyond doubt that we never lose anyone we love, they may pass over and be out of sight for a while, but from lifetime to lifetime we will play out different roles with our loved ones and the reunion in between lives will be magical and wonderful as we 'plan' our future life and what roles we are going to play next.

I believe, 'The ties that bind' are definitely *'LOVE'* and they can *never* be broken.

The happy ending to this story is that my eye never bled again from that day to this, nor did I need a hysterectomy as I'd been advised, and best of all Greg and Karen now live on the Island only minutes away. I love a happy ending. Don't you?

REFLECTIONS

I gazed in the mirror and what did I see?
A strange reflection looked back at me!
Gone was the girl with the chestnut hair,
The gleaming smile, without a care,
The hair was now silver the skin was now lined,
But the eyes held my gaze both patient and kind,
Filled with the memories of all they had seen,
The good and the bad, and the bits in between!
I closed my eyes to recapture my youth,
That girl of my childhood searching for truth,
She at once was before me, eager and keen,
Only to blend with whom she had been.
A warrior wild, a native, a slave,
A priestess, a milkmaid, a soldier so brave,
A poor starving widow begging for food,
"Please just a few pennies, I must feed my brood"
A caring old healer, hunted down as a witch,
Hung on the gallows and thrown in a ditch,
A humble young cripple, legs cruelly deformed,
Left to die in the gutter with no one to mourn,
A mean pauper's grave was all he was given,
But angels gathered round as he passed to heaven.
Life after life, the visions rolled on,
Many faces and names until all were gone.
Once more in the mirror I looked to see,
Sighing, I realised the reflection was me,
The silver hair, the skin now lined,
The eyes holding my gaze, still patient and kind,
Every soul I had been or am likely to be,
Dwells here in my being for all eternity,
I now understood, the lesson was whole
The eyes truly are 'The Windows of the Soul'

CHAPTER 38

THE NEXT STEP ON 'THE PATH'

On 4th of April 2000 the shop had been running for two years and the business was flourishing, so I really felt that I had something to celebrate. With my hand on my heart I can honestly say that I'd just experienced the happiest and most fulfilling two years of my life. To dream, create and build a business, so dear to me, from nothing was something I hadn't thought I was capable of, but with the help of my third dimensional customers and friends, who loved the place as much as me, I had succeeded and I felt extremely proud and very blessed. The emotion I had bound up in the place was beyond words and I was totally and utterly absorbed with what took place there giving it everything I had in return.

Some weeks after our celebrations a lady came into the shop and introducing herself as Pam, asking if I would display some flyers advertising forthcoming workshops at a local centre for personal and spiritual growth. The centre was housed in a large mansion set in its own beautiful grounds and it was somewhere that had intrigued me since its opening. Telling her I would be more than happy to display the flyers we fell into easy conversation after which Pam was happy to browse around the shop telling me it all looked very interesting. Just then a very elegant elderly lady came in and approached the counter asking if I was Linda.

"Yes, I am and how can I help you?" I replied.

"Oh, I do hope you can dear", she said, before introducing herself as Margaret a member of the local Hospice committee. It transpired her mission that day was to ask me if I would be the guest speaker at their spring fund raising event.

I was stunned and also very flattered as the hospice movement is such a worthy cause. Immediately I thought of my dear friend Betty and how comfortable they had made her and how kind they had been to Harold in her last few days on Earth.

"Yes, of course I'll do it." I replied, without hesitation. "But my only cause for concern is the subject I talk about. Do you think your audience will accept it?"

Margaret was adamant, telling me that the entire committee was in agreement with her choice of speaker for this event, before admitting it had already taken her a week to summon enough courage to come in and ask for my help. Accepting my involvement as a foregone conclusion I then asked when and where the venue would be and was surprised to learn that the committee wanted to make sure they had a speaker for the event before making any other arrangements.

At this moment Pam, whom I'd almost forgotten was in the shop, stepped forward and apologizing for eavesdropping told Margaret that she might be able to help with a suitable venue and not quite believing what I was hearing Pam proceeded to offer the spiritual centre for the fundraiser.

Margaret gave Pam a rather bewildered look as they had never met before and like me had only just made Pam's acquaintance. Seeing her initial reluctance Pam picked up a brochure from the counter and showed Margaret pictures of the centre whereupon they began talking animatedly, leaving the shop together minutes later announcing that they would return.

The next day Margaret popped in to thank me and to tell me the date had been set for the 17th of May at the spiritual centre. It seemed Pam had invited her to the centre the day before to have a look around, she'd even been invited to stay for lunch while they discussed the arrangements for the event. Margaret, waxing lyrical on how beautiful and perfect the place was and expressing the unbelievable 'good fortune' that had led her into my shop at the very same time Pam had been there. Thinking, to myself, this sort of thing happens all the time I decided discretion might be the better part of valour and merely asked her if she didn't think her 'Guardian Angel' might have directed her just at the right moment.

The intervening weeks sped by very quickly and before I knew it the eve of the event was upon me. Closing the shop early I was busy selecting an assortment of crystals to take with me when I heard a tap on the window. It was Pam.

"I've just called in to wish you well for tomorrow, not that you will need it"

"That's very kind of you Pam, but I think I need all the good wishes I can get because I'm feeling rather nervous."

"I don't think you have any need to feel nervous. Pam replied, "Because the day I offered Margaret the spiritual centre as a venue I had no authority to make such an offer. It was as if I couldn't stop myself from saying it, like my mouth was working independently of my brain, but amazingly my superior never questioned it and just agreed to the event. That's why I don't think you have any need to worry this event is obviously meant to be, like it was all pre-ordained."

Telling her she'd made me feel a whole lot better I saw her out of the shop and her parting conspiratorial wink made me smile. Immediately I felt my confidence return knowing that once again Spirit had given me the confirmation I required.

That night I'd gone to bed hoping I would sleep soundly in preparation for the following day, but sleep would not come. Lying there in the darkness willing myself to drift off seemed to push the chance of a decent rest further away. Dickie, as usual, had dropped off in minutes and was lying on his back snoring contentedly, much to my annoyance, when into my peripheral vision I became aware of a pinprick of light in the corner of the room. To my amazement the light began to grow until it was about the size of a football, pulsating and hovering mid-way between floor and ceiling, just a few feet away from where I lay! Fascinated by the mysterious globe the light held me transfixed and I felt as if I was being hypnotized, but despite the strangeness of the event I felt very calm, very calm indeed.

At that moment Dickie rolled over in his sleep to face the same direction as the light phenomena and immediately sat bolt upright, pointed to the light and shouted, "What the hell is that?" Quietly and calmly without taking my eyes away from the light I reached out to touch him, "It's alright, it's only the Light, now go back to sleep." Not another word was uttered as he lay down again and calmly turned over apparently still fast asleep, but I knew on some level of his being he'd seen the Light too.

Continuing to focus on the globe the most amazing thing happened as a flow of thoughts filled my consciousness telling me that everything would be all right the next day and not to be afraid. Assuring me that I was in service to the 'Light' and I would be carrying out the work I'd come here to do promising me 'They' would always be with me, loving me and guiding me forward on my Path.

Feeling rather like a computer being downloaded with data I lay there for some time bathed in the rays of this beautiful pulsating light whilst it continued to feed information into my consciousness. The only problem was, just like a computer, it was in some weird language which I could not understand and I was unable to translate any more details other than the above, but I knew that some part of my being understood and was making perfect sense of it all, even if the conscious Linda could not.

As the stream of information abated the Light began to diminish in size getting smaller and smaller until it became a pinprick once more before finally disappearing completely. Lying in the darkness, warm and comforted, knowing something really special had taken place before drifting off into a peaceful, dreamless sleep. On waking the next morning I asked Dickie if he remembered anything of what had happened the night before, amazingly, but not surprisingly, he couldn't remember having seen a thing!

The fundraiser turned out to be a wonderful day and all went well, just as Spirit had promised it would be. Once again I had been helped to fulfil another ambition because I'd always wanted to do something at that particular centre and now I had. Who says dreams don't come true! Thank you so much my invisible friends.

CHAPTER 39

STEPPING INTO 'THE 5TH DIMENSION'

As I've already mentioned impromptu healings were a common occurrence in The 4th Dimension. These events would usually happen whilst I was in conversation with someone or sometimes if they had chosen a rune and were reading the interpretation when something deep within would be triggered and the person in question would start clearing and releasing. These healings were often accompanied by a lot of tears so I always kept a good stock of paper tissues handy. On many such occasions the thought crossed my mind that it would be beneficial to have somewhere private to retire to, but unfortunately there was no room for expansion in my little shop.

Towards the end of the year 2000 I began to have dreams about a healing room. So real were these dreams I felt compelled to do something about them and soon came to realize that this wish was another part of my destiny. Investigating the possibility I discovered a large empty unit tucked away in a quiet part of the mall only a few yards from the shop. Having been used as a junk-come-storeroom for some time it was in a very bad state of repair and no one to my knowledge had ever run a successful business from there as it was tucked away and not in the main thoroughfare.

Nothing ventured, nothing gained, seemed to be my motto these days so with that thought in mind I arranged a meeting with the manager of the mall who invited me to his office in Douglas the following week for a meeting. Whilst waiting in the reception area of a large corporate building I quietly tuned in and asked my guides and angels to go ahead of me and help make his mood receptive to my request.

When I was eventually invited into his office Mr. B strolled over and shook my hand before sitting down beside me asking what all the mystery was about and what I was hoping he could do for me. Explaining the purpose of my journey and my reason for wanting the unit, because I had decided it was best to be truthful, just in case he didn't like the idea. After making my request I sat back and waited for his response, but before I could mention rent and how I couldn't afford much he assured me that my proposition was OK and he was prepared to let me rent the unit at a nominal rent on the condition that I funded the decoration and repairs necessary. Continuing, he advised me that he didn't really understand all this spiritual stuff, but if his conditions were agreeable he would have a one year lease drawn up at once.

I couldn't have wished for a better result and could have kissed him, but suppressed the urge to do so, shaking his hand instead, and thanked him quickly before he had a chance to change his mind. Mr B obviously had a heart or Spirit had done an enormous amount of work before I'd got to him as the rent agreed was not to be sniffed at and as it had been his suggestion and not mine I certainly wasn't going to argue.

Floating out of his office I quietly thanked Spirit for what must have been 'their' influence. After all he didn't know or understand anything about spiritual matters, to that much he'd confessed, but I knew, even if he didn't understand that he had just been used for the next part of 'the plan'.

The work started in earnest during the Christmas holidays of 2000. The new unit was too large for a small healing room so Dickie and our friend Graham partitioned it off to make one small and one large room. Over the next few weeks my long suffering husband worked hard every night and at weekends to turn what had been a dilapidated shed for want of a better description into two beautifully decorated rooms, 'The 5th Dimension Meeting Room' and the smaller '4th Dimension Healing Room'

Having received guidance before taking the lease on these premises I had been informed that this would not be a permanent arrangement, but only for the initial twelve months. Finding this quite puzzling I decided to go ahead with everything regardless on the misguided assumption that my guidance might be wrong.

Over the next twelve months we held workshops on a monthly basis with facilitators and mediums from the Island. John also came over from Wales on a number of occasions throughout the year and a very popular facilitator he proved to be as his workshops were always full to overflowing with a waiting list of people wanting to join in on his next one. We also held meditation classes on a twice-weekly basis, my friend Jody and I taking a class each on two separate nights.

We had great fun during that year and I met and made friends with a lot of new people and I sincerely hope that those who chose to take part in what took place there benefited equally as much as myself.

CHAPTER 40

PAM AND SYNCHRONICITY # 2

It was during the early summer of 2001 that Pam's path would cross with mine once more in a sequence of amazing synchronicities. It all began in very similar circumstances to the first time we'd met when she called in to deliver some more flyers advertising their forthcoming workshops. Pam enquired as to how my workshop and healing rooms were progressing and asking what type of workshops I would be holding. Informing her of the events I had lined up for the summer I was surprised to find she was very interested in one of them.

After Pam left the shop I perused the flyers she had left on the counter only to find one of the lectures really appealed to me as it was on the subject of synchronicity and was to be held the day before my birthday. Knowing as soon as I'd read the flyer that I just had to attend and would look upon it as a birthday treat.

Later that day Jody called in and during the course of our conversation I showed her the flyer pointing out the lecture on synchronicity. Scanning the sheet she told me she would be more interested in the evening devoted to Dreaming, a couple of weeks earlier. Deciding we'd go together to both lectures I rang Pam straight away to book our tickets and make sure we could get in to both lectures, nothing like striking while the iron is hot.

A few days later Pam popped her head around the shop door smiling and exclaimed, "It's my turn now I'd like to book a place on one of *your* workshops."

Inviting her in while I made out a ticket for her I went to take a card from the appropriate pile, but unfortunately, I'd run out of cards for The 5th Dimension meeting room which I was using for workshop admission tickets and had to use a 4th Dimension card instead.

After writing on the card and handing it to her I watched as she picked up my pen from the counter and crossed out the number 4 replacing it with the number 5.

"There," she announced with a smile "now I know exactly where I'm going, to The 5th Dimension."

A few days later Rags and I jumped into the car and headed to Andreas for one of our walks and to check out a house I'd seen in the estate agents window. For some reason that particular day I felt the need to visit the church at Andreas, it is the church where I was married and where my father, my grandparents and a lot of my ancestors are buried. The church is surrounded by fields in such a lovely setting as the views all around the churchyard are inspiring looking out over the open countryside and up towards the northern hills.

I'm sure you will recall 2001 was the year of the Foot and Mouth epidemic that swept its devastating way through the British Isles, but fortunately for the Isle of Man it came through unscathed, although we still had to adhere to all of the preventative measures necessary. Not having taken any of this into consideration when I'd set off that day Rags and I arrived at the church lane to be greeted with a notice restricting dog walking around the church. Continuing towards the village I 'asked' Rags where were we going to walk now and was rewarded with the grunts and growls of a very unhappy dog desperate to get out, so quickly signalling I turned the car into the road on which I'd lived as a child.

Parking opposite the back entrance to the village shop we jumped out Rags in the lead, desperate to sniff and explore. Moments later we were meandering our way along the road in the direction of the estate of houses at the top of the hill where I'd grown up. It was wonderful as I sauntered along my head full of childhood memories of past times and the people who had lived in the village in my youth, though most had now passed on. Rags followed happily at my heel, sniffing to her hearts content, she was in doggy heaven as this was not one of our usual walks and there were lots of new scents for her to savour.

As I walked along reminiscing I remember asking myself how long had it been since I'd last walked this stretch of road, 'not in a very long time' came the reply. Still engulfed in my reverie I stepped off the pavement to walk across the entrance to a private estate my attention instantly being drawn to something lying in the road only to find on closer examination that it was one of my business cards. Laughing to myself at the 'coincidence' I continued walking up the hill towards my old home. Having taken only a few steps a voice in my head told me to go back and pick up the card because something was written on it. So insistent was the voice I could not disobey and retracing my steps bent down to retrieve it.

The card was soggy and the printing had run having obviously been left lying in the rain for some time. Straightening up I realized I was facing into an estate of private houses and there right in front of me was the house I had come to see! Amazed to say the least I then turned my attention to the card and on turning it over my heart skipped a beat as someone had indeed written on the reverse, and that someone was me, it was *my* writing and *my* signature! Recognizing it as a ticket of admittance for a forthcoming workshop I stood in the middle of the road wondering which of the six people currently booked on that particular event had lost their admission ticket. Feeling in that moment my only option was to ring all six of them I turned the card over again and immediately knew who it belonged to as only just discernable, printed on the damp card was a crossed out number 4 and in its place a number 5 had been written.

Knowing I was holding the card I'd recently given to Pam, but not knowing her surname or where she lived I felt my only choice would be to ring her at work the following day. The feelings I was experiencing in my body at that moment were overwhelming, tingling all over as though my heart was going to burst right out of my chest, the euphoria was intense. Knowing without doubt something special was taking place and these events were trying to tell me something or lead me somewhere, but tell me what and lead me where? These questions mysteriously were all still waiting for answers.

Mid morning the next day I rang the centre looking forward to sharing with Pam the amazing coincidence of how I had found her ticket. Luckily it was she who answered the phone. Telling her I had something belonging to her I asked if she could guess what it was and she replied by telling me in a rather puzzled voice that she couldn't imagine which of her possessions I had obtained. Before I could launch into my story she told me how bizarre it was for me to ring her just at that moment because she was currently holding something in her hand that belonged to me! Now it was my turn to be puzzled and I listened to her laughing as she explained she was issuing the tickets Jody and I had booked for the forthcoming events. This was becoming more involved by the minute, one synchronicity after another and the cogs in my brain were revolving faster than ever trying to make sense of it all when Pam brought me back to reality by reminding me that I hadn't told her the reason for my call.

Launching into my story of the previous day I was to learn that Pam lived on the estate where I'd found the ticket and although she wasn't aware she'd lost it she knew something had blown out of the car one wet and windy afternoon a few days earlier and deciding it was only an old receipt she'd never bothered to retrieve it. When I'd finished the story Pam had to agree it was rather an amazing 'coincidence' after all it was only by default that I had actually been walking along that piece of road, and for the first time in years. That I of all people, should find her ticket, which had been lying there for days untouched by anyone else, was nothing short of a miraculous.

You may think that would be an end to this story but the synchronicities continued. A few days before the lecture at the spiritual centre another strange thing happened when I was engaged in boring housework and deciding to relieve the boredom chose a CD to listen to while I worked. Switching on the music centre I found it was tuned into the local radio station and before I got chance to flip it on to CD mode something caught my attention that made my ears prick up. At that precise moment Dr Neale the gentleman who was to be the speaker for the synchronicity lecture was being interviewed. Sitting down I listened intently fascinated by what he had to say, and as the interview came to a close he requested that anyone who'd been listening who had experienced any interesting synchronicities to please contact him by e-mail.

Knowing it was no coincidence that I'd switched the radio on at just the right time to catch his interview I felt compelled to e-mail him immediately giving just my name and telling him I would be in attendance at his lecture on Friday night and would very much like to speak with him afterwards about the synchronicities that were happening to me. Feeling sure that all the recent activity was guiding me to this man I'd come to the conclusion that spirit really wanted me to meet him.

I received a brief e-mail from Dr Neale to say he was looking forward to our meeting after the lecture and would love to hear about some of my experiences. By the day of the lecture I could barely contain myself and the day seemed to drag by as it does when you are waiting for something special. Jody and I were in extreme high spirits that evening as we made our way to the spiritual centre looking forward with anticipation to the lecture and meeting other like-minded people who would be attending. A light supper was served beforehand to give us all the opportunity to get to know one another before we were ushered into the conference room. Jody and I unfortunately were the last to enter the lecture room by which time the only empty seats were on the front row.

What a disappointment the evening turned out to be, Dr Neale seemed a very nice man, but talked endlessly about Freud and Jung and expounded their theories on synchronicity. In common with most of the audience Jody and I found it really heavy going and at one point during the evening I thought there was going to be all out mutiny. Dr Neale expressed the opinion that he was confused about the so called 'New Age' movement with the belief in Spirit and the use of crystals and so called complementary therapies and healing modalities, labelling them all 'quack' medicine.

To this statement an angry middle aged woman asked him if he'd ever read The Celestine Prophecy, James Redfield's account of what is happening to humanity at this time in Earth's history and the huge part that synchronicity, as our guidance, plays. Somewhat taken aback by her outburst Dr. Neale admitted that he hadn't even heard of it, let alone read it! An audible gasp went around the room and I think Dr. Neale was probably the only person in the room who had not read The Celestine Prophecy.

The people who had gathered there that evening wanted to discuss and presumably like me share their experiences of synchronistic events with Dr. Neale, but unfortunately that was not the sort of evening it turned out to be. Disappointed by the content of the evening I did not make myself known to Dr Neale and Jody and I made our getaway as soon as the lecture ended.

Exclaiming to Jody on the way home I questioned how my guidance could be so wrong as I'd felt so sure everything was leading me to this man. After an evening in his company I realized our interpretation of synchronicity was poles apart and I was left totally confused. Putting it down to over zealousness on my part I thought there must be something more that I was missing.

By the following Saturday I'd put the disappointment of Dr. Neale's lecture out of my head having been too busy to dwell on it. During the afternoon there was a constant stream of customers, like a tide ebbing and flowing through the shop. Sometimes on a Saturday afternoon I'd counted as many as fifteen people crammed into my little shop, all at the same time, absolutely phenomenal.

On this particular Saturday afternoon I was in deep conversation with a customer while a number of other people browsed around when I became acutely aware of the door opening and another energy coming into the shop and to my total and utter surprise it was Dr Neale.

"You've got to be Linda," he said, extending his hand in welcome.

Stammering an affirmative I asked him how he'd known where to find me. Telling me it had been easy as he'd just had lunch with friends who lived on the Island and during the course of which he'd felt compelled to ask them if they knew who I was which of course they did and they'd sent him in my direction. Then the dreaded question came as he asked why I hadn't stayed behind after the lecture. Telling him I was not sure he'd be so keen on talking to me when he knew my reasons for avoiding him the previous week I was rewarded with a smile and a carefully judged, "I'm listening."

By now I was really warming to this middle-aged American man because he knew I was about to criticise his lecture and was still prepared to stay and listen to my comments. After sharing my thoughts of what the people at the lecture were looking for, and expressing that it was not Jungian and Freudian theories. Accepting my derogatory comments with good grace he asked if he could stay a little while longer in the hope that things would quieten down and we would get the opportunity to talk. So, inviting him to sit in the 'Healing Chair' and partake in the energy of The 4th Dimension, I noticed him give me a questioning glance as if to say, "I'm not so sure about that."

Spirit pulled out all the stops that Saturday afternoon and sent all the right people in with all the right questions and problems and Dr Neale was able to witness first-hand the workings of one of the so-called 'New Age' stores he disliked so much. I myself dislike the label 'New Age' because it is hardly 'New Age' as the concept of the shop is as old as time itself.

Dr Neale stayed all that afternoon quite happy to sit in the chair and be part of the flow of energy that was the '4th Dimension'. At closing time when the customers had all departed, reluctantly, Dr.Neale stood up saying, "I've been in a number of these 'New Age' stores, but I can put my hand on my heart and tell you I've never come across a store such as this. It is wonderful, just wonderful, thank you for letting me stay and be a part of it."

Smiling I told him I'd enjoyed his company and that I knew he would take the energy of my little shop back to America with him before inviting him to choose a crystal to keep as a reminder of his afternoon in 'The 4th Dimension'. After choosing his crystal we hugged for a long while acknowledging our connection in Spirit before saying goodbye. I knew then that my guidance hadn't been wrong after all, as I had definitely been meant to meet this soul.

CHAPTER 41

LEAVING

I've already mentioned that before I opened the healing rooms I'd been given guidance that it would only be for the initial twelve months. This is the story of that guidance, together with some more that I found totally unbelievable. Again it is quite fragmented and there are many stories within the whole, so I will subtitle each one chronologically, as it happened.

LUCY

This story began on my birthday, the 7th of July 2000, six months before I signed the lease on what were to become the 5th Dimension meeting room and healing room.

That morning a middle-aged lady whom I'd never met before came into the shop with a younger woman. The older woman walked straight over to me and said, "I have a message for you, please listen to what I have to say."

The younger woman, her daughter-in-law was browsing and never lifted her head from what she was looking at, but by way of explanation said, "My mother-in-law is a medium."

Lucy, as she introduced herself proceeded with the message, "I am being told to inform you that you will not be here too much longer, you are not going to be far away at first and the work you will be doing is what you do here only without the distraction of the shop. It will only be for a short period of time, approximately twelve months."

While this was taking place the daughter-in-laws mobile phone rung and she whispered into it at the far end of the shop with her back to us so as not to disturb our conversation. Thanking Lucy for her message she winked at me as she left the shop and said knowingly, "Don't forget what I've told you today, it is important."

I had no idea at that time what the message meant, but Lucy's path would cross with mine again very soon. That evening when I arrived home Dickie had a surprise for me.

"No cooking for you tonight love I've booked us in at the bistro for a birthday treat."

"Oh lovely, no cooking and better still no washing up." I replied, laughing.

Running a hot bath with added aromatherapy oils I lay in the warm fragrant water and went over the events of the day, the enigmatic message from Lucy being the most fascinating. Emerging from the bathroom half an hour later feeling totally relaxed and rejuvenated and not knowing if it had been the effects of my leisurely aromatherapy bath or the thought of not having to cook dinner or a combination of both, I felt great and was buzzing all over with a sense of anticipation.

Arriving at the bistro Dickie and I were ushered to our table and given a menu each to peruse. Within minutes of being seated I heard the door open behind me and what sounded like a group of people coming in laughing and chattering in high spirits. There was something vaguely familiar about one of the voices, but not one I could readily recognise. The group of people were shown to the table next to us and turning to smile in their direction could scarcely believe who I was seeing, it was none other than Lucy and her daughter-in-law, accompanied by presumably her husband and son. We laughed and both said together, "Fancy meeting you again."

Lucy's daughter-in-law leant across their table and said, "That phone call I took in your shop this morning was from my husband he was ringing to tell me that he'd booked this table for us tonight as a treat for his Mum. I was really glad she was in deep conversation with you because we wanted to surprise her, you see it's her birthday today."

"Well that's another coincidence because it's my birthday today too." I revealed.

"Really" Lucy interjected, sounding very surprised.

Lucy gave me a mysterious look saying, "I know I was guided to meet you today and give you that message. I've already told you it is very important and it will all make sense to you when the time is right. Our 'chance' meeting again tonight is just a confirmation of that."

After our chance meeting the night of our joint birthdays I didn't expect to see Lucy again, but as fate would decree our paths were to cross, one more time.

ZOROASTER

By early February 2001 I was almost ready to open the new rooms and was busily trying to plan workshops for the coming months when one night I was awoken by a voice, "It is time to take the next step, you must let go of the shop."

Sitting bolt upright in bed I sensed the space around me expecting to 'see' the owner of the voice I'd just heard, but there was no-one. Glancing over at the clock I noticed it was exactly 2am. Lying down again I turned over and went promptly back to sleep putting the incident from my mind as 'only a dream'.

Dear reader I almost hear you groan and say doesn't she know better than that by now. Apparently not!

The following night at exactly 2am I was awoken again with the same message and sitting up in bed I tried to locate the voice which seemed to be coming from somewhere in the room, but in actuality I believe was inside my head.

Strangely the voice that had given the message was different to the voice I normally hear when speaking to myself. I was now wide awake, but in contrast to the night before I was not allowed to go back to sleep and was kept awake.... all night. The voice was insistent in a nice sort of way as it kept saying over and over, "It is time to take the next step, you must let go of the shop." And just as insistently I would reply, "But I can't do that so don't ask me."

On and on it went all night long backwards and forwards like a game of ping pong until glancing at the clock I discovered it was 6am and finally I surrendered.

"OK you win, if this is what you want me to do, I will do it, but can I please get some sleep now?" Within seconds I was fast asleep, but only for about an hour or so as I awoke just before the alarm went off which is most unusual for me.

I lay there looking at Dickie who was still asleep and wondered what he would think of the announcement I was about to make and I didn't have long to wait before I found out.

"Are you mad woman? Why would you want to do a stupid thing like that? It's a good business." All of this and more was his reply to my news.

Poor Dickie, none of it made any sense to him and I know it sounded crazy when I tried to explain to him as to how I'd arrived at my decision because to be quite honest it sounded crazy to me too. To agree to give up a flourishing business, one that I had started from nothing, built up, and loved beyond anything. Was I mad as Dickie had suggested?

That whole week went by in a blur, my head spinning and my brain scrambled wondering if I should follow this guidance or just forget the whole episode. Finally, confiding in Jody and completely at my wits end I said, "I don't know what to do, have you got any suggestions?"

Jody, as ever, was the voice of reason when giving advice to someone else suggested I stay calm and see what happened next before I made any life changing decisions which was probably very good advice under the circumstances. Before leaving the shop she invited me to her home that weekend for a massage as she thought it might help me to relax and unwind.

Arriving at Jody's home on Saturday evening to find she had set up the therapy bed in the centre of her small living room which was warm and inviting with a beautiful calming atmosphere the only light being that of shimmering candlelight. Just being there made me feel more relaxed than I had felt all week. Jody left the room while I undressed and lay down on the therapy bed covering myself in a deliciously soft warm towel that had been draped over the radiator, feeling more than ready for what I felt sure would be a wonderful pampering experience.

Jody returned after having mixed some aromatherapy oils and while warming her hands told me that she wanted me to relax totally and that meant…..no talking. I had to laugh, she knows me so well.

It was a wonderful, pampering experience and after what must have been more than an hour I felt totally relaxed, my bones having turned to jelly beneath her expert hands. Lying face down Jody completed the session by giving me some healing, being totally aware of what she was doing I surrendered myself to the process.

Jody, being extremely psychic then became a catalyst for the most amazing experience. "There is a man with you and next to him there appears to be a silver incense holder swinging back and forth. Can you smell the incense burning?"

That was the trigger. It was all I needed. Immediately I was transported in my mind to somewhere other than Jody's warm little room and I found myself in a church. A large engraved silver incense burner dispensing its sweet-smelling aroma was swinging back and forth in front of me accompanied by the sound of hypnotic chanting.

Jody's voice broke into my vision, "Linda, where are you?"

"I'm in a church." I managed to tell her.

A shaft of light was streaming through a narrow window into the gloomy incense-filled interior of the church coming to rest on a large ancient book lying open on a very old engraved wooden lectern. My awareness was drawn to a man standing next to the lectern dressed in a flowing black robe with a tall hat or headgear of some kind. Unable to make out his features he looked to me like some ancient prophet or priest, but I wasn't a bit afraid because I could sense he was smiling.

Jody's urgent voice broke into my vision, "What's happening now?"

"I'm with an old man, a priest I think."

"Who is he? Ask him who he is." Jody urged.

In my mind I asked the priest his name and immediately he raised his arm and drew a huge 'Z' in the air. At this point I almost laughed out loud at his gesture as it reminded me of the adventures of ZORRO. After the priest had drawn the letter 'Z' in mid air I was 'fed' a number of letters in rapid succession which I repeated out loud so Jody could hear, O's and R's and T's and S's. They poured in so rapidly I couldn't make sense of them, and laughing told Jody I must be making this up because it was such a jumble of letters, there could be no such word.

Jody was unable to make anything of it anymore than I could, but even after all of that it didn't stop the proceedings. To my amazement the vision continued to play like a film. I was now becoming aware of a crowd of 'beings' behind me in the aisle of the church. The man in black was beckoning me forward pointing to the open book and smiling, I could not see him smiling, but could sense that he was. Stepping over to the lectern I looked down at the ancient tome, the beam of light still playing on the open page, but to my utter disappointment it was in a language I did not understand.

"I'm sorry, I don't understand." I relayed telepathically to the priest, feeling rather inadequate.

Sensing that I was in the presence of a magnificent 'being' he continued to smile benevolently when into my mind I became aware of him saying, 'I AM the Light', then with more force behind it, 'I AM THE LIGHT' follow me.'

Extending his arm as if to usher me somewhere I allowed him to guide me as he turned me around to face the back of the church. Looking down the length of the aisle and very aware that the other 'beings' were moving to one side to let the high priest and myself pass. It was still very gloomy and I couldn't make out much of the interior, but I could see what appeared to be sunlight streaming through the partly open door at the far end of the church. The little procession made its way towards the door, the high priest and me in the lead while the other beings following close behind.

Reaching the door 'my friend' the priest turned to me and said, "It is now time for you to take the next step my child, do not be afraid."

"I am not afraid." I answered confidently, but not really feeling that confident inside.

As if by magic the door opened fully and I found myself standing on the threshold of the church staring out into open misty space that I could only liken to being thousands of feet up in an aeroplane amongst the clouds, the only difference being the brightness, like sunshine without sun.

Jody's voice broke in again insistently, "What's happening?"

"He is asking me to take the next step." I replied.

"Are you going to take it?" she asked eagerly.

"Yes, I feel I must." I said, finding it difficult to speak now, just wanting to continue with my vision, not knowing what to expect when I took that step, but confident that I was indeed going to take it because it felt right.

Taking a deep breath in my vision and shutting my eyes I stepped boldly forward into space not knowing if I was going to drop like a stone to the ground or soar like a bird through the clouds to find the source of that elusive sunshine.

Becoming instantly aware that I had stepped onto firm ground I opened my eyes to take in the location. The church had disappeared and now all around me was beautiful open countryside. A patchwork of green fields and softly undulating landscape surrounded me which was very similar to my beloved glacial hills on the Island's northern plain, but somehow subtly different.

What was it that was so different? I asked myself, before I becoming aware of what it was. There was not a house, a road, an electricity pylon or another living soul in sight and I found myself completely alone standing atop a small hill bathed in the most beautiful 'Light', feeling completely at peace. I stood there quietly drinking in the atmosphere of this special place when suddenly a beam of light emanated from the sky entering my heart and I let out a huge sigh ... and the vision ended.

Coming back to reality I filled in the gaps for Jody where I had become enthralled with my vision and could not speak. We chatted for some time afterwards about the vividness of the experience wondering what it all meant, and who the enigmatic priest could be as he was not a being I had been consciously aware of before. However, the one thing I had come back positive about was the decision to go ahead and let go of the shop and I couldn't believe how positive I felt about that.

On Monday morning after this experience Rosemary rang for a chat opening the conversation by asking what kind of a weekend I'd had, excitedly I recounted my tale of what had taken place at Jody's on Saturday evening and on reaching the part in my story about Zorro and all the letters that had spilled into my mind Rosemary immediately burst in with, "Oh my God Linda, it was Zoroaster, I know it was Zoroaster."

As she said the name Zoroaster I started to shake and shudder as energy ran up and down my spine. Over the years I have come to realize that this was confirmation from my HS of what my friend was telling me, but the name Zoroaster meant nothing to me, never having come across it before.

Rosemary who is a very spiritual lady and also extremely well read told me he was an ancient priest/prophet and there was actually a religion based on his teachings. Astounded that I'd never heard of the religion, but I knew by the way I felt that there was a connection between this being and myself. Relieved that I had not made the name up after all and that there had been such a person, but the question was, what did he want with me?

After the conversation with Rosemary I sat quietly to contemplate on what had just taken place and as I sat in silence certain events from the past few months were dropped into my mind. I found myself remembering the year before when I had been on my first cruise around the Greek Islands with my spiritual friends Carol and Janet. The thoughts that were dropping into my mind were about the last day of the cruise and our final destination, the island of Santorini, somewhere I had never heard of before this trip.

The girls and I were on deck watching the island come into view when suddenly out of nowhere I was struck with a pain in my chest and the nearer we got to the island the worse it became. The ship dropped anchor out in the bay or caldera the island being what was left of an extinct volcano and we along with many other tourists were then transported to the jetty on Santorini by a succession of small ferry boats. It was an 800 foot ascent from the jetty to the little whitewashed village perched at the top of the cliffs and the only way to get there was by donkey up an almost perpendicular zigzag pathway or by cable car. Carol and Janet opted for the donkey ride, but unfortunately I couldn't even consider it as the pain in my chest was so bad it had to be the cable car for me. We all met at the top before wandering through the maze of little streets until we arrived at a particularly beautiful viewpoint and sat down to drink in the panorama and watch the sunset which was breathtaking.

From where we sat we could look all along the quaint little village, perched as it was on top of the cliff, with its whitewashed houses clinging to the cliff-side, which made it look like a giant cake, the whitewashed houses like icing running down over the edge. The view then swept majestically down into the caldera where our cruise ship lay anchored and from our vantage point the ship looked like a small toy way below us, its decks lit up with a myriad of dancing lights in readiness for the approaching evening. We sat there for some time and took a number of photographs of the stunning scenery as the sun slid slowly into the calm waters. We then watched transfixed as the priests arrived in a procession for evening service in the church nearby, wearing their high black hats with their long flowing black robes sweeping the dusty ground.

When the sun had set completely we meandered back through the streets right to the far end of the village where there were no street lights or tourists. We stood in the darkness looking down over the village below listening to the muffled music coming from the bars and the chatter of the people walking through the narrow streets on that beautiful barmy evening, each of us deep within our own thoughts.

The pain in my chest was excruciating and I remember standing in the darkness with my hand on my heart trying to ease the discomfort I was feeling, when through the still, dark evening came the sound of distant chanting, presumably from the church we had noticed earlier. This chanting had the strangest and most profound effect on me. I began to cry silently in the darkness, tears rolling down my cheeks as something touched deep within my being and at that precise moment the pain in my chest/heart miraculously disappeared!

Remembering too that when I got back from this holiday I was addicted to the chanting I had heard that night and had purchased a CD which I was compelled to play over and over again, as if to draw the energy of it into every cell in my body. Had Zoroaster been trying to come through back then I wondered. As this thought evaporated from my mind another one dropped in to take its place as only a couple of weeks previously, Julie and my grand-daughter Hollie, who was only two years old at the time, had called to see me. Hollie was always on the lookout for a book with pictures whenever she visited the shop, unfortunately she was often disappointed, but on this particular occasion she had picked up a small paperback book from one of the lower shelves of the bookcase. It was a book full of colour photographs of ancient sites around the world, not one I could recall ever having looked at before and Hollie had handed it to me saying, "For you Nana."

On the page Hollie had shown me was a very familiar photograph of a beautiful sunset looking down from a cliff top and out over a bay far below where a cruise ship lay anchored in the calm waters. The caption beneath the photograph was, 'Sunset over the Greek island of Santorini, also known in ancient times as the Island of Thera thought by some to be Atlantis.'

Not only that I could see the photograph had been taken from the exact spot where we had sat outside the Greek Church when we had visited Santorini some six months before. All these events must be connected in some way or why else would I be thinking about them. The conclusion I came to was that Zoroaster must have been trying to get through to me all those months ago, but I had not been aware of him at the time.

The very next day more confirmation came my way when Harold popped in for his daily chat. Within minutes of walking through the door he shuddered and told me he was aware of a man in a long flowing black robe wearing some type of tall headgear who was telling him to inform me that he had drawn close to 'help me with what I had to do next.' Thanking Harold I then explained about the events of the weekend telling him I believed the being he had just described and channeled had to be one and the same…..Zoroaster.

That night I rang my friend and teacher John wanting to share with him my decision to follow my guidance to let the shop go and also about the details surrounding the appearance of Zoroaster.

"Well fancy that" he laughed, after completing my story. "Now I've got another confirmation for you because I have a large encyclopaedia open on my desk as we speak and it just happens to be open on the page about Zoroaster and his faith!"

I was flabbergasted to say the least, but this was only the beginning of Zoroaster's confirmations. Never having heard of him before the last few days he made sure I did in the weeks to come as practically every book I picked up had a reference to Zoroaster!

MY SECOND MEETING WITH LUCY

All of the above was very intriguing to say the least, but there was still more to come. The following week Lucy appeared in the shop telling me she had arrived on the Island late the night before and that she had been asked by Spirit to come and see me first thing the next day. She proceeded to give me the same message she had the first time we'd met which by now was more than nine months before.

"The time is now right and the help is in place for what you must do next."

When she had finished I shared with her the news about the healing room and meeting room and then about the guidance I'd been given as regards leaving the shop saying, "What you told me last year seems to be making some sense at last although I can't imagine why I'm only to have the rooms for twelve months or why I must leave the shop."

"All in good time" Lucy answered, enigmatically. "All in good time"

Lucy was right of course, it wouldn't do to know what was around the corner as we would never learn anything that way.

"Now dear, I think my job is done here and I wish you well on your voyage of discovery, but don't forget, listen to your heart, always listen to your heart, because your heart will guide you Home."

Lucy hugged me and with a knowing wink left the shop never to be seen again from that day to this.

Not long after this meeting the entire mall was sold and in due course I was informed by the new landlord that when my years lease had expired on the meeting room and healing room the new rent would be put up to the full price, unfortunately not one I could afford, especially if I was to give up the shop.

However, I had become aware since opening the rooms the reason for taking them on was to bring the Light into that space which was indeed part of my destiny and the destiny of those people who joined me in the work that took place there. Now I understood the guidance I had received and everything was falling into place, this was just another experience I needed as part of my journey.

'THE WHITE BROTHERHOOD' AND THE SIGN OF THE 'SIX POINTED STAR

A few weeks after the above events and fast approaching May Bank Holiday life had settled down somewhat and thankfully I had received no more revelations. Since accepting the guidance to leave the shop I had made it known locally that the business was up for sale, but I could feel a deep restlessness growing inside of me which I did not understand. Having followed my guidance I just wanted the business to be sold and everything over and done with as quickly as possible, but things very rarely turn out the way you expect them to, this much I had learned.

On May Bank Holiday weekend Dickie, being a motorcycle racing enthusiast, had gone away with some friends to an event in Ireland, giving me the weekend to myself. After a leisurely breakfast on Sunday morning I felt a strong urge to sit and read so I went to my bookcase which is full of second-hand metaphysical books I had collected over the years, a lot of which I had not yet had time to read. Picking a small tattered volume from the bookshelf with a deep inner knowing that this was the book I needed to read I settled myself in the sun porch with the sun streaming in on what was a glorious day.

Opening the book the first thing I noticed was a hand written date inside the front cover. It read 3/6/1927. No wonder it looked a bit battered, it was more than 70 years old! It was a book by Grace Cooke the medium who channelled White Eagle and set up the White Eagle Lodge at Liss in Hampshire. Anyone who is familiar with the teachings of White Eagle will know how beautiful and simple his philosophy is and I for one owned a few of these books and loved them, but this particular little book was one I had never read before.

It was Grace Cooke's own account of how she was guided to set up the White Eagle Lodge in England. Explaining how she had first come to work in spiritual service for the *White Brotherhood an ascended energy, endeavouring to shine light into the hearts of humanity around the world.

Having read maybe only twenty pages or so I could scarcely believe what I was reading. Grace was informed by her guide of a person who would make himself known to her only as 'Z' and was told that he would come as a messenger from his 'Master' who was part of the White Brotherhood and that she would presented with a symbol that would be proof of his validity. That symbol would be a six-pointed star.

This guidance was to be fulfilled some months later when such a person did indeed seek her out to help her establish the White Brotherhood work in Britain and when she asked 'Z' about his 'Master' he had answered, "He is all Love and He is all Light, and this is his symbol" offering her a little silver six pointed star!

Staring at the page I could feel the shudder of recognition course through my being and knew the book was *speaking to me.*

Well, I thought, my 'Z'... Zoroaster has certainly made himself known to me and over the course of the next few weeks the symbol of the six-pointed star was to come at me from every angle, and every time it did I would say, "Thank You" and "Please keep guiding me in the right direction"

* Ascended Masters ... Jesus, Buddha, Krishna etc.
Note: The six-pointed star is the symbol of the Christ Consciousness... 'As above, so below'

FLORA

By the middle of summer I was beginning to have serious doubts as to whether the business would sell as nobody had yet come forward and expressed a serious interest. How could I bear to leave it? I had asked myself on more than one occasion, but I knew that I must and thought how sad it would be if it just had to close.

These thoughts were uppermost in my mind as I wandered round my little shop on that beautiful day the door wide open and the warm summer sunshine streaming in. The whole place was alive with dancing rainbows reflected through the beautiful window crystals when a mature lady, a stranger to me, stepped in through the open door and put a stop to my reverie. Smiling at me with a lovely warm smile she asked if she might browse.

"By all means" I replied moving back to stand in the sunshine of the open door.

After a few minutes the lady asked if it would be possible to buy a pack of Angel Meditations Cards like the ones I had on display in a small casket on the counter. They are a particularly nice deck of cards and I loved to work with them, but unfortunately, I didn't have a pack left for sale, the deck on the counter being my own deck which I left on display for people to use. Apologizing I offered to order some telling her they would probably arrive before the weekend.

The lady looked crest-fallen, "That's a great pity because I return to the mainland before the weekend."

Looking into her eyes I found myself saying, "I would like you to have my deck, they're well-worn I'm afraid, but I feel you must have them."

"You can't do that." she protested.

"Yes I can." I replied. "I don't know why, but I really want you to have them."

Adamant that I wanted no payment I knew I just had to give my Angel Cards to this total stranger! Finally she accepted and popping them into a bag I handed them to her saying, "I know you will love working with them as much as I have"

"Now I have something I want to give you" she replied smiling, "It's a message from Spirit. Is there anywhere private we can go?"

In a sort of semi-dream-like state I picked up the shop keys and locked the door and we proceeded round the corner to the healing room. I'd never done such a thing before and I wondered why I was doing it now! Showing the stranger into the healing room I locked the door behind us so we would not be disturbed.

We sat opposite each other on two easy chairs as she introduced herself as Flora and told me that she was the visiting medium at the local Spiritualist Church in Douglas. Firstly she gave me a message about my family which was very much the sort of information you would receive through a medium at a demonstration of clairvoyance when suddenly the temperature dropped sharply and it went extremely cold, I could feel myself shivering even though it was a beautiful warm day outside.

Flora began to speak again only now her voice sounded somewhat different. She told me that there were three high beings around me the first being a Chinese Mandarin whom I had been consciously aware of only once before. The second was a Native American Indian with two feathers in his head band whom I'd been aware of on a number of occasions and the third was a high priest in a black flowing robe whom I presumed must be Zoroaster. Flora then sat bolt upright in the chair almost as if she was sitting to attention and stared at me with a slightly glazed expression. "You will not be in this place much longer. Do not be afraid to step away, but we tell you this, you have much more to do yet and your work will touch thousands before it is time for you to leave the Earth Plane."

I'm not sure if it was because of how cold I had become or the content of the last part of Flora's message, but my whole body was shaking. Flora regained herself and stood up slowly stepping forward to hug me and I could feel my heart begin to race as I couldn't help but notice she was wearing a beautiful silver six-pointed star around her neck!

Smiling to myself I then knew that she was the predicted messenger just as my guidance had told me, but feeling rather overawed and disbelieving at the content of Flora's message because I couldn't imagine what I was possibly going to do that would touch thousands of people.

Thanking Flora and wishing her well I was happy I'd given her the Angel Cards for nothing because she had just given me something in return that no amount of money could ever buy.

ANITA

Shortly after the above event with Flora I received a telephone call from Carole who was one of my regular customers.

"Hello Linda, I'm just calling to tell you Anita is on the Island and would like to see you, she has something very important she wants to tell you. Can you come in the next half-hour? Sorry its short notice, but she says it has to be tonight as she goes back to the mainland first thing tomorrow morning. Please say you will come, it sounds urgent."

Carole runs a B&B in Douglas and takes in the visiting mediums for the nearby Spiritualist Church which was how Flora had found the shop. After giving me directions on where exactly to find her

B&B I set off on what was a very wet and misty trip to Douglas. Following Carole's directions I turned into a terrace of large Victorian houses in a cul-de-sac with not a parking space in sight!

It had already taken me much longer than I expected to get to Douglas because of the bad weather on the mountain road and was feeling more than a bit frustrated as I exited out of the cul-de-sac back onto the main road. A few yards further along the road was a large wine store with its own car park and as luck would have it the barriers were up so I drove straight in and parked.

Jumping out of the car and about to lock the door all my keys fell off the key ring jangling and bouncing in different directions as they hit the wet ground. Cursing out loud I bent down to retrieve them just as someone came out of the wine store and shouted, "I wouldn't park there if I was you love, I'm just about to lock the barriers for the night, they won't be open again until eight tomorrow morning."

My keys falling off the key-ring at that precise moment was no accident because if they hadn't I would have been stuck in Douglas until the following morning. Driving back up the road and into Carole's cul-de-sac, thankfully my luck was in, as a car pulled away leaving me a parking space right outside her door. Spirit really wanted me to get this message whatever it was about and 'They' were going to make sure I got to Anita without any mishap.

Carole answered the door and led me into a large airy dining-room telling me Anita would join me soon and she would make sure we would not be disturbed. Thanking Carole I told her I was puzzled by Anita's request and asked did she know how it had come about.

"Remember a few weeks ago when I was in your shop, you said how much you admired Anita's gift and would love another sitting with her, but not at the church. Well, I mentioned it to Anita tonight over dinner and straight away she said she had to see you tonight it was very important. That's all I know."

This would only be the second time I had met Anita face to face the first time being when Harold and I had our sitting in the Spiritualist Church. Anita was such a busy woman I found it hard to believe that she was making space on her last evening on the Island for someone she had only met once before. My musings came to an abrupt halt as Anita entered the room and closed the door purposefully behind her.

"We won't be disturbed Spirit will make sure of that" she said confidently.

"Spirit will only allow in the people who need to be present and tonight that is just you and I. This will be an important sitting for you so listen carefully to what is being said and don't forget when you answer me speak up loud and clear I'm a little bit deaf you know and I hear Spirit better than I hear you. OK."

Without further ado Anita sat down opposite me and went straight into the sitting. Firstly she gave me wonderful proof of survival of loved ones by name and character even my great-grandmother came through and gave her correct name accompanied by a message to give to Mum which was marvellous and confirmed by Mum when I told her.

Then Anita's voice changed subtly and I felt strongly that her control had just been taken over as she continued to channel in quite an authoritative manner which I felt might be Zoroaster.

"I am aware you are following the guidance you have been given to leave the shop, but you do not understand why. Do not waiver from this path for this is the route you must take. There is a book to be written by you that will reach out to many people and you will need to understand the workings of the computer to help you with this task. I am aware that you do not like the world of technology and I am also aware that you own a computer of which you are afraid. Learn to master it! Do not let your lower mind worry over the whys' and wherefores' of your business as everything is in hand. Divine Timing is everything."

The sitting I realized was over when my attention was drawn to the neck opening of Anita's blouse and there on a silver chain resting in the hollow of her neck and winking back at me was a tiny six-pointed star!

Anita's message and her necklace was to be the last confirmation I would receive from Spirit about the guidance I'd been given, and in all things I was to learn Divine Timing is everything.

Volume II

COINCIDENCE

+

SYNCHRONICITY

=

'GUIDANCE'

A Personal Journey

CHAPTER 1

THE DAWN OF A NEW DAY

On a cold and grey November day in 2001 I found myself unlocking the door of my little shop for what I knew would be the last time. Letting myself in I sat down in the infamous 'healing chair' and waited for the new owners to arrive, knowing that I had already said my goodbyes, now there was just the formality of signing over this very special part of my life.

Dickie and I had visited the shop the day before to take some video footage as I wanted something tangible to keep for that moment when my failing memory might grow so dim that I could not remember what a special place I/Spirit had created. Wandering around the shop oblivious to Dickie and his recorder, I re-lived some of the experiences that had taken place there. The laughter and the tears, the healings, and the endless cups of tea and coffee served to the souls who entered the shop as strangers and left as friends, not just with me, but with each other. And not forgetting of course, the good natured rivalry over whose turn it was to sit in the 'healing chair'.

Yes, my head was full of special thoughts and memories, but I hadn't failed to overlook the auspicious date which was to be my last day as the owner/caretaker of The 4th Dimension Body Mind and Spirit Shop. Throughout my journey with spirit I had become aware that the numbers 11/11 were always a significant sign that spirit were at work in my life and as today was 11th November I sent up a silent prayer of gratitude, confident that everything was going to plan, even if I was yet to be made aware of it.

As the new owners approached the shop door a sudden wave of panic pulled me back from my reverie and my happy thoughts were replaced with those of fear as I doubted my ability to let go of my beautiful creation, a dream that I had so lovingly nurtured and breathed into life. Quickly reprimanding my ever present 'Doubting Thomas' for even thinking such a thought I chased away what was only a fleeting moment of indecision. Deep down inside my very being I knew spirit had other plans for me and leaving my little shop was something I *must* do. Within moments all parties had signed the contract, it had only taken seconds and now my beautiful creation was no longer mine.

Wishing the new owners well in their exciting venture I was amazed at how emotionally detached I suddenly felt and striding across the car park in the direction of my car the only thought that crossed my mind was how strange it felt not to lock up before leaving, but I was not even tempted to look back.

Minutes later I found myself driving towards the most northerly tip of the island, not a difficult thing to achieve when you live on a very small island surrounded by sea. I had no conscious reason for taking this route, but less than ten minutes later I found myself parking the car just a few hundred yards from the lighthouse and old fog-horn. Staring blankly out to sea thinking about the situation and my emotional numbness, I couldn't quite get past the fact that I didn't feel any sense of loss. Surely it couldn't be right to have no feelings on such a momentous change in my life's events? My head full of nothing but unanswerable questions I decided to take a walk along the Ayres.

Opening the car door I suddenly felt something, if only physical, as an icy blast blowing in from the Irish Sea almost bowled me over. The sea was very turbulent where the waters meet at the tip of the island and the waves crashed to the shore leaving foaming mounds of froth along the tide line. Above me seagulls' were wheeling and calling against a leaden sky and the relentless wind seemed to be blowing from every direction at once.

Attempting to stroll along a pathway that led through the clumps of heather I struggled to stay upright as I was pummeled by the gusts and squalls coming in of the sea, but I enjoyed the welcome cold on my cheeks, at least I was feeling something even if it was only the biting wind.

I'd been walking for some time when I suddenly felt the need to stand still. Obeying my guidance and spreading my arms wide I felt like a bird about to take flight. In that wonderful moment I felt so alive and filled with spirit, and I could feel my connection with everything around me, I was Pure Love, Joy, Peace and Belonging all rolled into one blissful feeling. Throwing my head back I raised my face toward the leaden sky and shouted, 'Thank You' toward the heavens although my words were instantly borne away on the gusting wind. Thank goodness there were no onlookers as I would have appeared to have been behaving very oddly indeed and not for the first time or last I might add.

Making my way back toward the car I thanked spirit once again for filling my emotional void so spectacularly. Now I felt ready for whatever the future might hold.

CHAPTER 2

THE PROMISE

I'd made a promise to spirit before giving up the shop that once that aspect of my life was over I would write a book about my spiritual awakening and I had every intention of fulfilling that promise. Imagine my amazement when only a few weeks after leaving the shop I received guidance asking me to set up a spiritual library. Scarcely able to believe that spirit had required me to relinquish my cherished shop, now I was being guided to start something else ... as well as write a book!

Choosing to ignore all the synchronicities and confirmations that normally bombard me when spirit have requested some action on my part I informed them rather boldly, but very politely, that I had no intention of running a library, reminding them of their previous desire for me to write a book. The reply I received back from spirit was equally as bold, "Oh, but my child you will do this when the time is right as it is an important part of your journey."

After the above exchange the synchronicities stopped and I breathed a sigh of relief and settled down to the preparations for Christmas. Before I knew it the festivities and all that they entail had passed and the day had arrived for Dickie and Christine to return to work. Kissing them both before they left I bade them hurried goodbyes as I had plans for my precious time once I was alone in the house.

Racing into the bedroom I retrieved my word processor and plonked it down on a small table in the sun room where I intended to work. I'd bought it a few months after going into business with the intention of using it for ordering and book-keeping only to find I did not understand a word of the gigantic book of instructions that came with it! Completely overawed and totally bamboozled by the manual's techno-speak I'd become disenchanted very quickly and relegated the poor old word processor to gather dust on the top shelf of the wardrobe, which is where it had remained.

Luckily for me I knew how to type, save and print and thankfully that was all I needed to understand for the task I had been set. Sitting in the sun-porch bathed in morning sunshine I switched on enthusiastically with all the flair and panache of someone who knows exactly what they are doing. My fingers hovered expectantly over the keyboard ready to write, but I remained inert staring blankly at the screen and the blank screen stared straight back. We stayed like that for some time, the word processor and I, just staring at one another. Not one word came into my mind. My thought processes seemed totally devoid of any signs of life!

Thoroughly disheartened I sat for a further ten minutes willing a title into my brain, but to no avail. The enthusiasm and excitement I had felt earlier evaporated into thin air and in a fit of pique I unplugged the wretched machine, marching back into the bedroom and returned it to the top shelf of the wardrobe where it could gather some more dust. Even as I carried out this meaningless task I knew I was really annoyed with myself for quitting so easily.

All the while Rags had been sitting patiently beside me and now she trotted excitedly behind me, no doubt thinking that as I was on the move there may be the chance of a walk. And that is exactly what I decided to do, thinking a walk in the winter sunshine would bring some clarity to my senses.

It was a lovely sunny winter's day with clear blue skies and after a rejuvenating walk by the river we returned home much refreshed. Rags raced passed me as I opened the door, making straight for her water bowl to quench her thirst, while I sat down at my dressing table to brush my hair. Staring, trance-like, at my reflection in the mirror the title to my book just dropped into my head, I hadn't even been consciously thinking about it because my head was still full of our country walk, but there it was out of nowhere, 'My Journey to the 4th Dimension... and beyond'.

Half an hour earlier I had been unable to think of anything and now I had this brilliant title. Staring into the mirror I expected to see some creative genius staring back, but it was still me, only now my mind was racing and I had to get started ... straight away.

Setting about the task in hand, and for the second time in less than an hour I hauled the much abused word processor out of pre-mature retirement to take pride of place in the sun-room. The little room was flooded with golden light and the cloudless sky remained the most beautiful shade of blue as the frost from the previous night had all but melted and an assortment of small wild birds had gathered to have breakfast on the bird-table just outside the window.

Once more I was filled with enthusiasm, sure in my mind that this time I would not let the dreaded blank screen get the better of me. Purposefully and very proudly I typed the title I'd been given moments earlier across the centre of the page and having done this I found myself and the blank screen eyeballing each other once more, nervously waiting for inspiration to strike.

Always having proclaimed to those closest to me that I could talk a book and most, if not all, agreed with me! But, now as I sat facing my nemesis I realized that it wasn't experiences to write about that I was short of only an appropriate place to start. A short while later having made up my mind to begin with my dabbling with a Ouija board in my teens I set off at a great pace, fingers dancing over the keyboard, recalling the experience as I typed. This was more like it, now that I had started I felt the rest would flow because all I had to do was let my memories roll like an old film and write it down as I went along.

That first day of writing just flew by, and after my false start I wrote most days, anything from an hour to three or four hours depending on how I felt and what else was going on in my life. My project was progressing well until the day Christine's friend called at the house and finding me typing in my usual spot in the sun-room asked idly what I was so busy doing. By way of explanation I told him I was writing my autobiography, but his response came as something of a shock when he enquired what had been so special about my life that I should want write about it!

Although I know he had not set out to hurt my feelings my bubble of self confidence burst and in that moment all the enthusiasm I'd felt about my project just drained away leaving me totally deflated. Without meaning to he'd sown the seeds of self doubt into very fertile ground and as they grew I convinced myself he was right, 'who on earth would want to read about me and my life?'

After Christine and her friend left the house that day I shut down the machine and placed it back on the top shelf of the wardrobe to gather more dust. How effectively the words of others can change the course of our actions and by listening to someone else's opinion instead of trusting my own guidance I had delayed the inevitable.

This was a wonderful lesson for me on how easily we can give our power away to others and in this instance I take full responsibility, because I chose to hold onto what was said to me, allowing myself to be hurt by it. We each have a choice in every moment to hold on to negative thoughts or petty injustices that we then carry around as baggage, effectively stopping the wonderful flow of Universal Energy and inspiration. My advice would be choose not to take such comments on board and walk away with your head held high and your dreams intact.

In August 2002 I awoke one morning so inspired that I just knew I had to start writing again. As soon as Dickie and Christine had left for work the word processor was out of its hiding place and set up in the sun-room in double quick time, all ready for the next phase of my project. Although I felt madly inspired at that precise moment I did not have a thought in my head as to what I was going to write, but the next minute my fingers were flying over the keyboard at a rate of knots that I found almost impossible to keep up with! Trying desperately to read what my fingers were writing I found myself laughing, laughing so much in fact there were tears in my eyes. It was one of my mother's favourite stories detailing the night I was born and the events that had ensued (Chapter 1, Volume I)

No sooner was the chapter finished than my fingers once more took on a life of their own and danced across the keyboard. This time however, the effect on me was quite different as I found myself writing about the traumatic events of losing both my father and grandfather whilst still very young (Chapter 2 of Volume I). As I typed a pain developed in my chest around the area of my heart, a tight, constricting pain which made it difficult for me to breathe. It felt so physical and so real that I was almost sick and began to wonder if I was actually having a heart attack! Tears rolled down my cheeks unchecked, obscuring my vision of the screen, but my fingers continued to type until thankfully the pain began to subside and by the time I had finished writing the chapter it had ebbed away completely.

Realizing that these chapters and the amazingly cathartic experience I had just undergone were the obvious opening chapters of my book I took my lead from that famous song from Mary Poppins, 'Let's start at the very beginning, it's a very good place to start' and decided to start my book at the beginning of my life here on Earth as Linda which of course was 'the most perfect place to start'.

Having no doubt at all that I'd just experienced a wonderful and energetic release, and the emotional baggage that had kept me trapped within the pain of my father's death for the past forty years was now gone and the incredible lightness I felt was unbelievable. No wonder I had been so inspired to write that morning, it had obviously been time for me to 'Let go' and something huge had shifted on an energetic level, leaving me free to continue … or so I thought.

Within weeks my husband's partner became ill and I was enlisted to help out in their car repair business, running round the Island picking up parts and towing in cars that had broken down etc. There was only a short respite from this disaster when my aunt and uncle arrived from New Zealand for a six week stay and within days of waving them goodbye, my eldest daughter Julie, broke her leg, making me chief cook, bottle washer, chauffeur and full time Nana to my granddaughter Hollie and her Mum for the next eight weeks. In all that time no writing got done which was a lengthy period of time for the old word processor to gather more dust, and on more than one occasion I remember thinking it was just as well I no longer had the shop as I would not have had the time to devote to it. Sadly, I was beginning to feel a bit of a victim as I had understood my guidance to suggest that giving up the shop would set me on the next step of my spiritual journey. Devoting my time to all and sundry, even if they were my earthly family, did not seem like much of a next step to me, but 'The Universe' has its own agenda and timing, all you need is an abundance of what the majority of humanity, including me, has in very short supply and that is patience with a capital P.

Eventually my life resumed a more mundane pattern and I was able to return to writing, finding time over the next couple of months to complete the book. Having kept my promise to spirit and written the book I stored it away, after all, it was about my life and my experiences, some of which were extremely personal. It was my baby and I wasn't sure at this stage that I wanted to share it with anyone else, least of all the general public. So guess what I did with it? Absolutely nothing!

However, if spirit has a purpose for something or someone they will find a way of accomplishing their task and in no short time I received a visit from a friend who lives in Africa. During her visit she dropped into the conversation that a mutual friend of ours had told her I'd written a book and asked was this information correct. Replying in a hesitant affirmative my stomach churned when she asked if she could read it. That mischievous gremlin 'lack of confidence' reared his head and I tried to make the excuse that it was only in manuscript form, but refusing to take 'no' for an answer she left a while later with my manuscript tucked under her arm.

Returning a few days later she handed over the manuscript telling me how much she had enjoyed it and asked when I was going to publish. Delighted that she'd not only read the book, but had apparently found it a good read and thought it worthy of publishing I gave the lack of confidence gremlin a quick elbow in the ribs and wondered how, as a novice author, I could go about publishing. Suddenly, I remembered an article I'd cut out of the newspaper months before, about a new publishing company who offered fledgling authors a way of putting their manuscript into book form. In my current highly excitable and newly self confident state all I had to do was remember where I'd put the cutting. Although on a conscious level I had absolutely no idea where to look by 'chance' I found it in the first place I did look!

Over the next few weeks after contacting the publishing company and with the help of a very special man, the owner David, my book was published and ready to be set free on the public at large. Janine, the new owner of my shop offered 'The 4th Dimension' as the venue for a book signing and given the circumstances and title of my book I considered this a very fitting locale and accepted gladly, but on the night before the book signing I had the most peculiar dream.

The Dream…

As an adult I found myself in one of the old outside toilets at the primary school I attended in Andreas Village. This toilet block has long since been demolished to make way for an extension to the school, but in the dream it was exactly as I remembered it in my youth. I could even smell the pungent aroma of the horrible 'Bronco' toilet paper we had to use. To my utter surprise and horror I realized I was about to give birth and within moments was cradling the newborn in my arms. Overwhelmed with the love I felt for this precious little being I held the babe gently in the crook of my arm while banging on the old wooden door with my free fist, trying desperately to get out, but the door would not budge. Eventually I resorted to yelling for help to alert any passers by that I had just given birth.

Magically the door opened and I ran out onto the schoolyard that I remembered so well from my youth, almost fifty years before, but to my horror, the yard was full of people with their faces hidden by a masks. Presumably 'they' had been lying in wait for me and began firing missiles of small rocks and stones in my direction. My only thought was to protect my precious baby and ran across the yard feeling the occasional thud as another projectile made contact with my body.

Rounding the corner of the schoolyard I could see the school gates directly ahead of me and made a frantic dash for the exit where my old school friend Chris was standing. Crying out to her for help a large missile hit the small of my back and my legs buckled beneath me as she snatched the baby to safety. Falling to my knees and supporting myself with my freed hands I turned to look at the schoolyard to face my mysterious adversaries, but to my utter amazement the yard was completely empty, there was not a person in sight.

The dream ended at this point, but so real had this experience been that I'd actually felt the physical pain in my body while dreaming, the blow to my back being the most painful. I'm writing about this dream some twelve years since having dreamt it and it is as clear in my mind today as it was then.

My interpretation of this dream is as follows:-

1. Trapped in a confined space relates to my own self limitation.
2. The birth signifies the creation of the book.
3. Asking for help … is calling upon my Higher Self/Spirit
4. The door magically opening is self liberation and the ability to move beyond self limitation.
5. Adversaries wearing masks signifies fear of the unknown and exposure to those with opposing views.
6. Assault by missiles is simply a fear of criticism.
7. My friend waiting at the gates denotes the presence of Spirit.

Wow! What a dream to have the night before you throw your personal life out into the public domain for all to read and go through with a fine tooth comb. But, I'm happy to say that's exactly what I did and most importantly I have never regretted it.

Including this chapter was important for me so that I could share with you how my original book was born.

Just a final thought. Throughout our lives, all of us, on occasion, will experience prophetic or important dreams. Please, never underestimate the power of your dreams, especially those just before you awaken. Don't doubt your Higher Self/Spirit will use any and every method at its disposal to capture your attention to get the message across.

CHAPTER 3

THE HAUNTED VILLA

The sequence of events in this chapter would have a bearing on many more similar experiences that would show up for me over the next few years, some of which I will share with you in this book. Honestly, I have to tell you that this is an area I would never have consciously ventured into myself, but obviously my Higher Self had different ideas.

Just a couple of weeks prior to signing over the 4th Dimension Dickie and I visited Portugal for the first time. We were accompanied on the trip by my two cousins, Elaine and Greg and their respective partners Jimmy and Karen, as well as Elaine's two teenage sons, Gary and Sean.

Because we were such a large party we decided to go self-catering and spent many hours deliberating over the various options open to us, finally deciding on a very rustic looking villa with shuttered windows and cascading bougainvillea overhanging the patio. The villa had its own private swimming pool which 'sold' it as far as the lads were concerned, so paying our deposit we waited with great anticipation for the day of departure to arrive.

In what seemed like no time at all the big day arrived and in very high spirits we set off to the airport en-masse, our expectations brimming over as none of us had stayed in a villa before and we couldn't wait to see if it lived up to the promise of the picture in the brochure.

On landing in Portugal the plane disgorged its happy band of holidaymakers with us amongst them. A coach was waiting to transport us to our destinations and after about an hour or so and feeling more than a little travel weary the driver finally announced the next stop would be the villa St. Jaime.

Walking through the villa gates the sight that greeted us was less than inspiring as workmen were scurrying about finishing what appeared to be last minute jobs on the old villa. One of the men, the supervisor I think, seemed friendly enough and he babbled away in rapid Portuguese, presumably apologizing for still being there, although he could just as easily have been telling us to catch the next flight home. Doffing his battered cap he backed out of the property closing the gates behind him, but strangely his workmates were already on the other side of the gate and practically running up the road! Watching them go with what seemed like unnecessary haste we all commented on what an unusual welcome we'd received.

The boys, excited by their release from the long coach journey were already in the house, running up and down the stairs, and in and out of the rooms looking to see what the villa had to offer. Hearing them laughing and calling out to us we picked up our bags and followed them inside.

The first thing we all noticed as we entered the villa was the pungent smell in the air, stale and musty as if it had been shut up for a long time, which seemed strange to me because we had arrived in October, almost the end of the season, not the beginning.

Downstairs consisted of two double bedrooms, kitchen and dining area and a large lounge with a huge sliding window out onto the patio overlooking the pool. There was also a curious little round room tacked on to the lounge with an open hearth and cushioned seating around the wall, presumably a little snug for cold Portuguese winter nights. However, as I walked into one of the back bedrooms downstairs I was overcome with a peculiar sensation, the hairs stood up on the back of my neck and a chill ran down my spine. Performing an about turn I walked straight out again knowing I wouldn't be able to sleep in there and hoping I would not be asked to.

Just then Greg and Karen called us upstairs to say we were going to have the two bedrooms on the first floor, so that Jimmy, Elaine and the two boys could all be together on the ground floor. Letting out a huge sigh of relief I sent up a silent prayer of thanks, although this was tinged somewhat by guilt at the thought that 'someone' was going to have to sleep in that oppressive room and as it turned out is was to be Gary and Sean.

The next day I was lazing by the pool reading the book I had brought with me and enjoying the winter sunshine while everyone else was playing cards on the patio. Spotting me sitting on my own Gary came over to join me, but he did not seem to be his normal carefree self and I ventured to ask him if anything was wrong. Drawing closer to me and replying in a very low voice so no one other than me could hear, he confided that he did not like the villa and did not want to stay.

Not remotely surprised by his comments he eventually told me what it was that made him feel this way. During the night it seemed he had become conscious of another person in their bedroom, a female who most definitely did not want him or his brother to be in there. Not wanting to tell Sean in case it spooked him, and who had apparently slept through the experience, Gary was desperate for me to believe his story. Promising not to tell anyone and that it would be our secret I was pleased to see him look a little happier, just sharing what he had felt seemed to have helped. Gary, who is obviously a very sensitive lad, had now confirmed the sensations I'd had on our arrival the day before.

That afternoon we ventured out to explore the surrounding district to find our bearings and see what was on offer locally. Unfortunately, I'd bought new sandals for the holiday and not having worn them in before our arrival my feet were soon covered in very painful blisters. On our return that evening we prepared our meal hoping to eat al fresco on the patio, but were forced inside as the weather deteriorated and the rain poured down in torrents. After our meal we played dominoes and cards, while Jimmy read an English newspaper he had purchased earlier in the day. Finally, deciding to retire for the night, the dominoes and cards were put neatly back in their box and the paper folded and left on the dining table in the lounge. Before climbing the stairs to our room I shot Gary a knowing smile as if in some way to comfort him, even though I was aware he did not want to go back into *that* bedroom, he returned my smile, but said nothing.

About two o'clock in the morning we were awoken by the sound of almighty crashing coming from downstairs, as if someone or something was wreaking havoc in the lounge, but for some indefinable reason not one of us got out of bed to investigate!

Congregating in the lounge early next morning we were scarcely able to believe the evidence of our own eyes as the room was an area of devastation. The paper had been torn apart and strewn everywhere while the dominoes and cards were scattered far and wide across the floor. The place looked like a bomb had gone off.

On discussion it transpired that everyone had heard the crashing the night before, but had all been too frightened to leave their respective bedrooms. After further talks everyone admitted they had felt spooked by the place from the very moment we'd arrived, but had chosen to say nothing as they had not wanted to spoil the holiday for everyone else. It was only Gary who had shared his fears with me.

Over breakfast that morning we all agreed to get on with our holiday and enjoy ourselves no matter what or who might be sharing the villa with us. After breakfast everyone wanted to go off for the day, except for me. My feet could not stand another pounding as blisters on my heels resembling small bunches of grapes made walking too painful. Opting to stay at the villa to put my feet up and read while everyone else went out to explore I had to re-assure 'the gang' that I would be fine even though they all expressed their reluctance at leaving me in the villa alone.

Once they'd gone I speculated on what could possibly happen to me, after all it was daylight and the sun was actually shining, which was not an every day occurrence on that holiday. Whilst it wasn't quite warm enough to sit outside I wanted to enjoy the morning sunshine, so sliding open the patio door I pushed the large sofa into the sunlight and sat down gazing out onto the garden and pool. The beautiful bougainvillea cascading down over the pergola in all its glory was a sight to behold and was covered in buzzing bees and spectacular butterflies. Lying full length on the sofa in a shaft of sunlight I sighed with contentment, the events of the previous night were rapidly vanishing in my mind and being replaced by the promise of a beautiful day.

Picking up my book I was soon engrossed, when suddenly I became aware of feeling very chilled even though I was sitting in the direct sunlight and froze mid breath, conscious that I was no longer alone. Coming from the direction of the downstairs bedrooms I could hear footsteps making their way across the tiled floor towards me. Resisting the temptation to turn around and look because I knew without doubt I was on my own as no one could have entered the villa without passing me first. The footsteps by this time had stopped directly behind where I was seated on the sofa, but instead of feeling fear I was aware of a wave of calmness washing over me.

In my mind I questioned the 'person' as to who she was, knowing without doubt it was a woman. This made her very angry and she rounded on me with a torrent of questions of her own. Her thoughts came thick and fast into my consciousness as she tried to find out why a collection of strangers had invaded her home. The tirade continued and became threatening as she assured me we would all be made to leave when her husband, Carlo, arrived. Then in a more quiet pathetic tone a thought came into my mind like a whisper as she uttered a quiet plea for the whereabouts and return of her husband.

Feeling her energy change from anger to despair I continued to question her trying to make my thoughts gentler. Telling her I might be able to help her find Carlo if she could tell me her name, I soon discovered I was in the presence of a Louisa Rodriguez. She even went to the trouble of telling me how her name was spelt making it quite clear it ended in 'GUEZ' as it could apparently be spelt differently. Having established an understanding of sorts she 'told' me that Carlo had been ill before 'disappearing' and she had found herself alone in the villa. In my thoughts I could hear her weeping and calling for help to find him.

At this point, I'd become aware in my consciousness of a light in the corner of the room and felt very strongly that it was Carlo. It was obvious to me he'd passed over and so had Louisa, but not realizing it had become earthbound in her home. As gently as I could I explained to Louisa all of the above and that the villa was no longer hers, it was now a holiday home. Communicating to her that we were all sorry if we had upset her and if she wanted I would try and help her locate Carlo so they could both move fully back into spirit.

Her relief that she could be re-united with her husband was

overwhelming, but she then expressed the thought that she had also lost her son, Alfonso. Feeling very strongly that Alfonso was still alive and well in this world I told Louisa so and thankfully she seemed to accept my feelings.

During this exchange I had been aware the light in the corner of the room was slowly getting brighter, so without further ado I asked Louisa to scan the area around us and to tell me if she could see a light. After a few moments the reply I hoped for came through my thoughts and I could feel Louisa experiencing a beautiful light. Telepathically I asked her to walk towards the light where I felt sure Carlo would be waiting for her and almost instantly the connection was broken.

Feeling Louisa and Carlo were finally re-united I wished with all my heart that they had now found peace ... together. Saying a prayer I blessed them both and felt my work here was done.

My confirmation came through that very evening when 'the gang' returned with the intention of eating out at a Mexican restaurant they'd spotted earlier in the day. Keeping the events of the day to myself I agreed to join them on the understanding it was not miles away because my feet were still very sore. They all promised me it was not far, so Greg led the way in a direction I had not yet explored. Rounding a corner not far from the villa and sandwiched between two new high-rise apartments was an old two storey building and on the gable wall in large faded letters, almost unreadable through time and weathering were the words 'Rodriguez Electrical Repair Shop'. That was the first confirmation and the second came a few minutes later when we arrived at the restaurant and were escorted to our table by a local, middle-aged waiter sporting the name badge 'Alfonso'.

Footnote

A short while after the above holiday when I next saw my cousin Elaine she told me she'd experienced something a few nights after the above events. She had awoken in the middle of the night and was aware of a male figure standing by the bedroom window and thinking it was her husband Jim she was about to speak to him when she realised he was lying beside her fast asleep!

Asking her what she did next she laughed telling me she'd pulled the covers over her head and kept them there until the next morning. Elaine and the others did not know about the experience I'd had, but I believe Carlo was taking a final opportunity to look around his old home before moving on fully into the afterlife with Louisa.

CHAPTER 4

THE GUIDING OWLS

One evening in the late spring of 2002 I decided to stay up late to watch a film. For some reason I didn't draw the lounge curtains that evening, which is most unusual for me, preferring instead to leave the large bay window exposed to the night sky. As I waited for the film to start I gazed absently out of the window focusing on the street lamp which was surrounded by tall trees about hundred yards away. The trees were swaying wildly in the wind and the light coming through the branches cast strange mesmerizing, patterns on the road below.

The film began and I watched with interest for some time until my attention was brought back to the window and found myself gazing, trance like, up the street to the moving trees. Hypnotized by the dancing shadows on the road beneath the lamp I became aware of movement and watched in fascination as a large winged creature made its way directly towards our house. Finding it difficult to drag my eyes away I sat rooted to the spot as the silhouette became clearer. It was a huge Snowy Owl the like of which I'd never seen before. Closer and closer the owl flew until it was almost at the window, swooping gracefully low, wings outstretched, I gasped as the most mesmerizing amber coloured eyes gazed straight into my own before performing a daredevil ascent up and over the roof. The experience almost took my breath away, but the look of recognition in those beautiful eyes I knew was something I would never forget.

After this experience I began to have owl dreams that were always about rescuing or protecting someone, although I never discovered whom I was rescuing or protecting. The time was obviously not right for me to understand, but sure enough more guidance was 'winging' its way towards me. Excuse the pun!

A couple of weeks after the above experience with the owl, Rags and I jumped into the car to find a nice quiet place to walk in the countryside. Having driven only a few miles from home I got the most incredible urge to stop the car at the entrance to a grassy lane bearing a public footpath sign. Directly opposite the lane was a very high whitewashed wall surrounding a farm yard, unfortunately the road was too narrow to allow me to park so I drove past. The urge was very strong within me to walk that grassy track and I vowed to myself that I would return another day, on foot, and without Rags.

The following day Harold (who you may remember featured in Volume I) rang to ask if he could visit. Harold had married in New Zealand the previous autumn and was now a full time resident in the Antipodes and was only back for a short stay to sort out loose ends on the Island. Happy to see Harold again, if only briefly, I invited him for coffee and as we sat chatting in the sun-porch he related a dream he'd had the night before.

Harold had dreamt that 'we' had been standing at the entrance to a grassy track which led downhill in the direction of the sea and behind us on the other side of the road had been a high white wall. Excitement rose in my chest as Harold described the very place I'd been compelled to stop the day before, but not sharing that fact with him asked for more details. He told me he had no idea where the place was only a conviction that it must be on the island somewhere, but was certain that he would recognize it if he ever came across it. My whole body was buzzing and asking if he would like spend the afternoon with me I was sure we were about to have another spiritual adventure.

Rags watched dejectedly as she sat on the back of the bay window armchair, her head bowed, sulking, as Harold and I reversed down the drive. Taking the same route as the day before we were soon within one hundred yards of the grassy footpath and rounding a bend in the road a high white wall loomed up ahead of us. As we passed Harold became very excited and confirmed that this was the place he'd dreamt about. Much to his surprise I told him about my experience the day before, admitting to not telling him earlier that day as I had not wanted to influence him in any way.

Harold was as perplexed as I was, but we both knew that for whatever reason we had been guided there, and parking the car where it was safe we made our way on foot back to the public footpath. By the time we reached the top of the track Harold was almost beside himself and kept repeating over and over again that we were visiting the location of his dream.

The track was overgrown and you could see it had not been used for quite some time, probably because of the foot and mouth restrictions the year before. We set off down the sharply inclined grassy lane and in no time at all a vista opened up before us that could not be fully appreciated from the road above. The view from where we stood was stunning as it looked out over 'The Ayres' which cover the northern most tip of the Island. The sea was a gleaming backdrop in the distance, the summer sunshine illuminated everything, and on the far horizon was the clear-cut silhouette of the Mull of Galloway.

Standing next to me, Harold gave an involuntary shudder as he mentioned once again that we were living his dream. Almost simultaneously we both pointed across the field at the bottom of the first hill where an outcrop of trees surrounded what appeared to be the remains of an old cottage. (I must point out at this juncture that I have lived in the north of the island all my life, but had never been on that path or known about that cottage before that very day).

As we reached the bottom of the hill a gate swung open into the field where the old cottage was nestled amongst the trees and glancing knowingly at one another we knew we had to go in. It felt like we were expected, and someone had left the gate open to welcome us. We made our way silently across the field toward the cottage where we entered into the energy of long ago and stood within the crumbling walls.

Harold stood in what had once been the doorway of the old croft and shuddered violently and I knew from working with him in the past that spirit had entered his body. Within moments he informed me that he had a gentleman with him who was waiting for his wife to 'cross over', but she was unable see him.

Harold's words were a catalyst for me as I began to rock gently to and fro becoming aware of a female presence. The sadness and utter grief she was experiencing were unbearable and very real to me and I could feel the ache of empty arms where once a child would have been cradled. Speaking softly to Harold from where I stood rocking, just loud enough so that he could hear me over the sound of the breeze that was playing through the overhanging branches. I shared with Harold that the man's wife was with me, but her grief at losing their only child was keeping her Earth bound preventing her from moving back into spirit.

With that knowledge we set about our work and did what we felt it right to do, which both Harold and I had done on the many occasions we had worked closely together in the past. Soon the atmosphere had lifted and a little breeze sent a shiver rustling through the new green leaves on the trees around us. We were alone again our companions in spirit were gone ... a family reunited after many a long year.

Thinking our work was done we made our way back to the open gate, but as we reached it we were made aware that we had to continue further down the track. Obeying our inward prompt, we strolled on taking in the sights, sounds and scents of the sea, enjoying one another's company. We were almost on the Ayres as the grassy track opened out onto flatter grassland, surrounded by gorse bushes glorious in the sunshine yellow of full bloom and giving off a beautiful coconut scent, the heady wafts of fragrance being carried along on the warm breeze.

Suddenly Harold stopped mid-stride and shivered violently and I knew instantly he was picking up on something as we both became aware of a female energy. Harold was being informed that she had not long passed into spirit after living a long life, but she had come to him to unburden herself.

It transpired that when she was only a schoolgirl she had been taken down this very track by an older man whom she had trusted. We both felt the male essence was a farm hand and a so-called friend of her family, but he had brutally raped her and then threatened to kill her if she ever told anyone. She had been so scared of any repercussions from this man she had lived her whole life in silence and had gone to her grave never having told a soul about her ordeal ... until now. Finally she furnished us with two names, her own and that of the perpetrator of this heinous crime, neither of which it would be wise to print here.

Thanking her for having come to us to share her secret we told her she was now free to move into the 'Light'. No sooner were the words spoken when we were startled by a great commotion in the gorse bushes behind us. Harold and I turning together were amazed and delighted to see a huge owl fly up from behind a gorse bush. Hovering over us for a few moments and holding us with its gaze before ascending into the clear blue heavens, winging away over the hills, and with it went the female presence we had both felt so strongly.

We knew in that moment that our work was finally done so we made our way slowly and contentedly back up the hill towards the main road chatting as we went. Harold commented on how big the owl had been and how unusual it was for an owl to be seen out in the middle of the day, while I shared with him my experience of seeing the beautiful snowy owl some weeks earlier and all the owl dreams I'd had since, expressing that every dream was about protecting and rescuing someone although I was never shown the person I was saving.

Our understanding of the recent events were now complete as it dawned on us why Harold been given his dream and why I had been compelled to visit this particular place the day before. We both laughed and remarked on how magical life was when you allowed spirit to direct you.

From that day to this I have never seen another owl, either in the wild or in my dreams and I must add that I have never felt the need to return to the location of the above events and have never done so.

Footnote

About three years after the above story I was invited by Maggie, a good friend of mine, to speak at a meeting for her meditation group. Telling her that I would be delighted to come along enquiring how long she wanted me to talk for and what would she like me to talk about. Laughing, she replied I could talk for as long as I liked about any of my spiritual experiences. Thanking her for the invitation I told her that I would see her on the night in question and was looking forward to joining in the meditation beforehand.

The day soon arrived, but for some strange reason I had no clue as to which story or what if anything I was going to speak about. I couldn't believe it and I'm sure you, dear reader, can barely believe it either. Even as I walked into the meeting hall that evening with everyone gathered and waiting, my mind was a complete blank. A mental fog had settled like a shroud around my thinking process, but I circulated the room chatting quite happily to this person and that and praying they couldn't see that I was a bag of nerves underneath.

Before long Maggie gathered everyone to their seats to prepare for the meditation to begin. Within seconds of closing my eyes I had completely lost my friend's voice as she led us through what I'm sure was a lovely meditation, if only I could remember it! Completely and utterly absorbed in my own meditation/reverie/vision, whatever you would choose to call it.

I found myself floating above the earth in a shimmering, radiant energy body and from my vantage point, hovering high above the ground I could see Harold and the 'physical me' standing together on the grassy track on 'The Ayres'. The owl with its mighty wings outstretched emerged from the gorse bush just as I became aware of another presence around me which was similar in appearance to my own ... shimmering and radiant. It was none other than the female energy we had released that day on The Ayres and she was sending thoughts filtering into my mind.... giving me permission to tell her story. Thanking her and feeling instant relief course through my body as I understood that this was the moment the 'radiant soul' had been waiting for to reach me. The meditation over I sat peacefully now that I knew what the subject of my talk would be.

When everyone had returned from their meditation they were invited by Maggie to share whatever they had received. One of the ladies in the circle put her hand up and told the group she had no idea what it meant, but an elderly lady had appeared to her in meditation and had given her two names, insisting that she tell the rest of the group as there was someone present who would know who they were. The names she gave were that of the victim and the perpetrator that Harold and I were given in our experience with the owl. That was my cue to stand up and tell her story!

CHAPTER 5

TRAUMA

During the summer of 2002 my mother and stepfather asked me to look after their house and pick up the mail while they took a short holiday. I can almost hear you asking what is so unusual about such a normal request, but the sequence of events which ensued would prove anything but ordinary.

In the months before this request was made of me I had been suffering from a very painful and swollen left forearm, a flare-up from a badly broken arm that had been pinned and plated back in 1989. My arm having been duly x-rayed I had received a follow up appointment with the orthopaedic surgeon where I discovered, much to the glee of the surgeon, that the pins and plates had to be removed as soon as possible as my body was rejecting them. He also explained that he could not promise me full use of my hand or arm after their removal as the original injury had been so extensive that the repair work had been a bit of a jigsaw puzzle. As he shared this information with me I felt a blow to my solar plexus like someone had punched me very hard in the stomach and needless to say left me feeling very uneasy about the forthcoming operation.

As luck would have it my good friend and spiritual teacher, John, was visiting the island the week after my appointment and I shared my anxiety with him. Without touching me he moved his hand over my arm and shoulder, sensing the energy in and around it before announcing with a smile that my arm would be fine and I had no occasion to worry.

The following week I received an official looking letter in a large brown envelope from the hospital inviting me for the planned operation. Reading the contents, I felt the punch to my solar plexus as I read the words 'trauma clinic'. Not able to explain the discomfort I felt within my being any better than that I intrinsically knew something was not right, not right at all.

A few days later, Mum and Henri went off on holiday. They were only going for a week, but Mum, being a bit of a worrier had made me promise I would call in each day to make sure everything was in order.

Letting myself into their home the next day I found a very official looking letter in a large brown envelope addressed to Henri, lying on the doormat. Its appearance was very similar to the one I'd received myself the week before and as I'd been instructed to open anything that looked urgent I tore it open. It was an appointment from Nobles Hospital in Douglas inviting Henri to attend the 'trauma' clinic and as I read the word 'trauma' I felt the now familiar punch to my solar plexus. Almost immediately the thought occurred to me that the trauma clinic was for people suffering from broken bones and as far as I was aware Henri was physically fit and well. Fortunately the appointment was for the week after they returned from holiday so I decided to do nothing about it, reasoning that they would be back in plenty of time to keep the appointment whatever it was for and in essence it was no business of mine.

The day before Mum and Henri were due back I was once again letting myself into their home when a strange feeling of déjà vu swept over me as I spotted another large brown envelope addressed to Henri lying on the doormat. Opening the envelope I discovered it was yet another appointment for the trauma clinic and once more I received the thump in my solar plexus as I read the word trauma.

The following day Mum rang to let me know they were home and to thank me for looking after the house. During the course of our conversation I asked her about the two appointments for Henri and apologizing for being unaware he had suffered some injury, only to find that he had not.

Mum told me, Henri, at a loss to know why he'd been invited to attend the trauma clinic had rung both his doctor and the secretary at the orthopaedic clinic at the hospital only to find that no one had a clue where the appointments had come from! The secretary had remarked quite pointedly that she was the only person to organize and send out appointments for the clinic and she'd not only, never heard of Henri, but the hospital number he had quoted from the letter was fictitious!

Mum finished her tale with a flourish by telling me Henri had tossed the appointments in the bin. Asking me what I thought about such mysterious goings on I didn't share my true feelings with her, but I knew exactly what I thought about this sequence of events. My over-riding feeling was my HS had been trying to warn me not to go through with the proposed operation. The possibility of losing the use of my arm and hand during a process which was undoubtedly going to involve more *'trauma'* for me was very definitely a step too far.

Now that I had figured out the guidance I'd been given all I had to do was trust it and without a second thought I rang the hospital cancelling the operation which was scheduled for the following Monday. As soon as I placed the phone back on the receiver my whole body relaxed and began to unwind, knowing without doubt I'd done the right thing.

This was a decision I'm happy to say I would never regret as almost from the moment I decided to follow my guidance the swelling and inflammation in my arm began to recede until I was completely pain free with a fully functioning arm. I could almost hear John's voice in my ears laughing as he reminded me there'd been no need to worry and of course he'd been absolutely right.

Master Numbers, Keys and Codes

This is a continuation of the previous story, which would turn out to be part of something much bigger. That afternoon, just after I had cancelled the operation my friend Maria rang inviting me to accompany her on a workshop at a local retreat that weekend. The content of the course was not something I was particularly interested in, but I found myself agreeing to attend if there were any places left. A short while later an excited Maria called to tell me she'd secured the last two places on the course and had managed to get us adjoining bedrooms for the weekend.

Caressing my inflamed, but by now not so swollen arm and trusting everything would be alright, I packed an overnight bag for my impromptu weekend away from home thinking as I did so that the retreat was a preferable destination to that of the hospital.

Maria and I arrived at the retreat in high spirits and were shown to our elegant adjoining themed bedrooms each complete with high open beamed ceilings. Maria's room was a pretty floral themed room and mine was a beautifully styled oriental room which I just loved as soon as I walked through the door. After unpacking our belongings we enjoyed a lovely supper where we met the other participants on the course, before Maria and I made our way back across the courtyard and bidding each other goodnight we entered our respective rooms.

I'd been looking forward to spending time in my gorgeous room ever since arriving, just to drink in the beautiful oriental surroundings. A little while later lying in bed trying to read something distracted me, and placing the book down on the bed I stared hard at the ceiling where I thought I'd seen movement, but there was nothing visible. Picking up my book again I resumed reading only to be distracted once more by something high up on the beams, but again when I looked there was nothing there. Deciding I must simply be tired as it was now past midnight I shut my book and laid it back on the bedside table, reminding myself as I did so, that we had an early start in the morning. Switching off the bedside lamp I closed my eyes in readiness for what I expected to be a good night's sleep.

Within minutes my eyes were wide open again as I had the strange and all encompassing feeling of being watched. Scanning the darkened room for some evidence of an onlooker my eyes were once again drawn to the ceiling beams. Then I spotted it. A small sphere of light high up on the cross beam above my bed. Intrigued by the phenomena I watched as it moved back and forth along the length of the beam. Completely entranced I lay silently as it hovered across the beam doing its tightrope act. When I was sure it was conscious energy of some sort I thought I must try and communicate with it and began asking questions to try and illicit who or what it was and what it wanted with me? For quite some time I persisted with my questions, but there was no response, until finally I suggested it leave me alone and let me sleep if it had nothing to say.

To my utter surprise at this juncture the sphere of light slowly descended from the overhead beam taking on a hazy body form that floated down beside my bed! After levitating around the bed 'The form' came to a standstill where it hovered in silence and I knew 'it' was reading my energy field, overwhelming me with a feeling of intent observation. Finally somewhat fed up with the one sided arrangement I reminded the apparently empty room that if whoever was present wasn't going to communicate they could kindly leave and let me get some sleep.

At some point I must have drifted off to sleep, but it was not a restful sleep and I was aware of tossing and turning for most of the night. However, the next morning I was up bright and early, showered and refreshed ready to meet the new day, despite having spent a very disturbed night. Knocking on Maria's door I waited for her to answer and was puzzled by a shuffling sound coming from within when the door slowly opened to reveal the sight of my friend still wearing her night attire. Looking tired and very dishevelled she gave me a bleary eyed look before telling me there had been a presence up in the beams and floating around her bed all night and she'd hardly had a wink of sleep!

Little did we know it then, but we were about to share another groundbreaking experience, for us at least. I firmly believe the visitation we both experienced that night was a precursor for what was to happen next in our lives, being part of our combined spiritual journey and the expansion of our consciousness.

Late on Sunday afternoon after having had a wonderful weekend we rather sadly packed our belongings into the boot of Maria's car ready to make the short journey home. We made our way down to the end of the long driveway where it meets the main road and waited as a car sped past, both commenting on the unusual number plate (777) on the speeding car, agreeing that neither of us had ever seen a triple number plate before. Minutes later Maria dropped me off at home after arranging to meet for lunch the following week in Peel.

The very next day a car cut in front of me in a dangerous place and cursing out loud as it sped away I noticed its number plate was 222. The day after that I was looking for a parking space when a car pulled out in front of me and my attention was drawn to the number plate, it was 555. The day after that I passed a car broken down at the side of the road, its number plate was 666! Knowing and sensing some internal shift taking place within me when my attention was deliberately drawn towards these triple sequences, but unfortunately I did not understand what was happening as I'd certainly never noticed these number sequences before, but now they seemed to be everywhere.

As arranged Maria and I met at a little tea shop in Peel the following week. For anyone who does not know Peel it is a pretty little fishing port on the West coast of the island and is famous for its ancient castle, new marina, and its beautiful sandy beach. We were shown to our table which looked out onto the promenade and were both excited to recall our events of the past week and for both of us they had an amazingly familiar theme. As we finished telling each other our similar stories and the high incidence of triple numbered car registrations our confirmation sailed past the window in the shape of car bearing the registration 333. We laughed out loud, but on another level we both knew there was something more significant going on.

Whilst driving home that day I sent a request to my HS asking for more information on all the triple numbers Maria and I were experiencing and a plea to understand the significance of the sightings. Having sent the question out there all I had to do was be patient and wait for my HS to reply, expecting the number sequences would stop now that I had asked for clarity. How wrong I was! They continued unabated, only now as well as car number plates there were same number sequences coming up on television adverts, in magazines, phone numbers on business cards etc. etc.

Approximately three months after asking the question the answer finally materialized when I received my new copy of Paradigm Shift, a spiritual magazine to which I subscribed. Ripping of the polythene cover and opening the magazine at random the article on the page leapt out at me, 'Numerology and Master Numbers'. Feeling a surge of energy travel through my body I had a strong feeling my answer may well have just arrived.

According to the article these 'Master Number Sequences' were now coming into the consciousness of humanity and many people around the world were becoming aware of them. Every time our attention is drawn to see these number sequences they act as a catalyst, unlocking keys and codes held within our energy body or blueprint for this life. In conclusion it maintained that this would only happen when our codes are ready to be triggered. Included below the main article was an interpretation of the sequences of numbers from 000 through to 999, in way of explanation as to what each number sequence meant to you, if you saw it. The article also pointed to the fact that as the new millennium progressed four digit Master Number Sequences would follow, for example, 1111, 2222, 3333 etc.

Throughout the entire reading of this article my HS had been sending ever stronger ripples of energy through my body confirming the truth of what my eyes were reading. Sighing deeply and thanking spirit for answering the question I'd asked three months before I finally understood the internal shift I'd felt when first noticing these number sequences.

As I write, it is now 2015 and this prophecy has already come about as I have been witnessing four-digit number sequences for almost five years now.

CHAPTER 6

THE CLEATOR CLAN

Isobel
Many years ago at the beginning of my conscious spiritual awakening I had the following experience which would turn into a very long and convoluted story with many parts woven together. As you read this tapestry of events I hope it will all make sense to you.

Arriving home one day after walking Rags I felt a strong compulsion to immediately leave the house again. So strong in fact I could not ignore it, and also knowing that I must go alone, much to the puzzlement of Dickie who thought I was crazy.

Driving very speedily towards the coast I knew without doubt I was heading towards my favourite beach at Andreas where I had spent many happy times in my childhood. Thinking my motivation was to watch the sunset and knowing that it had to be from that particular beach. Minutes later I was careering down hill through the twisting 'S' bends that lead onto the car park. Having parked the car I was about to get out when into my mind's eye appeared the vision of an old fashioned bicycle rolling down the hill toward me. Suddenly and without warning I became aware that the person I'd imagined sailing along on that old fashioned bicycle was now sitting beside me in the passenger seat!

The strangest sensation and stillness enveloped me as I became aware of a young woman of about twenty-five years old. Her dress was old fashioned and to my mind, turn of the last century, somewhere between 1890 and 1920s. A bit vague I know, but history was never my strong point. She wore a long tweed skirt and short jacket topped with a straw hat and brown lace up shoes. So real was this experience I could sense as well as feel the rough tweed of her skirt beneath my fingers.

Sitting there for some time in a state of neither, reality or unreality, I was beginning to wonder if the situation was a figment of my imagination when suddenly a name popped into my head. My companion it seemed was an Isobel Cleator. Feeling a little bit freaked and telling myself I was making it all up I decided it was time to go home. As soon as this thought entered my head Isobel disappeared, taking any thoughts I'd had of watching the sunset with her and leaving me convinced I'd imagined the whole episode.

On a beautiful calm evening a few weeks later I was once again compelled to make the same journey, only this time I found myself walking down onto the deserted beach, the shingle, dried seaweed and broken shells crunching beneath my feet. Sitting down on a stretch of sand above the high tide line I hugged my knees and gazed out onto the tranquil waters and watched peacefully as the sun slowly set in the West, my mind wandering to happy thoughts of childhood days spent on this very beach with my family and friends.

Suddenly the atmosphere around me changed, along with the feeling that I was no longer alone, and once more I found myself in the company of Isobel. This time I decided it would be different and I would not frighten her away by denying her presence, instead I would try asking her a question through my mind. Querying why she had appeared to me again I was surprised to learn that she loved this place as much as I did and it was our shared love and appreciation that had created our connection and deemed that we should meet.

Isobel's thoughts continued like a stream running through my mind and I learned that her mother had passed away when she was only young leaving her at home to look after the house and the needs of her father, but whenever she'd had some free time she'd made her way to this beach to walk and think and be close to nature just as I did.

Isobel's thoughts intimated there was more to our story and my connection with the name Cleator, and that this meeting with her was just to be a 'stepping stone' on my path. I have to confess at that point in my spiritual understanding I was not sure about any connection between myself and Isobel, but I had to agree with her about the love I felt for this beach and the surrounding area.

All very intriguing I thought to myself as the dialogue between us faded and Isobel vanished from my senses. The cocoon-like stillness that had surrounded us during the above exchange had now disappeared and I became acutely aware of the sounds of nature all around me. It was just as if someone had released the freeze frame and mute button on a remote control and everything had instantly come back to life. The sound of the sea lapping gently on the sand a few feet away from where I sat and the haunting cries of a few lonely sea-gulls as they made their final skim of the day over the calm waters was almost deafening. The sun had almost set, and the last remnants of the golden orb were now sliding slowly into the watery horizon casting a shimmering veil of gold across the Irish Sea.

Sending my thanks out to Isobel wherever in the ethers she was I made my way back to the car. Stopping briefly to look back over the beach I was completely overawed by the most glorious sunset as the clouds were now streaked in beautiful shades of red, purple, peach and gold. Sighing appreciatively I took in the breathtaking sight and thought about my exchange with Isobel, my eyes gazing out toward the horizon then heavenward. But wait ... was it my imagination or were my eyes playing tricks on me? The cloud formations appeared to be in the shape of angels! Was this a confirmation perhaps of my meeting with Isobel?

In reality it took quite some years for this story to fully unfold as many other threads were to be woven into this tapestry.

John Henry Cleator

In the summer of 2003, quite a number of years after the above events I was in a phone conversation with my aunt from New Zealand. During our conversation she told me that her god-daughter was to be married at Andreas Church in a few weeks time, but unfortunately she and my uncle could not attend. Offering to present the couple with a horseshoe on the 'big day' as a gesture from them she was thrilled and told me to take in every detail of the wedding dress to relay to her next time we spoke.

Just a few days later I visited an old friend who lives in Andreas Village. We were enjoying a cup of coffee and catching up with events in our lives when her husband arrived home from work, just at the moment I was telling her that Dickie had enrolled on a course to learn Manx Gaelic. Her husband left the room, returning a few moments later with a small, very old booklet in his hands. Offering me the book he assured me that Dickie and I would find it interesting, although he was anxious to have it returned when we'd had a chance to read it. Explaining to me he had acquired the book when clearing his father's house some months earlier after the old man had passed away and for some strange reason he had felt compelled to keep it. I looked down at the tattered old book in my hands, the title of which was simply 'Manx Yarns' by John Henry Cleator known as Juan Noa, someone who until that very moment I'd never heard of before.

The booklet went home with me, and Dickie and I both enjoyed the tales it contained which were written like poetry in a kind of old Manx slang. Propping it up on the lounge unit after reading it where I thought it would be easily seen and returned to my friend. Even though it was right in front of me it somehow became invisible or at the very least was exerting some hidden desire to remain in my possession, despite my best intentions to return it to its rightful owner.

The day after reading the booklet I was chatting to my mother when our topic of conversation prompted her to recite a poem, as she is often does. These recitations are memories from her schooldays more than eighty years ago and we often laugh about the fact she can remember reams of poetry learned decades ago, but she can't always tell you what she'd eaten for dinner. Gasping in astonishment, I recognized the words she was reciting were from the little booklet of Manx Yarns! On enquiring where she'd come across the poem and if she knew who'd written it I was disappointed to find that her memory only stretched as far as the surmise that it came from her childhood, but once more I felt the guidance of spirit as yet another synchronicity was not lost on me.

Some weeks later I found myself standing alone by the war memorial in the church grounds at Andreas, horseshoe in hand, neatly labeled with my aunt and uncles names on ready to present to the happy couple after they had taken their marriage vows. The small wedding party arrived, only a handful of people, the bride and her father arriving in an open horse-drawn carriage. I was given a few odd looks from the family as I didn't recognize any of them any more than they knew me. According to my aunt the young couple had met and fallen in love in Africa where the groom was a vicar and the bride a missionary worker and even though the prospective bride had lived most of her life in Liverpool she was insistent they return to the Isle of Man so she could marry in the church she had been baptized in, which was of course Andreas.

Waiting patiently outside in the sunshine while the service took place I was eventually rewarded by the sight of the newly weds, but instead of getting back into the waiting carriage they made their way into the old graveyard. Intrigued, I watched from my position by the war memorial as the bride bent down and laid her bouquet on a nearby grave.

As the happy couple returned to the front gates I was waiting to meet them although they looked at me uncomprehendingly, after all I was a total stranger to them at this small, very tightly knit family gathering. Stepping forward and smiling I introduced myself as I handed her the horseshoe and explained the gift was from my aunt and uncle in New Zealand. Thanking me, the bride remarked that it had made her day and a deep sigh of joy escaped me as I made my way back to the car.

Arriving home after the wedding the first thing I noticed was the booklet of Manx Yarns still gathering dust on the lounge unit where I had placed it weeks before. Swearing silently under my breath for being so forgetful, especially when I'd just been in Andreas for another purpose, I decided to take it straight back before I forgot it again. Minutes later as I drove past the first entrance to the church a thought dropped into my head along with a knowing that I had to return to the churchyard. Indicating and turning into the second entrance to the church I parked the car against the outer wall of the old graveyard, not entirely sure of why I was there for the second time that day.

As I got out of the car I was compelled to pick up the old booklet from the passenger seat before making my way into the graveyard. The heavy latch on the ancient, wrought iron gate clanged noisily as it shut behind me making me wince as I stepped onto the pathway that led between the graves, wondering where the bride had placed her bouquet. Halfway down the path I spotted the bouquet lying on an old grave and kneeling down to read the name on the headstone recognized it immediately as the name my aunt had mentioned. It was obviously her grand-parents grave and this was her link with the little village of Andreas. My curiosity was now satisfied or so I thought and I made my way back to the gravel path, but instead of turning back towards the gate my feet chose to lead me further down the path between the graves. Walking slowly forward almost trance-like until I reached the boundary wall of the churchyard where I made an about turn to face back towards the church. At that precise moment the sun came out from behind the clouds and shone onto a headstone directly in front of me making sure I would not miss the inscription.

In loving memory of
Hilda May
Beloved wife of
John Henry Cleator
Who died July 7th 1943
Aged 62 years
Also
Cyril Vondy
Beloved son of the above
Who died in infancy
Marish y Chiarn son dy Bragh
Also
John Henry Cleator
'Juan Noa'
Poet, Playwright and Faithful Manxman
Beloved husband of the above
Who died January 2nd 1963
Aged 85 years
Son ver eh Currym da e Ainleyn Harryd

Marish y chiarn son dy bragh ......With 'The Lord' Forever
Son ver eh Currym da e Ainleyn Harryd .... For He shall give His
Angels charge over Thee

Note: Special thanks must go to my good friend Janet for translating the above Manx into English.

Staring in astonishment I realized this was not just any old grave, but that of the person whose booklet I held in my hand! It was none other than Juan Noa's resting place!

Surveying the headstone I noticed that when new it must have been sculpted from white marble, but through the passage of time was now weathered and covered in verdigris. To the left of the inscription carved into the marble was the image of a serene and beneficent looking angel, clothed in flowing gown, holding a wreath of flowers with a star shining brightly above her head radiating heavenly light down over the occupants of the grave.

I cannot adequately describe the thoughts, feelings and sensations that were running through my mind and body at that moment because if someone had asked me to find the grave of John Henry Cleator aka Juan Noa, I would not have known where to begin my search. Without doubt my footsteps had been guided and I'd been led to the very place where his mortal remains now lay, but not only that I noticed another connection because Juan Noa's wife had died on my birth date a handful of years before I was born.

Silently I stood beside his grave and asked the question why I had been brought here and soon thoughts filtered through my mind and were shared with my own;

Juan Noa: "My dearest child, you were led to my grave with the help of your guide and we will lead you to many more places of revelation until all becomes clear."

Linda: "What connection do we have?"

Juan Noa: "You love nature and the simple things in life as I did when I lived upon the Earth plane. We resonate ... we are in harmony ... we are 'One' and always have been. My work touches you because it is about gentler days gone by, full of fun and companionship, the simple pleasures of life that you wish for deep in your heart to return to the Earth. All is well my child, but there is much more to this story about the name Cleator and your connections with it. For your part, keep an open heart and an open mind and allow yourself to be guided."

The flow of dialogue dissolved in my mind and miraculously I was freed from the spot where I had been standing throughout this experience and was able, if not a little shakily, to get back to the car.

You may remember in Volume I, Eleanor's Story (chapter 22) that her name was also Cleator, as was Isobel's, which was much earlier in my journey and intriguingly she had given me a similar message to that of Juan Noa.

Millie

Things did not however move very quickly in the unfolding of the Cleator saga and I had to wait some years before the next installment, when once again I was compelled to walk another little road. This road is not far from where I now live, in an area where my ancestors, in this life, have lived for generations.

Never having been drawn to walk this particular little road before, it being very narrow indeed, I parked the car as tightly as I could to the hedge so as not to obstruct other road users. Rags jumped out raring to go, sniffing all the new scents and aromas, without a doubt she was in doggy heaven. Strolling along the road that sunny day feeling quite elated because I was exploring somewhere new, but on another level *knowing* this was exactly where I had to be on that day.

Rounding a corner about a third of the way along the road suddenly into my mind's eye appeared the vision of a young woman hurrying towards me, dressed in what appeared to be her Sunday best, although her clothes were very outmoded and the vision lasted no more than a few seconds.

The next day I felt compelled to return to the little road and once more I encountered the vision of the same young woman walking briskly along the area of lane I'd seen her the day before. Deciding that on this occasion it couldn't possibly be my imagination I asked her name and soon became aware of other thoughts mingling with my own.

The name Millie dropped into my senses with the information

that she was on her way home after attending a prayer meeting in the meadows held by a Mr. John Wesley. She was hurrying to return to her place of employment because she did not wish to enrage her master as there was much work to be done even on a Sunday. Asking Millie whereabouts she worked to my surprise the instant 'reply' was Ballacleator, a large farm house nearby that had been owned by my aunt and uncle and was where my beloved grandmother (Nana) had passed away in 1977!

The exchange between us now apparently over Millie disappeared from my senses. Going over in my mind what I'd just been 'told' I thought it very strange that a prayer meeting should be held in the meadows although I was gratified to realize that I'd been correct the previous day when I had assumed she was wearing her Sunday best clothes, but what about the revelation of her working at BallaCleator? Questioning, I asked myself, 'Could that be true or had I made that part up?'

The following day I was compelled to return yet again and found Millie hurrying towards me in the usual place. On this occasion I asked her where precisely the prayer meetings were held and in my minds eye I could 'see' Millie pointing down a grassy track opposite to where we were standing her thoughts informing me that Mr. Wesley held his meetings down that lane and across the meadow.

Knowing very little about John Wesley and the significance of his life and his connection with the Isle of Man my spiritual guidance was not prepared to let my lack of knowledge hold me back. Visiting my friend Rosemary a few days later, out of the blue, she plucked a little book from her bookshelf and asked would I like to borrow it. Rosemary is well aware I am very proud of my Manx heritage and proceeded to tell me that the book she was offering me had been written by a well known local character, now deceased. She explained that the author had collected a plethora of stories and knowledge about the history and local characters from the north of the island, during the last century, concluding that she felt an overwhelming desire to lend it to me.

That night I opened the book at random and to my amazement discovered the page was about the time John Wesley had visited the island and held prayer meetings in the countryside, even mentioning the vicinity of where I kept meeting Millie. What a wonderful confirmation because on a conscious level I'd known absolutely nothing about this period until I read the book my friend had been compelled to lend me.

A few days later once more I was urged to walk Rags on the little road. Strolling along in the warm afternoon sunshine I was deep in thought about the events of the past few days, while Rags, no doubt, was pondering on whether she would catch scent and sight of some bunnies to chase. We were almost at the place on the road where I expected Millie to appear when I heard a car approaching. Stepping onto the grass verge the car pulled up alongside me and to my surprise the driver turned out to be an old friend whom I had not encountered for a number of years. Sitting beside my friend in the passenger seat was an elderly gentleman dressed in tatty navy overalls and wearing a flat cap like some old farmer and although I didn't recognize the gentleman I was transfixed by his gaze and he apparently by mine. Speaking across my friend, who I have to say, gave us both very funny looks as the conversation progressed the old gent, in a slow Manx drawl, and with no prompting from me launched into a story about the ghosts he had encountered on this particular road!

When he had finally told his tale I asked if he knew anything about John Wesley's alleged prayer meetings which were reported to have been held in the meadows. Not quite believing my 'luck' I learnt that he actually grazed his sheep on the meadow where Wesley had preached. My friend was by now totally freaked out by what the old gent and I were discussing so I didn't take the conversation any further that day apart from asking the old man where I might find him if I ever needed to.

The very next day I sought the old gent out and found him tinkering with some ancient farm machinery in an old barn just up the road from where we had met the day before. Knowing that I would need his help because it would have been very foolish of me to go into the meadows unaccompanied as the land and the lane down which we had to traverse was private with a very ominous **Trespassers _will_ be Prosecuted** sign.

After a very friendly Manx grilling to find out who my family were and to establish if I was worth his time and effort, the old boy soon realized he knew most of the older generation and was not only happy to chat and accept me, but also the bar of chocolate I'd brought with me!

Ever since I'd known I would be visiting the meadows I'd felt very strongly that my friend Janet should come along and was very pleased when the old gent happily agreed to guide both of us to the exact spot where Wesley had preached and where Millie had been part of his congregation.

A couple of days later Janet and I met the old gent as arranged and he led us down the private lane past the ominous sign in the direction of a derelict cottage. The old man launched into a story from his youth as we walked telling us about the last occupants of the humble dwelling who all appeared to have met with very unpleasant ends! Continuing past the ruins we crossed an open field and into the meadow beyond where great clumps of marram grass made walking very difficult. Halfway across the meadow my car keys fell out of my pocket and hearing them drop I stooped to forage for them in the long grass, but just at that moment the old gent stopped dead in his tracks and pointed to an old hawthorn tree sitting atop a little mound on the far side of the meadow.

"That's the place Wesley preached," he said, pointing his gnarled finger in the direction of the mound before beating the hastiest retreat his old wellington booted feet would allow. It was almost as if dropping my keys had been a signal for him, letting him know he could accompany us no further on this adventure and that his part had been played.

This was to be an experience for just myself and Janet and as we made our way over to the mound my eyes were drawn upwards to gaze lovingly at Barrule the largest of the northern Manx hills standing so proud in the distance, etched against a clear blue sky. The thoughts that filled my mind in that moment was how much I loved my island home in any weather and all its moods.

Having reached the mound Janet and I closed our eyes and entered into our own sacred spaces. The gentle breeze wafted the fresh scent of the meadow over my face and through my hair as it seemed to enter every part of my being, renewing and refreshing me from inside out. Meditating for some time we blended our thoughts with the energy of those who had come to listen to John Wesley preach from this very spot all those years ago, including my enigmatic friend Millie. It was a beautiful experience and one I'm sure I would not have been allowed to miss.

After this experience I no longer met Millie on my walks and thought the whole episode was over and laid to rest, but I was to be proved very wrong as almost seven years after the above events I found myself standing in for my friend Elaine who was then the housekeeper at Ballacleator.

On my first day working there I had the overwhelming sense of being brought back to this house by Nana's presence, just the same as I'd felt when Elaine had got the job seven years before. Now for the first time in almost thirty years since my beloved Nana had passed away in this house I once again stood within its walls and I can tell you it was a very strange feeling.

That night I dreamt about Millie whom I'd not really given any thought to over the intervening years, but there she was as vivid in my dream as she had been when she first showed up in my consciousness seven years earlier.

In the dream she showed me her bedroom at Ballacleator which was one of the attic rooms on the third floor. It was very drab and drear, sparsely furnished, cold and not very welcoming. Millie appeared to have had nothing much of any value in her life, no treasured possessions of any kind, except for a home made cross crafted from straw, which lay on her pillow.

On waking the next morning I knew there was more to this dream, but as is often with dreams I just couldn't bring it to mind. The following day I made my way to Ballacleator with a strange sense of knowing that at some point during the morning I would have to visit the attic room Millie had shown me in the dream. The opportunity arose later in the morning when the owners left the house to go shopping and waiting a few minutes after their departure I slowly made my way up the three flights of stairs that led to the attic rooms. My heart beating madly in my chest with every step I took as on a conscious level I had no understanding of why I was doing this other than out of curiosity. Reaching the top landing I tiptoed towards what I believed to have been Millie's room many years previously and placing my hand on the latch with my heart in my mouth, I slowly opened the door and entered the small musty smelling room festooned in cobwebs.

A single bed covered in an old-fashioned bed-spread was pushed into the corner of the room and next to it stood an old wooden chair. The room, it was clear, had not been occupied for many a long year and was not too different in its appearance to the room in my dream. Suddenly, Millie was there in my minds eye, smiling in welcome and 'telling' me she had brought me to this place to help me understand who she was and what she meant to me.

Standing on the threshold of Millie's room I closed my eyes and allowed her thoughts to filter into my mind. They were not nice thoughts as they were of beatings and abuse and I winced not wanting to 'see' what I was 'feeling' as Millie showed me her life. The hard work, the beatings and the abuse that she had endured, but at the same time I was feeling the dignified silence she had maintained throughout a life that had been cowed into submission. Her faith had helped her through a very hard life and I knew then that those prayer meetings in the meadows with Mr. Wesley must have been a little 'light' in her darkness.

A resonant shiver ran through my being as I stood on the threshold of what had once been Millie's room and in one blinding flash of knowing all the forgotten information from my dream returned. A moment of illumination was upon me as I realized that I was Millie and Millie was me or to be more precise Millie was a part of me. Finally, after a number of years I had received confirmation on another part of my life and journey.

Thank you to Millie and Nana for having guided me to return to this house that meant so much to us both for very different reasons because it had been the place of Nana's transition back into Spirit, but had been a place of enlightenment for me.

I would like to dedicate the following poem to Millie and her religious belief, which no doubt helped her through this physical life.

THE TAPESTRY

Candles burning brightly from a sconce upon a wall
Illuminate a tapestry hanging in a hall,
Each thread is interwoven with tender loving care
All the colours of the rainbow, each and every one is there.
The picture tells a story of a Soul born to this world,
The journey He had chosen, here in stitches is unfurled.

*

A babe nestled in a manger, a bright and shining star,
Three wise men come bearing gifts, having travelled from afar.
A youth with distant memories of some elusive goal,
And then a man full grown, remembering his role,
To love and to respect all life upon our Mother Earth,
This is what He promised before coming here at birth.

*

His wisdom came so easily from His blending with 'The Source'
To live and love without condition could be His only course.
Some felt a deep connection to this kind and beautiful Soul,
And after speaking with Him,
Began the search to make their lives more whole,
He shared His love with all He met along life's rugged path,
But some He met were cruel men, filled with fear and wrath,

*

His life it was not wasted, His message stays the same,
Now it's the time for us to continue in His name.
Each one of us has a tapestry, in the process of creating,
Just take a look inside your heart and see what you are making.
What colours do you see? What visions does it hold?
Is it the life you want to live and in your heart enfold?

If the answer's 'No' dear friend, it may be time to live life differently,
"But how can I make the changes to become the person I want to be?"
Fill your heart with Love until it's so full it overflows,
This is by far the best way to help your Soul to grow.
It won't be long before you see the world's a different place,
Your Love shines out and touches others you will see it in their face.

*

And when life is almost over and you feel you've played your part,
It's time to look inside once more and view the tapestry held within *your* heart
Is each thread interwoven with tender loving care?
Are all the colours of the rainbow to be found in there?
When you've asked yourself these questions, become quiet and very still,
And listen to the answers that come at your own will.

*

Candles burning brightly from a sconce upon my wall,
Illuminate my tapestry hanging in my hall,
Each thread I've interwoven with tender loving care,
Every colour of the rainbow I have lived and hand stitched there,
My tapestry is finished and held within my heart,
Now I can say,
"I am ... the very proud owner of a priceless work of art!"

*

CHAPTER 7

THE OLD POST OFFICE

As I mentioned in the introduction, not long after leaving The 4th Dimension in 2001 a lot of guidance had come my way about opening a spiritual library which you may remember I declined. Politely and rather enigmatically I was informed by spirit that when the time was right I would fulfill that particular guidance as it would be an important experience and very much a part of my journey.

It was now the summer of 2003, and ever since the turn of the year I had been experiencing a deep feeling of restlessness, knowing, without being told, that our time at our present home was coming to an end. As the year progressed the feelings became stronger with each day that passed, although I had mentioned this to no-one. My husband was unlikely under any circumstances to leave the house he loved and had worked so hard on over the past 22 years, let alone leave his beloved garage, knowing the only way he was likely to be parted from it was if he was dragged out kicking and screaming! Being a motorcycle enthusiast he had arranged his private work space perfectly for his needs and it would often be full of his motorbike mad friends tinkering and exchanging words of advice on engines, clutches, pistons and such like.

One day that summer I was in Andreas walking Rags when a sugar low hit me and I found myself entering the newly extended shop for what I thought was a bar of chocolate. After choosing my chocolate and browsing around the newly refurbished shop, I eventually made my way to the counter where the shopkeeper was waiting. Without thought or hesitation I promptly asked him what he was planning to do with the now empty original premises. Asking me if I was looking for premises to rent, rather bemusedly, I told him that I thought I might be, but in actuality until that very moment I'd not consciously been thinking about acquiring a location for anything!

The shop keeper took my rather vacant expression in his stride and explained the old shop was not available, but went on to say the now defunct Post Office at the top end of the village was vacant and had been for a couple of years and would that be of any use as he knew the woman who owned it. Not really knowing at that point what I had in mind I nodded my acceptance and left with not only my bar of chocolate, but also a scrap of paper containing a scribbled telephone number.

Within minutes I found myself sitting outside the old cottage that until a couple of years earlier had housed the post office in what had once been the downstairs parlour. On arriving home the first thing I did was to call the scribbled number to enquire if the property was to let and finding that it was I made arrangements with the owner to meet her there the following day. It seemed 'my' mind was made up, although I'm not sure by whom!

Pulling up outside the old post office the lady owner was already standing at the door waiting for me. Smiling, she shook my hand and after a few exchanged pleasantries she proceeded to unlock the outer door that opened into a tiny entrance porch. A strong smell of damp assaulted my nostrils as the door opened, but that was nothing compared to the odour that greeted me as the inner doors were thrown open. Entering a small oddly shaped room the aroma was so powerful it was like being hit by a nauseating tidal wave, both overwhelming and eye-watering.

The room I found myself standing in was far from ideal for any project you could think of, let alone a library. The ceiling was covered in ancient peeling lime-wash and festooned with cobwebs dating back into antiquity, while the plaster on the walls was damp and crumbling. Beneath my feet the floor was covered in ripped and tattered linoleum that bore the tell tale signs of mice, and maybe bigger rodents, who had been running in and out through a gap under the board which served as a division between this room and the room next door. The smell of rodent urine and droppings added to the overall aroma of putrefaction and I'm sure from this description you can almost smell it too! All in all the poor old post office was in a very sorry state of disrepair, the only obvious reminder of its former life was an ancient safe bolted to the floor in the far corner, just like something from a 'Wells Fargo' stage-coach office, if you were given to watching old black and white westerns.

Trying to assess what would have to be done to make the place usable I decided an ancient counter that had once been used for the post office would have to be ripped out and a new wall erected to separate this room from the little room next door which was already rented out and used to store animal feed. The place didn't even have a toilet as the door to the rest of the cottage had been boarded up years ago. If I were to rent this room I would have to make very good friends with the landlord at the public house nearby, just to use their conveniences.

Inside my head I could hear my voice screaming at me to get out and never come back, but even though that voice was screaming very loudly another part of me knew that this was where I had to be. My mind was doing somersaults when I became aware of the lady speaking to me, asking me if the room would be suitable for my needs and I could scarcely believe it was me speaking when I told her that it would be perfect!

The owner then asked what plans I had for the little room and I told it was to house a spiritual library. Rather pleased at this idea and assuming it to be a Christian library she confided in me that she was a Methodist lay preacher! Stammering, as I could envisage a problem arising, I crossed my fingers behind my back and admitted that the books I intended to keep were not only about Christian belief, but about the many different pathways to finding God/ 'The Creator'/ 'All That Is'/ 'Faith' and uncovering our true selves in the process. Continuing my discourse, I asked if what I sought to share with others wasn't pretty much a similar message to the one she was sharing with her congregation and to my amazement she agreed.

Having obviously made up her mind that I was a 'sure bet' she told me she would be willing to rent me the room on a monthly basis, at a nominal rent, on the condition that I was to refurbish it at my own expense. Dumbfounded at my response, I found myself agreeing to the terms she had set down before telling her rather brazenly that I would not need the premises until the following spring?

Stepping outside into the July sunshine we stopped to admire the view as it opened out over farmland towards Andreas Church. From where I stood I could almost pinpoint the location of my father's grave and feeling a tingle run down my spine I acknowledged the presence of my Higher Self and with it came the realization of being guided.

During a regression, some years before the above events, I'd been taken back to before I was born into this particular life and found myself in a place of beautiful light where I met with a radiant soul who introduced himself as my prospective father. Agreeing to come into this life as his daughter he informed me that he would pass back into Spirit whilst I was only a child, although he would continue to guide me from 'The Higher Planes of Light' helping me to experience the lessons I had chosen before arriving here as Linda.
(The information in the above paragraph was given to me before I came to understand that we choose our lives, our earthly family members, and also our destiny… the good and the bad experiences of life, before we are born. This came as a great surprise to me when I channeled the above as it was not part of my conceptual thinking or understanding at the time.)

My soon to be new landlady was quite happy to stand chatting in the summer sunshine and asked me questions about my family background … a very Manx trait. Unbelievably, it turned out she knew my mother and I also discovered that she was the last person to have seen my father alive almost 50 years before as she had been visiting her husband who had occupied the bed next to my father on the night he passed away.

So that was that, it seemed I was going to run a library, but not until the following spring by all accounts. It appeared the information I'd been given by spirit after leaving my little shop was coming true.

Destiny beckons

Arriving home that day my head was full of questions and buzzing with excitement about this new venture, but at the same time wondering how all of the above would work out. Opening the door I picked up the mail from the doormat and gave an involuntary shudder as I crossed the threshold as once more I acknowledged the overwhelming sense that it was time to move. Dropping onto the sofa I thumbed absentmindedly through the mail in my hand deciding to open a large white envelope first only to discover it was a flyer advertising a lecture on Numerology at the local retreat. Numerology is the science of numbers, a subject that I was by this point on my journey very interested in. The lecturer for the evening was a well known spiritual teacher whom I held in high regard having already met her on a number occasions, and after reading the flyer I just knew I must attend.

Around thirty people turned up on the evening in question all anxious to hear what the eminent lecturer had to share with us on the subject of Numerology. We were each given a jotter pad and pen and told that the first thing we would be doing was working out our Destiny number. To calculate your Destiny number we had to add up the day, month and year of our birth then reduce it down to a single number the exception being when it all added to 11, 22 or 33 which are Master Numbers.

Quickly scribbling down my calculations, excitedly I discovered my Destiny number was 33, one of the Master Numbers. When everyone had undertaken their calculations our speaker asked who in the room had a birth number of Number 1. Two or three people put their hands up and she proceeded to tell them what their destiny number meant to them. Moving on to number 2 and number 3 and so on until we got to number 6, which of course was my birth number when reduced to a single digit.

Only myself and one other gentleman seated at the very back of the room put our hands up. The speaker then enquired if either of our dates had added up to a 33 before we had reduced it to number 6. Looking over my shoulder toward the gentleman at the back of the room I could see he was shaking his head, which only left me with my hand in the air. Focusing all her attention on me, sitting in the fourth row, she went into what could only be described as channeling mode. The information that came through her told me I had come to help anchor the Christ consciousness on Earth at this special time in history and that Jesus or Sananda as he is known on the inner planes of Light was working closely with me on this vibration. She also told me that I was a spiritual teacher holding the vibration of 33 and if I did not follow the guidance I was given I would spend my life as a Number 6. For those unaware of the destiny of number 6 please let me explain... A number 6 is a caring nurturing person who continually does things for other people while their own aspirations are forever on hold!

By now those people sitting in the first three rows had turned around in their seats to view the focus of the lecturer's intense channeling. Sliding down on my chair in an effort to escape the gaze of those gathered around me I could feel my face burning. However, the overwhelming feeling I had was being booted up the backside by my Higher Self as the message was loud and clear.

Spirit could not have picked a more public way of telling me to 'pull my finger out' and get on with what they wanted me to do. Knowing in my heart that it could be no-one else's decision other than my own to follow the guidance I'd been given to open a spiritual library... or to let it all go.

CHAPTER 8

THE ARRIVAL OF DANIEL and OUR NEW HOME

The week after viewing 'The Old Post Office' the feelings I'd been experiencing about needing to move house intensified. On a conscious level I told myself the girls were grown up and had left home and the house was really too big for our needs. Although, there was some deeper knowledge or feeling going on underneath my thoughts that was making me feel this way, but I just couldn't put it into words.

Feeling so unsettled within myself I decided it was time for a bit of Eva's beloved Feng Shui or space clearing, in the hope that sorting out my wardrobe and drawers would have a positive effect on me. During the process I came across a set of guided meditation tapes that I didn't recognize and had no idea how I had come by them. The tapes purported to teach you how to connect with your guide, access the mental planes and request and manifest the things you required in life.

Intrigued, feeling like a child who has just found an unopened Christmas present that's been lost under the bed for months I couldn't wait to try them out. Making my way to our little south facing sun porch and the tape player all thoughts of clearing up the mess I'd made and continuing my attempts at Feng Shui were gone from my mind.

Listening through headphones and following the visualization on the first tape I was delighted to find myself enveloped in the most beautiful energy. The next day I listened to the tape again and once more I felt the same beautiful energy envelope me. Sitting quietly afterwards I asked to be given a name for the energy that had surrounded me on both occasions and moments after asking the name

Daniel dropped into my mind. Picking up my angel cards I asked for confirmation before plucking a card 'randomly' from the pack and turning it over two beautiful blue eyes stared back at me from the most serene face and the name on the card was Daniel!

The next day I sat in silence to listen to tape number two which contained the manifestation exercise and sending my thoughts up into the mental grid as I was prompted to do I asked my new guide, Daniel, to accompany me. Speaking aloud I told spirit if it was for my highest good I would like to request a two bed-roomed bungalow with views over the open fields situated on the outskirts of Andreas.

A picture of what I'd just requested formed fuzzily in my mind and knowing in my heart exactly what I wanted I released both the request and the vision into the ethers.

Two days later I was about to leave Ramsey after a shopping trip when I remembered I needed a newspaper for Dickie. Driving back down the main street, eyes peeled for a parking space I eventually spied one outside the local estate agents. Returning to the car moments later my eyes were drawn to the estate agents window and became locked onto a photograph of a two bed roomed bungalow which was on a small estate, on the outskirts of Andreas. Trembling, my eyes gazed at the picture and before I knew what I was doing I was through the door and asking the receptionist for the details. Remarking that I was very quick off the mark because the bungalow had only just come onto the market that day and she'd only just sat down after putting the details in the window.

Feeling an energy rise up inside of me like nothing I'd ever felt before, my heart racing with the excitement of my discovery, I got back into the car and read through the information the receptionist had given me. Not only was it exactly as I'd requested in my meditation a couple of days earlier, but it was only 150 yards away from The Old Post Office! So, I raced home as quickly as possible to tell Dickie, hoping against hope that he would at least agree to attend a viewing.

To my surprise after explaining everything to my long suffering husband he calmly announced that there would be no harm in going for a look. I was amazed to say the least as during the journey home I had prepared myself for some resistance to my request, but to my delight there was none. This all seemed too easy and convenient to be true and I was sure spirit had to have a hand in the current unlikely coincidence as there could be no other explanation.

That night I went to bed and sent a prayer of thanks up to Daniel telling him, 'he didn't half work quickly' as I'd only asked for his help the previous day and the house I'd 'found' and its location were both perfect. As an afterthought I told him that I would really like to see his presence and perhaps he would be able to show himself to me one day. The prayer and my thanks having been voiced and left my lips I drifted happily off to sleep.

In what seemed like only minutes I was wide awake, eyes open lying in the darkness. Glancing at the bedside clock and inwardly groaning I discovered I'd only been asleep for a couple of hours. Without any prior warning I suddenly became aware that I was sitting in the darkness in the lounge, although I was also acutely aware that my physical body remained in bed! The 'me' that was sitting in the lounge watched intently as the kitchen door slowly opened and a shaft of the brightest light entered illuminating the whole room enabling me to see everything with complete clarity. Accompanying the bright light was the added awareness of a presence and I turned my head in what felt like slow-motion to witness a young man 'appear' through the open kitchen door. This image was illuminated by the most beautiful light, he seemed to be filled with light and it radiated both through and all around him.

Standing up from where I'd been seated I gazed directly and unflinchingly into the most brilliant clear blue eyes I'd ever encountered. Before me stood the most handsome young man, unbelievably dressed in modern clothing! In his ensemble of blue chambray shirt and casual slacks with what appeared to be soft leather loafers on his feet he reminded me of a young man I'd known 30 years before when I'd worked in the pharmacy who had sadly passed away in his early 30's from leukaemia. Now here I was standing before a 'being of light' that resembled the young man so much that I found it physically impossible to remove my gaze from his.

With all the confidence of someone who meets a 'being of light' on a daily basis I asked telepathically if he were Daniel, adding that if he was he hadn't appeared as I'd expected. Smiling at me with the most beautiful serene smile he spoke through my thoughts as a kind and patient teacher would speak to a slow learning pupil. He assured me that his appearance was to allay any fears I might have had, rather than appearing to me in his natural state as 'a being of pure light'.

Understanding completely that I had nothing to fear from this wonderful 'being' who had taken such measures not to frighten me the above exchange had been made and now there seemed to be no more need to converse. But, our encounter was not over and stretching out his arms towards me, palms facing upwards, Daniel 'invited' me into his energy field. As if in a trance, I extending my own arms out and moved forwards fully entering his energy field and placing my palms flat down on top of his. As soon as this contact was made feelings of Love, Bliss, Harmony, Belonging and Oneness coursed through my being like an almighty orgasmic wave! Words are completely inadequate to describe this event, suffice to say, it was the most powerful and overwhelming experience surpassing anything I'd previously encountered on my journey.

As the feeling subsided I found myself back in bed, and wide awake, as I knew I had been throughout this whole amazing experience. Knowing I had just been through a bi-location event where a person finds themselves in two places at once and both locations feel absolutely real. The blissful and very sexual feeling experienced is known as 'awakening the sleeping serpent' or 'Kundalini' and is a release of energy housed in the base of the spine which sometimes happens during intense spiritual experiences.

Dear reader, you may be laughing as you read this and thinking it was some kind of erotic dream or flight of fancy, but I can swear to you that when the above took place it was real, very real indeed.

Sad to say, this is the only time Daniel has ever appeared to me in physical form to prove his existence and believe me it is not for the want of asking him for a repeat performance! I can tell you I was floating on air for at least a month after the above events as I now knew beyond doubt that Daniel was real and truly active in my life and his energy was working with mine for my Higher Good.

The following week we met the estate agent at the property in

Andreas, but before entering he warned us that the house had been vacant for a number of months as the elderly lady owner had gone into full-time care. He was also anxious for us to know before we viewed the property that not a lot had been done to the place since its construction in the early 1970's.

Unlocking the front door we entered into a long narrow porch cum hallway, a pungent smell of damp assailing our nostrils as we noticed the walls were black with mould. Half expecting Dickie to recoil in horror and not want to proceed any further I was suitably surprised when he commented that he wanted to see more. Opening the door into the main hall of the house the estate agent stepped back for us to cross the threshold and stopping short we held each other's gaze and smiled. We both felt it and we both knew it. We were home!

After showing us through every room in the house the agent very discreetly went off into the garden giving us the opportunity to wander through and discuss things on our own. Revisiting every room we imagined what it would be like if we did this and that and where we would place various items of furniture. By the time we met the agent in the garden minutes later our minds were made up, we most definitely wanted this property and without delay offered the full asking price. Not bad considering two days previously Dickie didn't even know he wanted to move!

Now all we had to do was sell our house which sounded simple, but as anyone who has ever been in this position will tell you it is invariably not. Our offer had been accepted, but unfortunately only a few days later the rug was pulled from beneath our feet when a cash buyer stepped in. All our hopes, dreams and plans were dashed, but without fear of repetition I will say again that 'The Universe' has its own timing and what is for you, definitely won't go past you.

A couple of weeks after the above events once more I was in town shopping when I felt compelled to look in the estate agents window and there to my surprise were the details of the Andreas bungalow. Looking longingly at the details I suddenly became aware of someone waving frantically from inside the office and was confronted by an excited receptionist, phone in hand, insisting she had been just about to call to tell us the sale had fallen through and were we still interested in the house. Trying to control the rising sense of excitement in my chest I told her I was sure we would be, but I would have to speak to my husband before we took it any further.

It appeared we'd been given a second chance and I couldn't wait to get home and share the news with Dickie. After a little persuasion on my part he agreed to go for a second viewing just to make sure we felt the same about the place and I'm happy to say we did, so once again we offered the asking price and once again it was accepted.

The following week our house went on the market and within a couple of days we had our first viewing by a very nice lady named Pat who was looking to relocate to Ramsey from the south of the island. After polite introductions I sat in the sun porch and let the estate agent show Pat through our home and after only a few minutes they returned to the sun-porch with a request from Pat for *me* to show her around. When we had concluded the tour she announced quite confidently that my home would soon be hers because she loved it, and knew that this was where she was going to live.

Sighing happily to myself I waved them off promising to keep in touch with Pat about what was happening and secretly hoping that she would sell her home quickly because I felt she was the right person to be the next owner of our house.

Between that first meeting with Pat and our actually exchanging contracts it would prove to be a real roller-coaster ride of frustration and high emotions until the day all the players were in the right position as far as 'The Universe' was concerned and everything moved in beautiful synchrony, like the workings of the most expensive watch in the world, timed to perfection!

Conclusion

After Pat left our home on the day of her viewing I found a decorative seahorse which had come unstuck from one of the shower hooks lying on the floor in the bathroom and picking it up placed it on the window ledge above the washbasin making a mental note to glue it back in place. Pat and I kept in touch regularly as we rode the roller coaster that is the property market and during one of our angst ridden conversations she told me the details to our house were on her lounge dresser with her lucky seahorse placed on top of them.

Laughing, I told her the tale about the seahorse I'd found on the day of her viewing which was still sitting on my bathroom window ledge waiting to be glued back into place. Excitedly she requested I leave it exactly where it was because she saw it as a sign of her forthcoming ownership saying, "My lucky seahorse never lets me down!"

And indeed it didn't as Pat did become the owner of our house when quite suddenly all the players involved had miraculously moved into the right position and the huge well-oiled machine that is fate decided the outcome in our favour.

By a strange 'coincidence' on the morning we moved I found the seahorse broken clean in half, lying in the sink below the window ledge. It had played its part and was no longer required as our house was now Pat's home, something she had known and trusted all along. And we on the other hand were now the proud new owners of our 'heaven sent' if a little out-dated and dilapidated bungalow at Andreas.

A lot of hard work was on the cards as our new home and my new venture of the spiritual library were both in dire need of lots of tender loving care, but at least now I understood why my guidance had postponed the lease on the old post office until the following spring. Although the best thing of all was I wouldn't be relying on the public house conveniences now my home was only 150 yards away ... What a relief!

CHAPTER 9

'Kimmeridge'

On the 12th day of the 12th month 2003, a very auspicious date as far as numerology is concerned, Dickie and I moved to our new home in Andreas. We were as excited as a couple of children on the last day of term as we turned the key in the lock for the first time. Stepping inside, the pungent smell of damp assailed our nostrils, but nothing was going to dampen our spirits, it felt absolutely wonderful because it already felt like home.

After the removal men had emptied the contents of their van our new home was filled to the brim with cardboard boxes of varying sizes and black bin bags full of clothes and assorted household belongings giving the general impression we had just moved into a hoarder's paradise. Rags, fed up with all the chaos had found her bed, curled up and gone to sleep, whilst our two poor old cats meandered through the unfamiliar surroundings meowing loudly in distress as they picked their way through the mêlée of bags and boxes.

Dickie and I both fell into bed exhausted on that first night ready for a good night's sleep. We had placed our bed in exactly the same position as the previous owner, an elderly lady named Margaret, who was now living in a nursing home in Ramsey. Unfortunately her health had deteriorated and she was now only lucid for short periods of time and was living what remained of her life only partly in this world.

Before long Dickie was fast asleep and snoring loudly whereas I on the other hand was still wide awake and soon became very aware that there were three of us sharing the bed! Margaret, bless her, was lying in between us and appeared to be fast asleep, presumably in the place and position she had slept in for years. In my mind I gently called her name and told her she no longer lived there, but to no avail and despite my best efforts the presence of Margaret remained, happily sleeping where she obviously felt she belonged. It took another three weeks and a strange sequence of events, as well as moving the bed to a different position in the room before I would get a good night's sleep.

We had two cats at the time, one jet black and the other one a tabby. In those first few weeks in our new home, often out of the corner of my eye, I would see what I thought was our big tabby cat sitting by her feeding bowl in the kitchen only to see her moment's later sitting in the garden staring back at me through the kitchen window.

One morning Dickie had gone off to work and I'd just let both cats in after they had been out all night. By now they had their bearings and were thoroughly enthralled with their new location as our bungalow backs onto open fields and both animals wanted to be out at night exploring and chasing the wildlife. Tired after their nights exertions they'd wandered past me into the lounge and made for their favourite sleeping places and within minutes they were curled up and fast asleep, no doubt dreaming of chasing rabbits and mice.

Leaving them to their slumbers I walked into the hall closing the lounge door firmly behind me when I was suddenly overcome with a strange compulsion to go back to bed. The compulsion was overwhelming, so sliding back between the still warm and welcoming sheets I snuggled down and rolled over onto my side, wondering as I did so why I felt the need to be there. No sooner had I rolled over than I felt the unmistakable sensation of a cat jumping onto the bottom of the bed before padding up to drape itself along my spine where it snuggled closely into me and began purring very loudly. Lying there sure in the knowledge that both my own cats were sleeping soundly in the lounge and could not get into the bedroom slowly the realization dawned on me that this had to be the spirit of a cat.

Enjoying the warmth of its very real feeling body I could clearly hear it purring loudly which sent a vibration right through my spine. The name 'Smudge' filtered into my mind and with it the sure and certain knowledge that this had been Margaret's cat. After a few minutes I could stand it no longer and rolled over to take a look, but of course as soon as I did 'Smudge' disappeared and I realized in that moment that this was the cat I must have been 'seeing' around the house for the past number of weeks.

Feeling very aware that something had to be done as things were getting a little crowded in the bedroom department because now we not only had Margaret, but also her cat wanting a share of the bed! As always looking for confirmation to explain the unexplainable I asked my neighbour the next day if the previous owner of our house had ever owned a cat called Smudge. Not only was she able to confirm Margaret's cat had been called Smudge, but that Margaret had absolutely adored the animal who had been her constant companion as her health failed. The neighbour even remembered Margaret telling her that Smudge would jump up on the bed and snuggle along her back, its favourite resting place, and remarking on how devastated she had been when he'd died. Thanking my neighbour for sharing some background history on my new homes previous tenants I said goodbye grateful that she hadn't thought to ask me how I'd known the name of the cat!

After the above conversation or confirmation if you like, I was never aware of either Margaret or Smudge again. I like to think they had been reunited with one another on a higher plane or vibration where they were happy together again.

However, this would not be the end of this story and although Margaret was no longer in our bed she hadn't quite finished with me yet and another set of seemingly unconnected, but very connected events would occur the following spring shortly after opening the Inner Light Spiritual Library.

Margaret had named the bungalow Kimmeridge and from the moment we moved in I wanted to change it because the name meant absolutely nothing to us, not knowing what it was or for that matter where it was, if she had named it for somewhere in her past. Making my intention clear to 'The Universe' I sent up the message that when I had time to do so I would be giving the house a brand new name, something Manx and significant to us as the new Manx owners.

In the spring of 2004 I eventually opened the above library which you will read about in a forthcoming chapter. The first week it opened a lady came in and made a very strange request considering the purpose of the place, asking for a map of the UK. Why she thought I would have such an item is anyone's guess, but as we have already learnt spirit moves in mysterious ways. Telling her that whilst the library didn't possess a map I would be more than happy to pop home and fetch her mine. Against her protestations I left her in the library while I went home for the map, returning a few minutes later, map in my hand, much to her delight.

Opening the map out fully on my desk she searched for the location she required as I peered over her shoulder and almost instantly the name Kimmeridge leapt out at me as I discovered the name of my new house was a place on the Dorset coast.

A few days later Dickie and I anxious to get on with the modifications the house needed found ourselves in a local DIY outlet. Wandering around the store we came across a selection of electric fires, one of which captured my attention as it just happened to be called 'The Kimmeridge Suite'.

A couple of weeks later I received a picture postcard of an old tower on a grassy hillside overlooking the sea, and turning it over was delighted to read that it was from a relatively new friend, Gill. She had been one of the first people to find the library on the day it opened. Perusing the short message my eyes fell on the typed location at the bottom of the card 'The Clavell Tower', Kimmeridge Bay, Dorset. Now I'd been presented with the previously unknown word Kimmeridge three times in as many weeks and felt there had to be more to this sequence of events than Margaret's desire for me to know where the place was.

The following week Gill called into the library and asked if I'd received her postcard whilst apologizing profusely for not addressing it properly as she didn't know the name or number of our house having merely taken a chance on addressing it to Linda Watson, Andreas Village. Confirming that I had received it I was more interested to know why she'd sent me a postcard depicting Kimmeridge Bay if she hadn't known it was the name of our house. Dumbfounded, she told me it had chosen at ***random*** whilst on holiday in Dorset! Checking the postcard when I arrived home that evening I marveled myself that it had reached me with only my name as direction for the long suffering postman to deliver.

In August of 2007 I accompanied Gill and two other friends on a camping trip to Wiltshire with the intention of visiting the latest crop circles. Never having been to Wiltshire or entered a crop circle before it was another first and fascinating experience for me.

The whole trip was both fun and informative and on our last day we went on our final excursion only to find ourselves at a quaint old smugglers inn overlooking the sea by the name of 'The Square and Compass' in a small place called Worth Matravers. Cradling my half pint of local cider and closing my eyes I sat within the ancient walls of the old tavern and allowed myself to soak up the atmosphere while all around the chatter and laughter blended together to make an inaudible, but comforting babble.

In my mind's eye I imagined the smugglers of long ago sitting within these walls, raising their glasses and telling stories of heroic smuggling escapades and the plotting of more to come, interjected with the odd outburst of laughter as they recollected their narrow escape from the forces of 'The Crown'.

When I finally opened my eyes after being deeply immersed in my reverie I found the old man sitting opposite staring at me intently and was prompted to ask if he knew a place called Kimmeridge. My heart skipping a beat when he replied that it was only a couple of miles away from where I sat. Immediately and very excitedly I shared the information with the girls and moments later we were careering down narrow country lanes speeding our way to Kimmeridge ... and another date with destiny!

Within minutes of leaving the inn we arrived at Kimmeridge and the view was just as breathtaking as it had been on the postcard I'd received from Gill. Getting out of the car in the parking area just below Clavell's Tower, like an automaton, I made my way slowly to the cliff edge not quite believing that I was finally at Kimmeridge. Looking down onto the blue waters of Kimmeridge Bay I could see a small cluster of buildings along the beach road far below. The wind whipped my hair across my face as it gusted over the cliff top and the urge to cry was overwhelming as the emotions of love and happiness swept through me and I felt the presence of Margaret all around me.

The overriding sensation was one of satisfaction and I was aware of Margaret smiling because she had finally brought me to her beloved Kimmeridge. Now I knew how much this place had meant to her, not a vague feeling, but a sure knowing ... the penny had finally dropped!

As you have probably already guessed despite my best intentions our house remains Kimmeridge, but there is another episode to this story of Margaret and our shared love of our home.

<u>The Final Piece</u>

A couple of years after the above events I was invited to speak at a meeting of the local WI. Never, ever, having been a member of the WI or even thought of becoming a member I was puzzled at being invited, and even more intrigued to find the invitation had come from the chairwoman, who was none other than Margaret's daughter. Dickie was somewhat concerned when I expressed my intention of accepting the invitation as he thought most of the women present would be very religious and have no interest in the things I talked about. Defiantly, I told him I was giving the talk even if he thought I was mad and with a shrug of his shoulders he gave up the argument and left me to find out for myself what my reception would be like.

On the evening in question I have to admit I was met with a few stony faces and disbelieving looks just as Dickie had predicted. As I finished speaking Margaret's daughter, who'd been sitting on the front row, offering up quite a few 'can't believe it' looks herself, stood up to give the vote of thanks. But, just at that very moment I felt divinely nudged and found myself asking if I may be allowed to tell one more story, explaining that the story involved her mother and asked if she would mind me sharing it with everyone.

A rather puzzled chairwoman thankfully agreed and sat down again with a nod in my direction. Without further ado and before she changed her mind I launched into the story you have just read.

Looking out at an audience of mainly disbelieving faces I smiled at Margaret's daughter as I spoke and could see the emotion in her face as tears welled up in her eyes. When I'd finished my story I turned to her again and asked politely if she could confirm anything of what I'd just spoken. To my immense relief and the awe of the other listeners she confirmed everything from Smudge to

Kimmeridge, telling the assembly that the happiest times of her mother's life had been spent at Kimmeridge with her husband and family, concluding that when her mother had moved to the island she had named her house Kimmeridge in memory of all those happy times.

This was a lovely end to what had been, in my eyes, a beautiful story. It may have taken a number of years to reach its conclusion, but this is without doubt definitely, 'The End'.

CHAPTER 10

THE LADY IN WHITE

Most of my experiences overlap and happen over a period of days, weeks, months or even years, so while I was living through the happenings in the last chapter this story was also unfolding.

One very damp and dreary morning in the middle of January 2004 only a matter of weeks after moving to Andreas I happened to be standing on top of the hedge in our back garden, for no other reason than to enjoy the view. Since moving to our present home this has become my habit, especially on evenings when there is a beautiful sunset as our back garden faces West, over open fields.

At the top of the long narrow field beyond our garden stands a big old house which has stood there all of my lifetime. When I was a child it was a very grand old house which I used to imagine would be filled with all manner of beautiful treasures as the owners were quite well off in comparison to most of the parishioners. I remember the lady of the house from my childhood because she was always very elegant and beautifully dressed in finery and furs, but I always felt a little sad when I came eye to glassy little eye with the poor, long dead, furry creature that was more often than not draped around her neck. Along with her husband, a very tall and stately looking man with the manners of a real gentleman they cut a very dashing couple and were both pillars of the small Andreas community.

Standing on the hedge that morning my gaze came to rest on the old house, a sad and pathetic remnant of its former self as it stood an empty and neglected shell in a terrible state of disrepair. The elderly occupants I had known in my youth had long since passed away and the house had been bequeathed to a relative living in some far flung place who apparently had no interest in living on the island.

Reviewing my thoughts of the building's history and owners I was suddenly overcome with the most incredible urge to visit the place. As usual not stopping to question the rational of my behaviour I raced indoors and slipping on my coat and shoes called to Rags to follow me. Unfortunately, poor old Rags was now quite deaf and remained seated in her chair staring blankly out of the window, but as soon as I appeared with my coat on she was off the chair on her rickety old legs raring to go.

Soon we were on the narrow road that led up to the old house, Rags trotting proudly in front of me or as proudly as her poor old arthritic legs would allow, her cute little docked tail wagging from side to side like a mini metronome as she led the way. Minutes later we were standing between the crumbling pillars at the top of the weed filled drive that led to the rear of the house.

Without any hesitation I walked towards this damp and crumbling elevation, not quite believing what I was doing as I'm not normally given to trespassing. Standing entranced for a moment, gazing at the peeling paintwork on the back door as if I were looking at some wonderful work of art before continuing my exploration of the place. Almost as if someone was guiding my footsteps I found myself led around the corner of the building in the direction of the garden gate on the east gable of the house. Lifting the creaking latch and easing the old wooden gate open Rags and I entered the hidden garden. Unfortunately, the sky had darkened and it was beginning to drizzle so I pulled up the hood on my coat before gently closing the gate behind me.

There was a small lawn just inside the gate and in my mind's eye I could clearly see three children, dressed in old fashioned clothes, playing on the lawn. Two girls and a boy, who appeared to be the eldest, laughed and played in the summer sunshine! Although in reality it was a cold, drizzly January day. Oblivious to me, the children continued with their game as I moved past them along the path until I was at the bottom of the wide sweeping steps leading up to the front door. Then, to my surprise, what felt like invisible hands on my shoulders gently turned me around to face down the length of what had once been the garden, but was now nothing more than an overgrown field sporting brambles.

Closing my eyes I allowed my inner vision to take over and was astounded by the beauty surrounding me. The garden was breathtakingly decked out in all manner of colourful flowers and rambling roses, it was the height of summer and the whole place was alive and in full bloom. Behind me I could still hear the children laughing and playing when I became aware of a young woman reclining in a cane bath chair a little way down the central pathway. Relaxing in the warmth of the summer sun, dressed only in a long white nightgown, I guessed 'The Lady in White' could not have been more than thirty years old. Remaining within my vision for a while longer, until prompted to open my eyes where to my disappointment the beautiful summer garden, 'The Lady in White' and the carefree happy children were all gone.

The rain now falling softly and silently I found myself standing alone, save for Rags of course in the middle of a very overgrown and neglected garden which bore absolutely no resemblance to the heavenly garden in the full bloom of summer that I had just witnessed in my mind's eye. Once again I felt those invisible hands on my shoulders as I was turned to face the house, my eyes drawn up to look at one of the bedroom windows. A mysterious male figure returned my gaze and without doubt was communicating with me as I could feel and know his thoughts within my mind and they were telling me I'd witnessed what I'd been brought to see and now it was time for me to leave.

These thoughts were so powerful I did not require telling twice and made for the gate with Rags 'hot on my heels' as she had obviously received the same message. On the short walk home I wondered why I'd been brought to the house and shown these visions of the past, but as usual I trusted that all would be revealed at the appropriate moment.

Two days later the skies were darker than ever and the rain was still coming down in buckets when I answered the insistent ringing of my doorbell only to find my friend dripping on the doorstep. Inviting her in I made for the kitchen to put the kettle on, but calling me back she requested I put my rain coat on as there was somewhere *we* had to go immediately. This sounded intriguing, and asking her where we were off to in such a hurry, you can imagine my surprise when she told me she had an overriding compulsion to visit the old house up the road! Unable to explain why she needed to go there, all she was able to say was that it had to be today, and it was me that had to accompany her. Telling her that I'd visited the place for the first time a couple of days earlier, but had not told anyone about my experience, she held up her hand and prevented me from telling her any more.

Almost dragging me out of the house, such was her haste to get there she marched me through the estate and within minutes we were standing in front of the crumbling stone pillars at the rear of the house. A strange feeling of déjà vu swept over me and I shuddered involuntarily as I noticed the route she was taking was the exact one I had walked a couple of days earlier. Following after her a little reluctantly I traced her steps to the back door and then around to the east gable. The old wooden gate creaked and groaned loudly as we entered the garden and the rain which had started falling when I opened the gate a couple of days before suddenly and thankfully, stopped.

Bypassing what had previously been the lawn and centre of the children's activity without comment we moved further into the garden and down the central pathway. My friend suddenly stopped dead in her tracks and closing her eyes she began to speak, and without any prior knowledge she described the garden to me exactly as I'd seen it two days earlier. Telling me it was a beautiful summer day with the scent of roses hanging in the air and the borders were full of colour with sound of buzzing bees. Standing quietly with her eyes closed she suddenly announced that we were not alone and proceeded to tell me that a woman, dressed all in white, with blood spattered down the front of her nightdress was reclining in an old fashioned wheelchair only a short distance from where we stood. If there had been a passing stranger listening they would probably have sent for the men in white coats, but I knew what she could see and could not help telling her that I had experienced the same thing when I'd visited previously.

All of a sudden the vision was over my friend opened her eyes and grabbing me by the hand told me we had to leave immediately and that we could remain in the garden no longer. Her desire to leave was as powerful as mine had been and we headed for the exit in double quick time. Once on the other side of the gate she conveyed to me that the urgency to leave had been relayed telepathically. She seemed to have been given the same urgent prompt as me and although she had not been aware of a male essence she had no desire to go anywhere near the house again as her objective for whatever reason had been the garden and the invalid.

My friend is not often given to flights of fancy, but on the way home we discussed what she had seen in her inner vision, which was almost an exact account of what I myself had witnessed, apart from the children. Asking her why she thought we had been drawn to the dilapidated old house and allowed to see a very clear picture of what we assumed to be a happier and perhaps sadder time for the occupants, all she could answer was that if her life had depended on it she would have been unable to do anything other than visit that house on that particular day with me.

A couple of weeks later the village was buzzing with the news that there were plans to demolish the old house. Horrified when I heard this news because now I knew there were people still residing there, albeit in a different dimension. Not content with the gossip I took myself off to the house to find out the horrible truth for myself. Standing at the top of the drive I read the planning order for demolition which had been posted on one of the old pillars and wondered what I could possibly do to prevent the destruction of this once grand old building. The thought that it would be razed to the ground instead of being renovated and brought back to life distressed me terribly, but I also knew this was what I was meant to feel.

Whoever had led me there in the first place and allowed me to witness the continued existence of those long gone inhabitants and had then compelled my friend to confirm their existence surely they must be expecting some action on my part. Although I could not imagine what I could possibly do and reprimanding myself for my lack of faith I sent out a plea to the owner wherever they were, asking not to allow the travesty of demolition to go ahead. Reminding myself that if spirit were working through me and had gone to all the trouble of involving both myself and my friend then they must have some knowledge of the outcome and all of these events would not have been in vain.

Surprisingly, only a couple of weeks later the planning order was rescinded when the prospective developers unexpectedly pulled out of the sale!

Shortly after the above events I happened to be in the village shop where I met with Billy, an old farmer friend of mine. Calling me over, Billy introduced me to the woman he was talking to, telling me she was an old friend he'd not seen for years. Happy to enlighten me, Billy began to recall events from their childhood when the woman standing in front of me had often stayed with her relatives in the 'old house' for her summer holidays. In fact, that was why she was on the island at present as she had inherited the house and had come to view the property and decide what to do with it!

Feeling spirit moving within me as that particularly interesting snippet of information fell on my ears I knew instantly that this was the moment spirit had been working towards. My window of opportunity had arrived!

Without hesitation I found myself telling her I hoped that when she sold the property it would be on the proviso that it would be restored to its former grandeur and to my amazement she agreed whole heartedly, making me, a stranger, the promise that it would not be bulldozed. The old house was sold shortly thereafter and to my delight 'the owner' kept her promise and it is now in the process of being restored and extended keeping the original structure intact.

What a magical result! The web of Spirit never ceases to amaze me.

CHAPTER 11

'THE INNER LIGHT LIBRARY' COMES TO LIFE

In April of 2004 I took possession of the key to the smelly little room that would become the 'Inner Light Spiritual Library', and without even taking a second look at the place I handed it straight over to my friend Janet and her husband Michael, who is a builder.

After Janet and Michael's inspection of the dilapidated little room they called in to tell me what needed to be done and Janet remarked on the fact that she had felt my presence in the room as soon as she'd entered. Feeling Janet was probably picking up on the energy I had been 'projecting' there since the previous summer because I had not actually set foot in the place since my initial viewing. However, I was pleased to have her tell me that it had a very positive energy despite the awful mess it was in.

In no time at all Janet and Michael had the major repairs completed with new carpet laid and the book shelves installed. On the night before the opening I was alone in the library filling the bookshelves when suddenly I became aware of a presence behind me. I continued with the job in hand, resisting the temptation to turn around, when eventually, finding my voice, I spoke aloud into the apparently empty room telling the invisible presence that they were welcome. Instinctively I knew the presence was there to help direct all those who needed to find the library for whatever reason. As I finished speaking a beautiful feeling enveloped me, like I was being hugged by a huge marshmallow, filling me with the all encompassing sensation of love and well being, it was heavenly.

The Inner Light Library was now ready to open its doors to the public as I knew the final piece of magic had just arrived and looking around me I was well satisfied with the finished effect. The smell of damp almost, but not entirely replaced by the smell of paint and new carpet, and thankfully I no longer had to worry about the pitter patter of tiny feet and the unwelcome company of little furry friends.

Sitting quietly I pondered on what was going to happen next as I was at another new beginning not only in my home life, but in my spiritual life as well. Change on every level seemed to be the order of the day as I experienced a life full of endings and new beginnings, and as to what the future held, who knew?

Once the library was open those already awakened to their spirituality sought it out despite its very remote location and others found it by chance in the most unusual ways. Quite often people would stumble through the door commenting on the fact that the road outside seemed to have an invisible mesh which somehow guided them across the threshold! Others who found themselves in the library could not explain why they were there nor could they explain what they were hoping to find, but all of them admitting to 'knowing' on some level, that at that particular moment in their lives the library was the place they needed to be.

It is my firm belief that once guided to the library people were exposed to the energy it contained and this 'energy' acted as a catalyst for those souls ready to open and awaken to their Higher Selves. For my part I feel extremely blessed and privileged to have witnessed the change that took place in many of those who crossed the threshold of the 'Inner Light Library' from where they began their own personal journeys of discovery.

It didn't take long for the library to become a meeting place, not unlike the 4th Dimension had been and I viewed it more as a service to the spiritual community of the island as many healings, meetings of like minds, and some very bizarre and truly magical things happened whilst I was in those premises.

The week the library opened I attended a lecture at a local spiritual retreat not far from where I now live. The lecturer for the evening was a Mr. Tony Neate who is a very well known and respected figure within the spiritual fraternity and has channeled spirit and written many books on spiritual and metaphysical matters over a great number of years. Never having met him before I was looking forward to the experience as his lecture was about bringing through information from a higher mind, commonly known as channeling.

Sitting in the lounge that evening with all those gathered for the lecture I recognized quite a few faces that I'd known from my time in the 4th Dimension. One of these ladies made her way over to tell me how much she'd enjoyed my book, which had been on sale for only a couple of weeks. Overhearing our conversation the woman sitting next to me then asked what my book was about. Swelling with pride (how egotistical of me) I informed her it was a simple autobiographical account of my spiritual awakening.

Introducing herself as Maggie, she inquired as to whether I had brought any books with me, and on hearing I had a few copies in the car she immediately insisted on buying one. Venturing that the current venue was probably not an appropriate place for me to set up business Maggie refused to take 'no' for an answer and to my acute embarrassment another lady who had been eavesdropping on our conversation also wanted a copy. Moments later, frog marched to my car by both ladies and after securing a book each we returned to the gathering. Feeling extremely nervous about the whole book selling thing I asked them both to hide their books in case the establishment thought I was networking.

Once back inside, the three of us fell into an easy conversation and both Maggie and Sandy expressed great interest in the library and promised they would seek it out in the near future. Our conversation was soon interrupted by the housekeeper as we were ushered into the dining room for supper where Maggie sat down opposite me at the large dining table while Sandy seated herself alongside me. A few minutes later an elderly gentleman entered the dining room and sat down in the only remaining seat at the table, next to Maggie. After a polite 'hello' to her table companion Maggie began rummaging about under her seat before producing my book and sliding it across the table toward me, in full view of everyone. Smiling disarmingly at my mortified face Maggie then proceeded to ask me to sign it! Embarrassed and blushing to the roots of my hair I shrank into my seat in the hopes no one had noticed her actions which I found a little disconcerting as I'd asked her to hide the volume not bring it out for public scrutiny.

The elderly gentleman sitting next to Maggie could not help but notice this little drama unfolding and scooping up the book as I pushed it back across the table began to read the back page before locking me in his gaze and asking if I was the author. Admitting that I was the author, while cursing my new 'friend' Maggie under my breath, he turned the book over in his hands and introduced himself as Tony Neate, saying, "I'd love to buy a copy of your book Linda, it sounds very interesting, and if I like it I will review it in my next newsletter."

Maggie was instantly forgiven, whether by chance or by design she had achieved a remarkable coup and Tony, true to his word, did in fact give my book a glowing review in his next newsletter that went out around the UK.

CHAPTER 12

THE MISSION

The following week a familiar face popped around the library door, it was none other than Sandy. She had confided in me on the night of the lecture that she was experiencing some spiritual 'problems' although she had not gone into detail and had promised to seek me out at the library with the intention of sharing her worries. In the quiet of the library I discovered she had attended Tony's lecture because she herself was channeling, but with no prior knowledge, she was finding it difficult to cope with everything that was coming through. Without some help or guidance she felt she had no control and was becoming extremely fearful and miserable, eventually begging me to help in some way. Not entirely sure I could give her the help she required I reluctantly agreed, on the understanding that my friend Rosemary could be part of the process too.

Together Rosemary and I worked with Sandy for some months as she underwent many healing sessions where we helped her to let go of things from this life and many other lives too! Sandy for her part tried desperately to dispel the fear and insecurity that dwelt within her so that she could stand in, and feel comfortable with her own power and potential as a true channel for Spirit. Her channeling, when she allowed it to come through was very 'interesting' bringing through some very high beings, but unfortunately in her untutored state she also allowed some of a lower vibration to air their views. Thankfully, it was fairly easy to distinguish between the two.

A few days before my 50th birthday I was in the library when the door opened and in walked Sandy looking the happiest I'd ever seen her. Telling her I wasn't expecting to see her on that particular day she remarked she had felt compelled to come. She was hardly through the door when she motioned that she must write and quickly I passed her a clipboard with some blank foolscap paper attached to it. As soon as Sandy took possession of the clipboard she sat down heavily in the wicker chair next to my desk and began to scribble furiously. I did not disturb her as it was apparent to me that she had entered a trance-like state which lasted for quite some minutes before she stopped scribbling and sat staring blankly at the page in front of her.

Offering the clipboard to me I gazed incredulously at what had been a blank piece of paper minutes earlier, but was now filled with signs, symbols, squiggles, spirals, arrows and patterns of all kinds. Sandy then began to channel verbally, telling me I was to be in the library at 7am on the morning of the 7th of July and that I was to light a candle before meditating, during which I would be given guidance.

The message that Sandy had brought through had felt loving and true to me and I felt sure it had come from a 'higher being'. Sadly, Sandy, on the other hand, was absolutely horrified that I could possibly be taking it seriously as she could remember nothing of what had just happened, which is not unusual in these circumstances. With what I hoped was a reassuring smile I told her I certainly was taking it seriously and that I had every faith in her ability to bring through wonderful messages from spirit.

Always up for a bit of excitement and a challenge I had already decided to keep my appointment with whomever or whatever may or may not turn up in my little library on the morning of my birthday.

On the morning of the 7th July 2004 I was up at the crack of dawn and arrived at the library just before 7a.m. to experience what I hoped would be another 'date with destiny'. Letting myself in as quietly as possible in an effort not to disturb the tenant who lived in the flat above, I lit a candle as instructed and then settled myself into the little blue wicker chair in the corner of the room next to the old safe. The wretched thing had had to remain when I took on the library because it weighed a ton and was bolted to the floor making it impossible to move, however, I had draped it in voile which camouflaged it nicely.

Closing my eyes to meditate I called on my HS, Daniel and my other guides and inspirers and welcomed in the presence of whoever

I was supposed to be meeting that morning. Before long the vision of a grassy hill dotted with small gorse bushes came into my mind's eye and I recognized the place instantly. Standing on top of the hill I was enjoying a 360 degree view when words began to flow into my consciousness, informing me that I had been guided to the library on that particular day to receive vital information about a mission I had agreed to undertake millennia ago! This was all news to me and became even more confusing when I was told that the *safes* that I had been led to were symbols of the work I was about to undertake.

Let me explain, as well as the monstrosity I was currently sitting next too there had been an un-moveable safe in the 5th Dimension healing room too.

My mind reeling with symbols and missions the thought flow continued and I was told that just like the lock on a safe the correct 'combination' had to be used to unlock and reveal the secrets and treasures stored within. Agreeing with this analogy I dared to say I still had no idea of what I'd agreed to do, only to be to be informed that I would be shown and helped to understand.

Once more the vision of the grassy hillside entered my mind's eye, only this time I was walking around the hill carrying a singing bowl in my hand! Never having owned or played a singing bowl in my life the vision continued with the bowl singing in my hand, as I walked slowly around the hill, three times to the right, then twice to the left and so on. As the vision unfolded I made a careful note of what was happening, but as it faded my head was still full of questions. When was I to do this? What would happen when I did? And exactly how was I supposed to wander around what was ostensibly private property without trespassing?

Inside my head a gentle voice addressed me as child and told me not to allow fear to 'own me' as all would be taken care of, telling me the mission would not pass me by as it was mine by design! I was then given the number 18 as a clue to when I would perform my task. Opening my eyes I sat for a moment trying to take in all that had just happened when my eyes fell on the clipboard with Sandy's written channeling still on the uppermost sheet. Absentmindedly I picked it up and was immediately overcome with a very strange sensation as inside my body and brain everything appeared to be moving into a new place and I could 'feel' the mechanism of cogs turning and sparks igniting within me. In that moment I knew exactly what all those strange squiggles and symbols meant! I could read them like it was written in plain English. The previously illegible graphics were information about a new energy entering into the Earth and how vortices around the globe would be opened into the 'Light' to release old energies that had lain buried in the darkness for millennia while others would be sealed.

On many occasions after that day I picked up Sandy's sheet of squiggles, but I could not tell you any more than I have outlined above. It was only in that moment straight after meditation that I seemed to have full clarity, and with that clarity I inherently knew I was holding the key to everything in our Universe … if only briefly.

Blowing out the candle before leaving the library I thanked Daniel and the other beings that had been with me, promising to do my best with the information I had received and stay alert and aware for more to come in. Arriving home a few moments later I found Dickie eating his breakfast and was prepared to be cross examined about my early morning escapade, but when I told him I'd been to the library he just rolled his eyes and shrugged his shoulders. Thankfully he did not question me any further, which was a bit of a relief as I was having a hard time believing all that had just happened myself, let alone try to relate it all to a doubting husband.

Later that day I was back in the library when my friend Janet called in with a present for my birthday and opening my gift I could hardly believe my eyes when the contents revealed, of all things, a beautifully carved Tibetan singing bowl!

Witnessing my delight, my friend told me she had discovered a stall selling them at Tynwald Fair, a couple of days earlier and had immediately felt it would be just what I wanted. Janet being a very intuitive lady had obviously been well 'tuned in' and it would be reasonable to suspect that spirit may have had a hand in her choice! Placing the singing bowl in the palm of my hand I began to play, and found to my utter surprise and delight that I was able to make it sing as if I'd been doing it all of my life … or maybe many other lives?

The entire day had been magical and I think it is fair to say I will never forget my 50th birthday.

CHAPTER 13

ENTER ELAINE

The following week, just as I was allowing all the excitement and the guidance of my birthday to sink in a lady entered the library that I recognized instantly as we had passed one another whilst out walking on numerous occasions over the past few weeks, but had never exchanged more than a polite 'hello'.

From the moment she spoke I took a liking to this stranger although I found myself wondering if she really was a stranger as there was something very familiar about her. Whatever it was I couldn't put my finger on it at that precise moment, but somewhere deep inside of me I felt I knew her very well. Not thinking it prudent to share my feelings at our initial meeting I decided to wait and see how things progressed between us. She chatted away easily, telling me she had passed the library on a number of occasions while out walking, each time wishing she could come in for a browse, but unfortunately the library had been closed.

As I jotted down her details on a membership card I discovered she was working at a large mansion on the outskirts of the village, but was saddened by the fact that since taking up residence in Andreas she had felt completely disconnected from another and more important part of her life as a medium. Without any prompting she went on to explain that apparently losing her ability to channel was making her feel depressed and completely shut down.

These words were hardly out of her mouth when she sat down heavily in the whicker chair next to my desk, her head slumping forward as her chin came to rest on her chest. This sudden collapse made me wonder if she was unwell, but before I had time to inquire her demeanour and posture appeared to change. Her body seemed to fill with a different energy to that of her own, and brimming with confidence and self-assurance she raised her head, sitting upright in the chair and began to channel!

The little library was full to bursting with the presence of the 'being' Elaine was channeling and the feelings I was experiencing were so beautiful, radiant and sincere. There was no way she could have possibly known the information she brought through that day matched with the guidance I'd been given on my birthday the week before. Without doubt the information I had received on my birthday was being confirmed through my new found and soon to become good friend Elaine. Our paths having crossed repeatedly over recent weeks only to culminate in this experience where information could be passed on was obviously all part of my ongoing guidance.

When Elaine opened her eyes I thanked her for the message and reassured her she was definitely not 'shut down' or 'switched off' if that performance was anything to go by and she responded by telling me she was as surprised as me by what had just happened. Anxious to know who she was channelling I was a little disappointed when she refused to tell me on the grounds that I would probably laugh. Promising I would not laugh, and that I had experienced a lot of strange things over the years she eventually told me that it was Saint Francis of Assisi!

Gratified by her trust I told her the energy in the library had betrayed the fact that she was channeling a very high being and that I felt very humbled by the experience. Elaine left the library a little while later beaming from ear to ear, somewhat elated at her re-found abilities, especially when I told her the message she had brought through was very meaningful to me.

My head hurt thinking about recent events and the confirmation from Elaine of my still to be accomplished mission. I felt as though a hamster in a wheel had taken up residence, currently preventing me from thinking clearly. In an effort to take my mind of the subject I picked up the TV guide to see if there was anything worth watching on 'the box'. Reading through the blurb of the late film, 'Stigmata' I decided that it was definitely not the kind of film I could watch when suddenly out of the ethers a kindly voice dropped into my head telling me I *must* watch it!

Later that evening Dickie went off to bed commenting that he didn't think the film I was about to watch was my usual 'cup of tea' and I'd be better of in bed. Making some lame excuse as to why I wanted to see it I settled down somewhat bleary eyed to watch something I didn't really want to see! Having sat through probably about an hour or so of the film a clip of a monastery garden flashed onto the screen and there to my surprise was a life size statue of none other than Saint Francis of Assisi! At that precise moment the same gentle voice I had heard earlier in the evening advised me that I could now go to bed.

The next day Rosemary and I were sitting in the library chatting when the door swung open and a very flushed Elaine rushed in demanding to speak to me outside alone ... immediately. Following Elaine out on to the pavement, expressing my concern at her rather flustered appearance, she blurted out that I would never guess what had happened the day before, but suggested it must be something pretty exciting.

Not able to contain herself any longer Elaine recounted the tale of her return to work the previous day when the new head housekeeper had taken her into the basement to check the store rooms. One of these rooms was kept permanently locked, but they had found a key on the housekeeper's chain and gone in for a look, only to find it full of boxes containing spiritual books and videos, not unlike the contents of the library. Elaine continued with her story telling me she had picked up a video from the nearest box only to find it was about the life and times of none other than Saint Francis of Assisi! Telling me she had almost fainted when she'd read the title because she saw it as a confirmation of the 'being' she'd channeled in the library.

When she'd finished her amazing story and was sure I'd taken on board the wonderful confirmation she'd received only half an hour after channeling in the library Elaine calmed down a bit, and I was able to tell her that I had also had confirmation the night before, although I'd had to wait a little longer to receive it.

I can't aptly convey in words the feelings we were sharing in that moment, but I think we knew something very special was taking place in both our lives. We now knew that we had not come together by chance, but by design and the design could only have been engineered by spirit. Making our way back into the library we joined Rosemary who had remained engrossed in her own thoughts as we'd made spectacles of ourselves outside on the pavement!

Elaine, still quite breathless from her tale proceeded to invite me for dinner the following Friday night which I accepted without hesitation as I desperately wanted to get to know this lady better. Even more intrigued, I was to discover she had also invited a young man she'd met recently at the Spiritualist Church who she was keen for me to meet. Looking over at Rosemary who had been sitting quietly throughout our conversation, Elaine extended an invitation for her to come along too. Rosemary accepted instantly, but as she spoke I felt something hit me really hard in the stomach, so hard in fact I almost cried out.

After telling us she would expect us on Friday evening at 7pm Elaine returned to work leaving Rosemary and I alone in the library. We had both accepted Elaine's kind invitation, but every time I thought about it I felt strongly that Rosemary should not be there.

The invitation was the best part of a week away, but on that Sunday I was compelled to visit my friend Ruth who lives on the other side of the island. In my haste to get to Ruth I had neglected to let her know I was coming and arriving at her home early on Sunday afternoon I was greeted by a look of surprise as she opened the door. As I began to re-tell the events of the past weeks Ruth promptly held her hand up to stop me speaking and told me not to say another word! Wondering why she had cut me off so abruptly I meekly followed her as she walked trance-like into the kitchen.

Ruth is a very practical human being and despite one or two hiccups where her true or Higher Self and on occasions something less desirable have broken through can usually be relied upon to take a focused and organized stab at problem solving and keeps her own spiritual awareness to her self. From her rather vacant appearance it didn't look as if today was going to be one of those days.

Asking again for the chance to tell her what had been happening I was not rewarded with an answer, but became aware of a far-away look in her unfocused eyes, to be followed moments later by an unusual sing-song voice issuing from her lips as she began to channel. The odd sing-song voice echoed around the kitchen and frighteningly she appeared to have grown in stature and was now looming over me as I sat at the kitchen table. Above me her body had begun to sway back and forth and the voice had taken on a threatening quality and was warning me that if I carried out the guidance I'd been given I would be killing not only the 'being' now confronting me, but many others like it!

To say I was amazed would be an understatement as Ruth could not possibly have known what I had been asked to do and she had not given me the chance to tell her before the current bizarre circumstances. Towering above me as I sat at her kitchen table stunned into silence and utter disbelief, her eyes wide and wild with rage and whatever was currently residing within her. The message that boomed around the room was one of anger and despair and over and over my ears were assaulted with the knowledge that my 'light' was so bright that it was blinding her/it.

Without any prior warning she then made her way out of the back door into the garden where she threw herself onto the ground writhing on her belly and trying to burrow her fingers into the earth like a huge earthworm! Never having witnessed anything quite like this before I was not sure how to handle it, but with soft words and coaxing I gently managed to bring her back inside away from any nosy neighbours prying eyes. My friend trying to dig her way into the ground was not something I wanted them to see.

It took some time for Ruth to fully come out of trance and when she did she was at a loss to know what had happened. All she could remember was seeing the brightest light she had ever seen when she looked at me and said she had never experienced anything like it before. As for me, I now understood my compulsion to visit my friend on that particular day as she had been chosen as 'the messenger' and this was a message I really needed to hear before I carried out my mission.

These beings, whoever they were, presumably dwelled deep within the Earth and were expressing fear on an energetic level in anticipation of what I was being asked to do. When I thought about it later Ruth was the perfect messenger with her great love of the earth and all things growing therein, but I can't help feeling she'd have been happier if they'd found another means of communication.

What or whoever Ruth had channeled had 'thrown down the gauntlet'. A challenge had been placed before me and there was now a choice to be made, to follow my guidance and carry out the mission or to abort ... and only I could decide.

Ruth asked me to leave her house shortly afterwards because she was still aware of a presence around her and felt that if I removed myself from her home whatever I'd encouraged in might leave with me. Driving home I thought deeply about the information I'd just received and was upset to find that the work I'd promised to carry out was going 'kill' or at the very least alter the states of many thousands of beings who dwelled deep within the Earth. Struggling with the knowledge that I was the one who would have to make the decision, but also knowing deep within myself that the guidance I had received this far was genuine.

That said I felt great compassion for these fear filled beings that had presumably lived in a dimension of darkness within the Earth for millennia and it was only natural for them to be afraid as darkness was all they knew. But what I had been given to understand was that my mission, if I accomplished it, would bring 'Light' into the Earth that would benefit all life that dwelled within and lift all beings into a higher dimension ... a higher plane of being.

CHAPTER 14

COME DINE WITH ELAINE and a MYSTERY GUEST or THREE!

The following week went very quickly and soon it was Friday, the day of our dinner date at Elaine's. Not having seen her all week I was looking forward to our evening and sharing with her what had happened at Ruth's. The only cloud on the horizon was the uneasy and inexplicable feeling that remained with me each time I thought about Rosemary being there.

Just before leaving home to open the library on Friday morning I received a phone call from Rosemary to say she would not be going to Elaine's that evening as she had been unwell the evening before and did not feel up to socializing. My stomach softened when I heard her words and for this I apologize, having no words of explanation for my feelings as I was sorry my friend was unwell.

Arriving at Elaine's home that evening promptly at 7 o'clock which is very unusual for me, as the rest of my family holds the firm belief that I will be late for my own funeral! Ringing the doorbell I was greeted by a smiling and very flushed looking Elaine, presumably from slaving over a hot stove preparing dinner. Pushing a stray lock of hair from her perspiring face she led me into the lounge and introduced me to a very solemn looking young man called David before scuttling back into the kitchen.

It was immediately obvious to me that there was something very different about David, but when our eyes met I was utterly transfixed and felt myself held by some unseen form of magnetism. Despite my inane babble David never uttered a word, preferring to stare without emotion, at me, around me, and through me, rather like he was viewing an interesting bug under a microscope. Eventually I realized that David's somewhat bizarre and non-communicative behaviour was because he was preoccupied by reading my aura and energy patterns which left me wondering how on earth I would get through the rest of the evening with this very intense young man.

To my immense relief Elaine reappeared and ushered us to the table commenting on Rosemary's absence as we sat down. At this point David spoke for the first time telling us flatly that Rosemary was never meant to be present and that only the three of us were destined to meet on that particular evening. Glancing at one another Elaine and I had no answer to such an informed statement, but somehow I understood.

Then as if someone had taken control of my mouth I asked if his parents knew he was a 'walk in'. David's answer was curt and to the point and I was informed in no uncertain terms that his parents only requirement was to know he was their son. In her innocence Elaine managed to ask what a walk-in was, but was totally ignored by David who lacking any obvious signs of emotion informed us that not only did he know when he accepted the role of 'walk-in', but that he had no intention of discussing his role. Poor Elaine looked on in bewilderment as she'd lost the thread of our conversation completely, and if it was possible became more flushed and flustered than when she'd been cooking.

A walk-in is a 'higher being' who through an energetic agreement with the in-dwelling spirit of a human continues with their Earth life and mission. This normally only happens when the original inhabitant has an important mission that they have failed to fulfill.

After the meal we adjourned to the lounge where I sat on the sofa opposite to David who had returned to the chair he'd been sitting in when I arrived. Elaine soon appeared from the kitchen and placed a steaming cup of tea for each of us on the coffee table before sitting down in an armchair next to David. No sooner had Elaine made contact with the chair than both she and David relinquished their control to higher beings and began to channel! For almost an hour they took it in turn to channel what could only be described as cosmic information, some of which concerned the mission I had agreed to undertake.

Confessing as I write, that on a conscious level a lot of it went completely over my head, although I'm certain that somewhere in the deepest reaches of my being it was all perfectly acceptable and understood.

When the channeling came to an end Elaine and David behaved as if nothing had happened and both appeared to be totally unaware of the time elapsed. Elaine even looked surprised to find that our tea was stone cold and offered to make a fresh pot. David immediately declined her offer and thanking her for dinner abruptly pulled on his coat before departing with the enigmatic statement that if he needed to find me, or the library, he would know exactly where to come without direction from either of us!

Elaine and I exchanged puzzled looks expressing the opinion that it had been something of a 'wow' evening, in more ways than one. Daring to ask how well she knew David I was to discover she'd met him at the spiritualist church only a couple of weeks earlier and had felt sorry for the somewhat despondent and lonely young man, and had invited him for dinner. It was only after doing so that she had to admit she wasn't sure she could get through a whole evening with the intense young man on her own which was the reason she'd invited me and Rosemary. Elaine apologized for roping me in, but I told her I didn't mind in the slightest because I felt it had been meant to be.

Asking her what she remembered about the evening it turned out to be very little as Elaine's memory had stopped with the arrival of the tea. She had no idea she'd channeled nor could she recall what she'd brought through, as the information was probably only relevant to me and the task I was to perform. Just like Sandy's scribbles in the library not a lot of it made any sense to the conscious me. If I had to sum up the bizarre evening, I would have to say, metaphorically speaking, it was like a kindergarten pupil being taught by senior lectures from university!

THE RETURN OF THE ANCIENTS

At the dinner party I had promised Elaine the loan of my font writer and told her I would drop it off when I got chance. So on a very foggy night the following week I found myself ringing Elaine's doorbell, font writer in hand. A smiling Elaine greeted me and welcomed me with a warm hug before ushering me into the sitting room and producing tea and biscuits.

Elaine sat down next to me and before she could pick up her cup of tea her head slumped forward as it had done on both previous occasions when I had been a spectator as she went into channel mode. Elaine's demeanour altered as she lifted her head and began to speak with the voice of someone I imagined to be a small, kindly Chinese gentleman, who proceeded to give me further information about my forthcoming task. Sitting spellbound, I listened to the guidance I was receiving, not quite believing or fully understanding what was happening until Elaine appeared to be coming out of her trance only to be immediately taken over by another much more commanding 'being' who continued the flow of information with a greater degree of authority.

This came as quite a shock to me as Elaine is a very quiet and gentle soul and the being she was now channeling exuded an awesome power and the strength behind the words gave me an instant boost of confidence. I was informed that the day I had to carry out this work would not pass by unnoticed, in fact I would be left with no doubts at all about what it was I had to do, and all I had to do in the meantime was to trust and keep my faith.

Relinquishing their hold on Elaine she was able to join me once again in the comfort of her lounge where we drank our tea and chatted about the information that had just been delivered through her. As it happened Elaine had some news of her own that day and I discovered she would be visiting her daughter, in America, at the end of the summer with a view to living there permanently. This news saddened me somewhat as I felt I was not ready for her to leave my life just yet.

The summer slipped by until one day in early Autumn I awoke with the phrase, 'Today is the day' repeating over and over in my head. Bleary-eyed I squinted at the calendar and discovered it to be the 18th of September and somewhere in my sleepy head a light came on as 18 had been the number I'd been given during the meditation on my birthday a couple of months before. Obviously today was the day, the day I'd been reminded about and given information about on so many occasions over the last few weeks. The high beings that had channeled through Elaine and David, whilst reluctant to put an accurate date in my head, had been emphatic that the correct date for my mission would not pass by without my knowledge.

Jumping out of bed and giving Dickie a bit of a surprise in the process, as I am usually quite lethargic in the morning, I prepared his breakfast in double quick time and hurried him off to work. He was completely unaware of the guidance I had been receiving over the past few months and I had kept him in the dark on purpose because I was not sure if he would have accepted it. I'm sure he already considered me a 'sandwich short of a picnic' and I was concerned that the current situation would have confirmed his worst fears. As soon as Dickie's van had disappeared around the corner I quickly slipped on my coat and boots and was out of the door like a 'greyhound out of the traps' speeding off in the car to yet another date with destiny.

The church clock was striking 9 o'clock as I parked the car in the village car park and opening the door I could hear the sound of children, their voices carrying easily on the still morning air as they filed into school. Grabbing my singing bowl from the passenger seat, carefully wrapped in a plastic carrier bag, I ran up the quiet country lane.

Arriving at my destination gasping for breath, I was confronted with an unexpected dilemma as the lower part of the hill from my vision was now completely overgrown with gorse making it impossible to carry out the exact performance I had been shown. Sending out a request for help I was immediately led a little further up the hill towards a hawthorn tree that stood alone near the summit. Without further ado I retrieved my singing bowl, tucking the plastic bag into the depths of my pocket and began to play. In my mind's eye I followed the steps, circles and the symbols I had been given until without warning my bowl stopped singing at the precise moment I completed the visualization.

My heart beating loudly in my chest I waited patiently for some sign of recognition that the task was now complete. A clap of thunder or a bolt of lightening maybe, but there was no thunder or lightening only a deep feeling of what could best be described as a knowing in my heart that I had accomplished what I had been asked to do. The vortex, having been sealed for millennia, was now open and light had entered into the darkness. Standing in silence on that lonely hillside I sent thoughts of love to all those beings that had dwelled for millennia within the darkest dimensions of the Earth as I now believed they were 'One' within 'The Light'.

Returning my singing bowl to its much maligned plastic carrier bag I made my way down the grassy track and onto the little ribbon of road that led back to the car park. A large house stands on that stretch of road and on that particular morning I could see four children, whom I had never seen before. Like little sentinels in a line from the smallest to the largest they stood on the hedge overlooking the road. As I approached them I noticed the tallest and presumably the eldest child had his right hand held above his head as if he was about to throw whatever it was he held in his clenched fist. Reluctant to be the recipient of a shower of pebbles or whatever it was he was holding and by way of deflection I asked why they weren't at school. The smallest child answered, telling me they didn't go to school and that Mummy taught them at home. By this time I was standing directly beneath them on the road, and looking up made eye contact with the eldest boy whose gaze held a sense of knowing and recognition and letting out a gasp opened his hand and let his missiles of choice, a palm full of blackberries, fall onto the grassy bank. Smiling to myself I walked away, but I could feel their little eyes boring into my back and I couldn't help feeling what a strange encounter I'd just had.

Arriving home a short while later I was surprised to find Elaine standing on the doorstep, smiling and telling me she knew I'd accomplished my mission! How could she possibly have known? But after agreeing with her that I had indeed carried out my mission we jumped up and down on the doorstep hugging each other like a couple of schoolchildren let out to play after a particularly hard maths lesson.

Inviting her in I was to find that the moment I'd been on the hill doing my 'thing' she'd been in the village shop and had experienced a sensation of completion that was so strong she'd had to come and see me to confirm it for herself. Sadly she had also come to say goodbye and to tell me she was flying out to America the very next day. Later that day and with a very heavy heart I bade her goodbye believing that I would never see her again.

Conclusion

A couple of days later, two things happened to complete this story. The first was preceded by the urgent ringing of my doorbell, only to find a woman I barely knew standing on the doorstep offering me a book as a donation to the library, telling me she'd tried to read it but couldn't understand a word. Thanking her for such a kind thought I took the book from her outstretched hand and felt a surge of energy coursing through my body accompanied by a strong feeling that I should read it myself before I put it into the library. Later that day I settled down to read the book which was by a very well respected medium who had written many books over a good number of years. After reading only a handful of pages the following information jumped out at me;

'The Ancients' are returning to Earth to carry out their missions to open the vortices that they sealed before 'The Fall.'

If ever I needed confirmation for what I had just done, this was it! I also believed the children I'd encountered standing on the hedge were none other than Ancients themselves ... overseers if you like, and it had been part of their destiny to witness me as I came back from fulfilling my mission. Only weeks after my mission I'd been out walking with Rags along that single track road and was not surprised to find the house empty and the children gone, never to be seen again.

After receiving the above confirmation I felt the need to meditate on all that had taken place. My meditation over I had a strong compulsion to sit at the computer, which is a very strange urge for me I can tell you, but I allowed myself to be led and began typing questions onto the screen. The most important question I asked that day and the uppermost thought in my mind was would I ever see Elaine again? To my amazement the answer I had not been expecting instantly flashed across my mind, my fingers typing furiously as it came through:- 'Elaine would be returning in the not too distant future and we would be working together very closely when she did return'.

At this point I thought I might have been making it all up and it was more a case of wishful thinking that I would see Elaine again. Nevertheless I printed the sheet off and filed it not quite believing the answers I'd just been given. I would just have to wait and see if the information I had received would come true.

MOTHER EARTH

The 'Great Earth Mother' spins silently through space,
If only we could see the pain written on her face
"Pain?" most may ask, "What do you mean?"
"The Earth looks the same as she has ever been."
The Earth is our Mother, both to you and to me,
But, there are none so blind, as those who will not see.
Her children have treated her badly I fear,
But, there are none so deaf, as those who will not hear.
'Mother' has been ravaged by mans' eternal greed,
For what they have thought are 'things' that they need.
Her belly has been filled with garbage galore,
Her body is bursting, but still we shout 'more'
Her skin has been covered in concrete and clay,
Her breathing is laboured. What more can I say?
Her forests are felled by mans' greedy hands,
Turned into arid desert lands,
Her seas are a boiling toxic broth,
In certain places they foam and froth,
No fish can live in this poisonous foam,
No mammal can call this place its home.
The dolphins and whales decide to retire,
Returning once more to a plane, much, much higher!
'Mother' decides she has had enough,
Watch out children … it's going to get rough.
Her body violently shudders and shakes,
Devastation is everywhere after the 'quake.
Her seas rise up into tidal waves,
Crashing to shore … only few to save'
Her volcanoes' erupt with mighty power,
Her children run and hide and cower,
The aftermath is a terrible sight,
How can we ever put things right?
This lesson is a hard one and not easy to ignore
"We are willing to listen … we cannot take more"
The answer is simple to those who can hear,
"Respect your Earth Mother and hold her very dear!"

# CHAPTER 15

THE RECONNECTION

Earlier in the summer of 2004 Rosemary had encouraged me to borrow and read a book called The Reconnection by a Dr. Eric Pearl. Excitedly, she described it as an inspirational read and informed me that a mutual friend of ours and herself had booked on the course in London later in the year for 'entrainment' by the author, Dr. Eric Pearl.

Over the next few days I read the book as instructed and found it very interesting, although I was not as enraptured as Rosemary had been and placed it under my desk in the library intending to return it to her when she next visited Andreas. That Saturday afternoon friends from the south of the island, whom I had not seen in a long time, called to see me and during the course of our conversation I felt prompted to show Rosemary's book to Peter. Pulling it out from underneath the desk I offered it to him and asked if he'd ever read it. To my amazement Peter's face flushed bright red at the sight of the book and told me he could not believe that out of all the books in the library I had chosen this particular volume to show him.

Intrigued at this turn of events I had to find out what was so special about the book and questioned him further. With a guilty nod in the direction of his partner he told me he'd booked himself on this very course only the night before, but hadn't yet mentioned this fact to his wife. Viewing us behaving suspiciously Peter's wife chose this moment to rejoin us and having eavesdropped on the last part of our conversation asked him what he was up to. Poor Peter had to come clean and admit he'd booked the course the previous evening and had intended to tell her over lunch, but unfortunately the appearance of the book had pre-empted this scenario. Fortunately for him it caused no particular dismay to his wife who not being of a similar spiritual mindset is none the less very supportive of Peter's enthusiasm in this area.

Finding that both Rosemary and Mary who he knew well would also be attending the course Peter then suggested I join them and make it a party of four. Thanking him for the invitation I declined politely as I didn't think it was really for me. Accepting my excuse he reminded me it would only take a couple of clicks on the computer if I decided to change my mind and shaking his head at the magnitude of the coincidence he had just experienced they left.

Rosemary visited the library the following week and I returned her book telling her Peter would be on the same course. This pleased her as she is very fond of him and expressed the opinion that if I was to join them it would make a lovely group. Sorry to disappoint her I was still convinced it wasn't for me and anyway I already had more commitments than I could cope with and quite apart from anything else I had no one to man the library whilst I was away.

A few weeks had gone by when I received a phone call from Rosemary who was distraught, telling me Mary had pulled out of the London trip. Mary had double booked herself for the weekend in question and as the other course was on the Island she'd decided to go to that one instead. Insistent and almost desperate Rosemary pushed the fact that there was now a space on the course, and in the hotel room, and the three of us were bound to have a good time together. Feeling sorry for her because I knew the excited anticipation she had been experiencing as the course drew nearer, so finally I capitulated and agreed to go.

Peter was almost as thrilled as Rosemary had been when I spoke to him later that evening, telling me he was now really looking forward to the trip and that the three of us going together felt just right. Putting the phone down I reflected on the fact that I was now going to London to take part in 'Reconnection entrainment' when I had steadfastly maintained that it wasn't my thing. Life and Spirit constantly make changes to our pathways, sometimes without us even noticing, but I couldn't help feeling my current direction had another hand involved.

November soon arrived and the three of us travelled to London together, staying in a hotel a few streets away from the workshop venue where we walked back and forth each day between the two.

Thinking we had travelled a long way to attend we were amazed to meet the other students on the course, some of whom had travelled a lot further than us as there were attendees from all over Europe, all intent to be in the presence of Dr. Pearl and to be entrained with The Reconnection energy.

It was a hectic and mind-blowing few days that I would find difficult to explain to anyone if they had not experienced it for themselves. On the final day immediately prior to the closure of the workshop Dr. Pearl gave a closing speech while the participants had to lie on their therapy beds, eyes closed, listening to his words. High above me, somewhere out in the Universe, my consciousness hovered as Dr. Pearl's words filtered through my mind and being;

"I am speaking to those of you whose *Dharma it is to take with you The Reconnection and use it for the highest good of all, to help raise the vibration of human consciousness on the Earth plane. Not all those of you gathered here will feel the need to take up this opportunity, but those of you who do, will know I am speaking directly to them."

*Dharma = destiny

My body was alive and my mind was on fire at his words as my consciousness floated somewhere beyond my physical self and I knew without doubt 'The Reconnection' was going to play a big part in my life from that moment on.

The extraordinary experience that had been 'The Reconnection' entrainment was now over and it was time to return to the hotel for the last time before travelling home to the Island. Leaving the workshop venue, Rosemary, Peter and myself walked back to the hotel chatting excitedly to one another about all that had taken place over the past few days. Suddenly my eyes were drawn to the name plate on the wall at the end of the street, Clerkenwell Street, I could not recall noticing it in the previous days even though we had walked many times through the street in both directions. It appeared to have a somewhat hypnotic effect on me and it began to repeat over and over like a mantra in my mind. For some unknown reason the name had been brought to my attention and one thing was certain I was unlikely to forget it!

Making our way to the airport later that afternoon we found we had time to visit Watkins spiritual book store, which for me was like entering heaven or at the very least like a child being allowed to run free in a sweet shop! On entering the shop and employing my usual ritual of asking to be led to the book I needed most I very quickly pulled a book from the shelf and giving the back cover a quick once over decided to go with my intuition and purchased it without even opening the book to look inside.

A little later whilst waiting in the departure lounge I received my first confirmation of the perfection and rightness in having taken part in 'The Reconnection' when I started to read the book I'd just bought.

Confirmation No.1 'In the first few years of the second Millennium many humans will be 'entrained' to a new energy coming from a specific area of the Universe. This energy will be passed from human to human exponentially from those that have been 'entrained', thus helping to raise the consciousness of humanity into the 5th Dimension.'

The above quote was almost word for word how Dr. Pearl himself had explained The Reconnection. How fantastic was that?

Confirmation no.2

When I returned home that evening and after sharing my story of the past few days with a rather bored husband, we settled down to watch a film, which just happened to be set in London. After only a few minutes, to my utter amazement, there was a shot of the lead character leaning up against a wall with a brass name plate next to him displaying in big bold lettering, Clerkenwell Street.

Confirmation no.3

The very next day an article in the newspaper jumped out at me just begging me to read it. The article was about a film star who had just bought an apartment in Clerkenwell Street, London. Now I knew without doubt, even after my initial reluctance, the Universe had once again led me to the right place, at the right time, with the right people, for wherever my journey was taking me next.

CHAPTER 16

'KLINGONS' ON THE STARBOARD BOW!

Now a fully qualified Reconnective Healing practitioner I couldn't wait to advertise and hone my skill. There was just one problem, I would have to use the library on the days it was closed to conduct my healing sessions because my spare room at home which would eventually become my healing room was still piled high with boxes from our move the year before.

POSSESSION
One of my first clients was a very kind, spiritual gentleman, someone I had known personally for many years and having heard about Reconnective healing he thought he would like to give it a try. We met at the library on the day of his appointment with my therapy bed set up and the room nice and warm ready for his healing session. Before we embarked on the healing we chatted comfortably together as I filled in his client information form and queried his reasons for attending. Discovering that for the past year or so he had been suffering from a peculiar heaviness in his chest, which always seemed worse whenever he was participating in any kind of spiritual work. It seemed the medical profession, after tests, had drawn a blank which was when he began to suspect that something energetic might be causing his problem.

As soon as the healing began and my hands came into his energy field an outpouring of bad language issued forth from his lips, directed at me. Stepping back from the bed I was in a state of shock as the poor man clasped his hand over his mouth and tried to stem the flow of obscenities. Apologizing for the outburst, maintaining he had no control over it and begging my forgiveness he asked me to continue. Although I was a little reluctant when he told me his chest now felt much worse, like someone was sitting on him.

Extremely puzzled by his behaviour and knowing the gentleman well I knew this was definitely out of character for him. However, I returned my hands to his energy field and could instantly feel an unusual energy rising off his chest. Lifting my hands to follow the energy I found my palms instantly sucked back towards his body by some invisible and very powerful magnet.

'Leave me alone you fxxxxxg bitch, I'm going nowhere, I belong here, now Fxxx off!'

The poor man clasped his hands over his mouth again writhing with embarrassment and blushing profusely. In that moment I realized that I was dealing with something I had only ever read about, but here I was in this extremely uncomfortable position where I couldn't just walk away and leave the poor soul. Feeling I had to do something, and quickly, the only thing I could think of was to call on some 'Higher help', and mentally reaching out to Archangel Michael I asked him to sever the cords holding whatever entity I was currently dealing with from my client. For my part I struck up a telepathic communication with the indwelling 'entity' telling it as lovingly as I could, that this was not where it belonged and it was now time to enter into the 'Light of the Higher Realms' where it would be welcomed home.

In what could only have been minutes, but seemed like a lifetime, the struggle was over and the entity was gone. To my immense relief I felt my client relax and without batting an eyelid continued with the healing session, feeling it necessary for me to behave as if this was something I was used to dealing with on a daily basis.

Jumping off the bed when the session was over my client hugged me and beaming from ear to ear told me that not only had the weight gone from his chest, but that he felt absolutely wonderful. Leaving the library a little while later with an unaccustomed spring in his step while I on the other hand was in a state of shock! I may have kept it well hidden from my client until after he had left, but I can tell you, I was shaken by the event. This was my first experience of 'one on one' spirit release, but as it turned out it would not be my last.

SANDY

Just prior to the above event Rosemary and I had been helping Sandy. It had been our hope that she would gain clarity and confidence through the weekly processes we had taken her through. Unfortunately, everything Rosemary and I tried with Sandy was to no avail and she was becoming more desperate and depressed as the weeks passed. Unable to trust in her own guidance or her inner power we had almost given up hope of ever helping her.

Rosemary and I were already at the library preparing ourselves in readiness for our session with Sandy when she arrived and announced that she had a strong feeling that she was on the verge of a breakthrough. Whilst we were delighted to hear this, our previous experience told us not to hold our breath until we could see some definite improvement in Sandy's outlook and spiritual state.

Almost as soon as we entered into meditation the sound of very heavy breathing filled the little library. Both Rosemary and I opened our eyes at the same moment and looked at one another as we realized the sound was coming from Sandy and we watched in fascination at what was unfolding in front of our very eyes like a scene from a horror movie. All we could do was call in our team of angelic helpers and ask Archangel Michael to help us hold a gentle, 'Light' filled space for the working out of what appeared to be a struggle between good and evil.

Sandy, apparently completely unaware of us writhed in her chair as her head tossed back and forth from side to side as if she were a rag doll being given a good shaking. Eyes bulging, she bared her teeth like some wild animal, making the most unearthly sounds and retching violently before finally spreading her legs wide as though in the final stages of labour as she appeared to be trying to expel some invisible and presumably satanic entity from her physical body!

Meanwhile Rosemary and I just continued to hold a space of 'Light' and our nerve, for what seemed like hours. When the fight was finally over Sandy was returned to us, a little punch drunk, but none the worse for wear although vowing never to let her control be taken against her will again.

She had learnt a very valuable lesson.... And so had we!

SOMETHING 'WICKED' THIS WAY COMES!

Late one very stormy evening, a few weeks after the above events, Dickie and I were watching television when suddenly the telephone rang which made us both jump. It was almost 11.30pm and picking up the receiver I waited for the bad news, as people ringing late at night are usually the bearers of bad news. The bearer of the news happened to be the current partner of my close friend Dawn. He was not a particularly nice man and someone whose company I avoided if at all possible. Knowing their relationship was a very rocky one I had advised her on more than one occasion to get out off it.

However, the voice on the other end of the phone was one of fear, so I listened to what he had to say. Asking me to listen, I got the impression he was holding the phone out in front of him, but all I could hear was a male voice booming and ranting in the background. When I could get him to listen to me I asked him to turn the television off so I could make some sense of what I was supposed to be listening to, only to be told the voice I could hear was Dawn and he was scared stiff because he thought she was possessed. Having heard my friend throwing a wobbly on a number of occasions I knew the voice in the background was definitely not hers. More than aware by now there was some kind of spiritual emergency going on and I could tell by the tone of his voice my caller was very afraid and just wanted me to get there as quickly as possible.

Advising him that I was on my way I gathered up a couple of things I felt I might need for my mercy dash and left my poor husband questioning the sanity of a wife who flies out of the house late on a stormy Saturday night. Telling Dickie I had no choice but to go as the situation was really quite serious, I grabbed my coat and made for the front door, and a date with destiny that required me to drive through a raging storm first. Shrugging his shoulders, Dickie let me go, having given up the argument some years previously.

Weather wise it was the worst night of the year with torrential rain and winds gusting up to 80 mph. The police had announced a 'do not travel' warning as there were branches, debris, and in some cases trees blocking roads all over the island.

My friend Dawn, unfortunately for me, lived in a remote farm house up a long and winding track surrounded by trees, at least a twenty minute drive away from my home. On the way there I had no time to think about what I would be walking into as I was completely focused on driving my little car which struggled against the gusting wind. The rain lashed down quicker than the windscreen wipers could take it away and I veered from one side of the road to the other dodging fallen branches and debris. Feeling I was definitely being challenged by spirit I eventually pulled up at my friend's house some 40 minutes after leaving home! Little did I know that the race through the storm was only one of the challenges I would encounter before the night was out.

Gathering up my bag from the passenger seat along with the few things I had thought it necessary to bring with me I battled my way to the front door, grateful that the sensor light came on when I entered its range, at least now I could see where I was going even if I could not imagine what I was walking into. At this point I had not realized that the most important thing I would need that night was my faith and trust in the Light of the higher realms and the beings that work with and through me.

Moments later a shaken and ashen face answered my urgent ringing of the doorbell and I was unceremoniously blown into the room by a fearsome gust of wind. I have to admit to not liking this man, but his whole countenance exuded fear as he thanked me for coming out on such an awful night. Asking where my friend was he nodded towards the closed kitchen door from where a repetitive banging could be heard. This concerned me more than his apologies about calling me out and his lack of knowledge of what he described as 'this spiritual stuff' and I got the distinct impression he'd rather be anywhere else than there, preferably the pub.

In answer to his pleas for help and telling him I would do my best, although I could not promise results as 'possession' was not my field of expertise, I left him to open another can of beer while I took a deep breath and called on my 'team' as I prepared to face whatever was waiting for me in the kitchen. Slowly opening the kitchen door I found the room to be in complete darkness and flicking on the overhead light I warily ventured in. The methodic thudding sound becoming louder I became aware of Dawn slumped against the far wall, her knees drawn up under her chin, her head bowed. As I approached her she threw her head back and it cracked violently against the wall before dropping forward onto her knees once more. Kneeling on the floor beside her I softly spoke her name and was rewarded as she lifted her head to look at me, but I was shocked to discover the eyes boring deeply into my own were totally unrecognizable to me! Filled with loathing and hatred, those eyes were not Dawn's as they held an astonishingly evil and mesmerizing quality. Repeating her name I was relieved to be released from the evil gaze as she lowered her head to her knees just moments before swinging it back against the wall with another sickening thud. Wincing, I realized that this was the rhythmic thudding I'd heard from the other room and to make matters worse a male voice suddenly boomed out of Dawn almost knocking me over and bouncing me of the kitchen wall;

'**The person you speak of is gone, she is no more, I am in control now, she is mine, now be gone and leave me alone**'

Standing in my own power and holding myself within the 'Light' I ignored the voice and tried once more to speak to Dawn, telling her I'd come to help and that I needed her to listen to my voice and respond only to me. But before I could get all the words out whatever it was inhabiting her made it's presence felt again;

'**I have already told you, she is mine, I am all powerful. She will not disobey me**'

Once again Dawn's head was sent crashing into the kitchen wall with a resounding thud. Having reached the point of no return I could stand it no longer, it was time to do something as I couldn't just stand there and watch my friend's head be beaten to a pulp by some invisible entity. Opening my old Bible I removed a printed sheet I had kept there for some years, it was a prayer of sorts and had been given by my spiritual teacher who had advised me to keep it for an occasion such as this. Its presence safely tucked away between the pages of my old Bible it had not entered my head for years and only the phone call earlier in the evening had brought it to mind. In fact when I'd put the phone down it was the first thing I'd thought of.

Obviously the occasion my mentor had foreseen years before had eventually arisen!

Almost as if the 'unwelcome guest' knew what I was planning the kitchen suddenly filled with the booming voice of the entity informing me again of how powerful and how in control it was. Doing my best to ignore 'it' I began to speak in a loud voice and addressed myself directly to Dawn because I was certain she still inhabited her physical body and hope upon hope was still able to hear me. Encouraging her to listen and focus only on my voice I began to recite the prayer, faltering a little when Dawn/entity stood up and loomed over me, continuing to rant and rave while glaring at me with those awful, evil eyes. Taking no notice I stood firm within the 'Light' and continued to recite the prayer whilst all the time urging Dawn to concentrate on my words. Suddenly, to my utter amazement Dawn began to undress and with every item of clothing she removed the aggressive male voice that had been emanating from her dissipated until eventually she stood before me completely naked and silent.

As I finished reading the prayer Dawn had opened her eyes and blinking incredulously, in her own voice, asked me what I was doing there. Thankfully, the eyes now staring back at me definitely belonged to my friend. However, she was even more incredulous and more than a little embarrassed at her current state of undress, but had no memory at all of the evening's events.

Sending out a silent prayer for her seemingly safe return I helped her to bed and then did my best to reassure her partner that everything was alright. Closing the door behind me I walked wearily back to my car glancing at my watch in the glare of the outside security light and was amazed to discover it was almost 3am. Thankfully the storm had abated so the drive home would be easier than the outward journey had been, assuming there were no trees across the road.

Moments later I slumped into the car only to become aware of a familiar presence. It was the same malevolent presence that had been with me in Dawn's kitchen! Evil and cloying it was now permeating my car! It was 3am and I was very tired with still a long drive ahead of me on debris strewn roads and believe me I was in no mood for any more 'aggro'. Strangely the emotion I felt most was anger and I told the presence that if it thought it could frighten me it was hitching a lift with the wrong lady as I'd already had enough of it's nonsense for one night and if it had any sense it would F*** right off while the going was good! Amazingly 'the thing' disappeared and I was once more alone in the car, my mission for that evening apparently over.

With hindsight I do believe that I was going through a spiritual initiation of sorts whereby you are challenged again and again with similar circumstances. The objective is to see if you will stand firm within your own power trusting in your faith and the support of Spirit to guide you or be filled with fear and run away from the challenge. I think I stood up to that particular challenge fairly well, but please God, no more like that, or at the very least not for a while.

CHAPTER 17

THE FLOWER OF LIFE

On Valentine's Day 2005 Rosemary and I embarked on a journey to Oxford to visit our mutual friend Eva who had organized The Flower of Life workshop to teach us how to activate our 'Merkaba' or 'Light body'.

Neither Rosemary or myself are experienced travelers and having successfully negotiated our plane and train journeys the relief as we finally approached Oxford took over and we were now behaving like a couple of excited school children. We had no idea where Eva actually lived, our only concern now was hoping Eva had made it to the station to meet us, but we need not have worried as we could not have missed her if we'd tried. We had hardly made it onto the platform when Eva bounced up the steps, her usual exuberant self, all smiles and hugs, dressed in a bright fuchsia pink coat and wearing her trade mark, oversized gold ear rings. .

We were soon making ourselves at home in Eva's obviously Feng Shui'd apartment and after allowing us a few minutes to sort out our bags she insisted on taking us to a mystery shop which she described as one of her favourite places. Rosemary and I had been travelling most of the day and we'd have much preferred a cup of tea and a chat, but when an excited Eva told us it would only take a few minutes to get there we gave in not wanting to disappoint her.

As it turned out Eva was right, the emporium was quite close and to our surprise turned out to be a huge bookshop, which delighted both of us. The place was full to the brim with spiritual, metaphysical and alterative literature. The three of us were in a state of bliss and if we hadn't been enrolled on a workshop I'm sure we would probably have spent the entire four days of our holiday in there. As I have mentioned earlier in this book it is my habit when entering an establishment like the one I had just found myself in to ask for guidance to select an appropriate volume for the place or circumstances I was currently involved in. Having done just that as I'd crossed the threshold a few minutes earlier I wandered through the vast shop stocked with tens of thousands of books and found my hand reaching out and lifting a very small book from the shelf in front of me.

Not surprisingly I'd never heard of the book I now held in my hand the title of which was 'An Introduction to The Keys of Enoch'. The author was a stranger to me as well and went by the name of J. J. Hurtak. Whether male or female I had no clue until I read the fly leaf, but the energy now coursing through me was enough of an indicator for me to know that for whatever reason, I'd been led to this particular book and I would have to buy it. Making our respective purchases our shopping expedition over, we arrived back at the flat only minutes before Armana, the workshop facilitator arrived. Eva had also invited her to stay as the course was being held in her apartment.

Later that evening the four of us ventured out to eat at a small Indian restaurant in the high street, another favourite haunt of Eva's, where we were meeting a couple of her friends who would also be joining us on the workshop. It being Valentine's night the restaurant had been decked out accordingly and the management of this little eatery had clearly gone to a lot of trouble to create what they felt to be the correct ambience for the occasion. We were shown to our table by a charming Indian gentleman through a sea of red and pink balloons with a vast array of accompanying hearts and flowers, where two other ladies of similar ages to ourselves were waiting. At first we felt a little incongruous, a group of middle-aged ladies and that's putting it politely, sitting on our own in the middle of a restaurant decked out in hearts and pink and red balloons to celebrate romance.

However, within minutes of us being seated a large group of young men arrived and sat at the table next to us and not long after that the table opposite was occupied by eight young women who all appeared to be going solo for the evening. I remember wondering what had happened to the age of romance and looking around the room was pleased to see a few smaller tables dotted about, presumably waiting for those still up for the romantic challenge of St. Valentine night.

Once all the introductions had been made we settled down to peruse the menu and very soon the waiter was scurrying off to the kitchen with our order. I should mention at this point that prior to enrolling on the course, Rosemary and I had received an information pamphlet outlining all aspects of the training and giving us a fairly detailed description of Armana and amongst her other skills listed it mentioned her ability to channel the *Ascended Masters.

*Enlightened Beings eg. Jesus, Buddha, Krishna etc.

As is usual with a group of people who have met because of their mutual interest we were all getting along well when my attention became focused on Armana. Sitting next to me I had noticed she was breathing very strangely and knowing from past experience of others I'd watched channel I was fully aware of what was likely to happen next.

My first thought was, not here, not now in a restaurant full of people. Too late, Armana was on her feet in seconds and trance-like reached across the table to point her finger at one of the ladies I'd just been introduced to. The poor woman, who obviously had no idea what was going on shot me a questioning look as Armana's outstretched finger touched her heart and she began to channel. Armana was completely oblivious to everything around her as the 'being' she had brought through assumed complete control and was speaking very loudly. Unfortunately, our new acquaintance, the poor woman who was the focus of Amana's interest had burst into tears and become highly emotional. The rest of us meanwhile were in awe of what was happening whilst being fully aware that we would be the subject of much speculation by the other customers in the restaurant.

If only the 'being' could have waited until we were back in Eva's flat and away from prying eyes, I thought. But nevertheless, fascinated by this utterly breathtaking display and trying to retain the content of what was being channeled I was also inwardly cringing and wondering if instead of serving us a meal the owners might politely ask us to leave.

As Armana finished speaking the poor woman sitting opposite

gradually regained her composure. Maybe I imagined it, but I felt there had been a huge shift in her energy field as her appearance seemed altered by the experience as she now gave the impression of being lighter and more open, as though the guidance she had received had resonated with her on a very deep level.

By now I'm sure we were all hoping Armana would come out of her trance, but no such luck and without warning she turned her attention to me! To my absolute mortification she placed the palm of her hand between my breasts and started to move it in a circular motion which made me blush to the roots of my hair. I know I'd been hoping to see her channel the Ascended Masters, but not in the middle of an Indian restaurant full of gawping onlookers! Sending up a silent plea I asked for someone, anyone, to stop her, but no one intervened and she continued to massage my chest as a flow of information was shared with me. To this day I could not tell you what was said although I know it was fantastic. It left her lips and entered my ears, but was then completely erased from my conscious mind. Bizarre, I know, but true.

When she had finished with me she continued on around the table giving a channeled message to each and every one of us and after what seemed like only minutes she sat down heavily, her head falling forward, her chin resting on her chest as her breathing returned to normal. Back from her trance Armana then continued chatting as if nothing out of the ordinary had happened and as if by some pre-arranged secret signal the moment she sat down the waiters arrived at the table to serve our meal.

Glancing at my watch I couldn't believe that almost an hour and a half had elapsed and taking a cautious look around I noticed many of the other diners had finished their meals and left the restaurant. Expecting the head waiter to apologize for the delay in the arrival of our meal I was to be disappointed, apparently time had ceased to exist for him too and with his face wreathed in smiles he organized his staff as if everything was right on time and it had only been minutes since our order had been taken to the kitchen.

The happy throng of mildly inebriated young lads from the next table stopped to share a few words and a joke or two with us as they got up to leave and we apologized for what we perceived to have occurred at our table only to be told they hadn't witnessed us doing anything other than chatting! Shaking my head it slowly dawned on me what had taken place as Armana had just given us a perfect example of what The Flower of Life was all about.

The Merkaba or Light body is a counter rotating field of energy that enables multi-dimensional travel. Fortunately whilst inhabiting it you become invisible to those inhabiting a space in a lower dimension as it actually raises your vibration to a degree whereby you become invisible. To put it simply you are able to see those inhabiting lower dimensions, but they can't see you.

That night in the restaurant Armana had moved into her Merkaba field and encompassing all of us had raised us all to a higher vibration so that we had effectively become invisible. So it was true, Armana's channeling had been completely hidden from those collected around us and only our own lower density selves had been aware of what was going on. With understanding I could now consign my initial horror at what had taken place that evening to my mental trash can, conveniently labeled, 'lack of understanding'. Thus accepting the evening as a magical experience I felt privileged to have been a part of.

The next day we all met in Eva's flat for the workshop where Armana, smiling benignly at everyone, sat quietly for a few minutes while we took our seats before standing up, clearing her throat and commencing the proceedings by reciting the following;

Kadoish, Kadoish, Kadoish, Adonai Sabbayoth

Assuming her recital to be some kind of prayer and curious to know what the words meant I asked her the question only to discover it was a prayer designed to cleanse the space we were occupying before we started to work. Never having heard the prayer before I made a mental note to find out more about it because Armana had not exactly explained the meaning of the words, despite my request, and was intrigued enough to want to find a translation.

By the end of that first day my head was aching. I had learnt or thought I'd learnt a lot about sacred geometry, but I had the sneaking suspicion that there would be more to come, much more! If the rest of the weekend was as intense as the first day had been I wasn't sure my simple brain would take it. My head spinning, full to the top with all the information we had been given earlier in the day I lay down on my bed with the little book I'd bought the previous day, planning to read for a while and hopefully nod off. Reading the introduction I was amazed to read the very words Armana had recited that very morning;

      Kadoish, Kadoish, Kadoish, Adonai Tsebayoth

The shock of seeing the words written down almost took my breath away and I read those unfamiliar, yet in some way very familiar words over and over again in utter disbelief. Shutting my eyes I could see an imprint of them blazing against my closed lids. The words were radiant and burning not only into my vision, but into the very heart of my being, feeling the love and guidance of spirit all around me. Returning my attention to the little book I found an English interpretation printed directly after the prayer;

      Kadoish, Kadoish, Kadoish, Adonai, Tsebayoth
      Holy, Holy, Holy, Lord God of Hosts

So now I knew exactly what the prayer meant and not only had my question been answered in a mere few hours, but the guidance I'd been given when I bought the book had been spot on as well.

Gathered in Eva's flat the following morning for the second day of the workshop Armana once more took the floor and recited the little prayer. Putting my hand in the air I asked if I could share it's meaning with the rest of the group. Smiling sweetly and waiting patiently Armana listened as I shared my amazing story with the others. Everyone seemed impressed, even Armana, who admitted not actually knowing an English translation of the words she herself had been taught until that very moment. I'm more than aware there is usually one person at every workshop who thinks they 'know it all' and all I can do is apologize because on this occasion I think it was me, but in my defence it was more out of enthusiasm than one-upmanship. Despite my interruption Armana continued with her program for the next couple of days and I think I can speak for all who attended when I say we were sorry when it eventually ended. For myself I have to say I found 'The Flower of Life Workshop' extremely brain taxing, interesting, eye opening, and jaw dropping in lots of different ways.

But there was to be one more remarkable occurrence that I would like to share with you because on the last night of our stay in Oxford I experienced a spontaneous past life.

Lily

The course had worn us out and on the last night Rosemary and I packed our cases ready for our trip back to the island before clambering wearily into bed hoping for a good night's sleep. Eventually I drifted off to sleep only to be woken a couple of hours later by the overhead light going on. Like an electric shock it brought me back to consciousness in the middle of a dream. Grumbling at Rosemary for disturbing my dream, she made her way back from the bathroom and climbed into bed, apologizing profusely before switching the light off again. As soon as the light went off although now wide awake I was immediately back in the dream/vision I had been experiencing before being disturbed and sharing this fact with Rosemary she immediately began asking me questions.

Rosemary. Do you know where you are and what period of history you are in?
Linda. I'm in a place called Dunston, probably somewhere in the 1880s. I'm in the kitchen of a large house.
Rosemary. Do you know the name of the house?
Linda. 'The Manse' although I'm not sure I know what a manse is.
Rosemary. What are you doing?
Linda. I'm a house maid/scullery maid and I'm working for you Rosemary. You are the cook/housekeeper

In my vision/dream, I could see Rosemary quite clearly, even though it didn't look like her as she is now, but I knew without doubt they were one and the same energy. She was reclining in an old wooden rocking chair beside an open black leaded range where a huge, soot encrusted, cauldron hung over the fire. A dirty apron tied around her ample girth, she rocked to and fro, the rough fabric of her skirt sweeping the crudely tiled floor beneath the chair. Every so often she would take a pull on the long clay pipe she held in one hand and squint out across the kitchen from under a halo of frizzled grey hair which protruded from a grubby mop cap. I in turn was also very shabbily dressed, but quite young compared to the woman by the fireplace, perhaps twenty years old at the most. I was very aware that I was not well, my chest felt weak and I found it hard to breathe in the damp and fuggy atmosphere of the kitchen.

From my vantage point, near a small window which looked out onto an orchard I could clearly see items of laundry scattered over bushes to dry and I almost leapt of the bed when the cook's voice barked through my senses, "It's raining girl get out there now and bring the washing in."

In my mind the cook's voice screamed again, remonstrating with me for my lack of action so I made my way reluctantly for the scullery and the door into the orchard. As I reached the exit I became conscious of a hand being placed on my arm and an overwhelming sensation of love emanating from a young man entering the room. Looking into his eyes I recognized this person as the son of my best friend in this life and who is about the same age as my youngest daughter! However, in the past life I was experiencing we were the same age and he was somebody who loved me. Knowing him in my regressed state to be the handyman/under gardener, he held my arm and comforted me telling me not to be upset by the harsh treatment meted out by the cook as her bark was almost always worse than her bite.

This gentle moment in the past was quickly interrupted by the Rosemary of the present wanting to know what else I could see and looking around I took in the long vista of the kitchen. In the centre of the floor stood a scrubbed wooden table around which half a dozen workmen/labourers were seated eating. Taking in the scene I realized I knew each of the men who presumably laboured on the estate where I now found myself. Some of those I recognized and knew to be still alive in my present life as Linda, the others were people whom I'd known and who had passed over into spirit.

Once more Rosemary's voice broke into my thoughts asking me if there was a window I could look out from and agreeing that there was I described the scene beyond the orchard. To my left was a copse and to my right a row of trees, which gave way to a rolling landscape with a view of the church spire in the distance.

Strangely, as I described all of this to Rosemary I became aware I didn't need to look out of the window as I had a 360 degree view of my location! Knowing that the front of this house had two large pillars and a portico over the door, even though I was standing in the scullery at the rear and when I let my mind wander further afield I could clearly see a stone bridge spanning a stream with a huddle of small dwellings around the village green and although it was about half a mile away I was aware the village was well known to me.

In the darkness of the bedroom I could hear Rosemary asking if there was anyone else present who I was familiar with and I was suddenly overcome by a feeling of great sadness at the recollection of a girl of my own age, knowing she had belonged here in this grand house too, but unlike me, she was not an employee as she had been the master's daughter and her name was Sara.

Poor Sara had suffered from TB and only recently passed over leaving me with a feeling of deep abiding love in my heart for her, knowing without any doubt that despite our class differences we had been friends. As soon as I began to think about Sara I found myself immediately removed from the house and transported to the distant church I had 'seen' from the scullery window. Clutching a bunch of bluebells I stood beside Sara's freshly dug grave my sadness was complete and totally overwhelming.

Lying in the darkness of Eva's guest room, more than a hundred years apart from the event I was reliving the tears rolled down my face drenching the pillow and it was all I could do to answer Rosemary's insistent questions, eventually telling her through my tears that I thought I must be making it all up.

"One final question" Rosemary begged. "Where is Dunston?" Instantly I was rewarded with an outline of the map of England appearing in my minds eye with just one black dot placed upon it, presumably this was the location of Dunston.

Whispering to Rosemary I requested no more questions and turning over on my damp pillow I knew I was emotionally wiped out, but the ache in my heart and the tears rolling down my cheeks were both very real and very physical.

On arriving home the next day I went straight into my healing room to practice the meditation we had been given on the workshop as we were under strict instruction to perform this meditation daily for the next 21 days. Opening my eyes after the meditation a voice gently spoke within my mind reminding me to look at the map. The map of England as I had seen it the previous evening entered my inner vision, the black spot clearly visible, presumably marking the place of my supposed regression, so jumping of my meditation stool I rummaged through an old box in the wardrobe until I found the atlas.

Leafing through the index I found three locations named Dunston. There was a Dunston in Staffordshire and another in Tyne and Wear, and also one in Lincolnshire. Looking up each one in turn I found that Dunston in Lincolnshire corresponded exactly to the black dot on the map that I had been shown in my spontaneous regression! Thrilled that I had been given confirmation I sent a silent 'Thank you' to spirit and thought that was the end of the story.

However, *four* years later during a hypnotherapy training course in Liverpool I was chosen by the tutor to take part in a past life regression. After closing my eyes and taking me through trance induction my tutor took me on a journey where I had to imagine I was on a train moving backwards through the countryside, but also back through time. The further back I went the more vivid the surroundings became leaving Linda far, far behind. Prompted by my tutor I stepped off the train when it stopped at the destination I'd chosen and to my complete and utter surprise it was none other than Dunston village. Then the questioning began.

Tutor.... Do you know where you are?
Linda.... Of course I do, it's Dunston. It's where I work.
Tutor.... How are you dressed? How old are you? Are you male or female?
Linda.... I'm 19 years old and my name is Lily and I'm wearing my best clothes.
Tutor.... Where are you going?
Linda.... To 'The Manse' of course, that's where I work. I like my master he is a good and kind man.

I relayed this information back to my tutor as I had been asked to and also to the gathered students, even though I was no longer aware of them. The only awareness I had was the tutor's voice and the unfolding scene before me.

A story then began to unfold. I as Lily had been to visit my parents who lived a few miles away from Dunston and they were very poor. Lily, it seemed, had a brother and sister, both younger than herself.

Tutor.... How did you find yourself working at The Manse in Dunston?
Linda.... My parents could no longer afford for me to live at home, and there was no work to be found for me locally so a friend of my father's found me this live in job.

Instructed by my tutor to approach the house I found myself walking between the two gate pillars and along the carriageway towards 'The Manse'. The young man I'd met in my original regression was tending the garden, and stopping to speak to him I could tell he was glad to see me even though I'd been gone no more than a few days.

Once more my tutor prompted me, only now it was to enter the house. Heeding his request I found myself walking around to the back of the property because I knew, as a servant, I was not allowed to use the main door and was only allowed to enter through the scullery door that led into the kitchen. The house seemed very quiet, unlike the first time when the cook and labourers were in evidence. Following the request of my tutor I walked through the house and making my way into the wide main hallway I could see the double front doors straight ahead, but was attracted to a door on my left and crossing the hall entered a grand room at the front of the house.

Two walls in this room were filled from floor to ceiling with a library of old leather bound books and along the gable wall was a huge open fireplace with a grand old clock sitting on the mantelpiece. Unable to see anything that would confirm a date in history my tutor decided it was time for me to leave. Telling him I couldn't leave yet he asked me if there was something more I needed to see and replying that there was I retraced my steps through the hallway and began to climb the main staircase.

Entering a bedroom at the top of the staircase I found myself in a large ornate bedroom overlooking the front gardens. Immediately I knew it had belonged to my friend Sara, the master's daughter, who had died some months before. Sitting down on the bed I was overwhelmed with sadness and tears began flowing down my cheeks both in the past and the present as I re-experienced the heartbreak of losing her. As my distress was obviously manifest in the present and must have been causing my tutor some concern I heard him asking me to choose a happy memory and as if by magic Sara was sitting on the bed beside me. We were laughing and sharing girlish stories as I brushed her long titian coloured hair and I could feel the love and special bond between us.

Breaking into this wonderful moment the voice of my tutor told me it was time to leave. Pleading with him to stay because of the happy memories I was reliving with Sara she immediately vanished and I was alone once more. My tutor then asked if there was something else I had to do before I left. "Yes, yes, there is" I begged.

A highly polished dressing table with a large mirror was placed in the light of the windows and making my way over to it I admired the beautifully engraved silver brush and comb placed neatly on its surface. It was the very brush only moments earlier I had used to brush my friend's hair. Alongside the brush on a small glass tray was laid a beautiful silver brooch. Knowing that Sara had always loved the brooch and it had been her most prized possession, but also knowing I could not leave without it I picked it up and held it in the palm of my hand to admire. It was oval in shape with a scalloped edge containing a delicate pressed violet. Closing my fingers around it I became aware of Sara standing in front of me smiling. I knew then that everything was all right and it was time for me to leave and happily allowed my tutor to bring me back to the present.

On the count of five I opened my eyes to see the other students leaning forward in their seats, each one with tears in their eyes as they had obviously lived through this whole scenario with me. So real had this experience been that when I eventually opened my hand which was still closed from the regression, I half expected to see Sara's brooch nestling there.

I have to say that although I was back in the present day there was a little more to come and that night as I lay in the darkness of my hotel bedroom I became aware that I was back in Dunston churchyard as Lily, kneeling over Sara's grave, to place freshly picked bluebells in her memory. Knowing that they had been her favourite flowers I also knew it was now a year after her death. I then became aware of having a conversation with her and I could hear myself telling her it would not be long before we would be reunited because I too was about to die of TB. The happiness I felt in that moment over a hundred years ago, but also in the present day, was overwhelming. It seems even in my life as Lily I had believed that physical death was not the end.

Conclusion

I am sure I have mentioned more than once already that I'm a self-confessed techno-phobe and although I am aware that the majority of humanity in the so-called civilized world has been linked up to broadband for years I have had to be dragged kicking and screaming into the 21st century. In fact I have only just been switched on/wired up/connected to cyber space or whatever you like to call it, as I write this chapter, so I was prompted to do a bit of research on the web.

Searching the net for archive maps and pictures of Dunston, Lincolnshire my mind was well and truly blown when I found an old map dating back a couple of hundred years. 'The Manse' was marked clearly by name, situated just on the edge of Dunston village with the local church located less than a mile away! I even managed to find some very old sepia photographs dating back to the turn of the last century with views of the village itself showing the old stone bridge over the stream and with the huddle of houses around the village green, just as I had seen it in my original spontaneous regression.

This particular life is not so unlike the account I gave of Millie in the chapter about The Cleator Clan. Once again I'd been a lowly servant girl, no such grandeur as remembering a life of comfort and fame where I was Queen Elizabeth 1st, Joan of Arc, Cleopatra, or some other important figure from history with status, wealth and power. No, not for me, or maybe I just haven't stumbled across such a life yet!

However, I still find it truly amazing when I have these past lifetimes confirmed to me in such a wonderful way because it has helped me on many occasions to understand some of the different aspects of my nature in the here and now, in this life, as Linda.

CHAPTER 18

ELAINE'S RETURN

In the spring of 2005 my friend David the local Tarot reader offered to read my cards. Never one to refuse an offer such as this I sat with bated breath as he told me I was about to be reacquainted with someone from America and that we were going to work together, as a team, for spirit. This sounded very like the information I had received from spirit the previous year when Elaine had left for America and although she and I had exchanged a few letters in the interim nothing she had written had suggested she would be returning.

However, the very next day I received a letter from Elaine to let me know she was coming back to England to tie up some loose ends during which time she would be visiting the Island on business and would love to catch up. She was visiting the island because she had been invited, in her role as medium, to take the platform at the local Spiritualist church in Douglas for the May Day weekend service.

Seating myself amongst the congregation on the day of the service I watched as Elaine entered the church with the other dignitaries, and the small procession made its way to the platform. Looking out over the sea of faces she was able to pick mine out almost instantly and I was rewarded with a huge smile of acknowledgment. Happy as I was to see Elaine again I felt a shiver running through my being as our eyes met and I acknowledged the presence of my HS as it spoke through my body. Knowing then that there was another reason for the two of us to meet again and that my own channeling as well as the information David had given would probably prove to be significant.

After the service she walked straight over to me and we hugged as if we had not seen one another in years let alone not much more than six months. When I thought about it afterwards I realized that in total we had only know one another for about four months before she had departed for America.

Elaine told me she was staying with her friend Betty for the weekend and promptly invited me back for coffee and a catch-up chat. A little later we had barely made it up the steps to Betty's apartment when Elaine asked me if I knew of any live-in jobs. Rather bemused as I thought she was visiting briefly before flying back to America I was to learn her plans had changed and she was now looking to remain on the Island. Finding it very hard to comprehend this new turn of events as only the day before I'd heard of such a job, which was not only a few minutes distance from my own home, but was in the house where my beloved Nana had passed away almost thirty years before.

Elaine became very excited about the prospect of applying for the job and we immediately rang the people in question only to find that she was the only applicant and after a quick interview was offered the position. It seemed destiny was waving its magic wand yet again as the job came with a two bedroom bungalow a few yards from the main house and was exactly what she was looking for.

A few weeks later I found myself helping Elaine to move into her new home, but as I drove up the long narrow drive a shiver ran through my body and I acknowledged that this was the first time I'd visited this house since Nana's passing thirty years before. In that moment I had the strangest feeling that somehow Nana had helped orchestrate this event. (Refer to chapter 6 and the Cleator Clan for more information on this)

Elaine and I didn't know it at the time, but now that she was living just down the road from me spirit had begun to weave threads and spin a magic web that would eventually lead us on a number of adventures together. But before these adventures could begin there would be some other challenges to face and a sad event for me to experience.

CHAPTER 19

'AU REVOIR' MY FAITHFUL FRIEND

The first of these challenges would be to bid farewell, for now at least, to my faithful little friend, Rags. She had been a much loved member of the family for more than sixteen years and had been my constant companion throughout the time of my spiritual awakening. I am more than aware that we had made a decision to be together in this life, long before we came to Earth.

It had been obvious for some time that Rags was coming to the end of her Earthly life as her once sturdy little Yorkshire terrier frame had turned into a bony counterpart and her poor little legs had become weak and very arthritic. Over time her eyesight and hearing had been getting worse and now she was completely deaf and practically blind, trapped in a murky silent world. She was still able to feel the sun on her back though and enjoy the lovely scents around our garden, but I looked on heartbroken as she would sniff her way around the borders then get disorientated as she tried valiantly to find her way to the back door at which point I would have to go and retrieve her. But, I do believe in those last weeks she regained her sight, not in this world, but in the world beyond as she would stare into space and wag her tail, standing up on those creaky back legs, begging invisible 'beings' to pick her up, just the way she had done to me before losing her sight. I choose to believe she was seeing beings from the Higher Realms of Light.

I'm sure Rags knew it was almost time for her to leave me and those last few weeks were almost unbearable to witness. Each night as I put her into her bed I prayed silently that the angels would take her in her sleep and that I would not have to make the agonizing decision that I knew only I could make, but finally I was left with no other choice. As the days dragged on poor little Rags became more and more disorientated and completely incontinent until in the end the vet had to be summoned.

If I could say that putting a very much loved pet to sleep was heartbreaking and beautiful all at the same time that is exactly how it was. On that fateful morning the vet arrived and silently and respectfully prepared the injection that would end Rags life here on Earth, whilst I cradled her in my arms for one last time, telling her how much I loved her and thanking her for so many happy years together and all the adventures we had shared. Looking up at me with those sightless, yet all seeing eyes she conveyed with deep love and respect that permission had been granted. She understood that this was to be my final act of love for her, the gift of release from suffering that would propel her into a new life beyond the one we had shared together.... in moments she was gone.

Of course I was extremely upset knowing I was going to miss her physical presence terribly, even though I was aware her soul the very essence of her being would be was absolutely fine, but I had no idea that Rags would continue to surprise me from beyond the veil.

Only days after her passing I returned home from a shopping trip in Ramsey and turning the key in the front door heard a sound I never thought I would hear again, as coming from *inside* the house was the sound of Rags barking excitedly. I don't know how long I stood on the doorstep just listening to her barking, smiling to myself and thanking her for coming back to me in such a lovely way. Over the next couple of weeks the same thing occurred twice more and during those first few weeks after her passing our black cat would suddenly rush into the hallway and stop at the spot where Rags bed had been, dancing and playing with an invisible Rags, just as they had done when she was alive.

My belief is that our cat could still see Rags as all animals are very psychic and unlike humans do not have any barriers into seeing the worlds beyond our own.

Now, some ten years later, I still feel and see Rags in my mind's eye. Often when I am out walking or being guided by spirit on some adventure she is visible to me trotting along in the lead, her little docked tail happily bobbing back and forth like a furry finger pointing heavenward.

Rags still remains an ever present friend and inseparable companion as she continues to take part in my journey, albeit from another dimension. It is a lovely comforting feeling to know she is still around and I firmly believe she will be waiting for me when it is my time to return 'Home'.

CHAPTER 20

ROCKING ALL OVER THE WORLD

This chapter has many threads to it, each one of them relevant to the story which took most of 2006 to complete. I will subtitle each individual episode as I endeavour to weave them all together in an easily readable manner.

In January 2006 I happened to be thumbing through our local free newspaper, the Courier, when an advert on the situations vacant page caught my eye. Manx Heritage who promotes and maintains the sites of historic interest on the island were advertising for vacancies for the forthcoming season. Reading on I began to tremble knowing I was very interested, but only at one particular venue, The Grove Rural Life Museum on the outskirts of Ramsey.

Being very fond of this old house I have a strong empathy with it as I well remember the two elderly sisters who owned it during my childhood. They were the last in line of the original owners and these two proud and interesting spinsters had maintained the house exactly as it had been in their own youth. It had therefore remained a time capsule of life some 150 years in the past, even the outbuildings retained their original items of machinery and horse carriages. Because of my interest I had visited the house and tea shop which was squeezed into the Victorian conservatory, on a number of occasions over the years and in doing so had become quite familiar with the layout of the place.

Without further ado and with trembling hands, I took out pen and paper to apply for one of the vacancies, but as I wrote I imagined myself standing on the first-floor landing next to the nursery door at the top of the first flight of stairs. Beside me on this landing stood a large grandfather clock and raising my eyes I took in the upper landing where a large portrait of Janet Gibb, the original mistress of the house hangs. No matter where you stand on the lower landing Janet Gibb's eyes are watching you and no matter how hard I tried I could not shake this vision from my mind as I wrote. Moments later with my hands still trembling I slipped the application into the old Victorian post box outside the library, asking myself as I did so, 'why am I doing this?' No immediate answer offered itself in either the physical or the metaphysical realms so trusting in an outcome of some kind I let the matter rest as it was definitely out of my hands now in more ways than one.

Dickie and I were leaving the island in February for the trip of our lifetime to visit New Zealand. We had been promising ourselves this adventure for years and now that Rags was gone and the girls were grown up we no longer had any excuses and the trip was finally booked with our departure date mere weeks away.

With only a week before our departure to New Zealand I received a letter from Manx Heritage inviting me for an interview to be held at The House of Mannanan in Peel. Dickie drove me to Peel, remarking more than once on the journey that I was remarkably calm about the whole interview scenario. Telling him I was not a bit nervous because I felt *sure* they were going to offer me something. His reply didn't inspire confidence telling me there would be a lot of applicants for the seasonal jobs and I would be lucky to get one. Undeterred by his pessimism I breezed through my interview in front of a panel of five, full of confidence, as though it was something I had done on many occasions, when in truth I'd never been before an interview panel in my entire life.

As the interview came to a close I was informed that I would be contacted by post of their decision and thanking them waltzed back into the reception area where Dickie was waiting with a deep inner knowing that I would be working at The Grove, come Easter. However, I still didn't know why I'd applied for the job or what I should be expecting in a spiritual sense, nor for that matter where I was likely to be led in the meantime.

NEW ZEALAND ... 'AOTEAROA' ...
'THE LAND OF THE LONG WHITE CLOUD'

Just a few days before we left my aunt rang from Wellington to ask if there was anything special we would like to do or see on our holiday as she was keen to organize an itinerary before we arrived. Telling her I would love to swim with dolphins I was a little disappointed to find that nothing like that was available in or around the Wellington area, but she promised to contact my cousin Gary after speaking to me to see if he knew where this activity could be found.

Muriel was on the phone again the next day to say she'd just received an e-mail from Gary who lives Tauranga after speaking with him the day before. I quote:-

'Hi Mum, I found a flyer lying on the kitchen worktop this very morning advertising excursions to swim with wild dolphins from one of the local quays. Not sure how it got there, but has all the hallmarks of something to do with Linda!'

So it seemed I could now look forward to making my dream of swimming with wild dolphins whilst in New Zealand a reality. On the one hand how wonderful, on the other I hoped they provided very good buoyancy aids as I'm afraid of deep water and not a strong swimmer!

After a very long and tiring flight we arrived at Wellington airport in the middle of a violent thunder storm with hailstones the size of golf balls, the like of which I had never experienced before in my life. Thankfully my uncle was waiting to whisk us home which was only minutes away from the airport. We would be spending the first two weeks of our holiday with my aunt and uncle in Wellington before traveling up country to the little community of Kati Kati to spend the remainder with Harold and Jude, before flying home from Auckland.

It took us a little while to get over our jet lag, but on our first full day of sightseeing my aunt whisked us into Wellington City with a long list of things she thought we'd like to see. The first place we visited was the main government building known locally as 'The Beehive' because of its unusual design. Housed within are many ancient Maori artifacts and escorted tours around the building were on an hourly basis throughout the day.

Joining the queue we were soon ushered into a room along with about twenty other people where all our belongings, bags, shopping and cameras had to be left in lockers. Next we were given a lecture on how to behave whilst in the building and expressly forbidden to take photographs as all cameras had to be left in the lockers, being told that disregarding this advice was a punishable offence! As the guide finished speaking there was a bright and visible flash from behind me as if someone had taken a photograph and along with the rest of the crowd I turned to see who the culprit could be. All eyes were drawn to a very large Tongan man, dressed only in shorts and T-shirt, standing at the back of the room. The guide was livid and demanded the Tongan man hand over his camera immediately, but the poor man, giving an excellent impression of a rabbit caught in the headlights of a car, turned out the pockets of his shorts to prove he'd left his camera in the locker next door as requested. The flash we had all witnessed was apparently a mystery!

After the above false start we had a lovely day eventually returning to the family home on the outskirts of Wellington for our evening meal. During our meal my aunt suggested we drive to the top of Mount Victoria after sunset and watch the lights come on all over the city. We all thought it was a brilliant idea and about half an hour later we found ourselves getting out of the car just a flight of steps away from the summit of Mount Victoria. It was a full moon that night although low cloud had kept it hidden from our sight up until this point, but as I reached the top step and was about to stand fully on the summit of Mount Victoria the moon in all its brilliance slipped out from behind a bank of clouds and shone brightly on to a very familiar face. It was only the Tongan man from our encounter in 'The Beehive' earlier that day! Walking past me as he made his way down from the summit without recognition on his part, but for me, my body was on fire and the resonation of spirit was running up and down my spine as I knew something significant had just taken place and I was aware enough, by now, to know that this was no coincidence. To see the same man twice in the same day, in two very different places in a city of almost 200,000 people would have taken some very serious calculations of the odds. I felt my awareness was being tested by the above experience and our holiday had only just begun, but I was to find out as our adventure progressed that this was not just a holiday.

THE LABYRINTH

Let me begin by giving you the definition of a labyrinth.
At its most basic level the labyrinth is a metaphor for the journey to the centre of your deepest self or if you will your soul. The journey then brings you back out again into the world of form, but bringing with you a broadened understanding of who you truly are.

After the above events everything progressed fairly normally for the next few days and we spent our time doing all the touristy things like taking in the beautiful sights of Wellington and the surrounding areas. During our second week my uncle invited Dickie to join him and his friends for a round of golf at their local course which would leave my aunt and I to our own devices, an event I was to learn she had been eagerly anticipating for the past week as she wanted to take me to Frederic Wallis House. Not familiar with the place, I learned it was about an hours drive away at a place called Lower Hutt and interested to know more about the place my aunt handed me a brochure which provided me with the following details;

'Frederic Wallis House is a retreat and conference centre, the property was purchased in 1937 by Margaret Wallis to commemorate her late husband, the third Anglican Bishop of Wellington. Margaret Wallis's dream for its use was broadly inclusive and holistic in its nature, it was to provide a unique environment to the individuals who visited the house, to help them find peace and serenity within its walls and grounds and to contribute to the fulfillment of their hopes and aspirations, for their body, mind and spirit.'

The more I read the more I felt in tune with this lady who had long since passed on. Even though her husband had obviously been a very religious man it appeared that she herself had not been fettered by the boundaries and dogma of organized religion and I was excited at the prospect of visiting this place, even more so when I found out it had a large labyrinth in the grounds. Feeling spirit moving through my body as I read about the labyrinth, I felt very strongly that another adventure might lie ahead.

Setting off as soon as the men had left for golf, we arrived at our destination some fifty minutes later. There was an air of excitement about us and we behaved like a couple of kids playing truant for the day, but unfortunately our excitement was short lived as when we tried to enter the house a very nice receptionist explained, apologetically, that there was a convention taking place on that particular day and entry was restricted to only those attending.

As you can imagine we were both crestfallen and deflated by the news which must have been apparent to the receptionist, who, taking pity on us, offered to let us look around the extensive gardens in way of recompense. We were not about to turn the offer down so we quickly made our way around to the back of the house where a large lawn surrounded by trees and shrubs stretched out before us.

It was the most beautiful day. Above us the sky was azure blue, not a cloud in sight and the whole scene was bathed in wall to wall sunshine as we wandered through the garden chatting easily in search of the labyrinth. We had almost reached the bottom of the garden which was screened by low bushes and surrounded by large trees when suddenly and quite by chance we came across a small flight of steps leading down onto the most magnificent labyrinth.

Inside my chest I could feel my heart beating madly as I descended the steps knowing that my HS had brought me here and that I was meant to walk the labyrinth. Finding myself at the entrance my aunt knew what I was about to do so she settled herself on an old wooden bench to await my return.

Setting my intention for my HS to guide me before entering the labyrinth I entered into my silent space and walked slowly and deliberately following the meandering narrow pathway as it spiraled into the centre. Some fifteen minutes later I reached the centre with no thought in my mind as to what I was to do when I got there. The centre itself was composed of four tiles each one bearing a simple flower motif and I imagined they were emblematic of the 'seed of life' … 'the beginning of all things'. Remaining in silence until I was prompted by spirit I inwardly gave thanks to the four compass points, standing on each tile in turn as I did so. Then I gave thanks to Mother Earth acknowledging the flesh and bones of my body as part of the earth, the vehicle which enabled me to walk my path in the third dimension. Then I gave thanks to Father Sky acknowledging the air that I breathe which is my connection to the life in my body and 'The All That Is' and finally I gave thanks for my continued guidance on my journey through my life here on Earth.

Opening my eyes I remained standing on the central four squares of the labyrinth and from my vantage point I could see my aunt seated on the old bench looking over at me. Without thinking I told her how wonderful the experience had been and was amazed to hear my voice echoing around the labyrinth as though it had been issued from a loud speaker! The look on her face was one of astonished surprise and I'm sure mine must have been the same. I spoke again, just to test it hadn't been a fluke, but the same thing happened. Stepping off the centre point I spoke and my voice returned to normal? Hopping on and off the tiles a couple more times to prove to myself that where I stood was causing the effect, before accepting the bizarreness of the situation and following the labyrinth back to my point of entry. By the time I'd reached the bench I'd persuaded my aunt that she must try the labyrinth too and feeling very happy and strangely changed by the experience I watched as she meandered through the labyrinth in her silent space.

Sitting on the bench in such a peaceful place I sighed deeply as a shaft of warm sunlight shone through a gap in the canopy of overhanging trees. It was heaven and I rested quietly in a very deep contemplative place until I was suddenly jolted into the present by the arrival of a very moth-eaten old tom cat that had jumped up onto my knee. His general battered appearance suggested most of his lives had been used up and he was probably down to the last one of nine. Most likely a stray, he was very thin and looked short of a good feed and I tried very hard not to contemplate the flea population he was undoubtedly home to. Purring loudly he looked straight into my eyes with the strangest look of recognition then apparently well satisfied with his choice of lap he draped himself over my legs, front paws dangling over one side and his back legs dangling over the other. Within seconds he was completely relaxed and fast asleep, drooling, his tongue lolling through a gap where some of his ancient teeth were missing.

Thinking to myself that it was most strange for a stray cat to be so trusting of a complete stranger I could not quite believe what happened next as a beautiful and enormous butterfly appeared from nowhere and began to hover only millimetres from my nose! Like the cat it stared knowingly into my eyes for some time before proceeding to flutter around and around my head completing circuit after circuit in an almost ritualistic pattern. But at the exact moment my aunt exited the labyrinth the cat jumped down from my knee to disappear into the shrubbery and the butterfly flew away. I hadn't a clue what any of these unusual events meant, but deep within my being I knew they were all significant of something I was not yet a party to.

SWIMMING WITH DOLPHINS

We had spent two wonderful weeks in and around Wellington and had been on many excursions including a trip to South Island thanks to the generosity and kindness of my aunt and uncle who had devised and provided us with a packed itinerary. Not content with all they had already done my aunt and uncle planned to drive us up country to Harold and Jude's. Included in the trip would be an overnight stay in Rotarua to see the geysers and visit a Maori village before spending another night in Tauranga to visit their son, my cousin Gary and also my much anticipated excursion to swim with wild dolphins.

Arriving in Tauranga after a very long and tiring journey I could barely sleep as I was so excited at the prospect of swimming with wild dolphins the next day. I'm always up for a challenge and this would be my biggest challenge to date, conveniently having put to the back of my mind the fact that I am not a very strong swimmer and have always been extremely frightened of deep water.

The following morning held the promise of a beautiful day as the skies were clear and blue with not a breath of wind. Sending up a silent thank you for the glorious day knowing that the sea would be like a millpond which would be to my advantage being such a weak swimmer.

My aunt, although offering to drive us down to the quayside to catch the dolphin boat made it quite clear she did not want to come on the excursion with us, deciding instead to remain on dry land and dropping us off at the quayside some time later commented on the fact she thought us all mad before abandoning us to our fate.

The captain of the small boat we were about to board turned out to be a very friendly man along the lines of a rather shabby Captain Birdseye and after welcoming us aboard he was eager to make conversation as we waited for the remainder of the passengers. Discovering that we were from the Isle of Man, although my aunt and uncle had lived in New Zealand for over 40 years, he amazed us by telling us it was a 'Manxman' who had in a roundabout way inspired him to get into the dolphin excursion business. We all looked at one another in surprise and disbelief. What were the odds of Captain Birdseye knowing someone from a little island in the middle of the Irish Sea, half a world away?

My uncle, not content with this small piece of magic asked for the Manxman's name and discovered it to be that of someone he had been friendly with at school over 60 years before! If we were already flabbergasted this revelation left us reeling and I couldn't help feeling that this auspicious start was to set the mood for the rest of a very special day.

There were about ten of us on the excursion that day and as the tiny boat was only about the length of my living room all the seats on deck were occupied. The Captain requested we all change into wet suits before we left the quay so that we would be ready and prepared to get straight into the water should we come across a pod of wild dolphins. As soon as we were all 'togged up' in our wet suits we set sail in spectacular weather with everyone aboard in high spirits and looking forward to what the day would bring.

Sailing out of the bay we made our way around Mount Monganui, a small mount attached to the coast of Tauranga by a spit of land. About a mile out from the coast the water was the most beautiful shade of turquoise blue, but beyond that it turned into an inky blue where the shallow waters gave way to the deep ocean. Fervently hoping that we would not need to sail into the deeper waters I put the thought to the back of my mind.

We'd been at sea for about three hours with not a dolphin in sight and thankfully, to my relief, the small craft had hugged the coastline along the Bay of Plenty sailing along in the crystal clear waters.

Anchoring in a cove to eat our packed lunch we all expressed our impatience at not having seen any dolphins, whereby the captain had to explain that these trips were not a 'done deal' as we were looking for wild dolphins, emphasis on the 'wild' and that they could not be procured at will. I'm sure he must have been thinking he might have a mutiny on his hands if we didn't see any dolphins soon, but he'd hardly finished speaking when turning to scan the sea he pointed a gnarled forefinger out toward the horizon and yelled 'dolphins'.

Within minutes the anchor was up and the little boat raced off through the crystal waters at a rate of knots, heading straight for the inky darkness of the deep water. We sailed further and further out to sea crossing into the unfathomable depths of the ocean still scanning the horizon for the elusive dolphins. We were miles and miles out to sea and the coast was no longer visible when I first noticed the sky changing as above us the clear blue sky was being rapidly replaced by storm clouds, the wind was freshening and the sea was becoming very rough.

The little boat began to pitch and toss as the waves grew bigger and everyone else had disappeared below deck with the exception of the captain, Dickie and me. Dickie knew that what we were experiencing was the worst fear of my life and also that I'd experienced repeated dreams of drowning since being a small child. Encouraging me to follow the others and go below decks he knew there was a very real fear that being tossed about in a small boat in very deep water my fears might easily become reality, but I steadfastly refused to join the others below despite his protestations that remaining on deck was unsafe.

Yes, this was my greatest fear and nightmare all rolled into one, but I felt strangely detached, very calm and at peace with an inner knowing that if we should be pitched into the stormy waters and drowned, everything would still be alright.

Almost laughing as we clutched on to whatever we could to remain in place the boat lurched from side to side with the mast dipping towards the water and the spray hitting us square in the face. The look on Dickie's face was one of concern and disbelief at my apparent indifference as to whether we lived or died, but being the honourable person he is he remained on deck and kept me company while Captain Birdseye fought with the wheel, doing all he could to keep the boat afloat and steer a course back to the safety of the quay.

Once back on the safety of dry land I relinquished my desire to swim with wild dolphins because I knew my recent experience was not by chance as this I felt was a destined part of my journey to let go of my fears and allow myself to understand how far I had travelled... and not just in miles.

THE LONG AND WINDING ROAD

We spent the remainder of our holiday with Harold and Jude who like my aunt and uncle, were kindness itself and had also prepared an itinerary of many and varied excursions for our benefit. Whilst staying with them I received an e-mail from my friend who was picking up our mail, to let me know Manx Heritage had offered me a job at The Grove Museum for the coming season. The post was for only a few hours a week as a tour guide, but I just knew that those few hours would be for a special reason. This was just another piece in the jig-saw and I would have to wait patiently and see where these connections were going to take me.

Determined to make the most of our last ten days with Harold and Jude we went out on many excursions, one of which took us high up into mountains covered with ancient trees. Weaving along narrow winding roads as the road snaked up through the range following one hairpin bend with another until eventually we were thousands of feet high. We had just begun our descent down through the seemingly unending narrow roads when suddenly 'out of nowhere' a car coming up the mountain careered across the road towards us as it misjudged the hairpin corner. Harold was driving and took immediate averting action, swerving onto what gravel there was to be found at the side of the narrow road and coming to a screeching stop only an inch away from the edge. All of the above took only seconds to unfold, but I experienced the sensation that time had slipped into a lower gear and almost come to a standstill. My mind remained sharp and clear throughout and to my amazement my heart never missed a beat, I was calm and at peace, just like on board the dolphin boat the week before.

Peering out of the window as we set off again as I stared down into an abyss which fell away only a hair's breadth from the wheels of the car. My only thought was how very differently this scenario could have turned out and for the second time in a matter of days we had cheated death and I felt totally indifferent.

4 IS A MAGIC NUMBER

There were only days left of our holiday in New Zealand when I experienced the most amazing day with numbers. For a reminder about master numbers such as 11, 22, 33, 44, or 222, 333, 444 etc. Please refer to chapter five.

Being very aware that I might never get the chance to see Harold again, not on the physical plane anyway I felt whatever time we had left together was all the more special as we set out on yet another excursion.

We had been driving for an hour or so in a direction we had not travelled before when a car suddenly cut in front of us making Harold swear as he slammed his foot on the brake and blew the horn. The car roared away ahead of us and I couldn't help but notice the number plate was 444. Less than two minutes later we turned onto route 444 and within a mile or so two other cars had passed us with the number 444 on their plates. Intrigued I wondered why my HS was bringing all these numbers to my attention and as that thought entered my mind we past a large industrial estate where the numbers 444 at least 20 feet high were painted on the wall of a warehouse in bright red paint. I almost laughed out loud at the incredulity of it as there was certainly no chance of missing them.

The day continued in the same vain and eventually I lost count of how many 444's I'd seen, but strangely no one else in the car seemed to notice or if they had they'd not felt the necessity to remark upon it, which left me feeling these numbers were in some way only important to me.

THE FINGER OF FATE

All too soon our holiday was over and very reluctantly Harold and Jude drove us to Auckland airport where we would begin the first leg of our long journey home. Touching down in Singapore for re-fuelling we had to comply with safety regulations and everyone had to disembark, being ushered into a holding lounge within the airport buildings. The place was already full when we entered as everyone presumably was waiting for their planes to be re-fuelled too.

Dickie and I wandered around the huge lounge looking for somewhere to sit when we were suddenly alerted to a cry of 'Hey Boy' over the hum and background chatter of hundreds of people. 'Hey Boy' is a typically a Manx form of greeting and only normally used between friends. It certainly wasn't something we were expecting to hear bandied about in Singapore airport! Looking around we eventually spotted a couple of friends from the island waving frantically to us over the sea of faces in the lounge. Feeling spirit run through my body as I recognized them and making our way across the crowded room we laughed and exclaimed to each other the sheer coincidence of meeting in such circumstances. Especially when we discovered it was only a glitch in their timetable that had left them stranded in Singapore at the same time as us.

I could feel spirit's hand in all of this as the lady we had just met had retired from the Grove museum the year before and it was her post that I had just been offered! Sitting happily chatting in Singapore airport we discussed my position as her replacement, the news of which amazed her and I could feel the pieces of the jigsaw that spirit had been placing in front of me being neatly slotted together, but still did not know what or where it was leading to.

Although our holiday was over there was still more drama to come before we reached the safety of home as flying over the Himalayas a few hours later we hit a very bad electrical storm and the pilot announced that everyone must remain seated with their seat belts fastened, even the cabin crew. The plane tossed and pitched, like a bucking bronco while the lightening flashed and arced fiercely all around us when suddenly the plane dropped hundreds of feet leaving my stomach somewhere miles above. All around us people were screaming and crying, except for maybe a handful of staunch souls which amazingly included Dickie and me.

Sitting tight, enduring it all with a stiff upper lip, knowing that nothing could be done other than pray, and yes some people were fervently and visibly praying as we hit one air pocket after another.

Strangely, I did not feel the need to pray only to trust, even though all around me there was chaos and fear I felt nothing but calm and a sense of peace. Needless to say we did make it through the storm and arrived home safely, although the whole experience was to prove an important lesson for me.

THE LESSON: 'DO NOT FORGET TO ASK'

When we arrived home I felt so unwell I went straight to bed. Having experienced jet lag on our arrival in New Zealand I assumed that this must be what was ailing me although it felt somehow quite different. Remaining in bed for days on end, not wanting to get up, dressed, washed or even to speak to anyone. This was most unlike me. It felt as if I was in a huge black hole which could only be described as deep depression and despair, not an emotion I am too familiar with. The thoughts in my head were deep and dark, thoughts of suicide and impending death. Dickie had never seen me like this before and was getting very worried as the days dragged on with little improvement in my general demeanour.

Almost a week had past when I awoke one morning from the first sound sleep I'd had since our return and my overriding compulsion was to meditate. As this was the first interest I had shown in anything since our return I dragged myself out of bed on weak legs and staggered into my healing room where I sat down heavily on my meditation stool. Closing my eyes to meditate I sent up a plea for help and to my surprise I instantly witnessed myself sitting calmly on board the aircraft during that terrifying electrical storm. I could hear all those hundreds of people screaming and praying for their lives, but I was also able to see jagged lines of energy emanating from each person and to my amazement each and every jagged line was plugged into *me*.

Now I understood and could feel the resonation run through my body as my HS was showing me how I'd absorbed the other passengers' fear, like an empathetic sponge. Remaining calm and positive during the storm I'd sucked up their fear as they gave it off and since my return I'd been suffering from an overload of negative energy which of course often manifests itself as depression. With a sigh of relief I accepted the enlightenment my HS had given me and opening my eyes said the following;

'I choose in this moment to let go of all and any negative energy that I may have absorbed into my being unknowingly that does not belong to me. Thank you. So be it, it is done.'

Giving thanks to my HS for this miraculous revelation I then walked out of my healing room and back into my life as if nothing had ever happened, completely well and ready for the next leg of my journey.

MORE ENLIGHTENMENT

When I eventually made it back into the library after our return home and my period of 'incapacitation' I was greeted by the familiar face of Sylvia, one of my regular visitors, who had come to return a couple of books. She obviously had time on her hands and making herself comfortable in the chair next to my desk, settled down to hear about my adventures. As I began to tell her about the 444 sequences she gasped and grabbing one of the books she'd just returned began thumbing through the pages before passing it to me and announcing proudly that she'd just been reading about number sequences and this book would explain it all.

The book was none other than The Flower of Life by Drunvalo Melchesidek. A book, I might add, that I was already familiar with having had to read it before I took the Flower of Life workshop the year previous.

The page Sylvia had offered me told the story of the author's experiences in Egypt, which were somewhat similar to my own in New Zealand where the sequence 444 had shown up for him on a number of occasions. The conclusion he had made was that whenever the number sequence 444 repeatedly shows up the person involved is going through some sort of 'Spiritual Initiation'. After reading the page I was left with the feeling that I was reading this information for the first time and that I had not come across before, even though I knew I had.

Slowly I began to question all the events I had lived through in New Zealand and had experienced on the journey home. Had it been a spiritual initiation of some kind? And had Sylvia's HS in collusion with my own HS been compelled on that particular day to pop in and enlighten me? I felt the answer to all of the above was a resounding, yes!

Dear reader, just in case you were in any doubt, you are still reading the somewhat convoluted chapter 20.

STONEHENGE BECKONS

Not long after our return from New Zealand a very excited Rosemary called to let me know Sandy Stevenson, one of our favourite spiritual authors, would be touring the UK later in the year. As we had both read and re-read her book on a number of occasions and thought it very good I had to agree that an opportunity to meet her in the flesh would be wonderful. Sandy is resident in Australia so the opportunity to see her was very rare, but on this occasion she would be holding a workshop in Buckinghamshire, not too far from our friend Eva's.

A couple of days later Rosemary was back on the phone to tell me Eva had extended an invitation to both of us and our mutual friend, Margaret, to stay with her, which would allow us all to attend the workshop together, even offering to do the driving if we all clubbed together and shared the cost of a hire car. Not realizing it was all part of the plan spirit was formulating I saw it simply as an opportunity too good too miss and agreed to go.

One morning a few weeks later I received an impassioned phone call from a lady requesting a healing session and was insistent that it had to be on that particular day. Fortunately for both of us I was free, as having recently started my new job at The Grove my schedule was now getting a little top heavy, however as I was not working that day I invited her to my home for the session. Arriving a few minutes before eleven o'clock I ushered her into my healing room anxious to know what the urgency was, unfortunately she didn't have a clue why she had to see me only that she did. When the healing session ended she jumped up from the bed and announced she had a message for me and closing her eyes she uttered the following; 'Later this summer you will be taken to ancient places of high energy not on this island and there you will be approached by those chosen to carry out work of great spiritual importance.'

Opening her eyes she told me this message had been repeating itself over and over again in her head whilst she had been receiving healing. Telling me she felt much lighter after her session and was sure it had done her a lot of good she allowed me to escort her to the door. Thanking her for the message, although I remained a little puzzled at the mornings outcome and bidding her goodbye I returned indoors to answer my urgently ringing telephone.

A trilling Eva was on the other end of the phone hardly able to contain herself, as was usual, when she had some exciting news. Almost struck dumb I listened as Eva explained that a friend of a friend had secured passes for us too visit Stonehenge while we were away to attend Sandy's course. Not only that, but they were passes for inside the fence where we could get 'up close and personal' with the ancient stones and we would visiting the site at sunrise. Again I could feel the workings of spirit flowing through my body as I agreed with Eva how wonderful that would be, but while she was talking the message I had just been given was repeating over and over and I started to wonder where all this was leading, presumably to Stonehenge for a start.

'THE GROVE'

I was now working at The Grove Museum as a part-time tour guide having easily made friends with the other members of staff, most of which had worked there for a number of years, returning season after season. On my first day I was shown to my station by Jean the manageress. I'm sure you have probably guessed where my station was located, in the exact place I had envisioned as I wrote my letter applying for a job! At the top of the first flight of stairs, outside the nursery door, next to the grandfather clock and overlooked by the portrait of Janet Gibb hanging on the upper gallery. Not only that, Jean informed me before leaving me on duty that I would be standing on the very spot where Janet Gibb had died!

It was not long before I told Jean and her friend Barbara, who also worked there, about the strange phenomena and synchronicities that spirit sent me on regular occasions, explaining to them that it was a form of 'spiritual satnav', a guidance system of sorts. Bringing in a copy of my book, which I thought might better illustrate my point I watched them reading avidly during their tea breaks. I could tell they were both intrigued, although I was not sure if they saw the aspect of spirituality and guidance each story held within it, but they were more than happy to listen and find out more, even though secretly I think they thought I was a little mad.

A number of strange things happened during my summer working at The Grove, which was not surprising really as it is an old house with a lot of history attached to it. The first of which was the flickering lights, which occurred as another employee and I were standing on the downstairs landing discussing Janet Gibb. These phenomena occurred on a regular basis when Janet's name was mentioned and one of the new employees actually witnessed her walking through the house dressed the same as she appeared in her portrait. And I myself witnessed a middle aged man pulling on his riding boots in one of the bedrooms who had been seen on more than one occasion by others as well. It was apparent the whole house had an atmosphere and life of its own, which continued unabated despite the passage of 21st century onlookers.

Then there was the case of the missing antique candle snuffer, which, I was informed, had disappeared at least three seasons before. Jean thought it had been pilfered and was gone for good only to find it returned to the exact place it had disappeared from. No one had actually witnessed its return, but within a couple of days of me being stationed outside the nursery door there it was, back on the night stand it had disappeared from years before.

Only days after this event Jean arrived at work and very excitedly told me an item that had disappeared from her study at home had miraculously reappeared in the same place, and after giving her husband the third degree she'd had to admit neither of them knew how this had happened. Expressing wonder in what would or could happen next, Jean, smiling broadly at me went off humming happily to herself. I believe a shift had taken place in her consciousness, either from reading my book or listening to my stories and the belief in a magical world of guidance had returned to her thought patterns changing her perception of reality.

The summer rolled on and I was enjoying working at 'The Grove' when one morning Jean met me at the door and asked me to take a stroll to the bottom of the garden before starting work as she was confident there was something I should see first. Intrigued I made my way along the grassy pathway, through the leafy shade of the huge old trees, rhododendrons bushes and assorted shrubbery to the bottom of the front garden of this grand old house. Directly in front of me, almost at the boundary hedge where the garden meets the field beyond, someone had erected a tapered flagpole about 20 feet high, the tapered end having been buried in the soft earth.

Surveying it, from a few feet away, I could feel spirit coursing through my body and my heart was beating madly in my chest. I'd never seen anything like this before, nor did I have a clue to its purpose, but it was having an extremely strange effect on me. Walking up to the structure I placed my hands on the cool, clean white shaft and closing my eyes asked for guidance. As I did so my minds eye was filled with a vibrant line of energy coursing its way over the Manx landscape like a stream or flowing river of light. This river of light emanated from the direction of Snaefel, our only mountain on the Isle of Man, and entered the very spot where the structure punctured the earth, right at my feet. My HS also knew that this energy point was the meeting place of rivers of light that criss-crossed from puncture points around the Island. From where I stood the lines of energy then flowed from our shores to much further afield, but I was not privy to where these streams of energy led.

Opening my eyes I noticed a plinth a few feet away which attempted to give an explanation for the structure. It seemed the pole had been inserted in the ground to symbolize a huge acupuncture needle and that this one along with five more had been placed at ancient heritage sites around the island with the intention of releasing blocked energy, just as acupuncture is used in the human body. The Earth, after all, is a living body and a sentient being with blockages of 'her' own and the enormous wooden acupuncture needles had been put in place to help heal the planet.

I knew what I'd just experienced was meaningful and I also knew that for something so 'New Age' to be erected the very season I happened to be working there was unlikely to have been coincidental, as well as the fact it was very out of context with the historical atmosphere of The Grove Museum garden. As usual I was party to some huge spiritual plan, but in common with most of their achievements I was only going to receive bite sized chunks at any one sitting.

RITUALS OF OLD AND RIGHTS OF PASSAGE

The summer just flew by and soon it was time for me to leave 'The Grove' as my contract was only until the middle of August, by which time I think all that needed to happen there had happened. The following week I was off to Oxford with Rosemary and Margaret, we were all looking forward to staying with Eva and attending the Sandy Stevenson workshop in Chesham, but after receiving that mysterious message from a client earlier in the year I was more interested in our forthcoming trip to Stonehenge.

We'd only been in Oxford for one day before having to rise well before dawn to travel the distance required to reach Stonehenge to witness the sunrise. It would be fair to say that I was the most excited person on the trip with the message I'd been given earlier in the year repeating over and over in my head. Eva had hired a people carrier as she had invited three of her friends, Marilee, Hazel and Angela who would be joining us on the trip. I'd met Angela the year before on a previous visit to Eva and we had gotten on really well, in fact I'd sent her some poetry I'd channeled in 2004 as I'd found her a very sensitive and spiritual woman.

Arriving at Stonehenge just before dawn along with about fifteen other people, presumably all bearing passes like ourselves, Eva parked the car before introducing us to three Japanese girls with whom she was acquainted. Eva being Eva had managed to get them passes as well.

As we entered the sacred space that is Stonehenge we all separated and without speaking to one another dispersed amongst the huge monoliths. Reverently, in silence and respect, I marveled at the ancient hands of higher intelligence that had placed these magnificent standing stones. Wandering around the ancient site in a state of total awe and wonder I felt, rather than saw, the first rays of the sun as they fingered the horizon at dawn.

Suddenly I was drawn to stop and place my hands against the stone nearest to me and as I did so the three Japanese girls walked over and requested that I lead them in a meditation. Only too willing to comply, I instantly remembered the words of the message I had been given telling me I would be approached by those who were to carry out important spiritual work with me.

Asking that we join hands before closing my eyes I was instantly transported in my mind to 'The Grove' where my hands were placed on the cool shaft of the acupuncture needle erected in the garden. Speaking aloud to the assembled girls, words floated into my consciousness then out through my mouth completely by-passing my brain and I was aware throughout the meditation that our little group was enveloped in a beautiful swirling energy, not only emanating from The Grove, but many other places as well, and it was all linking and connecting with the massive swirl of energy now filling Stonehenge!

When the meditation was over we all hugged as if we were old friends, even though we had all been complete strangers until minutes before. I asked them if they had received anything during the meditation and unbelievably, but not unexpectedly we had all received a similar vision of a massive energy sweeping and gathering pace as it came towards Stonehenge only to swirl around us and the huge stones before exiting through the centre of the ring. Amazingly, we had all been aware that the energy had not only shot up into the heavens, but also down into the Earth at the centre of the circle.

As far as I could ascertain the work that we had come together to carry out at Stonehenge was now complete and as if to confirm this we were approached moments later by the tour guide who advised us our time was up, but the fantastic achievement of our Higher Selves managing to get us all there at the right time to fulfill our destiny would live on forever.

After our early morning visit to Stonehenge we had breakfast in a lovely café in Marlborough, accompanied by the three Japanese girls as well. If I thought the magic was over for the day, I was to be proved very wrong as Eva sped us off for a flying visit to Silbury Hill, North Kennet Long Barrow and then finally to The Uffington White Horse.

Eva made a wonderful tour guide pointing out all the places of interest along the way, but unfortunately by the time we arrived at The White Horse the unpredictable weather, that has become the norm for an English summer, had closed in and we were enveloped in thick mist and pouring rain.

Parking the car in a small lot reserved for sightseers Eva waved her hand towards the mist and announced triumphantly that we'd arrived, and The White Horse could be found by following a path currently invisible, on the other side of the road. She followed this statement with another that assured us the Dragons Hill was in front of us, although this too was hiding in the mist. As nothing was visible we had to take her word for it and we all sat in the car for a few minutes wondering what to do.

Apart from me no one seemed keen on trekking up the hill in the bad weather, so I eventually told them having come all this way I intended to see the White Horse which was followed with a lecture from Eva advising me to stay on the path so that I would not get lost in the mist.

Getting out of the car I pulled up the hood on my jacket to keep out the heavy rain. Luckily the jacket I had brought with me was shower-proof as I'd had many years of British summer weather to recommend the need for such a garment. I then set of walking up the track on my own not exactly sure what, if anything, I would be able to see when I reached my destination. Only yards along the track, which was moderately steep, I could just discern the shapes of people walking ahead of me in the mist and as I caught up with them I was delighted to see it was the three Japanese girls who had also decided to brave the inclement summer weather to view the White Horse.

We continued walking up the hillside, chatting about the wonderful experience we'd all had at Stonehenge and bemoaning the change in the weather. Thankfully it had stopped raining by the time we made it to the White Horse only to find that we were not alone. The ancient site was surrounded by many people standing like sentinels in the mist and it appeared we had arrived just in time to witness some kind of ceremony. The guardians in the mist silently invited us to join them, taking what seemed to be our place in the huge circle of people.

At the head of the White Horse a man and woman stood opposite one another, each holding a large conch shell to their mouths. They seemed to be the focus of the ceremony as they raised the shells to their lips and blew, issuing forth the most hauntingly beautiful sound I have ever heard in my life. The sound echoed around the wet and misty hillside and the vibration of it reverberated right through my body shaking it from its internal moorings making me feel as if I'd come alive from the inside out. After a few minutes the couple slowly lowered the huge shells from their lips and everyone gathered stood in awed and reverent silence. From where I stood, high up on the hillside, I watched, stunned, as the mist rose higher and higher with every passing moment to reveal the magnificence of a truly amazing view.

A colourful patchwork of fields and countryside opened out before us, like a page out of a child's pop up book and the scene was bedecked in all the beauty and glory of summer. The sun then burst out from behind the receding clouds and shone brilliantly over the landscape, turning the raindrops on the grass into a glistening layer of jewels that danced and sparkled in the summer sunlight. The whole scene looked as if some invisible hand had dusted it with gems.

The circle of gathered spectators remained within their silent space allowing the ceremony to settle deep within them and I'm sure, like me, they were marveling at the experience that had just taken place. Suddenly the silence was broken by the sound of a roaring engine and within moments the source of the noise came into view as a WWII Lancaster bomber flew up from behind the hill only to cross our line of vision at little more than head height. A great cheer rang out from the assembled crowd on the hillside as if we were living through a war time scenario and cheering our boys off on another mission. What a grand finale, whether planned or unplanned, to bring this amazing ceremony to a close.

Completely overwhelmed, I couldn't shake the feeling that I was straddling at least three time zones all at once. Not only was I in the here and now, but also in the 1940's and then, of course, I was standing where our Iron Age ancestors had carved out this beautiful monument, which obviously still had a very significant meaning for a lot of people in the present day. Laughing to myself, I couldn't help thinking that Eva and my friends' who presumably were still sitting in the car far below may have vanished into thin air by the time I got back, only to find myself permanently abandoned in a different era.

After the fly past by the bomber the gathering broke up into little groups chatting animatedly. The Japanese girls and I discussed excitedly how lucky we had been to have arrived at the very moment the ceremony began, even though we had no idea on a conscious level, what had been going on. Finally deciding we had all had a fantastic day, especially after our wonderful experience at Stonhenge in the morning.

Just as we started to make our descent we were approached by a young man in his thirties with a very expensive looking camera complete with zoom lens draped around his neck. Asking us if we had found the event amazing we took the opportunity to find out if he knew more about the ceremony than we did and let's face it that wouldn't have been too difficult.

An amiable young man, he was only too happy to tell us his story, which has to be said was just as unusual as any of ours. Some weeks previously he had felt compelled to visit St Michaels Mount, so compelled in fact, he'd taken a few days off work to go. The moment he'd arrived a similar ceremony to the one we had just witnessed was taking place, but with only a handful of people. Like us he'd been anxious to know what was going on and why he'd had the compulsion to visit on that day. Asking for information he'd been told the ceremony was intended to heal the Earth and open vortices that had been sealed for millennia. He was to learn that St Michaels Mount had been the first of such ceremonies that were planned to take place at many ancient sites throughout the length and breadth of Britain. In that moment he'd had an overriding compulsion to join the small group and had instantly given up his job of ten years to be part of what was going on. Telling us that the group had grown in number as they visited more and more sights, but that there were always a certain number of people, like ourselves, at each ceremony who were required only to be in attendance at one event. He explained this as a sort of witnessing contribution for a particular ceremony, at a particular site and after the release of energy they were free to continue with their other purposes, stating he was certain that any one who attended either by de-fault or compulsion was meant to be there.

Whilst he had been speaking I could feel the resonance of spirit running through my body confirming to me my need to have been there and somehow knowing it was all part of 'the plan' that linked to the work I had already carried out on the island and the initiations I had received in New Zealand.

When he'd finished telling us his story he asked could he take a photograph of the four of us as he obviously presumed we were all friends as none of us had enlightened him to the fact that we too had only come together on that particular day. So somewhere in the world there is photographic evidence of myself and the three Japanese girls smiling for the camera standing in the summer sunshine within the perimeter of The Uffington White Horse.

What an amazing day it had been, full of ritual and rites of passage from dawn until dusk. A day of meetings and spiritual revelations, although evidence of this fact may not be apparent, or perhaps it will, who knows? Surely, there could be nothing more to experience on this very special trip?

THE STRANGER AND THE SINGING BOWL

Before leaving for Oxford Elaine had thrust thirty pounds in English money into my hands requesting I find her a singing bowl while I was away as she had admired mine on many occasions, but had been unable to find one for sale anywhere on the Island. Tucking Elaine's money into a separate pocket in my wallet I promised to do my best not thinking there would be a problem in my finding a singing bowl as I was sure there would be some New Age or spiritual shops to be found in Oxford.

Arriving on Friday lunchtime I had all afternoon to shop and scoured the streets, but could not find anywhere that sold anything as exotic as a singing bowl. Saturday was taken up by our trip to Stonehenge and The White Horse and on Sunday we were all up early for our trip to Chesham and our intended workshop with Sandy Stevenson. Sadly, Elaine's hopes of acquiring singing bowl were fading fast.

Piling into the people carrier we set off to pick up Eva's friends who lived close by. One of which was an American woman called

Marilee. Securing her seat belt she announced that we would be meeting a friend of hers in Chesham who was from London and he would be joining us on the workshop, adding that we were meeting him at an eatery called 'The Drawing Room' which was a vegetarian restaurant, at 12.30 for lunch.

Eva as ever was a wonderful tour guide and drove us through the beautiful countryside through quaint little villages with picturesque thatched cottages on our way to Chesham. The first thing we did when we eventually arrived was 'suss' out the venue for the workshop, so that we could find it quickly after lunch.

Parking the car in the town centre we were a bit surprised to find the place like a ghost town, not a soul in sight. Never the less we continued up the main street searching for the restaurant where Marilee had arranged for us to meet her friend. Already late Angela took the lead and marched us down a side street, on the corner of which was a New Age shop. Wonderful! This was just the sort of shop I'd been looking for, but 'darn it' the place like every where else in Chesham was closed.

As I peered into the shop window I caught sight of a sign out of the corner of my eye down yet another side street which just happened to be the place we were looking for. I called to the rest of the group as they ambled up the street behind us, telling them we'd found the place we were looking for and to follow us.

Turning my attention back to 'The Drawing Room' I noticed a man standing by the door who hadn't been there the first time I'd looked. As soon as I spotted him I was overtaken by a very strange urge and found myself running up the street and straight into his arms! Holding onto him as if my life depended on it, kissing and embracing like we were long lost lovers, and even stranger, he reciprocated! For long moments we held each other, oblivious to anything or anyone, then slowly and deliberately we withdrew, staring into each others eyes awkwardly as we realized that we did not know each other from Adam!

Angela, rather puzzled by what she had just witnessed looked on as we very self-consciously and embarrassingly introduced ourselves to one another. Poor Angela, expecting me to introduce him as some long lost lover, didn't really know what to make of it all, any more than I did. James, as the man turned out to be called, remained with Angela and I, standing outside the restaurant as the others joined us. Fortunately for both of us only Angela had witnessed our show of affection and she was still reeling in some kind of post traumatic shock, but the surprises for both of us were not to end there as the lady owner met us at the door and welcomed us into The Drawing Room.

Heavily beamed and oozing with atmosphere she informed us that the building dated back to the 15th century, which we could easily believe as there was not a straight wall, floor or ceiling in the place. Knowing I'd never visited this place before in my life, but somehow it all felt strangely familiar to me. Handing us each a menu the proprietor led us into another room where my jaw immediately hit the uneven wooden floor because every available space was filled with singing bowls in varying size and decoration. Managing to retrieve my jaw I asked if they were for sale and found that not only were the singing bowls for sale, but also all of the artwork displayed on the walls both in that room and on the first floor of the building.

Angela finding her voice again after my erratic behaviour in the street made the comment that I wouldn't have any problem finding a singing bowl for my friend as there were certainly plenty to choose from, before laughing and shaking her head at the incredulity of the circumstances. Walking over to a table where a number of singing bowls were sitting just begging to be played, I picked up the one that had caught my attention as we'd entered the room. It fitted snugly into the palm of my hand and I immediately began to play it like an ancient Buddhist monk and I felt sure it had been waiting there just for me. Angela and I then made our way up the narrow wooden staircase to view the upper floor while I still was unable to shake off the strange feeling of familiarity the old place exerted upon me.

Eventually returning to the others and our lunch Angela asked me which bowl I was going to buy for Elaine. Knowing without doubt it had to be the first one to catch my eye I picked it up and turning it over in my hand I was not in the least surprised to see a little sticker on the underside displaying the price as £30!

Now there was just the mystery of James to be solved. Who was he? And why had we met under such strange circumstances? Of course I knew he was Marilee's friend from London and would be attending the course with us, but that was all I knew about him. During lunch James made a point of sitting next to me and as I was still feeling slightly embarrassed by the manner of our meeting earlier I was hoping he might be able to enlighten me on our obvious attraction.

As everyone else was engrossed in conversation James ventured to ask who I was, as on some level we were evidently no strangers to one another. Noticing there was a look of love, albeit tinged with bewilderment in his eyes I had to tell him that although I was also aware of a strong connection between us it had to be from another life as I wasn't normally given to running up to strange men in the street and throwing my arms around them!

Laughing, I asked him, "Do you come here often?" then adding more soberly, "This restaurant I mean."

He admitted he'd never been there before in his life, although commented on the fact that the place had a strange feeling of familiarity about it. Admitting that I felt the same the only explanation I could come up with was it may have been significant to us both in a previous life which would go some way to explain our behaviour when we met and the overwhelming sense of knowing one another. Not content, I then asked why he'd booked that particular restaurant for us to meet. Totally unaware of the significance of my question he told me he'd picked it at random from the yellow pages for places to eat in Chesham. Commenting the strange thing was when he'd rung to book he'd been told they didn't open on Sunday, but they would make an exception for him!

Feeling the resonance of my HS running through me I told him I believed spirit had guided us both to this very spot just so that we could meet again in the here and now. Shuddering with resonance from his HS, he smiled and had to agree. James and I were obviously meant to meet that day, but we could not shed any more light on a joint past life that we may have spent together in the small community of Chesham, other than what I have already outlined.

After lunch we all made our way to the venue for the workshop which turned out to be well worth the journey. It was lovely to meet the author of one of my favourite books, but I had a sneaky suspicion after my meeting with James and the events of yesterday the workshop had merely been the bait required to get me to England that weekend. The trip was not finished yet as we still had the evening left experience and with my prior knowledge of spirit I knew it was too soon to consider the weekend over.

Once back in Oxford we were all invited to Marilee's apartment where she prepared a lovely supper for us all before announcing that James, who was a singer/ songwriter would be providing the entertainment for the evening. Settling next to Angela on the sofa, imagine my surprise when James picked up his guitar and began to sing, because the song he was singing *I* myself had channeled some time previously.

Nudging me in the ribs Angela, who'd read my poetry, told me she found the lyrics almost identical to one my poems, and I had to agree. Barely able to contain myself until James had finished singing when the opportunity arose to ask when he'd written the song. Looking down the page to where he'd recorded the date I was amazed to discover that he'd written the song in August 2004, the same time that I'd channeled what I considered to be my poetry. Here was yet another connection between James and me and also amazing proof of the collective consciousness and the resonance of spirit.

For those of you unfamiliar with the collective consciousness it is a universal wide web, that requires no lap tops, telephone lines or electricity and given the right environment and circumstances we are all able to tune into this amazing sea of consciousness and channel through what we find there.

There could be no doubt that James and I were on a resonant link given what had happened between us that day and also maybe lifetimes ago. For his part he was absolutely amazed by the above coincidence, especially when Angela told him that she had owned a copy of those particular words for at least a year.

As we bade our farewells that night James gave me a piece of paper with his contact details and asked me to keep in touch as the past few hours had made the day one of the most special he could remember. Thanking him I agreed, and tucked his details away in a safe corner of my handbag, but to my disappointment when I got home and looked in that safe place the piece of paper was nowhere to be found! I never did find it and have accepted that James was one of those people who come into your life, maybe just the once, to fulfill an agreement that was made long before arriving here. These agreements are made before entering the Earth plane and our current consciousness has no knowledge of what we once meant to one another until an event such as this appears in your life. For whatever reason it is better to accept the joy of the moment and relinquish the past and I think James was just such a person in my life, and I in his.

The huge jigsaw of guidance that had taken most of 2006 to be conveyed to me was now complete and with a deep sigh Chapter 20 can come to a close as the compilation of lots of individual stories of initiation, challenges and guidance have been woven together.

All in all the whole year had been a wonderful adventure and I felt happy in the knowledge that I had kept all my spiritual appointments and had carried out those tasks I had contracted spiritually to do.

I hope you have found it readable, understandable, inspirational and enjoyable and those readers who have remained with me this far are awarded a 'virtual gold medal' for their endurance and perseverance!

CHAPTER 21

WHO YER GONNA CALL?

As I mentioned in Chapter 20 Elaine and I were about to be guided into the area of ghost-busting. We had become good friends since her return to the island and as she was now living close by we saw a lot of one another, meeting regularly for meditation sessions and long spiritual conversations. These were interspersed with very down to earth conversations that usually culminated in uproarious laughter and were nearly always accompanied by many cups of tea and coffee, plus the odd biscuit or three. You don't get to be a size 16 without consuming a biscuit or three!

Between 2006 and 2010 Elaine and I carried out a number of energetic house clearings. Anything from mansions, to modern semi-detached houses and we never advertised our services once as this work just seemed to appear 'out of the blue' and land in our laps, often in very strange circumstances as the following stories will bear out.

ONE MAN AND HIS DOG

I'd made arrangements with Elaine to meet at 2pm one afternoon with the intention of going for a walk in the country. On the day in question she eventually turned up at 3.30pm, red faced and flustered, apologizing for having fallen asleep in her chair. Relating this information is just to make you aware that the timing of the following events was totally random. Jumping into my car we set off to find a quiet destination for our afternoon ramble. Within minutes of leaving the house I had turned off the main road into a small side road and without thinking about it parked the car telling Elaine that this spot was as good as any for a stroll.

We had only walked a matter of yards up the lane when I suggested that we turn into an even narrower track. A puzzled Elaine asked where we were going and I told her my mother and her family had lived up this lane when she and her siblings had been young. We walked and talked and soon a grand house came into view which had been built on the site of the humble farm dwelling my mother had occupied as a child.

The magnificent house complete with stables stood before us and an amazed Elaine questioned the possibility of my mother ever occupying such a place. Laughing, I had to explain that in the time of my grandparents it had been a two up two down humble farm workers cottage, not the magnificent edifice currently on view. Turning up the grassy track we began the gentle climb into the surrounding Bride hills and I found myself telling Elaine about the original old cottage and barn, and what they had meant to me;

As a child my mother would often walk my sister and I up this lane to her old homestead. We walked with the seasons, picking bluebells and primroses in the spring, admiring the beautiful Dog roses and poppies that lined the hedgerows in the summer and staining our fingers with over ripe blackberries in the autumn. My mother loved to reminisce and those walks were usually full of repeated stories about her childhood and the things she and her brothers had got up to as she quite literally walked down memory lane. My mother and her family were the last people to live there in the 1930's and after their departure the cottage had become derelict and remained empty for years until it was finally sold and demolished to make way for the grand house now occupying where it once stood. Telling Elaine it had been a sad day for me when the humble remains had been knocked down she immediately picked up on my sadness and commented that this place must have meant a lot to me and encouraged me to continue with my tale.

'I never told anyone where I was going, not even mum. I would just get on my bicycle and come here to be alone and in my own space, this was my sanctuary away from the world. In the spring and summer throughout my teens, depending on the weather, I would lie in the long grass in what had once been the cottage garden listening to the sounds of nature all around me. I loved to watch the swallows dipping and diving overhead displaying their aeronautic skills, feeling the excitement in my tummy as they swooped so low over the ground they almost touched me. In wintertime I would just sit within what was left of the old cottage walls daydreaming and drinking in the peace.'

When I'd finished my story Elaine expressed the opinion that it was sad when things had to change and whilst I agreed told her I didn't think anyone could object to us walking up the old farm track to enjoy the view. We'd almost reached the top of the track when Elaine asked when I'd last visited the place and casting my mind back I realized I hadn't walked up this track since 1999 when I'd brought my friend Gill out to witness the total eclipse. Given that it was now 2007 it was definitely not somewhere I visited every day. Still my recollection of the eclipse was good, even if it was eight years ago and pointing over the gate we were leaning against I showed Elaine where Gill and I had sat in the field to experience the phenomena.

Miles away lost in the view and my own thoughts Elaine's voice filtered into my senses asking me why I'd chosen to come here today and I had to tell her that it had not been a conscious decision on my part, that in fact when I'd parked I'd been working on autopilot.

However we were not to enjoy the peace and beauty of the spot undisturbed for long as below us on the path we had just taken a man was walking his dog in our direction. We were both a little disgruntled at the prospect of company invading what we considered to be a somewhat hallowed space, but we were also underestimating the power of spirit at work, which it most definitely was, although at this point we were not aware of the fact.

Within minutes the dog had reached us and was obviously delighted to find two strange ladies, and I use that term loosely to describe us, who were willing to make a fuss of him. His tail wagged excitedly and his tongue lolled happily out of the corner of his mouth as he enjoyed the attention. Very shortly we were joined by his owner, who also seemed very friendly and was panting almost as much as his dog. Smiling widely he wished us a good day and told us how unusual it was to meet anyone up here, other than the farmer, proceeding to tell us that he'd walked this path on a daily basis for nearly twenty years and we were the first people he'd met.

Exchanging pleasantries for a few minutes about the beautiful view he then pointed to the mansion below us and commented on the fact that his mother-in-law had lived in the original old farm workers cottage back in the 1920s. Amazed at his revelation I responded by telling him my mother has also lived there her family being the last to occupy the dwelling sometime in the 1930s. Looking at me in bewildered astonishment he remarked on the unusual coincidence whilst for myself I acknowledged the resonance of spirit running through my body as he spoke.

Shaking his head in disbelief he pushed open the gate into the nearby field, his canine companion shooting off at a pace of knots a soon as the gate was partly open and tore off around the field like the devil was chasing him. Closely following the lunatic dog the man entered the field, turning to ask Elaine and me if he could show us something, telling us it was a mystery he had pondered on daily for some twenty years, then holding the gate open he waited patiently for us to accept his invitation.

Why he felt 'we' would be able to shed light on whatever was currently hidden from our view in this particular field was a mystery. We pondered for all of twenty seconds before following him totally unaware of what we were about to be shown, but allowed ourselves to be led over an apparently mundane and perfectly normal grassy hillside. The dog walker and his faithful friend, who had by now returned to heel after his mad cap exertions, made their way up the hill before coming to an abrupt halt a few yards ahead of us. Stopping beside him we found ourselves looking down into a huge cavity about twenty feet across and easily as deep. At first glance it looked as if a hungry giant had taken a huge bite out of the hillside. The friendly dog walker asked us what we made of it and we responded with bemused looks as neither of us had a clue.

Thanking us for at least coming to look at the site he added that in his opinion it must have been some kind of archaeological dig, although his mother-in-law could not remember anything like that whilst she lived in the cottage below. He then presumed to ask if I would mention it to my mother and find out if she could recall anything during her occupation of the cottage. Very much doubting it had happened during her childhood, knowing that if it had, it would have cropped up in one of her many stories.

Accepting his telephone number I told him I would ask my mother the next day and ring him if she could remember anything. Elaine and I bade the man and his dog goodbye, the latter who had remained sitting patiently by his master's feet, tongue still lolling out of the corner of his mouth panting, during the above deliberations. Retracing our steps across the field towards the gate remarking on our strange encounter as we went and watching as the man and his dog walked on up the hill playing chase and catch with an old rubber ball.

Arriving home Dickie was already getting ready to go out and was less than happy at my late appearance. Unaware the day had moved slowly into evening after the late start with our walk and the strange meeting with man and dog I had completely forgotten we had been invited to our friends' house to share a Chinese meal that evening.

Rosie and I have been friends since childhood having grown up together on the same estate. Her brother George, who now lived in Aberdeen, was on the island for few days and as we'd all gone to school together had been invited for a Chinese take out and a catch up. We all knew each other very well and were comfortable in one another's company and once everyone had been greeted and hugged we settled around the dining table to enjoy our Chinese meal. Rosie asked me how I'd spent my day and immediately I launched into the tale of my outing with Elaine. When I got to the part about the dog walker and his theories about the mysterious archaeological dig taking place in the Bride hills George began to laugh before telling us all, with a certain amount of confidence that *he* had been the person who had created the hole in the hill!

To begin with we all thought he was joking, but when he was able to give us details of the major drain laying operation and exactly where it had taken place during the early 1970s we started to take him seriously. What made the whole event even more poignant was the reason for George's sudden trip to the island was to attend the funeral of his old boss, the plant owner who had employed George to dig that huge hole in the hillside back in the 1970's!

I felt spirit coursing through my body as I sat at my friend's table as once more spirit had arranged all the players in the game to be in the right place at the right time, and within hours of the question being asked I had been provided with an answer to a puzzle the dog walker had pondered on for nearly twenty years!

I'm quite aware this story has dragged on a little, but thought it worthy of including, and you are probably wondering where the ghost busting bit went, well it's just about to arrive.

The following day I rang the dog walker and shared with him the revelation of the night before and he was absolutely astounded when he heard George's explanation for the missing chunk of hillside and couldn't quite believe the riddle he had pondered on for so many years had been solved so quickly.

Whilst we were chatting I told him these occurrences happened quite often in my life and that I had actually written a book about it, which he said he would like to read. The next day I dropped a copy of my book at his wife's place of work and a couple of days later he was back on the phone telling me he'd read the book and thought I was just the person he'd been looking for? Not knowing what was coming next I was actually relieved to find out he had a presence in his house and he wanted me to remove it. To cut a very long story much shorter, it was agreed that Elaine and I visit his home and energetically cleanse it, which we did, and as far as I am aware they have had no further disturbances.

I know this has been a very long winded story to get to the punch line, but it is just to help you understand how the spiritual network operates. As we travel through this third dimensional plane spirit works through us and others we may meet on our path and their intention is to get us to where we need to be, whether we think we should be there, or not, is totally irrelevant.

THE CURIOUS CASE OF A MAN... A WOMAN ... A GIRL ... A DOG ... and 'A VERY HAUNTED HOUSE'

This particular ghost busting came through my eldest daughter, Julie, who knew nothing about the work Elaine and I performed. Taking a call on her mobile phone during a visit to me one afternoon, I heard her tell whoever she was talking to that she would ask her mum if she knew of anyone who could help. Mildly surprised I waited with baited breath to find out what I could possibly help with only to learn that Julie's 'friend' had 'a friend' who required urgent assistance as she believed her home to be haunted. Asking Julie to get the phone number of the girl with the problem I promised I'd try and find someone who could help, not telling her that it was likely to be me.

It had not passed my attention that Julie had received the phone call whilst paying me a visit and I felt spirit were once again engineering events and that Elaine and I were being asked to rise to the challenge they had set before us.

Waiting until Julie had left the house before contacting the lady with the problem I was to discover that she and her husband had purchased an old terraced house a couple of years previously and were desperately trying to modernise it, but all their attempts at turning the place into the lovely family home they had envisioned were being constantly thwarted and the poor woman was now at the end of her tether.

It transpired that they had bought the place at a knock down price from the previous owners, assuming they had run out of money during their attempts to renovate, but considering the problems she and her husband were encountering she was now considering the possibility that they had been only too glad to escape from the place.

Emotionally she explained to me what had been happening since they had moved in. It appeared things that had been hung on the walls would be found lying on the floor the next day and no matter how many times they fixed the roof and sealed the walls that damp patches would reappear in a short space of time. The kitchen was another matter entirely as they would often come home to find all the cupboard doors and drawers wide open, even though the house had been empty all day. Effectively they had only been able to renovate half of the kitchen, the older part remained as derelict as when they'd moved in, as no matter how hard they tried every attempt at renovation had failed. Seemingly it wasn't just the humans that were being affected by the place as even the family's docile pet dog had turned into a cringing cur who spent his time baring his teeth at some invisible presence and cowering in the corner of the lounge. She also complained that the place was always freezing cold winter and summer and no matter how high or how long the heating had been on for it made no difference to the temperature.

Continuing with her story the lady confided that the most troubling aspect was the effect all of the above was having on her nine year old daughter. It appeared the child was too frightened to go into her bedroom and was finding it impossible to sleep and hadn't done so with any success since they moved in almost two years before! Her conclusion was that the house had to be haunted and wanted to stay the way they'd found it.

Whoever or whatever the presence in the house was and whatever it's intention it was disturbing the peace of the whole family and needed to be dealt with, so, promising her our help I fervently hoped and prayed that Elaine and I were up to the challenge.

A few days later Elaine and I met the lady at the house in question and it was agreed that she would take the dog for a walk while we did what we needed to do. Both Elaine and I were quite relieved that the dog was going out as it being rather a large and seemingly ferocious beast, even though the owner assured us he was a big softie. As soon as she had left the house we made our way up to the first floor landing and then up the stairs to the top landing where we were both compelled to enter the bedroom on the left. There was a sudden rush of cool air as we entered and I commented to Elaine that this must be the child's bedroom as it was very girly. I was somewhat taken a back when she answered me in a gruff male voice saying,

"As if it's not bad enough putting up with that old b***h downstairs, now you! I don't want you here, or her, or the girl, this is my room and my house, now get out!"

Returning to her normal mode of speech Elaine told me she had felt the presence of an elderly gentleman who had occupied the room we were now standing in and he, having died in the house, probably on the stairs, was now trapped on the upper floor. No wonder the poor girl hadn't been able to sleep, he didn't sound very friendly. We then did what we knew we had to do and Elaine being the medium brought through the presence of the old man and I negotiated with him until we were happy that he had moved on.

Leaving the upper floor we then turned our attention to the main bedroom where a huge damp patch was evident on the ceiling and the wall. As soon as she'd tuned into the energy of the room Elaine was able to hear a baby crying. Although I could not hear it I felt a deep sadness, a sense of grief and loss as though the room still carried the imprint of the sad occasion and the emotion of a mother who had lost her new born child, but it was only a memory not an actual haunting and we carried out a routine cleansing before moving out onto the landing.

Simultaneously we became aware of a woman in long old fashioned skirts, only the white lace collar at her throat lifted the black of her attire. Her skirts brushed the ground as she paced up and down along about a third of the narrow landing, stopping short of the bedroom door at the end, a lit candle held in her hand to light her way. She was a silent woman as no exchange or communication was passed between us. She just appeared to be keeping a silent vigil outside what had once been a bedroom, but was now a bathroom/utility room. We found out later, from the owner, that the last third of the landing including the bedroom at the end was a modern extension, so it had not been there when this particular lady had lived in the house. Again we did what we had to do, until we were satisfied, or as satisfied as we could be that she too had moved on.

Making our way downstairs Elaine came to a sudden shuddering stop about half way down and turned to tell me she thought that this was the spot where the old man from the upstairs bedroom had died. Moving swiftly on we went into the lounge and immediately entered into a very unwelcoming energy, it was an extremely unpleasant feeling I can tell you and the temperature was freezing despite it being a lovely spring day outside.

Suddenly Elaine shouted out in a very angry voice,

"Who the hell are you? I'm fed up with all these people in my house, I haven't given you permission to be here any more than that old b**d who swears at me from the stairs, or the people invading my kitchen and eating all my food!"***

Elaine was obviously channelling the trapped spirit, who still believing herself to be in her rightful place, was extremely disgruntled at what she considered to be interlopers. Once again

Elaine channelled while I explained and negotiated with the spirit. Thankfully we helped her to realize that she had passed away and with her acceptance and approval, we aided her into the light of the higher realms.

The funny thing about this haunting was that I knew the woman who had owned the house, we had been on nodding terms before she had passed away some 15 years before and she had been renowned in the town for having a very fiery temperament. I just knew that she had been the woman we had been dealing with as Elaine had brought through much more than what I have recounted above, mostly expletives!

Moving through the house from room to room, we retraced our steps checking the overall energy and felt quite satisfied with the result, but would the family feel the difference? Within minutes of concluding our second tour we heard the key in the front door and I whispered to Elaine that our timing was perfect as the owner with her dog, thankfully still on the lead, walked in.

Secretly hoping the feedback would be promising I asked her to take a walk around the house and let us know if anything felt different. Her reply was to lead Bruno, her over large dog, into the lounge and let him be the judge. We held our breath as Bruno walked calmly into the room and dropped into his bed on the far side of the lounge, yawned loudly then stretched out completely relaxed. His owner stood open mouthed before exclaiming that it was nothing short of a miracle as he had never previously entered the room without baring his teeth and cringing in the corner like some poor abused mutt. I couldn't help smiling to myself, poor Bruno, who was much more psychic than either myself or Elaine had probably been the victim of much verbal abuse since his family had moved to this house and I'm sure he'd been shouted at on many occasions with plenty of ripe language to boot if the lady whom we had just returned to spirit had anything to do with it.

ANGELS AT WORK ... EXPECT A MIRACLE

Never ever having advertised before, in the summer of 2007 I was compelled to place a small advertisement in the local paper, it read something like this;

Angel card readings and healing sessions available...Interested? Please call Linda (my telephone number)

I only ever received two replies to this advert, both of them worthy of mention for completely different reasons and the story of the first responders, although not about ghost busting, has merits all of it's own.

Twin sisters made the first request for my services for an Angel card reading a couple of days after the advertisement appeared in the paper. An appointment was duly made for the ladies, in their mid-thirties to visit me the next day. Adamant that their readings take place separately I left one sister sitting in the sun lounge whilst I took the other into the lounge where her sister would be unable to hear what was being said. As I shuffled the deck the first sister commented on how close they were to one another and how as well as being sisters they were the best of friends, sharing everything. I wondered briefly why, if they were such good friends they wanted their readings to be secret from one another, but feeling sure all would be revealed at some point continued with the reading.

Once the deck had been shuffled I let the lady pick her cards and as the reading progressed it became very clear that all was not well in her world. Bursting into tears she told me she was having mega problems with her husband, who was apparently beating her up and putting her through other forms of abuse. She continued by telling me this problem was her reason for seeking a reading as she was hoping the 'Angels' would help her make a decision about what she should do as she could no longer tolerate living in a life that was a lie. Begging me not to tell her sister what had happened during her reading, telling me she did not want her to worry, because as far as the sister was concerned having their cards read was just a bit of fun.

When her reading was over we chatted for a while about her situation and I commented on the fact that maybe she should confide in her sister as I was sure she would be very supportive under the circumstances, but she was adamant that she did not want her sister to know. So promising not to tell her sister the information I was now a party too, having temporarily forgotten that the 'Angels' often have different ideas.

A few moments later the second sister entered the room smiling to me and commenting on how she was looking forward to her reading. I had already cleansed the deck in preparation, so that no residue of her sister's energy would be left behind on the cards. Choosing her cards at random from the down turned deck and passing them to me, one at a time, she sat eagerly anticipating some happy news and must have been puzzled by the look on my face. The cards she had chosen were exactly the same as those her sister had picked only minutes earlier and as I interpreted them the same sad story as her sister's poured from her lips, begging me not to tell her sibling as she didn't want to upset her.

Now I knew why they'd wanted to see me on their own, and from an angelic point of view why they had come to me. Telling the second sister that I thought her sibling would understand and help her cope with her problems far better than she thought she would I suggested we ask her to join us. Promising her that everything would be alright I called her twin into the lounge where they shared their respective stories of physical and mental abuse at the hands of their partners. Many tears and much hugging and kissing later they promised they would resolve their respective marital problems and support each other every step of the way.

I watched in total awe and humility as this beautiful healing took place between them, because there is no doubt that is what it was. Bidding them goodbye I watched as they left my home arm in arm a lot brighter and lighter than when they had arrived now that they had been united fully through their contact with the angels.

Raising my eyes to the heavens I gave thanks to the 'Angels' for guiding them my way and using *me* as *their* instrument to help bring about this wonderful event.

CREATING YOUR OWN REALITY

The second responder to my advert rang the same week. The woman on the other end of the phone was quite adamant that she had known I was the person she required as soon as she'd read my advert. Asking her would she like a healing session or an angel card reading I was surprised when she declined both, only to discover it was to remove something 'quite horrible', (her own words), that had taken up residence in her home and was haunting her. Despite my many protestations and pointing out to her that nowhere in the advert did it mention that I performed ghost busting, she wouldn't take 'no' for an answer so eventually I gave up arguing and took down her details.

After picking up Elaine the next day and before setting off we 'called in' our team in spirit to help us with any work we may have to undertake at Joan's, the lady in question. The directions Joan had supplied led us to a relatively new block of sheltered houses on the outskirts of Douglas. Ringing the doorbell we waited patiently on the doorstep until we heard a shuffling/ clunking noise coming from inside. On opening the door, we discovered Joan was a very elderly lady shuffling about on a walking frame with terrible haunted look in her eyes, as they darted suspiciously everywhere.

It was already a hot day outside, but as Joan led us into her small bungalow it was as if we had just stepped of the plane in Majorca, like stepping into an oven, the heating must have been turned up to maximum, I almost fainted, it was sweltering. Going through the menopause at the time I was already overheating on a daily basis and there was a serious chance that I might die of heat stroke before we got rid of whatever was troubling Joan.

Leading us into the lounge Joan sat down heavily in her chair telling us she was housebound and therefore unable to get away from the horrible thing that had been persecuting her day and night for months. Picking up the local paper from the arm of her chair she showed me my ad circled in red ink. Waving it in front of us she repeated her remonstrations of the previous day, so emphatic about the 'boogie chasing' being the job for me. Making this statement with so much confidence she had a lot more conviction in my ability than I felt myself at that particular moment, but both Elaine and I were determined to do our best for this genuinely terrified and unhappy old lady.

Sitting in the lounge of Joan's small one-bedroom bungalow we listened as she recounted a truly harrowing tale about the beast that was haunting her and Joan's description of a hideously deformed face staring out at her from under a dirty hood we had to agree was pretty scary. Elaine sat holding Joan's hand in an effort to comfort her as I questioned if she could see the creature in the room. Learning from Joan that it had gone into hiding the moment we'd arrived and it hadn't been present the whole time we'd been there, but quickly adding that it didn't fool her, she knew the cunning beast was there somewhere as her wild eyes scoured the small room.

Giving Elaine a questioning glance I wondered if Joan may be a bit senile, before asking her if I could take a look around the house. The small property consisted of one bedroom, a bathroom, kitchen, hallway and lounge, so not a very big space for us to miss something as large and grotesque as Joan had described. Wandering through what was fast becoming an intolerable sauna and wilting a little more with each passing minute, I failed to pick up any malign energy. Returning to the lounge a few minutes later I found Elaine giving Joan some healing. By this time I was almost at the point of fainting and asked Joan if I could open a window. Her reaction to this request stunned me as she held up her hands forbidding me to open the window, saying, 'the 'thing' had told her the souls of her babies would be captured and taken to live in hell forever if she opened the windows.'

This possibility was causing her a great deal of distress and we began to realize there was something more fundamentally wrong with Joan when we discovered the babies she was referring to were a collection of photographs of long deceased pets, displayed on the sideboard.

By now I realized we were obviously dealing with something much more than a simple haunting and I began to think that Joan may be a little bit mad. Giving her the benefit of the doubt, for now, I sat down in front of her and taking both of her hands in mine I tried to find out who would be coming to steal the souls of her babies. Joan's eyes flashed with hatred as she tried, but failed, to name the two people she felt she should have been able to trust in her life and who had both in their own ways let her down terribly. With gentle encouragement we were at last able to discover that her husband had denied her the right to have babies as he did not want a family, hence the assortment of pets, and despite her very real affection for him he had failed to return her love and had embarked on a string of extramarital affairs and liaisons with prostitutes during their marriage.

The other person, who Joan merely described as 'the bitch' was in fact her mother. Already having guessed this to be the case I was somewhat taken aback when she told us that her husband had admitted to having had an affair with her own mother. Finally telling us that he had kept this revelation and various other sordid details of his life secret from her until he was on his deathbed and had only told her then because he wanted to die with a clear conscience!

Poor Joan had experienced an awful life at the hands of the people she should have been able to trust and even when she'd acquired her pets as surrogate children, her husband had made them unwelcome and hated them. Her eyes were filled with hurt and hatred and her face wore a twisted grimace as she described him as a bastard who only ever thought of his own self gratification.

By now Joan was sobbing loudly, she had let so much hurt out. Elaine who was shell shocked at the above revelations, her mouth open during the whole of the previous expose put a comforting arm around Joan's shoulder as she cried.

As Joan composed herself a light was coming on in my head and I was compelled to ask her how long she had been housebound and how long the haunting had been going on. The answer to both questions was five months. It was then apparent to me that when she had become housebound all her focus had turned inward, dwelling on the injustices she had suffered by the actions of her husband and her mother. The hatred, venom and un-forgiveness that she had held within her for these two people had eaten her up like a cancer and become her focus of thought. In effect Joan had unwittingly turned all the pent up hurt and anguish onto herself, as she had created and breathed life into the grotesque manifestation, filled with hate and loathing that was now haunting her.

Gently I explained all this to her I was pleased to see a faint smile appear on her lips. Although she couldn't quite believe that she had created such a grotesque creature with the power of her own mind, and was at a loss to know how to get rid of it.

I was very blunt in my advice and told her she should forgive and release both her mother and her husband and send them on their way with *her* unconditional love. Joan was reluctant at first, but after telling her this was the only way forward I could think of she agreed as Elaine and I would help her.

Knowing and trusting our team were on hand I then led Joan into and through a guided visualization where she met both her husband and her mother in a beautiful safe location. Elaine and I held a light filled space as Joan sat in her armchair with her eyes closed. We were aware of her communicating with the others, asking for and receiving forgiveness and before I brought her out of the meditation I heard her softly uttering "Mother, I love you and I forgive you."

It was a joy for both Elaine and me as we observed the change come over Joan, her body relaxed and the tiredness and anxiety drained from her face. There wasn't a dry eye in the room, tears were rolling down Joan's cheeks as well as ours and when she opened her eyes she appeared transformed, radiant, smiling broadly and looking years younger.

Thanking us as we left Joan admitted that she felt 100% better and she knew that it was now all over, even commenting on the fact how surprised she had been to say the word 'Mother', a word she had not uttered for years. And as if to prove it not only to us, but to herself she spoke the word aloud once more and we all burst into tears again, only this time they were tears of joy.

So to conclude this story, sometimes things are not always what they seem to be, as this first appeared as a haunting, but was actually a different manifestation altogether, but just as in need of healing.

CHAPTER 22

IS IT A BIRD? IS IT A PLANE? NO ... IT'S A 'UFO'

This story began way back in 1992, but did not conclude until 2009. Yet again there are many threads to this tale spanning quite a few years and I will endeavour to tell the story in as clear and concise way as I can.

One evening in the early autumn of 1992 my friend Gill and I were travelling to Andreas for our usual girlie night out. This was a weekly event for us and apart from it being a particularly foggy evening we were not expecting or had previously experienced anything out of the norm. The autumn mists had rolled in quickly as it got dark that evening and in some places you could hardly see a hand in front of you. As usual I was behind the wheel as Gill does not drive, and due to the misty conditions probably driving with a little more caution. Rounding a sharp bend in the road as we approached Andreas we were amazed as the sky above us lit up with a pulsating orange glow, which dispersed the mist in our immediate vicinity. Slowing until we were almost at a standstill we could see a huge craft hovering directly above us. It was black and triangular in shape about the size of a football pitch with a pulsating orange light at each corner, barely skimming the trees which overhung the road.

Poor Gill was terrified and grabbed my knee as she questioned me as to what it could be. I hadn't any more idea than she had, but I certainly didn't find it frightening, its presence only made me curious. Unlike Gill I had previously witnessed some other strange objects in the sky, but nothing as up close and personal as this and I was determined to follow it despite my friend's protestations.

The craft moved slowly ahead of us for a while before veering off across the fields in the direction of a small side road. Telling an almost apoplectic Gill that I just had to follow it and completely ignoring her desperate pleas that I shouldn't, I indicated to turn into the side road. Very aware that Gill was shaking like a leaf in an autumn gale, and before I could turn onto the smaller road, she let out a scream of terror. My scream very quickly followed Gill's, but was more from excitement than fear as the strange craft had suddenly shot directly up into the sky and vanished, leaving us once more on the dark road shrouded in mist.

Moments later we were driving into the village past the police station and the sports field where the local football team were working out. The pitch was floodlit, but it was no match for the light from the craft we had just encountered. Gill was still visibly shaking and I was glad we were only moments away from getting her a stiff and comforting drink in the presumed safety of the pub. But, only a few hundred yards from our destination, as if lying in wait for us, the craft appeared once more directly above us, its orange lights still pulsating and hypnotizing.

In Gill the re-appearance of the craft inspired only fear, and screaming again she pointed at it hovering above us as the lights pulsated in a gentle 'come hither mode'. Turning the next corner the pub came into view and I told a trembling Gill that I'd drop her off outside, but that I was going to follow the craft. Although terrified she refused to get out of the car and leave me on my own. Her fear of something happening to me because she'd deserted me far outweighed her fear of something happening to both of us and so we hypnotically continued to follow the low flying craft wherever it was leading us.

Before long we were turning into the old WWII airfield at Jurby where the craft/ufo was now hovering above the old guard house, apparently waiting for us. All for getting out of the car and going for a closer look because I was convinced that whoever or whatever was flying the thing had a purpose in leading us to this deserted place. Gill on the other hand was not about to let me out of the vehicle, grabbing a tight hold on me she told me in no uncertain terms that she was not letting me go. Poor Gill her voice was strained and trembling with emotion, but her determination and resolve to save me from myself and my curiosity held firm. She held on so tightly I could not break free, until once more the craft took our attention as it accelerated with phenomenal speed and disappeared straight up into the night sky, leaving us once more engulfed in darkness and fog.

The subject of our close encounter, very strangely, was never discussed between the two of us until a similar night about two years later. We had made our weekly trip to the Andreas pub on a rather foggy night, and were sitting in the lounge bar chatting when a friend of ours, who also lives in the village, came in and stopped to talk. To our amazement he commented on the thick fog currently shrouding the village and reminisced to a similar night a couple of years previously when his father had supposedly seen a UFO flying over the village. Laughing he took himself off to the back bar and left Gill and I staring at one another. We were both speechless for a few moments before accepting the unspoken, what we already knew to be true On that foggy night two years before we had actually witnessed and experienced something very strange, something very strange indeed.

'BEAM ME UP SCOTTY'

The next part of this story took place in the late summer of 1996 when John, my spiritual teacher came to the island to hold a workshop on dowsing. The workshop was being held in the grounds of a beautiful old house on the outskirts of Andreas, but to my great disappointment I was unable to take part because of work commitments.

On the evening of the workshop one of the girls who had attended called at my home offering me a scrap of paper and telling me that John would like me to call him on the number scribbled on it. Curiosity having got the better of me I dialled the number as soon as the messenger had left and after only a couple of rings John's familiar voice was saying, 'Hello Linda'. Puzzled, I wondered how he knew it was me, and as if in response to my unasked question I was to learn that the number I had dialled was X directory and I was the only person he'd given permission to use it as he was staying in the house alone. John told me he knew how disappointed I was at missing the workshop and wanted to invite me over to do some dowsing with him that evening. Only a few minutes after our conversation I found myself driving slowly up the long drive towards the elegant old house in a state of high excitement at the prospect of a one on one workshop with this very perceptive man.

John took me through the paces of the dowsing workshop he had taken earlier in the day as we wandered around the gardens surrounding the house. When he was satisfied with my efforts we walked through a small rose garden which led into what had once been a field, but had at some point been incorporated into the garden and was now complete with lily pond and fountain.

A little way into the 'garden' John stretched out his arm to halt my progress asking me to take my gaze down the length of the garden and to tell him what I saw. Focusing my gaze on a line of trees about 100 yards away I stared long and hard until my eyes became unfocused and I eventually saw something. John, who had been watching my face intently during this process, asked what I could see. Telling him I could see what appeared to be a shimmering heat haze, like the sort of thing seen above the road in very hot weather, but as it was now well into the evening and the air temperature had dropped I found my description somewhat at odds with the facts.

John smiled and told me what I was seeing was energy and according to him a very special energy. Then to demonstrate it's presence he asked me to hold my arms out in front of me as though I was sleep walking, and to walk forward into the shimmer. Having no idea about what was likely to happen and with my bare arms held rigidly to the front I left John where he was standing and walked towards the energy. I'd only taken a few steps when a feeling something like an electric shock ran up both arms and instantly dropping them to my sides I stepped smartly back in surprise. Inspecting my forearms for damage I noticed the hairs were standing on end and it felt as if the hairs on my head were doing the same. From behind me I could hear John laughing and telling me that the sensation I had just experienced was the result of standing in a charged energy field.

Feeling very excited, my curiosity having been piqued by the experience, I wanted to confirm it, so holding my arms out once more I walked back into the charged atmosphere. My whole body came alive and was tingling from head to toe as wave after wave of 'electricity' coursed through my being. Laughing and on a complete high I immersed myself in this strange energy field, throwing my arms into the air and reaching up to the sky I shouted out loud, "Beam me up Scotty".

If, like me, you are a Star Trek fan or 'Trekky', you will know this phrase very well.

By now I was almost in the centre of the garden twirling around in fevered excitement when out of the corner of my eye I noticed John smiling at me, still standing where he had been throughout my experience. I had been so carried away I'd almost forgotten he was there at all, but now that I'd become conscious of him watching me I reluctantly left the energy field and walked back to him, my head spinning and full of questions.

I hadn't even had time to formulate the first question before John asked me why I'd shouted, "Beam me up Scotty". My answer was simple as the sensation I'd had whilst pirouetting in the energy field had reminded me of the matter transporter used in the Star Trek series whereby you could disappear and re-appear somewhere completely different. Raising his eyebrows and smiling his enigmatic smile John then explained just how near the truth my explanation of the energy field was.

I was to discover that I'd been dancing about in an energy vortex, an inter-dimensional portal or doorway, which allowed craft to move between dimensions other to and including the one we exist in. I was to learn that there are many of these portals around our world and they are used by craft from other worlds who observe humanity and where required help with our evolution.

This unexpected information was so exciting especially as this particular portal was only a couple of hundred yards from where Gill and I had witnessed our UFO. But this would not be the end of the UFO saga, there would be more to come, much more.

MESSAGE FROM A MEDIUM

One summers morning during 2007 I answered the urgent ringing of my front doorbell to be greeted by a lady whom I knew to be a medium, she was someone I didn't know well and she had not visited my home before. Apologizing for arriving unannounced she told me her guide had given her no choice but to seek me out. Handing me a sheet of paper she explained that she had received this message the previous evening from a very powerful entity named Thoth whom she had never channelled before, but that I was mentioned specifically as the recipient of the message. Thanking her I took the sheet from her shaking hand and watched mystified as she quickly made her way down the garden path jumped into her car and drove away at top speed. It was almost as if she just handed me a ticking time bomb and desperately wanted to avoid being in the blast zone when it went off.

I could scarcely believe she had given me the name of Thoth, because at that particular time I met regularly with two other ladies for meditation and Earth energy work, one of which regularly channelled the entity Thoth for the work we were doing together.

Settling myself in the sun lounge I began to read in enthralled fascination and was not surprised to find the contents of the sheet dealt with extra-terrestrial visitation and the interaction of UFO's on our planet. It brought to mind the encounter Gill and I had undergone some years previously and echoed the conversation that I'd had with John about inter-dimensional doorways. At the bottom of the page written in bold letters should anyone else view the document was written, *'this information is for Linda Watson'*.

I'd hardly finished reading the channelled information when a text message arrived from my daughter Julie. Given what I'd just been digesting the start of the text was highly appropriate as it began with 'Hello Mothership'.

Less than two hours later Dickie arrived home for lunch carrying a thick paperback book and offering the tomb to me as he walked through the door explained the gentleman he'd been working for that morning had thought I might like to read it. The book just happened to be a comprehensive guide to all the UFO sightings and alleged landings during recorded history on planet Earth. I shook my head in disbelief as Dickie had only been working for this particular man and his wife for about a month and there was no way he could have known I would be interested in the subject of the book. Asking Dickie why a perfect stranger had given me a book such as this I discovered that during the morning the man had begun to question Dickie on whether he believed in UFO's and life on other planets. Dickie finding himself a little 'out of his depth' had deflected the question by saying that not only did his wife believe, but that she had actually experienced a close encounter.

On hearing this snippet of information the man had become very interested in meeting me and had produced the book for my perusal. Obviously this man was as interested in the subject of UFO's as I was, and given the synchronicities that had just taken place I felt we should meet as soon as possible because presumably some communication needed to take place between us.

Bob turned out to be a very clever, retired gentleman who had travelled the world extensively and was extremely knowledgeable about many things, but his main interest since retiring had become UFO sightings, close encounters and alleged abductions and the agenda of those aliens visiting planet Earth.

During our discussion Bob wanted to know about the sighting I'd had with Gill and grew very excited when I described it to him claiming he would have loved to have been there with us to witness it and then asked if I was familiar with the author Tim Good. As it happened I did know of his work as he is one of the most well known and respected investigative authors on the subject of UFO's in the world. At this point Bob announced proudly that Tim was a very good friend of his and that they'd worked closely together for many years before retiring. In fact he partly blamed Tim for his current obsession with UFO's and added that although Tim now lived most of the time in the USA they regularly kept in touch by e-mail. Picking up Tim's new book from the coffee table he offered it to me and remarked how he wished Tim could have been there to hear my account of our close encounter.

The evening flew by and soon it was time for me to leave and as Bob showed me to the front door he exclaimed how he had thoroughly enjoyed my company and how good it had been to be able to talk with someone who had similar interests to his own. It was apparent that he considered UFO spotting to be a little 'of the wall' and not a topic that you could discuss with just anyone, which from my own experiences I could fully understand.

Driving home that evening I pondered on my meeting with Bob and why our paths had crossed, although apart from our mutual interest I could come up with no explanation as yet. Arriving home I leant over to pick up the copy of Tim Good's book from the passenger seat, but the moment I touched the book a tingle ran through my body. By now I knew that tingle meant something, it was my HS speaking to me and in that instant I knew my meeting with Bob *was* meaningful and I was being asked to stay vigilant!

The next day I visited Rosemary who was very excited to show me a new channel she had found on the TV. Flicking through the channels she explained to me how she thought this channel was right up our street as it interviewed people who were happy to discuss the subjects we were interested in. As I waited for her to find the station the name Tim Good dropped into my mind and repeated over and over again. Rosemary then discovered the channel she was looking for and on screen an interview was just concluding and the lady interviewer was thanking her guest Tim Good!

Spirit were obviously not about to let the grass grow under my feet and the very next day I received a phone call from Bob with the request that I write an account of my close encounter and draw a diagram of what Gill and I had seen as he would very much like to send them both to Tim in the US. Bob was disinclined to e-mail the information to Tim as he was aware that Tim's e-mails were often intercepted and he wanted to post it instead.

Dropping off the information the following day I asked Bob to elaborate on why Tim thought his e-mails were being hacked and was told that those in 'power' were always 'watching' people like Tim and indeed the rest of us in case we knew something they didn't. He described them as the upper echelons of power, by which I assumed he meant the US government, but he wouldn't be drawn on the subject. The only other comment he made was that he hoped Tim would receive the letter with my account in it, although I couldn't really see why he wouldn't if it was properly addressed.

A few weeks later, by chance, I met Bob in town and asked had he received a reply from Tim about our sighting and learnt that they had exchanged e-mails over the past few weeks, but not surprisingly Tim had never received the details I had produced. Looking about to see if anyone was close enough to hear our conversation before continuing, Bob reminded me that Tim believed his mail was being intercepted and tampered with and the fact that the letter had not arrived seemed to prove his point.

I have met and spoken with Bob on a number of occasions over the intervening years and he has told me that Tim Good never did receive the account of my UFO sighting, although Bob did share with me some very interesting information and sketches that he had received from Tim. They were all accounts of UFO sightings from credible eye witnesses and their encounters were exactly the same as the one Gill and I had experienced. There was another compelling similarity that intrigued me, all the sightings were in roughly the same time period and all those he shared were from different locations in the UK.

A VISITATION FROM DOWN UNDER

The final piece in this saga happened during the summer of 2009. Arriving home one day I found an enigmatic message on my answering machine. The voice on the machine was female and had a broad Australian accent, the message was clipped and without character, emotion, or pleasantries, and went something like this;

"You do not know me, but I know of you and I have come to the Island from Australia to meet with you and receive information that you hold. That is why I am here. Please ring the following number to arrange a meeting as soon as possible"

As you are no doubt already aware I can't resist a mystery and I rang the number post haste. My call was answered by a lady with a refined English accent, obviously not the caller who had left the message as she actually sounded very pleasant, very unlike the cool disembodied voice that had been left on my answering machine. It soon became apparent that this lady knew about the contents of the message and told me I could make the arrangements for us to meet with her, as she would be driving the lady from Australia to see me. When I asked her could she enlighten me as to what this was about she declined, saying I would find out when they arrived, but it could not be discussed over the phone!

Now I was even more intrigued and spent the day wondering why someone, whom I did not know, would travel all the way from Australia to the Isle of Man especially to see me. As the original message had clearly stated that I had information the Australian required I was also a bit worried as to what that might be and my mind boggled for the rest of the morning.

The doorbell rang at precisely 3 o'clock. Knowing it would be my enigmatic visitors they were very punctual being right on time. Opening the front door to find an elderly grey haired lady and a younger woman who was obviously her daughter as the likeness was very apparent. Accompanying them was a short, stout, barrel of a woman who immediately asked me if I was Linda Watson. She spoke in a clipped broad Australian accent without a hint of friendliness or even the glimmer of a smile. Admitting that she had indeed found the person she was looking for I invited them in and asked them to join me for tea and biscuits in the conservatory. In way of reply the rude woman told me she had no time for tea and pleasantries as time was of the essence. The elderly lady smiled nervously at me, obviously aware of the others boorish manner, before suggesting there was time for a cup of tea whilst they explained to me what was going on.

Once we were all seated in the conservatory, cups of tea in hand, exchanging pleasantries, apart from the strange Australian lady who seemed blissfully unaware of her abrupt and unfeeling manner. I soon became aware that she appeared to be communing with someone other than those physically present. The mother and daughter had accepted their tea graciously and thanked me for my kindness, but 'the Australian' was intent on telling me her guides had led her to me and that they had told her I could supply her with the location she was looking for then sat stony faced, waiting for my response. Trying not to be put off by her terseness I told her I would try to help if she could give me a clue as to what location she was looking for.

Imagine my amazement when she proceeded to tell me she knew I had observed an unusual craft in the sky and that in the near vicinity of this sighting there was a vortex of which I also had personal experience. All of this was delivered directly and coldly without a thread of emotion. It was obvious she wanted to visit the energy field close to where Gill and I had seen the UFO many years previously. Telling her I knew where she wanted me to take her I explained that the property had been sold and the owner was in the process of building a huge barn and equestrian centre on the land. I then discovered the woman's mission and her reason for being so far away from her homeland was to seal the vortex before the horses arrived as they would be unable to withstand the rarefied energy the site produced, adding that it was my mission to take her there at once and that I would have nothing else to do. The little Australian woman was on her feet and raring to go as soon as I had agreed, which I felt was all I could do under the circumstances, after all I was not about to stand in the way of a woman and her mission, because I knew very well how that felt.

Leading the way I drove slowly watching in the rear view mirror as the intrepid trio followed close behind. We didn't have far to go and were soon getting out of our respective cars at the top of a private lane. Standing a few paces from me the abrupt Australian appeared to be communing with her invisible guides again and I waited until she opened her eyes and then pointing across the field towards the old house I explained where I had experienced the vortex in relation to the buildings. Pinpointing the spot wasn't difficult as there was now a huge crane in the garden in approximately the same place I'd asked 'Scotty to beam me up'. Reminding her that the whole area was private property and that she may need permission from the owner before setting foot on the land I was rewarded, once again, with a show of apparent rudeness as she walked away in the direction of the vortex, obviously she had received all the permission she felt she needed.

Sighing, I watched the strange little woman disappear down the leafy lane intent only on fulfilling her spiritual errand and knowing that my part in this mission which had begun many years previously with my sighting of the UFO was now over I made my way back to the car. Becoming very aware of being watched by her two companions, mother and daughter, who were now sitting in their car where they would presumably wait patiently for the strange, curt, little Australian lady to return. Waving to them as I passed their car they smiled beneficently in return, they had the appearance of two ageing guardian angels and I smiled inwardly at the amazing incredulity of the whole bizarre episode, but such is the way of life when you allow spirit free reign.

Footnote

I never saw or heard from the Australian woman or her companions again, not from that day to this, but I can tell you the equestrian centre was erected and to my knowledge nothing detrimental has ever happened to any of the horses so I have to deduce that the lady from 'down under' completed her mission and successfully sealed the vortex. I'm just very glad that I got the opportunity to experience it before she did!

CHAPTER 23

MESSAGE FROM 'THE MASTERS'

The final story in Volume II occurred in June 2010 and as in the preceding chapter began with finding a rather odd message on my answer phone. On this occasion I returned home to find a request for a meeting with a Penny Parks, a person I had met only twice before.

The message informed me that she would be on the island in a couple of weeks' time and that she had to speak to me on a matter of great urgency. Having not seen this woman in some years I had no idea why she needed to see me in person as she had failed to leave any hint of her intentions in her message. However, that familiar tingle ran up and down my spine akin to the flutter of a thousand butterfly wings against my bare skin and I knew in that instant that this proposed meeting would be something to do with my spiritual journey. Intrigued to find out what Penny wanted to tell me with such urgency and filled with excitement and the very human feeling of impatience I thought it unlikely that I would survive two weeks of waiting, but as it happened the time flew by as it usually does when you are immersed in a busy life.

The day before my birthday in early July I answered the phone to find it was Penny Parks and in her soft and serene voice I heard her tell me that today was the day for us to meet. Instantly I apologized, telling her I would have to re-schedule as I'd already made plans for the day and was more than a little taken aback when she told me I would have to cancel my plans as what she needed to share with me couldn't and wouldn't wait any longer!

Thankfully my plans could be easily re-arranged and being desperate to know what all the intrigue entailed I decided then and there to allow this woman, who was practically a stranger to me, to call the shots. Not normally given to manipulation by people I don't know very well or even those I do for that matter, but what can I say? It just felt right.

We had arranged to meet outside a small café in the centre of Laxey at 2pm and as I drove along the coast road to the small village a wave of panic swept over me as I tried to remember what she looked like, after all I'd only met her briefly on two previous occasions and that had been years ago. However my HS was not going to let me miss this particular meeting and as I pulled up in the car park my eyes were immediately drawn to a woman seated on her own at a table outside the café. Even though the place was alive with tourists it felt like she was the only person I could see and it must have been a similar feeling for Penny because as I stepped out of the car she waved warmly in my direction.

Penny stood out from the crowds around her with her long blonde hair falling over her shoulders and the folds of her beautiful diaphanous blue summer dress floating around her as she almost levitated across the road towards me. A look of pure serenity was etched on her pretty face and her overall appearance was almost angelic.

Greeting me with a hug she told me she would have known me anywhere and feeling almost hypnotized by her presence I agreed that I too would have recognized her, but in essence she had changed quite dramatically since we had last met. The confident and alluring person standing before me now was definitely not the woman I remembered from all those years ago, something had definitely and wonderfully changed about her.

Telling me we couldn't remain in such a public place to have our conversation as there were too many people milling about and the subject matter required privacy she asked if I knew of anywhere close at hand. Suggesting the gardens in the glen which were only a few minutes walk away she agreed instantly. As we strolled slowly towards the glen Penny shared with me how she had followed her guidance and moved from the Island to the south coast of England shortly after our last meeting. Once settled she had established a meditation and personal growth centre to help soldiers returning from the war in Afghanistan who were suffering from post traumatic stress syndrome. Penny continued by telling me she had spent many years working on her own personal and spiritual growth too, the results of which were evident to see. Commenting on the fact that she was now a completely different person to the one I remembered her whole face lit up as she laughed at my remarks and put the change in her appearance down to daily meditation, not only with the troops, but also with her own Higher Self.

Once I was aware of the things that had brought such a dramatic change in Penny I asked why there was such urgency that we meet, and where did I fit into the general scheme of things, after all we were little more than strangers. To my astonishment Penny laughed again and advised me that whilst we might consider ourselves almost strangers for the past month she had been receiving my name in her daily meditations. 'The Masters', she told me, had come through on a regular basis since making up her mind to visit the island and they had repeatedly asked Penny to seek me out as they had a message for me.

Totally blown away with this information I desperately wanted to know what the message was, but Penny was unable to tell me. All she knew was that the message would be given in the right place at the right time and today was the day it would arrive and that is why it was so imperative that we met.

By this point we had entered the glen and were walking along chatting easily together like old friends, passing a number of tourists sitting on a bench sunning themselves and enjoying a quick ice cream, presumably before making their way back to their respective coaches for the next leg of their trip around the Island.

We followed the path into the deeper shade of the overhanging trees, not consciously going in any particular direction we let our feet guide us onto the pathway beside the shallow, gurgling river. Penny then commented on the fact that this was somewhere she had never been before and I had to agree, in all my life I had never been to the place we now found ourselves.

Penny had become very quite and we walked side by side in silence under the overhanging trees until a few yards up ahead of us I noticed a low stone wall that bordered the narrow river, bathed in brilliant sunshine, which filtered down through a gap in the trees.

Suddenly a cold chill ran through me and I gave an involuntary shudder, knowing that I was acknowledging the arrival at our destination. To confirm my intuition Penny announced that we had reached the place we were meant to be.

Leaning against the low wall she tilted her face towards the sun. Closing her eyes the sun illuminated her delicate features and she appeared to be in some kind of reverie before whispering to me that 'The Masters' were present. My heart thumped in my chest as she spoke those words in the anticipation of what was to come, but in that same moment I became aware of the sensation of being watched. Looking past Penny to the opposite bank of the river, about ten feet away, to my amazement was the most spectacular heron I have ever seen and it looked directly into me with eyes that were wise and all knowing. In all my life I have never seen a heron that close, especially not in the wild. How could we not have spotted him when we arrived? And more importantly why had he not flown away?

My questions went unanswered, for now at least, as my focus was brought sharply back to Penny and I watched in awe and fascination as the largest and most beautiful dragonfly flew repeatedly around and around her head throughout the entire time she was channelling 'The Masters'.

The first part of the message was extremely personal to me and I will not divulge it here, but the most important part and the main reason why Penny had had to seek me out was that 'The Masters' wanted me to write another book. I actually shouted out at this point to say I was sorry, but I just couldn't do it. As a 'dyed in the wool' technophobe the thought of returning to a computer and starting again was about as welcome as a boil on the bum!

But, with their usual serenity 'The Masters' advised me that I had already written a book and that I could and would do it again. With a sinking feeling in my stomach I'd asked what they wanted me to write about this time and was relieved to find it was to be more of the same, a continuation of my first book. I listened as I was instructed to write about my experiences of working with spirit and that the book when complete would help to awaken and expand the consciousness of those who chose to read it.

Addressing me as 'dear one' they continued by reminding me that once a seed is sown it will lie dormant until the right moment for it to take on life and if others read my/spirits words their lives would never be the same again, as they would awaken and embark upon their own journeys.

As soon as the channelling finished the brightly coloured dragonfly flitted away across the river leaving me wondering if there was some significance in the presence of both it and the heron. Had they been there too witness the event? With that thought in mind I gazed across the water for another look at that gorgeous bird before we left this place and reeling in complete shock I realized the heron had disappeared. How could a bird the size of a heron take off in complete silence and without being noticed by us when we'd only been feet away? That was another question I couldn't answer, or at least not just yet.

Penny, being the channel, had no memory of what had just been said, which is often the case, so as we retraced our steps through the glen I discussed the contents of the message she had brought through. When I told her about the strange appearance and disappearance of the heron and the dragonfly, she, like me, concluded that they had both been an important part of the whole experience and definitely were significant.

When I said goodbye to Penny that day I thanked her and we hugged like old friends with a deep knowing that our paths may not cross again. She knew she had followed her guidance from 'The Masters' and her mission was complete. But, as for me, a new mission had just begun!

Footnote

The following day, which happened to be my birthday 'The Masters' chose to give me an unusual birthday gift, not one, not two, not three, but four, wonderful confirmations of our contact.

First confirmation

That morning I called in to see my spiritual friend Margaret and share my story of the day before. She sat spellbound throughout my tale with her coffee cup poised midway between saucer and lips. When I'd finished she told me how amazing she found it all and agreed that the heron and the dragonfly must have some significance before asking me if I'd like to pull a card from her new Tarot deck. I could see she was dying to try them out so I willingly obliged picking a card and handing it over to her.

Taking the card from my outstretched hand Margaret turned it over and gasped loudly, the look on her face was one of utter disbelief. Quite convinced that I'd picked a card with some unfortunate reading attached to it I couldn't quite believe my eyes when Margaret showed me the card I had chosen from a deck of 66 cards. Incredible as it seems the card in her hand was The Heron!

The picture on the card was a replica of the magnificent bird I had seen across the river when I was with Penny the day before, but the message on the card was even more significant as The Heron in this particular deck was known as 'The Scribe' or 'The Writer' and the definition in the little book that accompanied the deck was: - 'Someone who has the ability to communicate and work with the Higher Realms'

Second confirmation

Both Margaret and I sat in stunned silence as we read the message in the Tarot book until we both became aware of a tapping sound outside the window and turning in unison to our amazement a beautiful dragonfly was trying to get in through the partially open window.

Third and Fourth confirmations

That same day I received a lovely gift of a dragonfly necklace almost identical in size and colour to the insect I'd seen flying around Penny's head and I also received a lovely tea light lamp which when lit appears to have many dragonfly's flitting around the inside. These gifts came from two spiritual friends of mine and all I can think is 'The Masters' must have been looking over their shoulders and nudging them to buy the gifts they purchased for me.

Dragonfly

The spiritual meaning of the Dragonfly is; Dragonfly helps to move you past self created illusions that limit your spiritual growth. Dragonfly is mysterious and comes from another realm, a realm of magic and mystery and speaks to you of your pure potential, giving you the gift of inspiration and vision.

Afterthought on my message from 'The Masters'

Writing another book was not something that was high on my list of 'things I must do' and probably never would have been if it had not been for the above experience.

However, it seemed 'The Masters' had the confidence in me to write another volume, even if at that point I didn't have the confidence in myself. I knew then that I would just have to find it, and find it I did, and you, dear reader, are holding the proof in your hands or have been reading it on your computers or e-readers.

Unfortunately the writing of this book has taken me a number of years to complete, as life and all that it entails has a very annoying habit of getting in the way, or maybe I'm just making excuses for my own procrastination! Whatever the reason, I have finally kept my promise to 'The Masters' and can now move on to my next mission, if there is one, with the fervent hope that I'm not requested to write another book as the remainder of my life on Earth can't possibly be long enough to accomplish such a feat!

THE END... or is it?

I would like to complete this book with a quote from one of the most gifted minds in history:-

The Intuitive Mind is a 'Sacred Gift'

and

The Rational Mind is a 'Faithful servant'

We have created a society that honours

'The Servant', but has forgotten

'The Gift'

Albert Einstein

#0048 - 310717 - C0 - 210/148/22 - PB - DID1907748